Television Culture

Television Culture

John Fiske

METHUEN
London and New York

To Lucy and Matthew

First published in 1987 by
Methuen & Co. Ltd
11 New Fetter Lane, London EC4P 4EE

Published in the USA by
Methuen & Co.
in association with Methuen, Inc.
29 West 35th Street, New York NY 10001

Printed in Great Britain by Richard Clay Ltd, Bungay, Suffolk

British Library Cataloguing in Publication Data

Fiske, John
  Television culture: popular pleasures and
  politics.——(Studies in communication).
  1. Television programs
  I. Title   II. Series
  791.45'75   PN1992.5
  ISBN 0–416–92440–9
  ISBN 0–416–92430–1 Pbk

Library of Congress Cataloging in Publication Data

Fiske, John.
  Television culture.

  Bibliography: p.
  Includes indexes.
  1. Television and politics..2. Popular culture.
  I. Title.
  PN1992.6.F57   1987   302.2'345   87–20399
  ISBN 0–416–92440–9
  ISBN 0–416–92430–1 (pbk.)

Contents

Acknowledgments

The name on the spine of a book identifies only the hand that wrote the words. The voices that are assembled here are those of colleagues and students whose work I have read, or listened to at conferences, and with whom I have conversed to my enormous pleasure and profit over the years. I thank you all. Those whose words I have quoted directly are, I hope, adequately acknowledged in the references. Those others, whose input has been just as important if less direct, must be content with a more generalized expression of gratitude: they are mainly, though not exclusively, my colleagues and students at Curtin University of Technology, at Murdoch University, at the University of Iowa, and at the University of Wisconsin-Madison. In particular, the graduate students at Curtin, Iowa, and Madison have been intimately involved in the development of these ideas: they will recognize many, and may even feel responsible for some.

The individuals who have helped me directly include Bruce Gronbeck, whose generosity with his time and expertise has been exceptional, Mary Ellen Brown who has encouraged and criticized me every word of the way, Graeme Turner, David Bordwell, Ron Blaber, Noel King, Graham Seal, Jennifer Garton-Smith. My secretarial colleagues, particularly Rae Kelly at Curtin, and Evelyn Miller and Mary Dodge at Madison, have collaborated with me so effectively that they have at least doubled my own productivity: I wish all academics had colleagues as good as they.

I wish to thank, too, the benefactors of the A. Craig Baird foundation at the University of Iowa and the Brittingham foundation at the University of Wisconsin-Madison: the visiting professorships which their generosity made possible have played important formative roles in this book.

I gratefully acknowledge the permission given by the publishers of the following magazines to reproduce the photographs in figures 7.1, 7.2, 10.1, and 11.2: *Soap Opera Digest, Daytime Nighttime Soap Stars, TV Week, Fame,* and *Daytime TV.* Early versions of some parts of this book have appeared as journal articles as follows: parts of chapters 1 and 6 in *Critical Studies in Mass Communication* and in the *Australian Journal of Screen Theory,* part of chapter 9 in *Communication,* and part of chapter 13 in

Cultural Studies. I hope readers who have come across these articles will find that their development in this book will compensate for any sense of familiarity as they reread them.

And, importantly, I wish to thank those who contribute so much to my experience and enjoyment of television: my family, particularly Lucy and Matthew, my friends, all those who watch it with me, gossip about it with me and who are part, in one way or another, of the thorough implication of television into my everyday life. And not least of these are those who are so often cast as the scapegoats for the ills of capitalist societies, the producers and distributors of popular television. Without their products my leisure would be less fun, my teaching less stimulating, and this book impossible.

I apologize for the absence of illustrations to the transcripts of *Cagney and Lacey* and from *Miami Vice* in Figure 13.1: the fees demanded by the producers were beyond the scope of an academic book. I regret that their desire for additional profit overrode the value the illustrations would have had for students.

John Fiske
Dept of Communication Arts
University of Wisconsin-Madison
April 1987

Chapter 1

Some television, some topics, and some terminology

Any book about television culture is immediately faced with the problem of defining its object. What is television? And, equally problematically, what is culture? In this book I work with a definition of television as a bearer/provoker of meanings and pleasures, and of culture as the generation and circulation of this variety of meanings and pleasures within society. Television-as-culture is a crucial part of the social dynamics by which the social structure maintains itself in a constant process of production and reproduction: meanings, popular pleasures, and their circulation are therefore part and parcel of this social structure.

Television, its viewers, and the ways it functions in society, are so multifarious that no tightly focused theoretical perspective can provide us with adequate insight. The theoretical and methodological roots of this book lie in that loosely delineated area known as "cultural studies" which derives from particular inflections of Marxism, semiotics, post-structuralism, and ethnography. This area encompasses both textually inflected and socially inflected theories of culture, and requires theoretical, analytical, and empirical approaches to rub together in a mutually critical and productive relationship. The book will focus on the problem of how the textuality of television is made meaningful and pleasurable by its variously situated viewers, though it will also consider the relationship between this cultural dimension and television's status as a commodity in a capitalist economy.

But we start by considering television as a cultural agent, particularly as a provoker and circulator of meanings. How meanings are produced is one of the central problematics of the book, but a convenient place to start is with the simple notion that television broadcasts programs that are replete with potential meanings, and that it attempts to control and focus this meaningfulness into a more singular preferred meaning that performs the work of the dominant ideology. We shall need to interrogate this notion later, but I propose to start with a traditional semiotic account of how television makes, or attempts to make, meanings that serve the dominant interests in society, and how it circulates these meanings amongst the wide variety of social groups that constitute its audiences. I shall do this by analyzing a short

1

segment of two scenes from a typical, prime-time, long-running series, *Hart to Hart*, in order to demonstrate some basic critical methodology and to raise some more complex theoretical questions that will be addressed later on in the book.

The Harts are a wealthy, high-living husband and wife detective team. In this particular episode they are posing as passengers on a cruise ship on which there has been a jewel robbery. In scene 1 they are getting ready for a dance during which they plan to tempt the thief to rob them, and are discussing how the robbery may have been effected. In scene 2 we meet the villain and villainess, who have already noticed Jennifer Hart's ostentatiously displayed jewels.

☐ *Scene 1*

HERO: He knew what he was doing to get into this safe.

HEROINE: Did you try the numbers that Granville gave you?

HERO: Yeh. I tried those earlier. They worked perfectly.

HEROINE: Well you said it was an inside job, maybe they had the combination all the time.

HERO: Just trying to eliminate all the possibilities. Can you check this out for me. (*He gestures to his bow tie.*)

HEROINE: Mm. Yes I can. (*He hugs her.*) Mm. Light fingers. Oh, Jonathon.

HERO: Just trying to keep my touch in shape.

HEROINE: What about the keys to the door.

HERO: Those keys can't be duplicated because of the code numbers. You have to have the right machines.

2

HEROINE: Well, that leaves the window.

HERO: The porthole.

HEROINE: Oh yes. The porthole. I know they are supposed to be charming, but they always remind me of a laundromat.

HERO: I took a peek out of there a while ago. It's about all you can do. It's thirty feet up to the deck even if you could make it down to the window, porthole. You'd have to be the thin man to squeeze through.

HEROINE: What do you think? (*She shows her jewelry*.) Enough honey to attract the bees?

HERO: Who knows? They may not be able to see the honey for the flowers.

HEROINE: Oh, that's the cutest thing you've ever said to me, sugar. Well, shall we? (*Gestures towards the door.*)

□ Scene 2

VILLAIN: I suppose you noticed some of the icing on Chamberlain's cup cake. I didn't have my jeweler's glass, but that bracelet's got to be worth at least fifty thousand. Wholesale.

VILLAINESS: Patrick, if you're thinking what I know you're thinking, forget it. We've made our quota one hit on each ship. We said we weren't going to get greedy, remember.

3

VILLAIN: But darling, it's you I'm
thinking of. And I don't like you
taking all those chances. But if we
could get enough maybe we
wouldn't have to go back to the
Riviera circuit for years.

VILLAINESS: That's what you said
when we were there.

VILLAIN: Well maybe a few good
investments and we can pitch the
whole bloody business. But we are
going to need a bit more for our
retirement fund.

☐ The codes of television

Figure 1.1 shows the main codes that television uses and their relationship. A code is a rule-governed system of signs, whose rules and conventions are shared amongst members of a culture, and which is used to generate and circulate meanings in and for that culture. (For a fuller discussion of codes in semiotics see Fiske 1983 or O'Sullivan *et al.* 1983.) Codes are links between producers, texts, and audiences, and are the agents of intertextuality through which texts interrelate in a network of meanings that constitutes our cultural world. These codes work in a complex hierarchical structure that Figure 1.1 oversimplifies for the sake of clarity. In particular, the categories of codes are arbitrary and slippery, as is their classification into levels in the hierarchy; for instance, I have put speech as a social code, and dialogue (i.e. scripted speech) as a technical one, but in practice the two are almost indistinguishable: social psychologists such as Berne (1964) have shown us how dialogue in "real life" is frequently scripted for us by the interactional conventions of our culture. Similarly, I have called casting a conventional representational code, and appearance a social one, but the two differ only in intentionality and explicitness. People's appearance in "real life" is already encoded: in so far as we make sense of people by their appearance we do so according to conventional codes in our culture. The casting director is merely using these codes more consciously and more conventionally, which means more stereotypically.

The point is that "reality" is already encoded, or rather the only way we can perceive and make sense of reality is by the codes of our culture. There may be an objective, empiricist reality out there, but there is no universal,

Figure 1.1 The codes of television

An event to be televised is already encoded
by *social codes* such as those of:

Level one:
"REALITY"
appearance, dress, make-up, environment, behavior, speech,
gesture, expression, sound, etc.

these are encoded electronically by
technical codes such as those of:

Level two:
REPRESENTATION
camera, lighting, editing, music, sound

which transmit the
conventional representational codes, which shape the
representations of, for example:
narrative, conflict, character, action, dialogue, setting,
casting, etc.

Level three:
IDEOLOGY
which are organized into coherence and social acceptability by
the *ideological codes,* such as those of:
individualism, patriarchy, race, class, materialism,
capitalism, etc.

objective way of perceiving and making sense of it. What passes for reality in any culture is the product of that culture's codes, so "reality" is always already encoded, it is never "raw." If this piece of encoded reality is televised, the technical codes and representational conventions of the medium are brought to bear upon it so as to make it (a) transmittable technologically and (b) an appropriate cultural text for its audiences.

Some of the social codes which constitute our reality are relatively precisely definable in terms of the medium through which they are expressed – skin color, dress, hair, facial expression, and so on.

Others, such as those that make up a landscape, for example, may be less easy to specify systematically, but they are still present and working hard. Different sorts of trees have different connotative meanings encoded into them, so do rocks and birds. So a tree reflected in a lake, for example, is fully encoded even before it is photographed and turned into the setting for a romantic narrative.

Similarly the technical codes of television can be precisely identified and analyzed. The choices available to the camera person, for example, to give meaning to what is being photographed are limited and specifiable: they consist of framing, focus, distance, movement (of the camera or the lens), camera placing, or angle and lens choice. But the conventional and ideological codes and the relationship between them are much more elusive and much harder to specify, though it is the task of criticism to do just that. For instance, the conventions that govern the representation of speech as "realistic dialogue" in scene 1 (pp. 2–3) result in the heroine asking questions while the hero provides the answers. The representational convention by which women are shown to lack knowledge which men possess and give to them is an example of the ideological code of patriarchy. Similarly the conventional representation of crime as theft of personal property is an encoding of the ideology of capitalism. The "naturalness" with which the two fit together in the scene is evidence of how these ideological codes work to organize the other codes into producing a congruent and coherent set of meanings that constitute the *common sense* of a society. The process of making sense involves a constant movement up and down through the levels of the diagram, for sense can only be produced when "reality," representations, and ideology merge into a coherent, seemingly natural unity. Semiotic or cultural criticism deconstructs this unity and exposes its "naturalness" as a highly ideological construct.

A semiotic analysis attempts to reveal how these layers of encoded meanings are structured into television programs, even in as small a segment as the one we are working with. The small size of the segment encourages us to perform a detailed analytical reading of it, but prevents us talking about larger-scale codes, such as those of the narrative. But it does provide a good starting point for our work.

☐ CAMERA WORK

The camera is used through angle and deep focus to give us a perfect view of the scene, and thus a complete understanding of it. Much of the pleasure of television realism comes from this sense of omniscience that it gives us. Chapter 2 develops this point in more detail. Camera distance is used to swing our sympathies away from the villain and villainess, and towards the hero and heroine. The normal camera distance in television is mid-shot to close-up, which brings the viewer into an intimate, comfortable relationship with the characters on the screen. But the villain and villainess are also shown in extreme close-up (ECU). Throughout this whole episode of *Hart to Hart* there are only three scenes in which ECUs are used: they are used only to represent hero/ine and villain/ess, and of the twenty-one ECUs, eighteen are of the villain/ess and only three of the hero/ine. Extreme close-ups become a codified way for representing villainy.

This encoding convention is not confined to fictional television, where we might think that its work upon the alignment of our sympathies, and thus on our moral judgment, is justified. It is also used in news and current affairs programs which present themselves as bringing reality to us "objectively." The court action resulting from General Westmoreland's libel suit against the CBS in 1985 revealed these codes more questionably at work in television reporting. Alex Jones recounts their use in his report of the trial for the *New York Times*:

Among the more controversial techniques is placing an interviewee in partial shadow in order to lend drama to what is being said. Also debated is the use of extreme close-ups that tend to emphasize the tension felt by a person being interviewed; viewers may associate the appearance of tension with lying or guilt.

The extreme close-up can be especially damaging when an interview is carefully scripted and a cameraman is instructed to focus tightly on the person's face at the point when the toughest question is to be asked. Some documentary makers will not use such close-ups at all in interviews because they can be so misleading.

The CBS documentary contained both a shadowed interview of a friendly witness and "tight shots" of General Westmoreland. Such techniques have been used in documentaries by other networks as well.

Even the wariest viewer is likely to find it difficult to detect some other common techniques. "I can't imagine a general viewer getting so sophisticated with techniques that they could discount them," said Reuven Frank, a former president at NBC News who has been making documentaries for about 30 years.

(*NYT*, February 17, 1985: 8E)

There are two possible sources of the conventions that govern the meanings generated by this code of camera distance. One is the social code of interpersonal distance: in western cultures the space within about 24 inches (60 cm) of us is encoded as private. Anyone entering it is being either hostile, when the entry is unwelcome, or intimate, when it is invited. ECUs replicate

7

this, and are used for moments of televisual intimacy or hostility, and which meanings they convey depends on the other social and technical codes by which they are contextualized, and by the ideological codes brought to bear upon them. Here, they are used to convey hostility. The other source lies in the technical codes which imply that seeing closely means seeing better – the viewer can see *into* the villain, see *through* his words, and thus gains power over him, the power and the pleasure of "dominant specularity" (see chapter 2). These technical and social codes manifest the ideological encoding of villainy.

Most of the other technical codes can be dealt with more quickly, with only brief comments.

☐ LIGHTING

The hero's cabin is lit in a soft, yellowish light, that of the villains in a harsh, whiter one. (I am reminded of Hogben's (1982) anecdote about the occasion when he was given a hostile treatment in a television interview. He did, however, manage to convince the interviewer that his point of view deserved more sympathy, whereupon the interviewer insisted they record the interview again, but this time without the greenish-white studio lighting.)

☐ EDITING

The heroes are given more time (72 secs) than the villains (49), and more shots (10 as against 7), though both have an average shot length of 7 seconds. It is remarkable how consistent this is across different modes of television (see Fiske 1986b): it has become a conventional rhythm of television common to news, drama, and sport.

☐ MUSIC

The music linking the two scenes started in a major key, and changed to minor as the scene changed to the villains.

☐ CASTING

This technical code requires a little more discussion. The actors and actresses who are cast to play hero/ines, villain/esses and supporting roles are real people whose appearance is already encoded by our social codes. But they are equally media people, who exist for the viewer intertextually, and whose meanings are also intertextual. They bring with them not only residues of the meanings of other roles that they have played, but also their meanings from other texts such as fan magazines, showbiz gossip columns, and television criticism. Later on in the book we will discuss intertextuality and character portrayal in greater depth: here we need to note that these dimensions of meaning are vital in the code of casting, and that they are more important in the casting of hero/ines than of villain/esses.

Characters on television are not just representations of individual people but are encodings of ideology, "embodiments of ideological values" (Fiske 1987a). Gerbner's (1970) work showed that viewers were clear about the different characteristics of television heroes and villains on two dimensions only: heroes were more attractive and more successful than villains. Their attractiveness, or lack of it, is partly the result of the way they are encoded in the technical and social codes – camera work, lighting, setting, casting, etc., but the ideological codes are also important, for it is these that make sense out of the relationship between the technical code of casting and the social code of appearance, and that also relate their televisual use to their broader use in the culture at large. In his analysis of violence on television, Gerbner (1970) found that heroes and villains are equally likely to use violence and to initiate it, but that heroes were successful in their violence, whereas villains finally were not. Gerbner worked out a killers-to-killed ratio according to different categories of age, sex, class, and race. The killers category included heroes and villains, but the killed category included villains only. He found that a character who was white, male, middle class (or classless) and in the prime of life was very likely, if not certain, to be alive at the end of the program. Conversely characters who deviated from these norms were likely to be killed during the program in proportion to the extent of their deviance. We may use Gerbner's findings to theorize that heroes are socially central types who embody the dominant ideology, whereas villains and victims are members of deviant or subordinate subcultures who thus embody the dominant ideology less completely, and may, in the case of villains, embody ideologies that oppose it. The textual opposition between hero/ine and villain/ess, and the violence by which this opposition is commonly dramatized, become metaphors for power relationships in society and thus a material practice through which the dominant ideology works. (This theory is discussed more fully in Fiske and Hartley 1978 and in Fiske 1982.)

The villain in this segment has hints of non-Americanness; some viewers have classed his accent, manner, and speech as British, for others his appearance has seemed Hispanic. But the hero and heroine are both clearly middle-class, white Americans, at home among the WASPs (White Anglo-Saxon Protestants). The villainess is Aryan, blonde, pretty, and younger than the villain. Gerbner's work would lead us to predict that his chances of surviving the episode are slim, whereas hers are much better. The prediction is correct. She finally changes sides and helps the hero/ine, whereas he is killed; hints of this are contained in her condemnation of the villain's greed, which positions her more centrally in the ideological discourse of economics (see below).

These technical codes of television transmit, and in some cases merge into, the social codes of level 1. Let us look at how some of them are working to generate meanings and how they embody the ideological codes of level 3.

□ SETTING AND COSTUME

The hero/ine's cabin is larger than that of the villain/ess: it is humanized, made more attractive by drapes and flowers, whereas the other is all sharp angles and hard lines. The villain wears a uniform that places him as a servant or employee and the villainess's dress is less tasteful, less expensive than the heroine's. These physical differences in the social codes of setting and dress are also bearers of the ideological codes of class, of heroism and villainy, of morality, and of attractiveness. These abstract ideological codes are condensed into a set of material social ones, and the materiality of the differences of the social codes is used to guarantee the truth and naturalness of the ideological. We must note, too, how some ideological codes are more explicit than others: the codes of heroism, villainy, and attractiveness are working fairly openly and acceptably. But under them the codes of class, race, and morality are working less openly and more questionably: their ideological work is to naturalize the correlation of lower-class, non-American with the less attractive, less moral, and therefore villainous. Conversely, the middle-class and the white American is correlated with the more attractive, the more moral and the heroic. This displacement of morality onto class is a common feature of our popular culture: Dorfman and Mattelart (1975) have shown how Walt Disney cartoons consistently express villainy through characteristics of working-class appearance and manner; indeed they argue that the only time the working class appear in the middle-class world of Ducksville it is as villains. Fiske (1984) has found the same textual strategy in the *Dr Who* television series.

□ MAKE-UP

The same merging of the ideological codes of morality, attractiveness, and heroism/villainy, and their condensation into a material social code, can be seen in something as apparently insignificant as lipstick. The villainess has a number of signs that contradict her villainy (she is blonde, white American, pretty, and more moral than the villain). These predict her eventual conversion to the side of the hero and heroine, but she cannot look too like them at this early stage of the narrative, so her lips are made up to be thinner and less sexually attractive than the fuller lips of the heroine. The ideology of lipstick may seem a stretched concept, but it is in the aggregate of apparently insignificant encodings that ideology works most effectively.

☐ ACTION

There are a number of significant similarities and differences between the actions of the hero/ine and the villain/ess. In both cabins the women are prettying themselves, the men are planning. This naturalizes the man's executive role (Goffman 1979) of instigating action and the woman's role as object of the male gaze – notice the mirror in each cabin which enables her to see herself as "bearer of her own image" (Berger 1972): the fact that this is common to both hero/ine and villain/ess puts it beyond the realm of conflict in the narrative and into the realm of everyday common sense within which the narrative is enacted. The other action common to both is the getting and keeping of wealth as a motive for action, and as a motor for the narrative: this also is not part of the conflict-to-be-resolved, but part of the ideological framework through which that conflict is viewed and made sense of.

A difference between the two is that of cooperation and closeness. The hero and heroine co-operate and come physically closer together, the villain and villainess, on the other hand, disagree and pull apart physically. In a society that places a high value on a man and woman being a close couple this is another bearer of the dominant ideology.

☐ DIALOGUE

The dialogue also is used to affect our sympathy. That of the villain and villainess is restricted to their nefarious plans and their mutual disagreement, whereas the hero and heroine are allowed a joke (window/porthole/laundro-mat), an extended metaphor (honey and the bees), and the narrative time to establish a warm, co-operative relationship. Both the hero/ine and villain/ess are allowed irony, the use of which will be theorized and analyzed in chapter 6.

☐ IDEOLOGICAL CODES

These codes and the televisual codes which bring them to the viewer are both deeply embedded in the ideological codes of which they are themselves the bearers. If we adopt the same ideological practice in the decoding as the encoding we are drawn into the position of a white, male, middle-class American (or westerner) of conventional morality. The reading position is the social point at which the mix of televisual, social, and ideological codes comes together to make coherent, unified sense: in making sense of the program in this way we are indulging in an ideological practice ourselves, we are maintaining and legitimating the dominant ideology, and our reward for this is the easy pleasure of the recognition of the familiar and of its adequacy. We have already become a "reading subject" constructed by the text, and, according to Althusser (1971), the construction of subjects-in-ideology is the major ideological practice in capitalist societies.

This ideological practice is working at its hardest in three narrative devices in this segment. The first is the window/porthole/laundromat joke, which, as we have seen, is used to marshal the viewer's affective sympathy on the side of the hero/ine. But it does more than that. Freud tells us that jokes are used to relieve the anxiety caused by repressed, unwelcome, or taboo meanings. This joke revolves around the "feminine" (as defined by our dominant culture) inability to understand or use technical language, and the equally "feminine" tendency to make sense of everything through a domestic discourse. "Porthole" is technical discourse – masculine: "window-laundromat" is domestic-nurturing discourse – feminine. The anxiety that the joke relieves is that caused by the fact that the heroine is a detective, is involved in the catching of criminals – activities that are part of the technical world of men in patriarchy. The joke is used to recuperate contradictory signs back into the dominant system, and to smooth over any contradictions that might disrupt the ideological homogeneity of the narrative. The attractiveness of the heroine must not be put at risk by allowing her challenge to patriarchy to be too stark – for attractiveness is always ideological, never merely physical or natural.

The metaphor that expresses the sexual attractiveness of women for men in terms of the attraction of honey and flowers for the bees works in a similar way. It naturalizes this attraction, masking its ideological dimension, and then extends this naturalness to its explanation of the attractiveness of other people's jewelry for lower-class non-American villains! The metaphor is working to naturalize cultural constructions of gender, class, and race.

The third device is that of jewelry itself. As we have seen, the getting and keeping of wealth is the major motor of the narrative, and jewelry is its material signifier. Three ideological codes intersect in the use of jewelry in this narrative: they are the codes of economics, gender, and class.

In the code of economics, the villain and villainess stress the jewelry's investment/exchange function: it is "worth at least fifty thousand wholesale," it forms "a retirement fund." For the hero and heroine and for the class they represent this function is left unstated: jewelry, if it is an investment, is one to hold, not cash in. It is used rather as a sign of class, of wealth, and of aesthetic taste.

The aesthetic sense, or good taste, is typically used as a bearer and naturalizer of class differences. The heroine deliberately overdoes the jewelry, making it vulgar and tasteless in order to attract the lower-class villain and villainess. They, in their turn, show their debased taste, their aesthetic insensitivity, by likening it to the icing on a cupcake. As Bourdieu (1968) has shown us, the function of aesthetics in our society is to make class-based and culture-specific differences of taste appear universal and therefore natural. The taste of the dominant classes is universalized by aesthetic theory out of its class origin; the metaphor of "taste" works in a similar way by displacing class differences onto the physical, and therefore natural, senses of the body.

The meaning of jewelry in the code of gender is clear. Jewels are the coins by which the female-as-patriarchal-commodity is bought, and wearing them is the sign both of her possession by a man, and of his economic and social status. Interestingly, in the code of gender, there is no class difference between hero/ine and villain/ess: the economics of patriarchy are the same for all classes, thus making it appear universal and natural that man provides for his woman.

This analysis has not only revealed the complexity of meanings encoded in what is frequently taken to be shallow and superficial, but it also implies that this complexity and subtlety has a powerful effect upon the audience. It implies that the wide variety of codes all cohere to present a unified set of meanings that work to maintain, legitimate, and naturalize the dominant ideology of patriarchal capitalism. Their ideological effectivity appears irresistible. The resistibility of ideology is one of the themes that runs through this book, and later on, in chapters 5 and 6, we will return to this analysis, complicate it, and contradict its main implications. For the moment, however, it serves to demonstrate that popular television is both complex and deeply infused with ideology.

□ Some terminology

This book is not concerned with television as an industrial practice or as a profit-making producer of commodities, though it is obviously both of these, but attempts to understand it from the perspective of its audiences. For our purposes, then, television consists of the programs that are transmitted, the meanings and pleasures that are produced from them, and, to a lesser extent, the way it is incorporated into the daily routine of its audiences. We will concentrate on "typical" television – the most popular, mainstream, internationally distributed programs, for these are the ones of greatest significance in popular culture.

To understand television in this way we need to see it and its programs as potentials of meaning rather than as commodities. A program is a clearly defined and labeled fragment of television's output. It has clear boundaries, both temporal and formal, and it relates to other programs in terms of generic similarity and, more essentially, of difference. We know that an ad is not part of a program, we know when one program finishes and another starts. Programs are stable, fixed entities, produced and sold as commodities, and organized by schedulers into distribution packages. *Dallas* is the same program whether it is broadcast in the USA, North Africa, or Australia.

A text is a different matter altogether. Programs are produced, distributed, and defined by the industry: texts are the product of their readers. So a program becomes a text at the moment of reading, that is, when its inter-action with one of its many audiences activates some of the meanings/pleasures that it is capable of provoking. So one program can stimulate the production of many texts according to the social conditions of its reception. *Dallas* is a different text in the USA, in North Africa, and in Australia, indeed, it is many different texts in the USA alone. Texts are the site of conflict between their forces of production and modes of reception. The analysis we have just performed shows how the dominant ideology is structured into popular texts by the discourses and conventions that inform the practices of production and that are a part of their reception. But what it has not shown is how other discourses, other conventions can be brought to bear upon it that may conflict with the dominant ones structured into it. A text is the site of struggles for meaning that reproduce the conflicts of interest between the producers and consumers of the cultural commodity. A program is produced by the industry, a text by its readers.

To understand both the production of programs and the production of meanings from them, we need to understand the workings of discourse. This is, in itself, a multidiscursive term; that is, its usage varies according to the discourse in which it is situated. At its simplest, discourse is the organization of language above the level of the sentence: it is thus an extensive use of language. By extension it can cover nonverbal languages so that one can talk of the discourse of the camera or of lighting. This formalistic use does not get us very far, for it ignores the social and ideological dimension. Discourse is a language or system of representation that has developed socially in order to make and circulate a coherent set of meanings about an important topic area. These meanings serve the interests of that section of society within which the discourse originates and which works ideologically to naturalize those mean-ings into common sense. "Discourses are power relations" (O'Sullivan *et al.* 1983: 74). Discourse is thus a social act which may promote or oppose the dominant ideology, and is thus often referred to as a "discursive practice." Any account of a discourse or a discursive practice must include its topic area, its social origin, and its ideological work: we should not, therefore, think about a discourse of economics, or of gender, but of a capitalist (or socialist) discourse of economics, or the patriarchal (or feminist) discourse of gender. Such discourses frequently become institutionalized, particularly by the media industries, in so far as they are structured by a socially produced set of conventions that are tacitly accepted by both industry and consumers. In this sense we can talk about the discourse of news, or of advertising: these discourses still exhibit our three defining characteristics – a topic area, a social location, and the promotion of the interests of a particular social group.

Discourses function not only in the production and reading of texts, but also in making sense of social experience. A particular discourse of gender, for example, works not only to make sense of a television program such as *Charlie's Angels,* but also to make a particular pattern of sense of gender in the family, in the workplace, in school, in social clubs – in fact, in our general social relations. Social experience is much like a text: its meanings depend upon the discourses that are brought to bear upon it. Just as two differently socially situated people may make a different sense of the same text, so they may make a different sense of the same social experience.

This brings us to another characteristic of discourse: discourses are not produced by the individual speaker or author, they are socially produced; the meanings that they bear preexist their use in any one discursive practice. It is often said, somewhat enigmatically, that we do not speak our discourse bur our discourse speaks us. This means that discourse not only makes sense of its topic area, it also constructs a sense, or social identity, of *us* as we speak it. We all of us have an extensive repertoire of discourses that we need in order to make sense of the variety of texts and social experiences that constitute our culture. The analysis of a program can identify the main discourses out of which it is structured, but it cannot of itself identify the discourses that the viewer will bring to bear upon it to make it into a text that bears meanings for him or her. The discourses of the program attempt to control and confine its potential meanings: the discourse of the reader may resist this control.

So texts are unstable, unconfined. The ad and the program may be part of the same text in their interaction in the production of meaning and pleasure. Meanings are not confined by producers' boundaries between programs, but are part of the "flow" of television as experienced by its audiences. Neither is the television text confined by the boundaries of its medium: reading and talking about television are part of the process of making a text out of it and are determinants of what text is actually made. So, too, is our experience of other cultural media – books, films, newspapers, songs, and so on. The textuality of television is essentially intertextual.

An essential characteristic of television is its polysemy, or multiplicity of meanings. A program provides a potential of meanings which may be realized, or made into actually experienced meanings, by socially situated viewers in the process of reading. This polysemic potential is neither bound-less nor structureless: the text delineates the terrain within which meanings may be made and proffers some meanings more vigorously than others. The analysis of the *Hart to Hart* segment has shown how the conventional use of televisual codes has preferred a set of meanings that, and this is typical, fit well with the values of the dominant ideology. But other meanings may be made (see chapter 6): the text's polysemy or meaning potential may be realized differently. A white woman, for example, may find the window/porthole/laundromat joke offensive, and may read the heroine's concern for her appearance as evidence of her cleverness in being able to outwit the villain and villainess. The point to make here is that the motivation to exploit the polysemy of the program is social: the polysemy of the text is necessary if it is to be popular amongst viewers who occupy a variety of situations within the social structure. This variety of social situations is no harmonious relation-ship of roughly equal groups as modeled by liberal pluralism, but must always be understood in terms of domination and subjugation. The unequal distribution of power in society is the central structuring principle in under-standing the relationship of any one group to others, or to the social system as a whole. As social groups are neither autonomous nor equal, so too the meanings they produce from the text are neither self-contained nor equal. The more positive, feminine reading of the heroine's efforts to increase her attractiveness is not a self-contained, self-sufficient one: an essential part of its meaning is its relationship with, and difference from, the dominant meanings of female attractiveness in patriarchy. As the woman reader is socially positioned in a power relationship with patriarchy, so her readings of a text enter a power relationship with those preferred by the ideological structure of the codes that comprise it. Polysemy is always bounded and structured, for polysemy is the textual equivalent of social difference and diversity.

A textual study of television, then, involves three foci: the formal qualities of television programs and their flow; the intertextual relations of television within itself, with other media, and with conversation; and the study of socially situated readers and the process of reading.

The term "readers" may seem inappropriate for the watchers of television, but it is the term I use most frequently in this book. I also use the related terms of "viewers," "audiences," and "audience" to refer in different ways to the people who watch television. "Audience," in the singular, is the easiest term to understand – and dismiss. It implies that television reaches a homo-geneous mass of people who are all essentially identical, who receive the same messages, meanings, and ideologies from the same programs and who are essentially passive. The inability of the term "audience" to account for social differences and consequent differences of meanings means that it ascribes great centralizing, homogenizing power to television and its producers. Consequently it sees the audience as relatively powerless and undiscriminating, at the mercy of the barons of the industry. It sees viewers, in Stuart Hall's (1982) productive phrase, as "cultural dopes" who are unable to perceive the difference between their interests and those of the producers. Such a view of the television audience is surprisingly widely held, often by people who, on other topics, are capable of thinking quite clearly.

Pluralizing the term into "audiences" at least recognizes that there are differences between the viewers of any one program that must be taken into account. It recognizes that we are not a homogeneous society, but that our social system is crisscrossed by axes of class, gender, race, age, nationality, region, politics, religion, and so on, all of which produce more or less strongly marked differences, and that these social differences relate among each other in a complexity of ways that always involves the dimension of power. Social power is unequally distributed in society, so any set of social relations necessarily involves power and resistance, domination and subordination. The term "audiences" recognizes the heterogeneity of society and allows for that heterogeneity to be understood in terms of power relations.

The terms "viewer" and "reader" are more active than either "audience" or "audiences"; I use them with a considerable overlap of meaning, and thus, at times, interchangeably. But there are differences of emphasis between them. A "viewer" is someone watching television, making meanings and pleasures from it, in a social situation. This social situation is compounded of both the social relations/experience of the viewer (class, gender, etc.) and of the material, usually domestic, situation (which is also a product of his/her social relations) within which television is watched. The television viewer experiences a far greater variety of modes of watching than does the cinema spectator. "Viewing," then, is an active process that brings to television the social relations of the viewer (her/his point of view) and the material situation: viewing television news will be quite different for the woman who is cooking the family meal than for the man slumped in an armchair in front of the set. A viewer is engaged with the screen more variously, actively, and selectively than is a spectator.

"Viewing" is specific to television, "reading" is common to all texts. So the term "reader" means "the producer of texts, the maker of meanings and pleasures." This productive ability is the result of social experience or training, whether formal or informal. It is not an innate gift, but an acquired ability. It is a social practice, is ideological, and is the means by which sociocultural experience, the text in question, and its intertextual relationships, are brought together in a productive moment of interaction. The "reader" is less concretely situated than the "viewer" and is rather the embodiment of that central cultural process – the production of meaning.

17

Cultural processes are often referred to metaphorically as though they were economic ones. Bourdieu's (1980) metaphor of cultural capital is typical. By this he means that a society's culture is as unequally distributed as its material wealth and that, like material wealth, it serves to identify class interests and to promote and naturalize class differences. Thus, those cultural forms which a society considers to be "high," for example, classical music, fine art, literature, or ballet, coincide with the tastes of those with social power, whereas lowbrow or mass cultural forms appeal to those ranked low on the social structure. The point of this is that culture and class are closely interrelated but the discourse of culture disguises its connection with class. By using words like "taste," and "discrimination," and by appealing to apparently universal values such as those of aesthetics, the discourse of culture grounds cultural differences in universal human nature or in universal value systems. It pretends that culture is equally available to all, as democratic capitalism pretends that wealth is equally available to all. The fact that few acquire either culture or wealth is explained by reference to natural differences between individuals, which are expressed as differences in their natural talents or taste; this explanation hides the role of social class. The upshot of this is that naturally "better" people (i.e. those with "better" taste) appreciate "better" art (i.e. that which is "inherently" more universal, aesthetic) and therefore the value system that validates "high" art and denigrates "low" art is based in nature, and not in the unequal distribution of power in a class-divided society. Bourdieu's account of cultural capital reveals the attempt of the dominant classes to control culture for their own interests as effectively as they control the circulation of wealth. The consistent denigration of popular culture, such as television, as bad for people individually and bad for society in general is central to the strategy.

This theory of cultural capital explains the social function of culture as the provision of a system of meanings and pleasures that underwrites the social system structured around economic, class, and other forms of social power. Cultural capital underwrites economic capital. But the metaphor of the cultural economy must not be confined to its similarities with the material economy. The circulation of meanings and pleasures in a society is not, finally, the same as the circulation of wealth. Meanings and pleasures are much harder to possess exclusively and much harder to control: power is less effectively exerted in the cultural economy than it is in the material.

We need to extend the metaphor of cultural capital to include that of a popular cultural capital that has no equivalent in the material economy. Popular cultural capital is an accumulation of meanings and pleasures that serves the interests of the subordinated and powerless, or rather the disempowered, for few social groups are utterly without power. Popular cultural capital consists of the meanings of social subordination and of the strategies (such as those of accommodation, resistance, opposition, or evasion) by which people respond to it. These meanings of subordination are not made according to the dominant value system, they are not ones that make a comfortable sense of subordination and thus work to make people content with their social situation. Rather they are meanings made by a value system that opposes or evades the dominant ideology: they are meanings that validate the social experience of the subordinate but not their subordination.

This popular cultural capital requires a set of cultural competencies to "read" it. Brunsdon (1981), for example, argues that women fans of soap opera are highly "competent" readers. Cultural competence involves a critical understanding of the text and the conventions by which it is constructed, it involves the bringing of both textual and social experience to bear upon the program at the moment of reading, and it involves a constant and subtle negotiation and renegotiation of the relationship between the textual and the social. Cultural capital and cultural competence are both central to people's ability to make socially pertinent and pleasurable meanings from the semiotic resources of the text.

Pleasure results from a particular relationship between meanings and power. Pleasure for the subordinate is produced by the assertion of one's social identity in resistance to, in independence of, or in negotiation with, the structure of domination. There is no pleasure in being a "cultural dope": there is, however, real pleasure to be found in, for example, soap operas that assert the legitimacy of feminine meanings and identities within and against patriarchy. Pleasure results from the production of meanings of the world and of self that are felt to serve the interests of the reader rather than those of the dominant. The subordinate may be disempowered, but they are not powerless. There is a power in resisting power, there is a power in maintaining one's social identity in opposition to that proposed by the dominant ideology, there is a power in asserting one's own subcultural values against the dominant ones. There is, in short, a power in being different. These exertions of power are all available to the subordinate and as such are all potential sources of popular pleasure. Pleasure requires a sense of control over meanings and an active participation in the cultural process. One of the central arguments of this book is that television is so popular, that is, it is capable of offering such a variety of pleasures to such a heterogeneity of viewers, because the characteristics of its texts and of its modes of reception enable an active participation in that sense-making process which we call "culture."

Television and its programs do not have an "effect" on people. Viewers and television interact. So in this book I shall not talk about television's "effect," though I shall refer to its "effectivity." This rather ugly form of the word makes it more diffused and generalized, less specific. In particular it takes it

19

out of any direct relationship with a "cause." Television does not "cause" identifiable effects in individuals; it does, however, work ideologically to promote and prefer certain meanings of the world, to circulate some meanings rather than others, and to serve some social interests better than others. This ideological work may be more or less effective, according to many social factors, but it is always there, and we need to think of it in terms of its effectivity in society at large, not of its effects upon specific individuals or groups. "Effectivity" is a socio-ideological term, "effect" an individual-behavioristic one.

And finally, in this preview of some of the terms used in this book, we come to that most important and slippery concept of all – "culture." Culture is concerned with meanings and pleasures: our culture consists of the meanings we make of our social experience and of our social relations, and therefore the sense we have of our "selves." It also situates those meanings within the social system, for a social system can only be held in place by the meanings that people make of it. Culture is deeply inscribed in the differential distribution of power within a society, for power relations can only be stabilized or destabilized by the meanings that people make of them. Culture is a struggle for meanings as society is a struggle for power.

This book is structured into two unequal sections. The next two chapters, like the first half of this one, investigate the forces of cultural domination. They explain how the dominant ideology and the social groups that it favors have their political and cultural interests promoted by television. The rest of the book explores the ways in which television can serve the interests of subordinated and oppressed groups. For television is a complex cultural medium that is full of contradictory impulses which enable it, on the one hand, to make profits for, and promote the ideology of, the few, but, on the other hand, to promote an oppositional, intransigent, or, at least, *different* cultural capital for the subordinated groups that constitute the majority of our divided society.

Chapter 2

Realism

The *Hart to Hart* segment is "realistic," not because it reproduces reality, which it clearly does not, but because it reproduces the dominant sense of reality. We can thus call television an essentially realistic medium because of its ability to carry a socially convincing sense of the real. Realism is not a matter of any fidelity to an empirical reality, but of the discursive conventions by which and for which a sense of reality is constructed.

The most obvious is that it presents itself as an unmediated picture of external reality. This view of television realism is often expressed by the metaphors of transparency or reflection – television is seen either as a transparent window on the world or as a mirror reflecting our own reality back to us. It is significant that both these metaphors invoke a sheet of glass as an impersonal, noncultural medium of reproduction – the human or cultural agency in the process is masked: this means that the finished representation is naturalized, that it is made to appear the result of natural rather than cultural processes, it is taken away from the realm of history and culture and moved towards that of universal truth. Taking the metaphors to their logical extreme like this reveals their obvious inadequacy to explain the way that television gives us representations of the world, but some professionals still cling to what media theorists call "the transparency fallacy" (the first of our metaphors), and the use of the reflection one is quite common even in relatively thoughtful discussions of the medium. The way that I phrased it at the beginning of this paragraph does allow it some validity, for it does assume that it is *our* reality, not *the* reality, that is reflected; in other words it admits that reality is the product of people, and not a universal object that people merely observe from the outside. What I wish to do in this chapter is to study the ways by which television produces "reality" rather than reflects it.

Realism can be defined in a number of ways, for it is actually a fairly slippery concept capable of a variety of inflections. Ian Watt (1957) and Raymond Williams (1977) tend to define it by its content. Watt traces its origins to the rise of the novel in the seventeenth and eighteenth centuries. Realism developed alongside empiricism, individualism, humanism, and the bourgeoisie, so it is not surprising that it should share characteristics with all of them. For Watt realism depends on the belief in an objective reality that can be accurately experienced by the human senses: this reality is made up of an infinity of unique objects, people, places, and actions. So for him realism characteristically represents particular events happening to individualized people in specified places and time spans. The senses and experience of the individual are seen as the prime way of making sense of this universe of phenomena, and if social, moral, religious, or political ideas intrude, they must always be expressed within the forms of individual experience.

Raymond Williams (1977), whose historical perspective covers the nineteenth and twentieth centuries, lists three main characteristics of realism in drama: he finds that it has a contemporary setting, that it concerns itself with secular action – that is, with human action described in exclusively human terms – and that it is "socially extended." By this he means that it deals with the lives and experiences of ordinary people, not kings and social leaders; in particular, that inflection of realism which we may call "social realism" and which Williams's definition is inclining towards deals with the working class's experience of subordination in an industrial society. In so far as this is portrayed sympathetically (though not uncritically), Williams is able to add a fourth characteristic of realism, that it consciously interprets this experience from a particular political point of view, normally from the left. The first three characteristics explain realism's particular suitability for television: television's audience, like realism's content, is socially extended, unlike the more selective audiences of theater or many cinema films; television is particularly well suited to representing human action in human terms – its small screen and comparatively poor definition lead it to concentrate on mid-shots and close-ups of people acting, reacting, and interacting. Its repetition and its origins in studios rather than exterior locations lead it to rely on familiar interior settings of a human domestic scale that fit comfortably into the family room within which it is usually viewed. Television typically deals with the contemporary – this holds good as a generalization despite the popularity of historical drama as a genre. Indeed, critics like Feuer (1983) and Heath and Skirrow (1977) have identified as one of the defining characteristics of television its "nowness," the sense of being always "live" which it constantly tries to promote. Film presents itself as a record of what has happened, television presents itself as a relay of what is happening. Even at the micro level this sense of the present is conveyed by television's technical processes. Cheaply produced dramas, such as soaps and sitcoms, are normally shot with multiple cameras in the studio and have limited or no post-production editing. This means that the time taken to perform an action on television coincides precisely with the time taken to perform it in "real life" – dead time in the middle cannot be edited out as it is on film. This absence of authorial (or editorial) intervention adds subtly to the sense of realisticness, the sense that the camera is merely recording what happened, and to the sense of liveness, that it is happening now – the same perfect match between represented television time and the lived "real" time of the viewer is, after all, characteristic of genuinely live television, such as sport.

Marion Jordan (1981), in her excellent discussion of the social realism of the English soap opera *Coronation Street,* lists characteristics that are perfectly compatible with those of Watt and Williams:

> Briefly the genre of Social Realism demands that life should be presented in the form of a narrative of personal events, each with a beginning, a middle and an end, important to the central characters concerned but affecting others in only minor ways; that though these events are ostensibly about *social* problems they should have as one of their central concerns the settling of people in life; that the resolution of these events should always be in terms of the effect of personal interventions; that characters should be either working-class or of the classes immediately visible to the working classes (shopkeepers, say, or the two-man business) and should be credibly accounted for in terms of the "ordinariness" of their homes, families, friends; that the locale should be urban and provincial (preferably in the industrial north); that the settings should be commonplace and recognisable (the pub, the street, the factory, the home and more particularly the kitchen); that the time should be "the present"; that the style should be such as to suggest an unmediated, unprejudiced and complete view of reality; to give, in summary, the impression that the reader, or viewer, has spent some time at the expense of the characters depicted.   (p. 28)

Williams's emphasis on social extension and Jordan's on the working class should alert us to the fact that most American television realism is not "social realism" with its implied criticism of "dominant" realism. Television's world is much more centered on the middle class which provides its typical content and viewing position.

Our discussion of realism so far has concentrated on its content and the definition of the social world which it provides. We have looked at its form only to stress its so-called transparency. But form is just as much a bearer of meaning and culture as is content, and many would argue that, as a bearer of ideology, form is considerably more effective than content. Obviously the definition of the world and the agenda that constitutes the world are important, but it is the form that they are given that produces the point of view from which we look at them, and thus the sense we make of them, and, paradoxically, the sense they make of us. For making sense is always a two-way process: understanding the object necessarily involves defining the subject who is doing the understanding.

□ The form of realism

So realism can be defined by its form, as well as by its content. This relates it
to what it does rather than to what it is or what it shows (its content). Realism
does not just reproduce reality, it makes sense of it – the essence of realism is
that it reproduces reality in such a form as to make it easily understandable.
It does this primarily by ensuring that all links and relationships between its
elements are clear and logical, that the narrative follows the basic laws of
cause and effect, and that every element is there for the purpose of helping to
make sense: nothing is extraneous or accidental. Thus the flowers in the
Harts' cabin are not just accidental decoration, they signify the Harts' class,
taste, and wealth, and they also carry the values of being a popular hero/ine,
those that constitute attractiveness.

I have assumed that realism is typically narrative in form, and this assumption holds good; indeed some, such as Barthes (1975a), imply that realism is
always narratival; even a photo or a realistic painting is a frozen moment in a
narrative, and understanding it involves reconstructing the narrative on
either side of the moment presented to us.

This definition of realism is particularly relevant for television because it
admits of fantasy. *Wonderwoman* or the *Six Million Dollar Man* are "realistic"
because their "fantastic" actions and abilities conform to the laws of cause and
effect, they are related logically to other elements of the narrative, and work
according to what Belsey (1980) calls a "recognizable system."

Davies (1978/9) develops this point in her argument that Hollywood
cinema appeals as widely as it does not because it is a visualization of the
nineteenth-century realist novel, but because its realism is able to embody a
variety of popular forms:

> What we have in Hollywood cinema is not so much a transference onto the
> screen of the dominant realist narrative form (which was principally con-
> cerned with interior moral life) but a fusing of popular forms (melodrama,
> romance, adventure, Gothic thriller, detective story, etc.) with a realist
> *politique*. (p. 61)

Her use of the word "politique" is significant for it implies that the mode of
realism itself is political, is ideological. The politics lie in the way it "contains" the world within Belsey's "recognizable system." Realism is thus
defined by the way it makes sense of the real, rather than by what it says the
real consists of. Watt (1957) refers to this way of understanding realism when
he points to its historical conjuncture with empiricism, individualism,
humanism (or secularism), and bourgeois capitalism. The way we make
sense of a realistic text is through the same broad ideological frame as the way
we make sense of our social experience in the industrialized west (the art of

non- or pre-capitalist societies is rarely realistic), and both involve the way we make sense of ourselves, or rather, the way we are made sense of by the discourses of our culture.

One way in which we are made sense of is described in screen theory by the phrase "the positioning of the reading (or viewing) subject." We will be exploring the issues involved in the question of subjectivity in chapter 4: for the moment we need to note that the text produces a socially located position that it invites the viewer to occupy in order to understand it easily and unproblematically. Thus the *Hart to Hart* segment invites the viewer to "be" white American, male, and middle-class. Realism achieves this positioning of the reading subject through its form.

MacCabe (1981a) claims an essential formal characteristic of realism is that it is always structured by a "hierarchy of discourses." By this he means that a realistic narrative will contain a range of different and often contradictory discourses, which are usually explicitly recognized as such, but that these are low down in the discursive hierarchy. Taking precedence over them is an "unwritten" and therefore unrecognized discourse which tells the "truth," that is, it provides us (the reader-spectator) with a position of all-knowingness from which we can understand and evaluate the various discourses of the narrative. In fiction, this is provided by the implied author, in film and television by the filmic/televisual discourse through which the story is told; this comes down finally to how the camera and the microphone represent the real and how the editor puts the results together. Thus in the *Hart to Hart* segment there is a discourse of heroes and a discourse of villains, but the televisual discourse (which we have already analyzed into its elements of setting, lighting, dialogue, music, etc.) gives us the means to understand and evaluate both discourses and set them in a sense-making relationship to each other. This unspoken, unrecognized discourse which MacCabe calls the "metadiscourse" gives us a more privileged position than either the hero/ine or the villains. This position of spectatorial privilege from which the world makes perfect realistic sense MacCabe calls "dominant specularity."

This position of privilege is, as the word implies, one that is ideologically active. The *Hart to Hart* segment attempts to position us as white, male, middle-class Americans, and by adopting this comfortable and ideologically rewarded position we are not just making easy sense of the text, we are reproducing the dominant ideology in our reading practice and are thus maintaining and validating it. Ideology, according to Althusser (1971), is not an abstract, stable set of ideas that we unconsciously adopt, but a practice: it exists and works only through practices, and here we are concerned with the simultaneous and inseparable practices of making sense of the text and thus of constituting ourselves as subjects-in-ideology. By this I refer to the process whereby understanding the realistic, obvious sense of the segment requires viewers to adopt the social position and thus the social identity that the text has prepared for them. In this case it is that of the white, middle-class male. In doing this viewers are making a particular sense of themselves and of their social relations and are thus actively participating in the practice of maintaining the dominant ideology.

Closely related to the hierarchy of discourses and dominant specularity in MacCabe's theory is realism's inability to deal with the real as contradictory. Contradictions that may exist in reality are inevitably resolved in realism by the discourse at the top of the hierarchy. Colin McArthur (1981) argues against MacCabe here by citing an instance of television handling contradiction:

> In *Days of Hope*, there is a scene in which Pritchard, the gentlemanly Northern coal owner, lectures Ben and the three arrested Durham miners on the excellence of the British tradition of peaceful, gradual and constitutional reform while, in the background, the soldiers brought in to suppress dissent in the coalfield indulge in bayonet practice. (p. 308)

MacCabe's (1981b) answer to this clarifies the working of the hierarchy of discourses in the resolution of contradictions:

> What McArthur here confuses is the narrative's ability to state a contradiction which it has already resolved, and the narrative's ability to produce a contradiction which remains unresolved and is thus left for the reader to resolve and act out. In other words while McArthur looks simply for contradiction in the text, we must look at how contradiction is produced in the audience. In the example McArthur cites there is a contradiction between what the mine-owner says and what the picture shows. But this is exactly the classic realist form which privileges the image against the word to reveal that what the mine-owner says is false. In this manner our position of knowledge is guaranteed – we may choose to disagree with what the narrative tells us but if it has already placed us in the position where we are sure we are right, it has not questioned the very construction of that position. (p. 312)

This televisual metadiscourse which produces this position of "dominant specularity" for us uses a number of formal devices developed by Hollywood for what Monaco (1977) calls the "omniscient style" of the classic Hollywood realist film. This depends on motivated editing (sometimes called continuity editing, e.g. by Bordwell and Thompson 1986), and its essential components, the shot/reverse shot technique and the 180° rule, the eyeline match and the action match.

Motivated editing, which developed as the classic Hollywood realist style, tries to make the work of the editor and director as invisible as possible. It does this by giving the impression that the edits are always required or motivated by the events in the "reality" that the camera is recording; they are never the result of the desire to tell a story in a particular way. This produces the effect of seamlessness, of a continuous flow, with no manufactured joins or edges. Of course this is, in practice, all nonsense – television is heavily edited, with cuts occurring on average about every seven or eight seconds. This maintains a high degree of visual stimulation – constantly changing signifiers is a televisual characteristic – and seems to be required by television's less than imposing visual image and its typical mode of reception.

The shot/reverse shot (or shot/countershot) is a typical stylistic device of motivated editing, and it is worth looking at in some detail to work out how it produces this "realism effect." Let us take a specific, but typical, example, a short sequence from an episode of *Cagney and Lacey.*

As Cagney replaces the phone after a call from a man she has just met, the camera holds Lacey and her in a two-shot, establishing the spatial relationship between them. It is shot more from Cagney's point of view than Lacey's, and thus has Lacey in almost full face. This is "motivated" as it is she who opens the conversation, and Cagney's view of the phone call that we are most interested in:

☐ *Camera*	☐ *Dialogue*
Shot 1: Two-shot, focused on Lacey	LACEY: So he's gorgeous and he's not a policeman. Did he ask you out? /*cut*/
Shot 2: CU of Cagney	CAGNEY: He gave me his number. OK? /*cut*/
Shot 3: CU of Lacey	LACEY: Well, did you tell him you would go out with him? /*cut*/
Shot 4: CU of Cagney	CAGNEY: Did you hear the word "yes" pass these lips? /*cut*/
Shot 5: CU of Lacey	LACEY: I didn't hear the word "no" either. /*cut*/

(Cu = Close Up)

27

Each cut coincides precisely with a change of speaker, so the editing and camera work appear to be determined by the action: it disguises its highly conventional, planned form in favour of an appearance of naturalness. Caughie (1981) distinguishes usefully between the types of camera work that are appropriate to the two styles of realism that he calls the dramatic look at the real and the documentary look. By the dramatic look he refers to:

> the system of looks and glances which is familiar from fictional film, and which works to produce the consistency and movement of the narrative, placing the spectator in relation to it – the rhetoric, that is, of narrative realist film: eye-line match, field/reverse-field, point-of-view. This rhetoric centres the narrative: it establishes, within a world of events, scenes, characters, and little narratives, the line and the connections which are to be privileged. It orders the world into a readable hierarchy.   (p. 342)

This *Cagney and Lacey* sequence exemplifies his definition precisely. The shot/countershot (or field/reverse field) pattern is working here to position the spectator in MacCabe's dominant specularity. The establishing two-shot gives us knowledge of the whole scene: we then see each speaker from nearly the point of view of the listener. We know, in shots 2 to 5, through the conventions of eyeline match and the 180° rule, exactly whom each speaker is looking at and talking to, even though she is not shown on the screen. This knowledge given by the metadiscourse of camera work and editing is superior to that possessed by either of the characters: we "see" into each, under their words, and into the relationship between them more clearly than either of them can. Thus it is important that the camera does not replace one of the characters, does not position us exactly in her position, for this would position us as one of them and deny us this superiority. More importantly, it would also mean that the speaker would appear to address the audience directly and would thus appear to recognize our presence. The omniscience given us by this dominant discourse of the camera depends also upon our position as an invisible eavesdropper-voyeur who can hear, see, and understand all without the characters' knowledge. "Reality" is laid bare before us.

Another effect of these conventions of shot/reverse shot and motivated editing is what is called "suture." This literally means "stitching," and works in two dimensions. The first is within the film (or program) itself where it refers to the way that the construction of the film, the way it is stitched together, is made invisible by these conventions so that our experience of it is one of "seamlessness." The second is the way that it stitches the spectator into the narrative: by allowing the spectator to see and understand the action from (nearly) the points of view of the characters it maintains the impression that the screen gives us direct unmediated access to the action, and thus allows the filmic/televisual metadiscourse to remain invisible, unspoken.

This attempt at seamlessness is not confined to fictional realism. In news or current affairs programs location interviews are normally shot with a single camera trained on the interviewee. After the interview is finished, the camera is then turned onto the interviewer who asks some of the questions again and gives a series of "noddies," that is, reaction shots, nods, smiles, or expressions of sympathetic listening. These are used to disguise later edits in the interviewee's speech. When a section of this speech is edited out, the cut is disguised by inserting a "noddy," thus hiding the fact that any editing of the speaker's words has occurred. Without the "noddy," the visuals would show an obvious "jump" that would reveal the edit.

The camera work and editing in this *Cagney and Lacey* sequence have produced a "hierarchy of discourses." The lower positions in the hierarchy are occupied by the discourses of Cagney and Lacey which come from the social bases of the traditional woman who believes that a woman's happiness depends upon her having a "meaningful" relationship with a man, and that of the newer "liberated" woman who challenges this. These are both what MacCabe (1981a) calls "written" or "spoken" because they are explicitly part of the drama. The invisible metadiscourse, however, which takes hierarchical precedence over them, is not: it is the filmic/televisual discourse which, by explaining and making sense of the lower discourses, confers upon the viewer the position of omniscience. From here the viewer can understand the partiality of each woman's discourse, and thus can see that in "reality" the "truth" lies somewhere between the two.

Caughie (1981) contrasts these conventions of dramatic realism with those of documentary realism:

> By the "documentary look" I mean the system of looks which constructs the social space of the fiction, a social space which is more than simply a background, but which, in a sense, constitutes what the documentary drama wishes to be about, the "document" which is to be dramatised. Thus, *Cathy Come Home* and *The Spongers* wish to be about the social environment of sections of the community and the bureaucracy which oppresses them; *Days of Hope* claims as its subject the whole of the labour movement from rural community to organised labour. This attention to the social environment and to the community is what connects documentary drama with the ideology of naturalism. (p. 342)

He goes on to give a good example of this documentary look:

> At another, and I think more fundamental level, the documentary look finds its consistency in the rhetoric of the "unplanned" or "unpremeditated" shot: the camera surprised by the action. In the last episode of *Days of Hope*, Sarah and Philip are in a pub; Sarah raises her pint of beer and proposes a toast to the success of the General Strike; a voice off-camera

responds, "I'll drink to that"; Sarah, still in mid close-up, acknowledges the speaker, still off-camera; and only then does the camera pan round to look for the person who had taken it by surprise. The little scene denies a script, denies planning, denies rehearsal, and establishes in their place a complete world which the camera can only capture, cannot have constructed, a world which goes on beyond the fiction. .... It is spontaneous, therefore true. (p. 344)

Other differences that Caughie notes between dramatic and documentary realism include the dramatic's reliance on an invisibility of form and on a spectator who forgets the camera, whereas the documentary appears to use an objective, but recognized camera, and thus uses conventions like the hand-held camera, the cramped shot, and "natural" lighting, often supported by unclear or inaudible (and therefore "natural") sound. The documentary conventions are designed to give the impression that the camera has happened upon a piece of unpremeditated reality which it shows to us objectively and truthfully: the dramatic conventions, on the other hand, are designed to give the impression that we are watching a piece of unmediated reality directly, that the camera does not exist. This may seem paradoxical in view of the careful matching of camera scripting to dialogue and action, but the conventions of dramatic realism abound with such paradoxes, all carefully disguised.

The conventions of the dramatic look are ideally suited to the classic realism that makes the individual's experience the "natural" way of understanding reality. Those of the documentary, however, shift the emphasis onto the environment of the protagonists, onto social factors, and away from the individual. They are thus better suited to the politically aware social realism that Williams (1977) finds in *The Big Flame,* and that may be called "progressive" if not "radical" (see p. 46–7): they are consequently less common in typical prime-time television.

There is another scene, later in the same episode of *Cagney and Lacey*, when the conventions of motivated editing and shot/reverse shot are used differently. The scene opens with a shot of Christine Cagney at a restaurant table. The man she is waiting for (who is the one who had phoned her in the earlier scene) is seen through the window behind her. He enters the restaurant off-camera, speaks his first lines off-camera, and then enters the frame to join Cagney at her table. As he does so the camera pulls back to give the establishing two-shot:

☐ Camera	☐ Dialogue
Shot 1: Establishing shot: Cagney waits, the man enters the frame, and forms a two-shot	MAN (*off camera*): Hi Christine. CAGNEY: Oh, sorry, I just went ahead and ordered, I hope you don't mind, I'm kinda pressed for time.

MAN: Oh no, oh no, it's fine, I hope there's no problem.

CAGNEY: No, I have six and one half minutes. Besides, I wanted to see you. /*cut*/

Shot 2: ECU of man

Shot 3: CU of Cagney's reactions; his shoulder is visible

MAN: Oh good, listen, I don't remember if I told you but /*cut*/ last night was . . . different.

CAGNEY: Well the restaurant was anyway.

MAN: Do you know what I'm saying, Christine?

CAGNEY: Yes I do /*cut*/ (*she pauses*) /*cut*/ as I said, I went ahead and ordered basically whatever they had prepared, because – er – the truth is I don't know what you like to eat.

Shot 4: ECU of man
Shot 5: CU of Cagney, tighter than shot 3

MAN: I'm an adventurer, remember?

CAGNEY: That's right, where did you say you went to school? /*cut*/

Shot 6: ECU of man

MAN: University of Pennsylvania. /*cut*/

Shot 7: CU of Cagney

CAGNEY: Right, in Philadelphia.

31

MAN: Uhum.

CAGNEY: Right ... You went on a basketball scholarship?

MAN: Uhum.

CAGNEY: Right.

MAN: Is everything OK?

CAGNEY: It's perfect. Why?

MAN: You just seem a little nervous.

CAGNEY: Oh no, I'm just interested, I would like to get to know you. /cut/

Shot 8: ECU of man   MAN: I think we know each other pretty well. /cut/

Shot 9: CU of Cagney   (*Cagney looks at him.*) /cut/

Shot 10: Two-shot, as shot 1   CAGNEY: Oh thank you (*to waitress bringing their meal*).

(CU = Close-up, ECU = Extreme Close-Up)

Here the narrative emphasis and viewer interest focus upon Cagney's suspicion of the man and of her own attraction to him, so this motivates the editing to keep the camera on her and her reactions even when he is speaking, thus keeping her in shot for much longer than him. Her suspicion of him is conveyed to us by her tone of voice and dialogue: the unspoken televisual metadiscourse of the editing, camera work, and lighting "tells" us that her suspicion is justified. The "truth" of the scene lies in her experience of it, not in his. The editing we have already mentioned, but it is worth noticing how the camera uses the variants of the close-up shown in shots 2, 3, and 5. The man (shots 2, 4, 6, 8) is always shot in tighter close-up than Cagney is, and in chapter 1 we have noted that extreme close-up is more likely to be used to portray villains than heroes; this is not to suggest that the man is a villain, but to swing our sympathy away from him, to see him from Cagney's point of view. Cagney, at the beginning and ending of the scene (shots 3, 9), is shot in "normal" close-up. In shots 5 and 7, however, she is more worried about him and about her feelings concerning him, so the camera moves in slightly to convey this anxiety, but not far enough for the shot to become an alienating extreme close-up. The camera's attempt to position us physically and emotionally with Cagney is supported by the lighting: the man's face is slightly less well lit than Cagney's, and her hair has back-lighting to give her a "halo" effect. Both of these are standard conventions of realistic lighting used to position the viewer "with" one character and "against" the other.

The metadiscourse of television realism is giving Cagney's discourse hierarchical precedence over the man's, and makes the scene easily readable by us in our position of dominant specularity. It works to defuse the contradictions in Cagney's experience by "explaining" to us her suspicions of the man and of her feelings for him. Our understanding of the scene is omniscient, and therefore hierarchically superior even to Cagney's.

☐ Realism and radicalism

The theory of realism that we have been following so far is leading us to the conclusion that realism is inevitably reactionary, it finally represents the world to us in a way that naturalizes the status quo. This provides us with a point of entry to the debate that has lasted for at least the last twenty years about television's role in an industrialized society. This debate focuses around the question of whose interests does television serve, and whose, if any, are disadvantaged by it. It is a debate that, in one form or another, underlies the whole of this book.

For the moment I wish to confine it to the relationship between realism and radicalism, and by radicalism I mean a critical interrogation of the dominant ideology and of the social system which it has produced and underpins; this entails an awareness of the inequalities and of the arbitrariness of late capitalism, which in turn produces the desire to hasten social change and the willingness to work for it.

Analytically it is convenient to identify two main foci of this definition of radicalism, which correspond roughly to our two ways of theorizing realism – via its content and via its form.

The clearest example of the debate is that centered around the British television mini-series *Days of Hope* in *Screen* in the late 1970s. The main participants were MacCabe and McArthur, though Tribe and Caughie also made valuable contributions. Their articles have been collected in Bennett *et al.*, 1981: pp. 285–352. *Days of Hope* was a series of four television plays that told the story of the rise of the British labor movement from 1916 to the General Strike of 1928 through the experiences of three main fictional characters. It provoked numerous public complaints, which fell into two main categories – those objecting to the BBC's screening of "left-wing propaganda" and those questioning the historical accuracy of its details, whether of dress, setting, or action. It is significant that the complaints brought together questions of ideological truth or falsity and ones of realistic accuracy or inaccuracy. Ideology and realism are inseparable.

Tribe (1981) makes the point that the letters from the public concerning the veracity of the image – the clothes, the buttons, whether the army marched in threes or fours in 1916 – were not just concerned with historical accuracy, but that this concern was itself an ideological practice and related to the ideological work of the text:

> It can be suggested that this veracity of the image is the vehicle for the veracity of the history that it constructs. This history is itself conceived as the truth of a past, a set of political events that we can draw lessons from. The project of *Days of Hope* is thus associated with the writing of a popular history along historicist lines. This history is however recognised as Truth by the viewer not by virtue of the "facts" being correct, but because the image looks right. The recognition effect "that's the way it was" is a product not of the historicity of the plot but of the manipulation of the image. (p. 324)

The realisticness of the image directly affects its believability and thus is a vital part of the cultural form through which the ideological practice operates.

Obviously, *Days of Hope* was a potentially radical television drama, and was seen as unacceptably so by (presumably) right-wing members of its audiences. Its radicalism lay in the way it provided a realistic view of recent history from a self-consciously left-wing political viewpoint: it thus conformed perfectly to Williams's (1977) defining characteristics of realism – it was contemporary (or nearly), secular, socially extended, and explicitly political. It was broadcast in a capitalist society, and it attempted to present a left-wing, critical view of that society. So its content challenged the dominant ideology of the time, and even its harshest political critics, of whom MacCabe was the most articulate, allowed that it was "progressive" if not radical. Its progressiveness lay in the way that its content opposed the dominant ideology and its concomitant social system. But, according to MacCabe, it failed to achieve the status of the radical because its form was that of conventional dramatic realism. MacCabe admits the progressiveness of the content of

Days of Hope, but finally condemns it politically because its potential is defused by the way it is made sense of and understood within the ideological frame of bourgeois capitalism as it is activated by the drama's realistic form.

This may seem a tortuous argument, and to understand its more general theoretical implications we need to go back to the notions of the hierarchy of discourses, of dominant specularity, of contradictions, and of transparency. Realism for MacCabe is necessarily reactionary because it proposes a notion of the "truth" that is seen as factual, not as a construct of discourse and culture. This "factual truth" is conveyed by the unspoken discourse at the top of the hierarchy, which he calls the metadiscourse, and which positions the viewer at the point from which this truth is made to seem objective, adequate, and therefore natural:

> The simple access to truth which is guaranteed by the meta-discourse depends on a repression of its own operations and this repression confers an imaginary unity of position on the reader from which the other discourses in the film can be read.
>
> (MacCabe 1981a: 310)

It is the transparency of the metadiscourse (the "repression of its own operations") that guarantees its truthfulness because it disguises its arbitrariness and therefore its political effectivity. It positions the viewer in "an imaginary unity of position" which is a crucial point in MacCabe's argument, for it is this that denies contradictions, or rather provides a means of resolving contradictions that may be expressed lower in the discursive hierarchy. The point is that realism resolves contradictions and does not leave them unresolved and reverberating in the reader. Unresolved, active contradictions working in the reader's consciousness would destroy the unified position of dominant specularity, and the complacent acceptance of omniscience that goes with it, and produce instead discomfort, uncertainty, and an active desire to think through these contradictions not just in textual terms but in terms of the reader's social experience. This is the radical frame of mind that is the necessary condition for the desire for social change. The crucial distinction is the one between contradictions in the text (which realism can handle comfortably without disturbing its reactionary entrenchment) and contradictions in the reader (which are a precondition for radicalism, and which the form of realism can never produce).

In chapter 6 we will discuss an alternative, and more productive, theory of contradictions in the text, one that emphasizes the impossibility of resolving them finally. MacCabe's theory stresses the power of realism, even when dealing with radical content, to leave viewers always in a reactionary frame of mind because its form enables them to use the dominant ideology to make dominant sense of a radical movement and thus to defuse its radicalism.

35

Realism, in this view, is a reactionary mode of representation that promotes and naturalizes the dominant ideology. It works by making everything appear "realistic," and "realisticness" is the process by which ideology is made to appear the product of reality or nature, and not of a specific society and its culture. Thus, if the Hispanic villain in *Hart to Hart* had triumphed over the white hero, it would, in our society, have appeared "unrealistic." Similarly, though differently, if the ship's cabin had had square windows instead of portholes it would have appeared "unrealistic." Realism involves a fidelity both to the physical, sensually perceived details of the external world, and to the values of the dominant ideology. In this way ideology is mapped onto the objective world of "reality," and the accuracy of realism's representation of the details of this "real" world becomes the validation of the ideology it has been made to bear – and I use the term "made to" in both its senses of "constructed in order to" and "required to." Realism's desire to "get the details right" is an ideological practice, for the believability of its fidelity to "the real" is transferred to the ideology it embodies. The conventions of realism have developed in order to disguise the constructedness of the "reality" it offers, and therefore of the arbitrariness of the ideology that is mapped onto it. Grounding ideology in reality is a way of making it appear unchallengeable and unchangeable, and thus is a reactionary political strategy.

Chapter 3

Realism and ideology

□ Popularity

There are a number of questions raised by the previous chapter's discussion of realism and the construction of the viewing subject, particularly ones about its pertinence to television. For its origin is in film theory, and although film and television share many characteristics, they also have crucial differences. The most important of these cluster around the different conditions of viewing, but there are also related differences in the nature of the text, and in the conditions of production. These form the substance of later chapters in this book. For the moment I wish to discuss the relevance of the concept of a radical text to mainstream broadcast television.

Television is, above all else, a popular cultural medium. The economics that determine its production and distribution demand that it reaches a mass audience, and a mass audience in western industrialized societies is composed of numerous subcultures, or subaudiences, with a wide variety of social relations, a variety of sociocultural experience and therefore a variety of discourses that they will bring to bear upon the program in order to understand and enjoy it. For its own purposes television attempts to homogenize this variety so that the one program can reach as many different audiences as possible. It tries to work within what these different audiences have in common, but it also has to leave a space for their differences to come into play in their readings of the program. We will go into this more fully in chapter 5, but for the moment we should note that the way that MacCabe gives the text almost total power to position the viewing subject denies the differences between different audiences and between the meanings they can, and do, construct from the same program.

But these differences operate in a constant tension with cultural homogeneity. This common ground is to be found firstly in a shared dominant ideology and secondly in a set of textual conventions that producers and readers share because they are part of a common history and experience. Television is a conventional medium – its conventions suit both the audiences with their needs for familiarity and routinization and the producers, for established conventions not only keep the costs of production down, they also minimize the risks in the marketplace. The economic dimension of television gives it a conventional form, even when its content is more progressive.

Thus *Cagney and Lacey* can represent the social world from a feminine or even feminist point of view in a form (the conventional police series) which is conventionally masculine in its ideology. Admittedly this masculine form is tempered with elements from the more feminine form of the soap opera, but the prime conventions, and therefore the dominant ideology, are those of the patriarchal bourgeois form of the police series.

As we have seen, the effect of putting a socially interrogative view of the world into a conventional form is debatable. MacCabe also argues that the conventionality of the form will always, finally, defuse any radicalism. For him, the unwritten discourse at the top of the hierarchy, the metadiscourse, makes such perfect and comfortable sense that it denies the need for any further interrogation on the part of the viewer by producing a frame of mind, that of omniscience, that makes further social interrogation not just unnecessary, but actually impossible.

This argument ends in a similar place, although it gets there by a very different route, to that of the pessimistic Marxism of the Frankfurt School. Their view was that the culture industry of capitalism homogenized people into a mass, and deindividualized them by debasing their taste into that of the lowest common denominator. The combination of economics and ideology was so powerful that any oppositional or radical movement was immediately swallowed up or incorporated into the dominant ideology. Thus a show like *Charlie's Angels,* popular in the late 1970s, could be said to have an element of radicalism in that it showed three female detectives in roles that were normally confined to men. But the fact that they were cast and photographed to foreground their sexual attractiveness could be seen as a device of incorporation; that is, their radicalism was incorporated into the dominant sexist ideology through the form of their representation in such a way as to show that patriarchy can accommodate "the new woman" into its view of the world without having to make any adjustments of principle, only minor ones of detail. Similarly, the female window/porthole/laundromat joke in our *Hart to Hart* segment can be seen as an incorporating device.

In both cases the effect of incorporating signs of "the new woman" into patriarchy is to defuse any threat it might contain and to demonstrate patriarchy's ability to accommodate potentially radical movements within the existing power structure. In this way its grip on our social meanings of gender is actually strengthened.

One of the effects of incorporation that is relevant here is its ability to rob the radical of its voice and thus of its means of expressing its opposition. When the iconography of the punk style of dress was incorporated into

38

"fashion" by the industry, the punk subculture was robbed of one of its main means of expressing its opposition to the dominant order. So, too, the incorporation of a left-wing or feminine discourse into bourgeois patriarchy can rob these discourses of their radical qualities. Incorporation is a powerful ideological defense mechanism.

Barthes (1973) uses the metaphor of inoculation to explain a similar ideological process:

> One immunizes the contents of the collective imagination by means of a small inoculation of acknowledged evil; one thus protects it against the risk of a generalized subversion. (p. 150)

Thus television news will often include radical voices, spokespeople from trade unions, from peace demonstrators, or from environmentalists, but these will be controlled doses whose extent and positioning in the news story will be chosen by the agents of the dominant ideology. Similarly, bourgeois realism can contain radical and subversive discourses, but it places them low down in the hierarchy of discourses and thus enables them to "inoculate" the dominant ideology against the radicalism which it is apparently allowing to speak. The implication of this metaphor is that the dominant ideology strengthens its resistance to anything radical by injecting itself with controlled doses of the "disease." The incorporation theory of the Frankfurt School works the same way – capitalism is strengthened by the elements it incorporates from the oppositional, and by the voices it has robbed from the radical.

This position ends up by implying that all popular culture inevitably serves the interests of the dominant ideology, for it is this that provides the common ground between producers and audience-seen-as-consumers, and between different audience groups whose differences are thus minimized. It then produces the conventional form of the popular work of art which performs its work of positioning the viewer as a subject of and in the dominant ideology so effectively that any radicalism of the content is necessarily defused by the conventionality of the form.

This opens up the question of the nature of the viewing process by which sense is made of both the program and the viewer. This forms the substance of the next chapter; here I simply wish to point to one implication of McArthur's position that MacCabe denies – this is the ability and freedom of the viewer to bring extra-textual experience and attitudes to bear upon the reading of the program. Thus women have told me how much they enjoyed *Charlie's Angels* when it appeared on their screens in the 1970s, and that their pleasure in seeing women taking active, controlling roles was so great that it overrode the incorporating devices that worked to recuperate the feminist elements in its content back into patriarchy. The ideological tension between patriarchy and feminism was not resolved as clearly or completely as the theory of the hierarchy of discourses would have us believe; while the hierarchy is undoubtedly there in the program, it may well be that its ideological effectivity was confined to those viewers who lived their lives through the dominant ideological practice, or a close inflection of it, whereas those who found that the dominant ideology did not enable them to make adequate sense of their social experience, and who thus turned to an oppositional or alternative one, were able to bring this different ideological frame to bear upon the program and still make a sense out of it and find a pleasure in it that was *their* sense, *their* pleasure, not the one proposed by the program. In other words, the program can mean different things to different people – a male reading may differ from a female, female pleasure from male pleasure. In later chapters we will explore the implications of this more fully. For the moment we need to note that there is some evidence that the television program is a relatively open text (that is, a variety of meanings can be, and are, made from it), that these meanings may be socially determined rather than textually determined, and that it is through this openness and polysemy that the same program can be popular with a variety of audiences.

The final inability of the text to impose its "meaning" upon its readers requires us to reconsider the extent of the power that Althusser grants to ideology. This power to constitute people as subjects-in-ideology appears to be so great that resistance is almost impossible, yet without resistance to ideology, resisting or oppositional readings of texts would be unlikely, if not impossible. Gramsci's theory of hegemony grants resistance a far more important role than does Althusser's theory of ideology. Briefly, hegemony may be defined as that process whereby the subordinate are led to consent to the system that subordinates them. This is achieved when they "consent" to view the social system and its everyday embodiments as "common sense," the self-evidently natural. Gitlin's (1982) seminal account of the hegemony of television forms gives due stress to the role of resistance, but his analysis appears to demonstrate that this hegemony is almost irresistible. However, he does cite Blum's (1964) findings that black audiences frequently put down television programs while watching them as evidence that the consent of the subordinate is never completely nor finally achieved.

Mercer (1986a) argues that this question of consent is one that has been inadequately investigated. Consent has been assumed to take one of two forms:

> either this consent is – paradoxically – *forced* by means of a legitimising "dominant culture" or the force is *consented* to via a liberal conception which holds that the mainspring of consent resides in the sovereign and legal category of the individual. Either way the site of consent is reduced to a vacuous timidity and its cousins "pleasure" and the "popular" are similarly assimilated to either ideological effects or personal preferences. (p. 50)

Mercer argues that such simplistic notions of consent fail to locate it within a complex, elaborated culture such as those of industrialized societies. Consent can take as many different forms as there are different social and historical moments of its negotiation. And consent can only be negotiated within structures of domination, subordination, and resistance.

Hegemony is a constant struggle against a multitude of resistances to ideological domination, and any balance of forces that it achieves is always precarious, always in need of re-achievement. Hegemony's "victories" are never final, and any society will evidence numerous points where subordinate groups have resisted the total domination that is hegemony's aim, and have withheld their consent to the system.

Said (1984) links Gramsci's notion of hegemony to that of elaboration: "elaboration is the ensemble of patterns making it feasible for society to maintain itself" (p. 171). An elaborated culture is dense, complex, and above all diverse: "the real depth in the strength of the modern Western state is the strength and depth of its culture, and culture's strength is its variety, its heterogeneous plurality" (p. 171). An elaborated culture is one that is structurally opposed to the homogenizing force of the dominant conception of what a society and its subjects ought to be like, and its elaboration consists of a wide diversity of forms of resistance.

> Gramsci's insight is to have recognized that subordination, fracturing, diffusion, reproducing, as much as producing, creating, forcing, guiding, are all necessary aspects of elaboration. (Said 1984: 171, cited in Mercer 1985: 51)

Hegemony characterizes social relations as a series of struggles for power. Cultural studies view texts similarly, as the site of a series of struggles for meaning. The dominant ideology, working through the form of the text, can be resisted, evaded, or negotiated with, in varying degrees by differently socially situated readers.

□ Realism and discourse

Realism shares many of the characteristics that Barthes (1973) ascribes to myth (see chapter 8), and these all stem from its being a discourse (or, as Barthes calls it, a language) that hides its discursive nature and presents itself as natural rather than cultural, that is, as an unmediated product of, or reflection of, an innocent reality. When O'Sullivan *et al.* (1983) define reality as a product of discourse they are, albeit somewhat mischievously, contradicting head-on the belief in an objective reality, accessible to all on equal terms and representable objectively or transparently. Structuralism and post-structuralism do not deny the existence of reality: what they question is its objectivity, its accessibility, its representability, and, therefore, its naturalness. Reality, the argument goes, is only accessible through the discourses we have available to make sense of it. Perception is a process of making sense, and sense is a product of discourse. Nature, or objective reality, does not "make sense" on its own – we have only to look at the vastly different interpretations different cultures make of universal nature to see evidence for this assertion. Discourse, as we have seen, is not only a product of culture, it is also, in industrialized societies at least, the product of society, and the power of political relations within that society. A discourse will always stem from a socially (politically) identifiable point and will serve the interests of the groups around that point by making their sense of the real appear *common* sense: and common sense is, as Barthes (1973) says, "truth when it stops on the arbitrary order of him who speaks it" (p. 150). So, as critics, we must never be content with asking and revealing what view of the world is being presented, but must recognize that someone's view of the world is implicitly or explicitly, obviously or subtly, inscribed within it. Revealing the *who* within the *what* is possibly the most important task of criticism.

This is important, because in industrial societies resources and social power are distributed unequally. This may be obvious in the domain of economics, but it is equally true, if less obvious, in the related domains of culture and language: indeed it is one of the great myths of bourgeois capitalism, centrally inscribed into, and assiduously promulgated by, the educational system, that a nation's cultural and linguistic resources are freely and equally available to all. Stuart Hall (1982) briskly opposes this:

> Of course a native language is not equally distributed amongst all native speakers, regardless of class, socio-economic position, gender, education and culture: nor is competence to perform in language randomly distributed. Linguistic performance and competence is socially distributed, not only by class but also by gender.
>
> (p. 79, quoted by Hartley 1984a)

Discursive power, that is, the power to make common sense of a class-based sense of the real, is held by the same social groups who exercise economic power. But the difference between the exercise of power in these domains is crucial: economic power is open and obvious, discursive power is hidden, and it is its hiddenness, its "repression of its own operations," that enables it to present itself as common sense, as an objective, innocent reflection of the real.

Barthes (1973) calls this self-disguising process "exnomination":

Now a remarkable phenomenon occurs in the matter of naming this regime: as an economic fact, the bourgeoisie is *named* without any difficulty: capitalism is openly professed. As a political fact, the bourgeoisie has some difficulty in acknowledging itself: there are no "bourgeois" parties in the Chamber. As an ideological fact, it completely disappears: the bourgeoisie has obliterated its name in passing from reality to representation, from economic man to mental man. It comes to an agreement with the facts, but does not compromise about values, it makes its status undergo a real *ex-nominating* operation: the bourgeoisie is defined as *the social class which does not want to be named.* (p. 138)

Exnomination masks the political origin of discourse, and thus masks class, gender, racial, and other differences in society. It establishes *its* sense of the real as the *common* sense and, when it achieves this, invites (Barthes and MacCabe would say "requires") the subordinate subcultures to make sense of the world, of themselves, and of their social relations, through the dominant, exnominated discourse, and thus, according to Barthes, to identify ideologically with their oppressor:

By spreading its representations over a whole catalogue of collective images for petit-bourgeois use, the bourgeoisie countenances the illusory lack of differentiation of the social classes: it is as from the moment when a typist earning twenty pounds a month *recognizes herself* in the big wedding of the bourgeoisie that bourgeois ex-nomination achieves its full effect. (p. 141)

In precisely the same way, realism invites (or requires) groups subordinated by class, gender, and race to (mis)recognize themselves in the exnominated metadiscourse of the *Hart to Hart* segment. Discourses lower down the hierarchy can be named, and this in itself becomes a sign of their lower discursive status. To name a discourse, say, "feminist" or "Marxist" is to imply that other discourses, other points of view, are possible. Only that which is not named appears to have no alternative, only that which is not named can achieve the status of the natural, of common sense. In MacCabe's theory, the "unwritten" metadiscourse works so well because it is "exnominated." It has been one of the achievements of Marxist cultural criticism in the thirty years since Barthes first proposed this theory that capitalism can be named in the cultural and discursive domains as well as in the economic: feminism has achieved the naming of patriarchy in a very much shorter period.

The repression of the role of discourse in defining the real leads to tautology – the real is what is real, not the real is what I say is real. Television realism articulates "a classic relation between narrative and vision in which what we see is true and this truth confirms what we see" (MacCabe 1981c: 315). Barthes (1973) describes tautology at work in more detail:

> Tautology is the indignant "representation" of the *rights* of reality over and above language. Since it is magical, it can of course only take refuge behind the argument of authority: thus parents at the end of their tether reply to the child who keeps on asking questions: *because that's how it is.* (p. 153)

Those groups with authority (those that constitute what Barthes calls the bourgeoisie) try to prevent a struggle over meaning by naturalizing *their* meaning – their economic and social power is mobilized discursively, ideologically, and culturally to exnominate itself beyond the realm of potential opposition. MacCabe's account of the operation of the meta-discourse in realism is identical. As those with social power are, amongst other things, white, male, middle-class, of conservative religion, middle-aged, and living in an economically and politically powerful region, we may expect the metadiscourse of television realism to originate from that social point where these discourses intersect, and therefore to naturalize that point of view and to work towards establishing it as the common-sense consensus of the nation. It denies the subordinate (those groups that Barthes calls the oppressed) the means of articulating and understanding their subordination by denying them a discourse with which to speak and think their opposition. As Barthes (1973) puts it:

> The oppressed is nothing, he has only one language, that of his emancipation; the oppressor is everything, his language is rich, multiform, supple, with all the possible degrees of dignity at its disposal; he has an exclusive right to meta-language. The oppressed *makes* the world, he has only an active, transitive (political) language; the oppressor conserves it, his language is plenary, intransitive, gestural, theatrical: it is Myth. The language of the former aims at transforming, of the latter at eternalizing. (p. 149)

What is important here is Barthes's suggestion that the oppressed must have one discourse that derives from their material social existence, the discourse of emancipation that aims at transforming the world, which no amount of social, economic, or cultural power can deny them. There is thus always a point from which hegemony can be resisted and social change motivated. MacCabe seems to deny the possibility of this point preserving its existence within or in spite of the structures of power and domination ranged against it.

□ Television and social change

The arguments that television is always an agent of the status quo are convincing, but not totally so. Social change does occur, ideological values do shift, and television is part of this movement. It is wrong to see it as an originator of social change, or even to claim that it ought to be so, for social change must have its roots in material social existence; but television can be, must be, part of that change, and its effectivity will either hasten or delay it. Thus series like *Charlie's Angels* and *Police Woman* in the 1970s, despite their numerous incorporating devices, were part of the changing status of women in our society, and could not have been popular in a period when women were firmly confined to domestic and traditional female roles. The tension in the programs between the portrayal of the liberated, active, strong woman and the incorporating devices of patriarchy was never wholly resolved to patriarchy's advantage, however much textual theorists might point to textual evidence that "demonstrates" that it was. Not all viewers read television programs according to the textual strategies encoded in them. The problem with much traditional textual analysis, whether its impulse has been ideological or aesthetic, is that it has tended to produce an authoritarian, even "correct," reading of a text, and has tended to ascribe to the text the power to impose this reading on the viewer. We are only just beginning to produce a theory of the text and consequent methods of analysis that can cater for the activity of the variety of viewers to make a variety of meanings out of the same text.

A similar problem confronts theorists, like MacCabe and Kaplan, who call for a radical text. Kaplan (1983a), who is primarily concerned with gender politics rather than class politics, finds four main characteristics in radical feminist films: her list summarizes the strategies that radical theorists in general call for to defeat realism as the dominant mode of patriarchal capitalism, and as such is easily adapted to apply to television and film in general, rather than to feminist film specifically. The first of her four features of radical texts is:

1. They focus on the mode of representation, on film or television as a machine producing illusions of the real, they draw attention to the (televisual) process and use techniques to break the illusion that we are not watching television, but "reality" (p. 138).

This echoes MacCabe's claim that part of the subject matter of any radical film or television program must be the process of making the program. Claire Johnston (1973), quoted by Kaplan, makes a similar point in her call for a radical feminist cinema:

> Any revolutionary must challenge the depiction of reality; it is not enough to discuss the oppression of women within the text of the film: the language of the cinema/depiction of reality must also be interrogated, so that a break between ideology and text is effected. (p. 28)

Similarly, Caughie's (1981) "documentary look" at least calls attention to the role and presence of the camera – it reminds us that we are watching a representation of the real. Against this, we must note that it does not make explicit the social point of origin of its metadiscourse, but instead presents this metadiscourse as one of objective facticity, of the "truth." This may be why its techniques appear to be more suited to progressive social realism than to radicalism.

Kaplan's other features of radical texts are:

2. They refuse to construct a fixed spectator, but position the spectator so that s/he has to be involved in the processes of the film, rather than passively being captured by it. Distanciation techniques ensure the divorce of spectator from text.

3. They rather deliberately refuse the pleasure that usually comes from the manipulation of our emotions.... They try to replace pleasure in recognition with pleasure in learning – with cognitive processes, as against emotional ones.

4. All mix documentary and fiction either (a) as part of the belief that the two cannot ultimately be distinguished as filmic models or (b) to create a certain tension between the social formation, subjectivity, and representation. (p. 138)

This sort of implied call to action on the part of the producers derives from a belief in the power of the text to produce a radical frame of mind in the spectator and thus to effect, if not originate, social change. This seems to me to overestimate the power of the text, to misplace the origins of radicalism and of social change, and to underestimate the role of the reader in the construction of meaning. In the rest of this book I shall argue that television inherently has the first two of Kaplan's characteristics of a radical text, and that their coexistence with the opposing characteristics of a reactionary realist text is the reason why television can be popular without being totally reactionary. Kaplan and MacCabe both have doubts about whether the sort of radical film or television program they want would be popular, but neither of them addresses the problem of popularity and its relationship to radicalism or progressiveness. The radical text, in its rejection of the dominant conventions for representing reality, tries to exclude the dominant ideology from any role in the production of meanings from the text. But in a mass-industrialized society, where our cultural life is dominated by the products of industrialized cultural production and distribution, the conventions of that culture industry, with their necessarily close relationship to the dominant ideology, have become the agents of popularity, accessibility, and understandability, and thus have to be taken into account in a theory of popular meanings within a mass culture.

Social change in industrial democracies rarely occurs through revolution, which is the sociopolitical equivalent of the radical text. Rather it occurs as a result of a constant tension between those with social power, and subordinate groups trying to gain more power so as to shift social values towards their own interests. The textual equivalent of this is the progressive text, where the discourses of social change are articulated in relationship with the meta-discourse of the dominant ideology. *Cagney and Lacey* is a progressive text because the discourses of feminism are articulated in a constant tension with those of the dominant ideology of patriarchy. The presence of the dominant ideology and the conventional form of realism through which it works are necessary to ensure the program's popularity and accessibility, but do not necessarily deny the progressive, oppositional discourses a space for themselves. Rather they provide a frame within which such oppositional discourses can be heard and their oppositionality made part of the substance of the drama.

The ability of the realistic form to contain oppositional discourses without defusing them completely is predicated on the ability of the viewer to read radically, and to give these discourses semiotic priority over the dominant ideological framework. This is the concern of chapter 5; I wish to close this one on a note of doubt that realistic television is necessarily reactionary.

Chapter 4

Subjectivity and address

The role of the subject as the central site of the sense-making process has been given a lot of attention in recent critical theory in general and screen theory in particular. It is not an easy concept to grasp, first because the word itself has such a long history of varied and abstract usages and second because the concept is in conflict with that commonsensical notion that is the basic assumption of so much capitalist and empiricist thought, the notion of the individual.

Theories deriving from both structuralism and Marxism require us to replace the notion of the individual with that of the subject. This is not to deny that we are all individuals, that is, that we inhabit different bodies with different and unique genetic structures, but it is to say that that part of us which forms our individuality is essentially biological, part of nature, and does not, therefore, form a major part of the study of culture. What cultural studies are concerned with, of course, is the sense that various cultures make of "the individual," and the sense of self that we, as individuals, experience. This constructed sense of the individual in a network of social relations is what is referred to as "the subject."

O'Sullivan *et al.* (1983: 231–2) trace three main usages of the word subject:

(1) *subject as in political theory* – the citizen as subject of the state or law. This sense implies the subject's lack of freedom of action with respect to the power to which s/he is subjected.

(2) *subject as in idealist philosophy* – the thinking subject; the site of consciousness. This sense implies a division between subject and object, between thought and reality, or between self and other. Hence subjectivity in this sense is the representation of that which appears to the self as opposed to that which is taken to exist in fact.

(3) *subject as in grammar* – the subject of a sentence (as in subject-verb-predicate), and hence the subject of a discourse or text; that which the action is about or determined by.

The first usage of the word often carries the implications of being subject *to* forces of social power – we are subject (or subjected) to the law, for instance, or to parental authority. The phrase "loyal subject of the queen" is an example of this usage with its connotations not just of socially determined behavior and the attitudes that go with it, but also of a sense of identity that originates from outside, rather than inside, the individual. This last is important for it points to the major difference between subjectivity and individuality: subjectivity is the product of social relations, whereas individuality is seen as the product of nature, or biology.

O'Sullivan *et al.* (1983) dismiss the second usage rather brusquely on the grounds that

> in this sense, subjectivity is the site of consciousness but it suggests a free-floating consciousness or unitary identity which then appears as the *source* of action and meaning rather than their product. The implicit individualism of this philosophical position fails to account for the role played by social relations and language in determining, regulating and producing what any one "thinking subject" can be.   (p. 232)

Their dismissal of idealist philosophy is justified, but they could have pointed out that the theories of Freud and Lacan have produced a relation between the individual and subjectivity that stresses the social and linguistic dimensions, and thus contrasts with the individualism of idealist philosophy.

The third usage brings the role of language, of discourse, and therefore of texts into the discussion. The theory here is that a piece of discourse is not only uttered or received by the subjectivity, but also produces it. Our subjectivity is the site of the sense that we make when we are speaking or listening but the sense that we make is not only a sense of the text or discourse, but is also a sense of our self, of our subjectivity itself.

Our subjectivity, then, is the product of social relations that work upon us in three main ways, through society, through language or discourse, and through the psychic processes through which the infant enters into society, language, and consciousness. Our subjectivity is not inherent in our individuality, our difference from other people, rather it is the product of the various social agencies to which we are subject, and thus is what we share with others. These social agencies are so numerous and interact with each other and with the social experience or history of each of us in so many different ways that the theory does not lead us to a reductionist, conformist view of society – clearly all subjects of white, patriarchal capitalism do not think in the same way, nor do they construct identical senses of their own identities; but equally clearly, all such subjects do have something in common that distinguishes them from subjects of other social systems. This separation of the subject from the individual allows us to understand why biological females, for instance, can have a male subjectivity, why blacks can make white sense of the world, and why members of the working class can understand themselves and their social experience in ways that serve the interests of the middle classes. The theory of the subject also denies the unity of the individual and her/his experience: individualism teaches that our experience and history are unified by our unchanging self into a coherent, unified development through time (if there are discordant bits that refuse unification, there is a whole industry of psychotherapy to help cure the problem). The theory of the subject, however, proposes that as there are contradictions between the agencies of society, so there will be contradictions in the subject. We may, for instance, have grown up in an unchallenged patriarchy, but have been subject to feminist discourses and agencies, and thus have contradictions built into our subjectivity which enable us to watch and gain pleasure from shows as different as *Hart to Hart* and *Cagney and Lacey*. As O'Sullivan *et al.* (1983) put it, "just as we are subjects of and subjected to these various agencies, so our subjectivity is a contradictory mix of confirming and contending 'identities'" (p. 232).

☐ The social subject

Let us look first at the way that our subjectivity is constructed on the social dimension. Hartley (1983) lists seven types of subjectivity (which he defines as a "structure of accessed identifications"):

> I'll suggest seven of the more important identifications that are available or encouraged. They are what I'm tempted to call the seven types of subjectivity: namely *self, gender, age-group, family, class, nation, ethnicity*. The list is both abstract and analytical (I don't have a textual warrant for it), and in the concrete instance of television it is not even a list, since the seven categories get very mixed up, and some are encouraged more than others (family more than class), whilst others don't co-exist very peacefully (some notions of nation with some types of ethnicity).   (pp. 69–70)

What Hartley is looking for here is what he calls textual processes and representations that may encourage reader identifications. In order to make sense of the *Hart to Hart* segment, the viewer is encouraged to identify with white, male Americans, family-oriented (the Harts are a close married couple, the villain and villainess a divided pair), in the prime of life (which is a mix of high physical and sexual attractiveness together with a degree of experience, maturity, and wisdom). These abstract social values or agencies are given concrete representation in the program, and together produce a unified subject position that the reader is invited to occupy in order to make easy, obvious sense of the text. The unity of this subject position is what makes it so acceptable in an individualist ideology (in which the individual is seen as both unique and unified) and this unity is the inevitable effect of realism which, as MacCabe (1981a) explains, is incapable of handling contradictions. This unified subject position denies any possible contradictions among these seven social agencies, and brings them together in a coherent whole within which each supports the others. So, for instance, there are no contradictions between whiteness and masculinity (despite the myth of black virility), there are no contradictions between whiteness and Americanness (despite the material existence of millions of non-white Americans) and there are no contradictions among class, gender, and age (despite the fact that they distribute power very differently in society). Hartley's list of seven is provocative and illustrative rather than exhaustive: he could well have added social agencies such as education, religion, political allegiance, region, urban or rural, and so on. Thus we somehow "know" (there is no warrant for it in the text) that the Harts are, for instance, better educated than the villains, that they are urban, from the north (there is a textual warrant for this, Jennifer adopts an exaggerated southern accent to say "That's the cutest thing you've ever said to me, sugar" in a way that constructs the south as deviant, the north as normal). We "know" all this because of the unifying, mutually supporting way in which these agencies work.

This support is organized by the ideological codes on the third level of Figure 1.1: they organize the social agencies and their meanings into coherence with each other, and then insert this textual coherence into the much broader and extra-textual ideological practice of making and promoting *common* sense.

The point to make here is that these social agencies are not confined to television: indeed, they work so easily in television realism only because they are representations of agencies actively at work in society. Television is able to construct a subject position for us only because these social agencies have been working all our lives to construct our subjectivities in equivalent ways. Ideology in general and television in particular try to deny contradictions between these agencies and to unify them into a mutually supportive structure, but our social experience is much more likely to make us aware of contradictions, tensions, and differences.

Television tries to construct an ideal subject position which it invites us to occupy, and, if we do, rewards us with the ideological pleasure that is provided by experiencing, once again, that our dominant ideological practice, apparently, *works*: the meanings of the world and of our subjectivities that it produces appear to make sense. It is, therefore, the pleasure of recognition. Of course, the degree of fit between these meanings and television's preferred ones will be determined by how closely the ideological practices of our everyday life fit with the dominant ideology. If our subjectivity conforms easily to the dominant ideology we will find little strain in adopting the subject position that television constructs for us: but some feminists, for instance, who oppose patriarchy's definition of gender difference, may find it impossible to match their subjectivities to the ideal subject position of the text, and thus would find the program unwatchable (unless they watched it theoretically and politically, reading it as another example of patriarchy at work, from which they could derive a wry, oppositional pleasure). Ideology may work hard through social and textual agencies to produce conforming subjects, but it can never be totally successful and in the next chapter we shall review work that reveals the power people have to resist the workings of ideology.

☐ The discursive subject

But for the moment we need to look further at the way our linguistic or symbolic systems work towards constructing our subjectivities. Language does not represent the world, but makes sense of it, for the world is not already divided up into neat categories that language names. But if language makes sense of the world, it makes that sense from a particular point of view. Any system of representation is inextricably linked to the social system in which it operates, and this linkage is active, not reflective. As Hall (1984) says, "a set of social relations obviously requires meanings and frameworks which underpin them and hold them in place."

Like all categorizations, our division of the constructors of subjectivity into the social, the linguistic, and the psychological is useful for analysis only: in practice the categories leak into each other, so that language and society are remarkably hard to separate out. Each of Hartley's (1983) seven types of subjectivity has its discourse through which much of its influence is exerted. A television news report on two white Australians sentenced to death in Malaysia was worded: "The two Australians will be the first westerners to die under Malaysia's strict anti-drug laws" (Channel 9, January 8, 1985). Here the overt discourse of nationality displaces the socially taboo one of race: the report invites us to make sense of the situation by using the categories of white/non-white rather than Malaysian/non-Malaysian, despite the way that "whiteness" has been disguised by the less politically loaded term "westerner."

In the second *Cagney and Lacey* scene (see pp. 30–2) the discourse of gender is working in subtler ways, for it underwrites a number of codes to discourage us from adopting the masculine point of view that is normal in patriarchal television. The narrative code gives the female the active role in the exchange, she controls the flow of knowledge and understanding. The camera concentrates on her, but differently from the way that attractive blonde women are normally represented in patriarchy: it interacts with the codes of acting, lighting, make-up, dress so as to deliberately make Cagney seem different from the passive bearer of the male sexual look. Instead, she is represented as a controlling, active person upon whom the camera dwells not in order to display her sexual attractiveness for the viewer-voyeur, but to explore and convey the manner in which she is controlling the scene.

Althusser (1971) places great importance on that aspect of discourse which he calls "interpellation" and which corresponds roughly with what linguists call "mode of address." Both these terms refer to the fact that any discourse is necessarily part of a relationship between addresser and addressee, and that any such interpersonal relationship is, in turn, necessarily part of wider social relations. Interpellation refers to the way that any use of discourse "hails" the addressee. In responding to the call, in recognizing that it is *us* being spoken to, we implicitly accept the discourse's definition of "us," or, to put it another way, we adopt the subject position proposed for us by the discourse. The news story about the two white Australians sentenced to death in Malaysia interpellates us as white, post-Christian humanists with a history of colonial superiority, and, in making sense of the item in this way, we adopt that subject position and thus, in the act of viewing, constitute ourselves as contributing to the constant process which constitutes us as subjects-in-ideology.

Television adopts a variety of explicit modes of address besides the indirect ones of the news report or the denied ones of dramatic realism. These interpellative strategies include, at the other extreme, modes of direct address such as "There's nothing you can't do in your Holden jackaroo" (a commercial for a four-wheel-drive vehicle), or:

> I wonder if you remember this dramatic picture we showed you a few weeks ago of Mrs Barbara Carter of Halesowen. She was attacked by lions in the West Midlands Safari Park. Well after an experience like that you'd hardly expect Mrs Carter to be keen on uh seeing lions again. But today she visited a farm near Stratford on Avon to do just that. A report from Alan Towers . . . .
>
> (quoted by Brunsdon and Morley 1978: 47)

This linguistic recognition of the viewer's presence has its visual counterpart in the way that television personalities (news readers, hosts and hostesses, etc.) look at the camera and address it directly. This nonverbal direct address works through eyes, tone of voice, facial expression, and gesture in the same way as direct verbal address to construct an intimate, explicit viewing relationship. Brunsdon and Morley (1978) and Feuer (1983) in their studies of British and American news magazine programs note how the intimacy of this mode of address works to construct a complicity between presenter and viewer that provides a televisual way of living the ideology of the family: it recognizes and constructs the domesticity of the viewing subject as the appropriate site where meanings are made and thus as a selector of the discourses which constitute those meanings.

> Thus, the relationships which are established between programme and audience, which set the viewer in place in a certain relation to the discourse – here, a relation of identity and complicity – are sustained in the mechanisms and strategies of the discourses of popular television them-selves, but also by the presenters, who have a key role in anchoring those positions and in impersonating – personifying – them. The linking/framing discourse . . . re-positions "us" into – inside – the speech of the programme itself, and sets us up in a particular position of "knowledge" to the pro-gramme by (also) positioning us with "the team"; implicating "us" in what the team knows, what it assumes, in the team's relationships with each other, and the team's relation to "that other, vital part of *Nationwide*" – us, the audience.
>
> (Brunsdon and Morley 1978: 22)

Nationwide's team of presenters work to establish an intimate relationship with the viewer that attempts to overcome the contradictions inherent in the inequality of that relationship. On the one hand they work towards an identification between "us" and "them" into the "we" of the program-plus-audience. In this they assume the position of "our" representatives asking the questions and making the comments that they assume derive from our (and their) common sense. But, on the other hand, "we" can never be equal to "them": for the presenters control the textual discourse and propose the reading strategies appropriate to the item:

> MB: And while we move on with Bob up river to Norwich and the studio let's hear from another part of East Anglia, from Suffolk this time although you might think it was a bit of America. In Bicentennial year a report from Luke Casey in Leighton Heath:
>
> LC: This is part of a very polite invasion. Three times a week an American aircraft courteously deposits its cargo of United States citizens onto this seasoned soil of Britain. For most, East Anglia is their first, jet-lagged look at Little Old England, where even the language is different. Soon they'll be happily, if predictably, pitching into the battle between tomatoes and tomatoes, and the mystery of Wor*cester*shire Sauce. But first, they learn of our more pressing eccentricities.
>
> (Brunsdon and Morley 1978: 50)

This invites us to read the presence of US airmen in East Anglia in terms of domesticity and tourism. They are individuals slightly bemused by their first step on "Little Old England," not members of foreign armed forces here to fly nuclear bombers. The link attempts to rule out a political discourse as a reading strategy.

Such linkages work also to construct a unity in variety that is the hallmark of the program, and which, indeed, could be argued to be the hallmark of television itself. The preceding item had been about a trip on a sailing boat on the Norfolk Broads and the linkage used geographical proximity, tourism, and a tone of jokey domesticity to construct a unity between the two different and potentially contradictory items. It is easy to imagine the different framing that could have been given to juxtaposed items on East Anglia as a holiday playground, and East Anglia as a frontline nuclear base.

☐ Addressing the subject

This construct of unity in the program also works to construct an equivalent unity in the viewing subject. As the presenters embody the unity of the program, so we, in identifying with them, are interpellated as unified subjects repressing any discomforting contradictions in the sense that we make of the program and of ourselves.

Jane Feuer (1983) finds that David Hartman's mode of address in *Good Morning, America* works similarly to identify viewers with him in a way that produces a comprehensive unity in diversity:

> For – at least in the case of *Good Morning, America* – the mode of address *is* to a great extent its ideological problematic. It would not be accurate to say that the show "carries" certain ideologies which the viewer may then accept or reject. *Good Morning, America*'s mode of address both produces and reproduces its ideological problematic of family unity and national unity-within-diversity. According to an ABS vice-president, "The image of David . . . is one of traditional values; he's perceived as a family man." It does not take a psychoanalytic reading to see the members of the show's family are meant as an ideal family for us, an idealized bourgeois nuclear family with a daddy and (various) mommies, brothers and sisters, fragmented by space but together in time through the power of the television image itself. It is a family similar to many American families in its fragmentation, its mobility, its alienation, yet the *Good Morning, America* family is unified as a direct (it is implied) consequence of television technology. That is to say, television brings families together and keeps them together. (pp. 19, 20)

Ellis (1982) places similar emphasis on television's interpellation of the viewer as a family member, but, usefully, begins to question television's power to unify. He argues that scheduling is part of television's mode of address to the domestic viewer. It is based upon the premise of the wife/mother being at home during the day and then being joined by the children home from school at about 4.30. This shift is marked equally clearly by a change in both program type and advertisements. Then, at about 6.00, the father of the household is expected to return from work, so the early evening news is broadcast to gather him into the audience. This is typically followed by a "softer" local news and news magazine program aimed at bringing the mother back and consolidating the family audience for the prime-time viewing to follow. In Britain and Australia, children are assumed to go to bed at 7.30, so slightly raunchier programs can be screened then. Prime time drifts to a close as the "normal" family gets ready for bed at about 9.30–10.00 p.m., leaving the airwaves for more minority or serious (or cheap) programs. Only those with a particular interest or oddballs such as insomniacs are predicted to watch late-night television, those that fall outside the consensual "average" family.

Hartley (1985) in a stimulating article takes the idea of the viewer as family member even further. He argues that television attempts to speak to its audience as children: "TV is a paedocratic regime; that is, the audience is imagined as having child-like qualities and attributes, TV addresses its audience as children, and is characterized by child-like pre-occupations and actions" (p. 9).

There are benefits to the industry in such a construction of the audience as it provides a kind of bench mark against which producers can measure their practice. He gives a number of examples of producers speaking of the audience as children (from Gitlin 1983: 138, 188, 324). The Australian program manager quoted by Tulloch and Moran (1986) was even more explicit in the economics of this strategy: "Get the kids in at 6, 7, or 7.30 and the parents will watch too. Older people will watch shows for younger people, but not vice versa" (p. 198). The huge, diverse audience is, by these institutional constructs, made knowable and singular.

This conceptualization is shared by institutions other than those of the producers. The networks practice their social responsibility by acting *in loco parentis*, and regulatory bodies and codes of industrial practice define standards of speech and behavior according to a family's concern for the moral welfare of its children. In the Annan Report, for instance, even where adults are specified as viewers, they are identified as members of a family by their relationship to children:

People watch and listen in the family circle, in their homes so that viola-tions of the taboos of language and behaviour, which exist in every society, are witnessed by the whole family – parents, children and grandparents – in each other's presence.

(p. 246; quoted in Hartley 1985: 11)

In Feuer's (1983) extended family of *Good Morning, America*, television becomes the concerned and responsible parent, the viewers the sheltered and cosseted children.

This emphasis on the family viewer has some further consequences for television. The family viewer of television is quite different from the isolated individual spectator of cinema posited by screen theory. The family viewer does not always give the screen such concentrated attention, but watches more sporadically in between or while reading the paper, eating, or holding snatches of conversations. Television then has to work harder than cinema to draw the viewer in: its mode of address recognizes a form of viewing re-sistance or evasion in a way that cinema's has no need to. The television viewer's response to interpellation is partial, not total: the power of the text to position the reading subject is much less than cinema's.

Ellis suggests that television works to construct a "complicity" with the viewer that is more than the construction of the ideal family out of the "TV family" and the "real" viewing family of Feuer. He argues that television uses this complicity to win the viewer's consent to television's role as her/his "eye" on the world. The crucial "look" for cinema is that of the spectator at the screen, in television it is that of television upon the world. The look of the viewer is one of glances rather than the controlled gaze of the cinema spectator. This has some significant consequences.

Firstly it sets up "the world out there" in opposition to "the family in here."

The position from which TV's investigations of the world, both fictional and factual, can take place is determined by the creation of complicity. TV assumes that it has certain kinds of viewers and that it speaks for them and looks for them. Interviewers base their questions on "what the viewers at home want to know", drama bases itself on the notion of the family.

(Ellis 1982: 164–5)

"The world" becomes something that is potentially disruptive to the family, so the news constructs essentially negative and threatening versions of "out there," sitcoms enact the weekly contest between the forces that attempt to disrupt the family and the "nature" that holds the family together, soap operas explore the internal stresses of the family against the rarely achieved but powerful ideal of the "normal" family. Ellis argues that television's effect is to "isolate" the family viewer from the world, to center him/her in the home, and to construct a subjectivity that is entirely familial:

> Broadcast TV confirms the normality and safety of the viewer's presumed domestic situation. The viewer delegates the activity of investigatory looking to TV itself. TV returns a particular overall sense of the outside world to the viewer against which the normality of the domestic is confirmed.
>
> (Ellis 1982: 167)

But against this, Ellis argues that television does not totalize its views of the world into a coherent picture viewed from an uncontradictory viewpoint, because to do so would "sacrifice the generalized domestic address" which is necessary if television is to reach the wide variety of people who can be spoken to through the general interpellation as "member-of-a-family." The viewer who "glances" is a much more diversified subject with a more diverse set of relations to the screen than is the cinema spectator who "looks" or "gazes." Television's thrust towards unity in diversity never totally achieves its object: the diversity is always there, both in "the world" that television looks at from the lounge room and in the relationships that its viewers take up with the screen.

Hartley's (1985) account of the conceptual strategies by which television institutions construct for themselves an image of the audience-as-child, and the problems that it entails, has similarities with Ellis: such a singular focus works also to "unify" the audience. But the convenience of this conceptual strategy for the institutions does not mean that the audiences themselves have to share it, and clearly they do not. The pleasures that *Prisoner* (see chapter 5) or *The A-Team* (see chapter 11) offer children liberate them from their role of subordination in the family. Similarly music videos for teenagers and sport for men offer extra-familial reading positions and pleasures. While television sport may address men as extra-familial mates in male-bonding, Morse (1983) has shown that its eroticization of the male body can address women as feminine sexual subjects, not as mother-wife-consumer. Hartley (1985) goes on to argue that television is caught between competing needs – the need to appeal to and win over a wide diversity of audiences and the need to discipline and control those audiences so that they can be reached by a single, industrially produced, cultural commodity. In order to achieve this, television has to recognize that a diversity of audiences requires a diversity of modes of address:

> Far from seeking to fix just one subject position (least of all that of Ellis's "normal citizen"), television has developed a heterogeneity of modes of address, of points of view, of program genres, of styles of presentation. It is characterized, in short, by excess, providing its audience with an excess

of "positions" which nevertheless can be easily recognized, and offering an excess of pleasures which nevertheless can be disciplined into familiar, predictable forms.   (Hartley 1985 : 16)

☐ Psychoanalysis and the subject

The interaction between languages, their mode of address, and other social agencies is the one that best accounts for the role of the subject in the television viewing: however, we must not ignore the relationship between language and psychoanalysis in the construction of meanings, and in the formation of the subjectivity which is the site of the meaning-making process. This has been particularly influential in the development of screen theory, but less helpful in developing a theory of television and television criticism.

At the heart of this approach lies Lacan's belief that the unconscious is structured like a language and that the infant's acquisition of consciousness is in fact the acquisition of language, or rather of the means of making meaning. In early infancy, the child does not distinguish between inside and outside, between self and not-self: his or her perceptions of the external world take the same form as the perceptions of his/her internal states. The awareness that self is different from not-self, or the other, is the first meaning that the child makes and the first construction of difference upon which all meanings depend. This awareness of difference is at the heart of Lacan's view of infancy as the period in which the child simultaneously develops the ability to make meaning and enters into the meaning system always already awaiting her or him. The two processes are really one, for the child cannot, to use an instance central to feminist thinking, construct that most basic meaning of self, the one based on gender differentiation, without entering into the system of gender differences and the power relations between them that the culture already uses and which awaits the entry of the new arrival.

Lacan's account of the mirror phase is also based upon difference. In this, the infant sees her/himself reflected in a mirror and, in the realization that reflection and self are different but related, enters the world of the symbolic, the world where objects are not essences, but bearers of meaning. But the reflection is never merely that, for that would imply that it was inferior to the real, and Lacan argues that the reflection is more than the real and "improves" on it. The mirror phase occurs when the child's body is still inadequate and ineffective, and what the child sees reflected is his/her imaginary body, shorn of its physical limitations, so the symbolic is composed of both the imaginary and the real. Thus a photograph of a scene (which may be understood as a "fixed" reflection) is often more pleasurable to look at than the scene itself, for it can close the gap between the imaginary and the real, and pleasure derives from the extent to which this unity is achieved, this gap is closed.

Thus a child gets pleasure from his/her reflection to the extent that the act of looking allows the symbolic self in the mirror to merge the imaginary self with the perceived real self. Similarly images of women and men on the television or film screen produce pleasure in the viewer in so far as they allow the imaginary to be grounded in the representation of the real and thus to gain the guarantee that the imaginary is adequate because of its close relation to, if not total identification with, the real.

We must not allow this theory to imply that the imaginary depends upon an essential ideal of the self that is part of a universal, unchanging human nature. The fact that the unified imaginary world precedes the entry into the symbolic via difference means that the desire to regain this unity may well be a universal part of human nature, but the form of this unity and therefore the ways in which the desire is expressed and satisfied are determined by culture and are therefore ideological. The child's experience of the real occurs only after its entry into the symbolic and is determined by the symbolic system into which s/he has entered. If both the symbolic and the real are culturally determined, as any system of difference must be, the form that the imaginary takes in its struggle to unite them must also be the product of culture, not nature.

This is important, because it means that the imaginary, the subconscious, pleasure, and desire are all cultural constructs, or at least culturally inflected, and are not unchanging and unchangeable aspects of human nature. An essentialist reading of Freud and Lacan is politically unproductive in that it misrepresents constructs of a patriarchal society, such as phallocentric language and the Law of the Father, as human nature and thus excludes them from the agenda of social change. Such an essential view of the subjectivity would first deny the power of different social experiences to produce different subjectivities and thus different ways of understanding, and second, would see the language system, particularly as manifest in a film text, as necessarily reinforcing the subjectivity that has already been produced by the symbolic system that both producer and reader of the text share. Lacan's and Freud's theories on the creation of the subjectivity (and of the unconscious) in the infant need to be given a cultural rather than an essentialist inflection, for only then can they accommodate the role of social experience in the construction of the subject, and the development of contradictions within the subjectivity, and its ability to change over time.

Television is experienced by, and constructs, a variety of social subjects rather than a singular psychoanalytic one, and the Lacanian account of the construction of subjectivity which has proved fruitful in the study of cinema is not so applicable to television. Feuer (1986) suggests that the "individual" spectator posited by cinema is pre-Oedipal and thus is appropriately under-stood by a Lacanian model, but the family television viewers are post-Oedipal, socialized, and thus require a socially derived theory of subjectivity rather than a psychoanalytic one. This requires us to develop a model of the reading subject and his/her relationships to the text that can account for differences amongst socially constructed subjectivities. Screen theory, with its emphasis on the text that is common to all readers, and on psychoanalytic processes which are equally common, has produced a model of singular textual effectivity and singular reading subjects. In the next three chapters we will diversify our account of audiences, of the meanings proposed by the text, and of the reading relations through which text and reading subject interconnect.

Chapter 5

Active audiences

☐ Text and social subjects

When audiences are understood as textual subjects, as in MacCabe's work, they are seen as relatively powerless and inactive and MacCabe and others such as Heath developed this view into the orthodoxy of screen theory. But a few dissenting notes were struck in the pages of *Screen* and a number of writers such as Morley (1980b), Willeman (1978), and Neale (1977) began to challenge this view of the subject, particularly by insisting on the difference between the socially and the textually produced subjects. The social subject has a history, lives in a particular social formation (a mix of class, gender, age, region, etc.), and is constituted by a complex cultural history that is both social and textual. The subjectivity results from "real" social experience and from mediated or textual experience. The actual television viewer is a primarily social subject. This social subjectivity is more influential in the construction of meanings than the textually produced subjectivity which exists only at the moment of reading.

Willeman (1978) writes:

> There remains an unbridgeable gap between "real" readers/authors and "inscribed" ones, constructed and marked in and by the text. Real readers are subjects in history, living in social formations, rather than mere subjects of a single text. The two types of subject are not commensurate. But for the purposes of formalism, real readers are supposed to coincide with the constructed readers. (p. 48, quoted in Morley 1980a: 159)

Morley (1980a) went on to investigate empirically this difference. He took the issue of *Nationwide* that Brunsdon and he (1978) had analyzed and showed it to groups of between five and ten viewers. He also showed a later issue to another group. The groups were defined primarily by occupation, though he also noted their gender and race. The occupations included apprentices, bank managers, teacher-training students, arts students, black girls, trade unionists, and so on. The screening of the programs was followed by an open discussion, usually of about thirty minutes: recordings of these discussions are the prime data with which he worked.

He chose groups because he wanted to trace the responses of socially produced subjects, and the social dimension would emerge from what groups had in common. Occupation was the prime definer of the group because it is a prime definer of class, and class, according to Parkin (1972) and Hall (1980a), is the most important factor in producing socially motivated differences of reading.

What Morley found was that Hall, in following Parkin (1972), had over-emphasized the role of class in producing different readings and had under-estimated the variety of determinants of readings. Thus the readings showed some interesting and unexpected cross-class similarities: bank managers and apprentices, for example, produced broadly similar readings despite their class differences; so, too, did some university students and trade unionists. We could explain these apparent anomalies by suggesting that the apprentices and bank managers were similarly constructed as subjects of a capitalist ideology in that they were both inserting themselves into the dominant system (albeit at different points) and thus had a shared interest in its survival and success. University students and trade unionists, however, were in institutions that provided them with ways of criticizing the dominant system and they thus produced similar and more oppositional readings.

This work of Morley helped to establish ethnography as a valid method of studying television and its viewers. The object of ethnographic study is the way that people live their culture. Its value for us lies in its shift of emphasis away from the textual and ideological construction of the subject to socially and historically situated people. It reminds us that actual people in actual situations watch and enjoy actual television programs. It acknowledges the differences between people despite their social construction, and pluralizes the meanings and pleasures that they find in television. It thus contradicts theories that stress the singularity of television's meanings and its reading subjects. It enables us to account for diversity both within the social forma-tion and within the processes of culture. Ethnographic study may take the observational form of Hobson's (1980, 1982) work in which she went into homes to see how women integrated television into their domestic and family lives. Or like Morley's (1980a, 1986) or Ang's (1985) work, it may use viewers' verbalizations of their responses to television, in which case it moves to an ethnography of discourse. Of course, Hobson talked with her subjects, too, and their discourses about the media in their lives are an important part of her data. Palmer (1986) combined observations of children viewing in their homes with interviews and questionnaires. All these studies, in one way or another, trace differences amongst viewers, modes of viewing, and the meanings or pleasures produced. This revaluation of the viewer requires a similar revaluation of the text. Textual studies of television now have to stop treating it as a closed text, that is, as one where the dominant ideology exerts considerable, if not total, influence over its ideological structure and therefore over its reader. Analysis has to pay less attention to the textual strategies of preference or closure and more to the gaps and spaces that open television up to meanings not preferred by the textual structure, but that result from the social experience of the reader.

Hall's (1980a) preferred reading theory was an early attempt to account for this theoretically. Briefly, he argued that viewers whose social situation, particularly their class, aligned them comfortably with the dominant ideology would produce dominant readings of a text; that is, they would accept its preferred meanings and their close fit with the dominant ideology. Other viewers, whose social situation placed them in opposition to the dominant ideology, would oppose its meanings in the text and would produce oppositional readings. The majority of viewers, however, are probably situated not in positions of conformity or opposition to the dominant ideology, but in ones that conform to it in some ways, but not others; they accept the dominant ideology in general, but modify or inflect it to meet the needs of their specific situation. These viewers would, Hall argued, produce negotiated readings of the text; these are readings that inflect the meanings preferred by the dominant ideology, to take into account the social differences of different viewers.

Thus a dominant reading of the *Hart to Hart* segment in chapter 1 would be made by a white, middle-class, urban, northern male, and would conform to the dominant ideology as it is encoded in the text. An oppositional reading might be made by a Hispanic member of the working classes, who would reject the dominant meanings and pleasures offered by the program because they opposed his interests; he might support the crimes of the Hispanic villain as revolutionary acts against white capitalism. A woman, however, might produce a negotiated reading, which accepted the ideological framework of the narrative, but negotiated within it a special significance for the heroine, her actions, and the values she embodies. She would thus see the heroine's capitalization on her looks and her jewelry as means of exercising female power within, but not against, patriarchy.

The limitations of this theory are that it overemphasizes class in relation to other social factors and that it implies that the three types of reading are roughly equal. In practice, there are very few perfectly dominant or purely oppositional readings, and consequently viewing television is typically a process of negotiation between the text and its variously socially situated readers. The value of the theory lies in its freeing the text from complete ideological closure, and in its shift away from the text and towards the reader as the site of meaning.

Just how far this shift goes is, of course, a matter of debate. Hall argues that while television programs allow a variety of negotiated or oppositional meanings, their structure always prefers a meaning that generally promotes the dominant ideology. It is the ideology in this meaning that is negotiated with or opposed. It is more productive to think not so much of a singular preferred meaning, but of structures of preference in the text that seek to prefer some meanings and close others off. This is an elaboration of Hall's model, not a rejection of it, for it still sees the text as a structured polysemy, as a potential of unequal meanings, some of which are preferred over, or proffered more strongly than, others, and which can only be activated by socially situated viewers in a process of negotiation between the text and their social situation.

Eco's (1972) theory of aberrant decoding is essentially similar. In this Eco argues that whenever there are significant social differences between the encoders and decoders of a text, then decoding will necessarily be "aberrant." By this he means that the text will be decoded by a different set of codes and conventions from those operating during its encoding or production, and the resulting meanings will thus be determined more by the social situation of the decoder than by that of the encoder. He concludes that for mass communication, whose texts by definition are decoded by a wide variety of social groups, aberrant decodings are, paradoxically, the norm.

In the rest of this chapter I shall detail some recent ethnographic studies of television viewers, and the evidence they provide of the viewers' ability to make their own socially pertinent meanings out of the semiotic resources provided by television. These studies make this chapter a pivotal one in the book. The preceding chapters have analyzed television's power to construct its preferred readings and readers. Subsequent ones will explore television's openness, its invitations to its viewers to construct their meanings out of its texts, and will thus require us to reevaluate the relative power of texts and viewers in the production of meaning and pleasure.

☐ Making meanings

Morley (1980a) was the first to put this semiotic and cultural theory through an empirical investigation. His work calls into question key aspects of the screen theory of classic realism, and its view of the relationship between the text and the reading subject, for it refutes the argument that the ideology in the structure of the text works almost irresistibly to position and construct the subjectivity of the reader as a subject in ideology. Bank managers and apprentices are *already* positioned towards the dominant ideology, so too are students and trade unionists. Reading the television text is a process of negotiation between this existing subject position and the one proposed by the text itself, and in this negotiation the balance of power lies with the reader. The meanings found in the text shift towards the subject position of the reader more than the reader's subjectivity is subjected to the ideological power of the text.

To be popular, the television text has to be read and enjoyed by a diversity of social groups, so its meanings must be capable of being inflected in a number of different ways. The television text is therefore more polysemic and more open than earlier theorists allowed for. As Hobson (1982) puts it: "The message is not solely in the "text", but can be changed or "worked on" by the audience as they make their own interpretation of a programme" (p. 106).

This means that reading is not a garnering of meanings from the text but is a dialogue (Volosinov 1973) between text and the socially situated reader. As Morley (1980a) says:

> Thus the meaning of the text must be thought in terms of which set of discourses it encounters in any particular set of circumstances, and how this encounter may re-structure both the meaning of the text and the discourses which it meets. The meaning of the text will be constructed differently according to the discourses (knowledges, prejudices, resistances, etc.) brought to bear on the text by the reader and the crucial factor in the encounter of audience/subject and text will be the range of discourses at the disposal of the audience. (p. 18)

The *Hart to Hart* extract in chapter 1 provides us with an example of a discourse in a text that can be read differently by the discursive practices of different readers. The window/porthole/laundromat joke occurs within the discourse of gender. Its social domain is gender difference, its location is the masculine position. It says that women can only make sense of the technical world by reducing it to the domestic. It therefore makes sense of the feminine in a way that serves the interests of the masculine, because it reserves competence in the technical, public world for men. It is therefore a bearer and producer of a patriarchal ideology. But it may meet a nonpatriarchal subject, and must be capable of being read from this subject position.

One way of understanding our subjectivity is that it is composed of the variety of discourses that we use to make sense of the social domains that constitute our social experience. Because our social experience has varied, and does vary, so much, our subjectivities are likely to be composed of a number of different, possibly contradictory discourses, each bearing traces of a different specific ideology. (A discourse bears a specific ideology and through that relates to the dominant ideology or ideology in general.) Stuart

Hall (1983) argues persuasively for the contradictoriness of the specific ideologies and discourses that comprise our subjectivity which requires us to see the subjectivity as disunited, as a site of struggle, not as a unified site of ideological reconciliation:

> As Gramsci said again, our personalities are not at all as we imagine them, as sort of unified boxes, but are full of very contradictory elements – progressive elements and stone-age elements. There is a true domestic woman inside the woman who is struggling to be a liberated feminist, there is the religious trace inside those of us who think we are fully secularized modern citizens, we are full of the rag-bag and debris of ancient ideologies which have lost their systematic form, but still hang about. Even when we don't think with these bits, we feel with them, which is one of the reasons why people in the modern world, who know that, for instance, sexual jealousy is one of the most extraordinary ways of dispensing with emotional energy ... once it happens get into an absolutely primitive rage. ... The notion that we are talking about a kind of rationally calculative system and figures of thought that just correspond to a rationally given economic interest does not describe the maelstrom of potential ideological subjects that we are.

The reader of the window/porthole/laundromat joke is not required to read it in the way preferred by the text. If the text's conservative patriarchal discourse of gender meets either a more liberal or more radical one in the reader, the joke will be decoded very differently (see chapter 6). But Hall implies that such a joke may be decoded in two ways simultaneously by the same viewer. A one-time sexist who is now liberated will be able to respond doubly according to both gender discourses which still exist, even if unequally, in his or her subjectivity.

Both the text and the subjectivity are discursive constructs and both contain similar competing or contradictory discourses. It is out of these contradictions that the polysemy of the text and the multiplicity of readings arise.

Hodge and Tripp (1986) provide good examples of multiple or contradictory readings made by viewers. They did not ask what effect television has on its audience, nor what use does the audience make of television; rather they asked how a particular television text, seen as a polysemic potential of meanings, connects with the social life of the viewer or group of viewers. They were concerned with how a television text is read, with how meanings are made by the active reading of an audience, and how this activity of reading can be explained in terms of a theory of culture, that is, the process of making common sense out of social experience. Their readers were school children and their work is based on an assumption about children that needs spelling out, because it differs from that which underlies so much of the research in this area: Hodge and Tripp assume that children are not fools or passive dupes able to be affected against their will and against their interests by the wicked stepmother called television. Rather, they assume that children are engaged in a constant active struggle to make sense out of their social experience, and that television plays an important role in that struggle.

Market research had found that one of the most popular programs with Australian school children was *Prisoner*, a soap opera set in a women's prison, and screened in the USA under the title *Prisoner: Cell Block H*. This appeared, on the face of it, to be a surprising choice for junior high school students.

Hodge and Tripp discovered that many of the children found, at varying levels of consciousness, and were able to articulate with varying degrees of explicitness, usefully significant parallels between the prison and the school. They perceived the following main similarities between prisoners and school students:

1. pupils are shut in;
2. pupils are separated from their friends;
3. pupils would not be there if they were not made to be;
4. pupils only work because they are punished if they do not, and it is less boring than doing nothing at all;
5. pupils have no rights: they can do nothing about an unfair teacher;
6. some teachers victimize their pupils;
7. there are gangs and leaders amongst the pupils;
8. there are silly rules which everyone tries to break. (p. 49)

In their discussions the children showed that they made meanings out of *Prisoner* that connected the program to their own social experience. A textual study revealed many parallels between prison and school. In both there were recognizable role types amongst staff and prisoners that formed recognizable and usable categories with which students could "think" their school experience – the hard-bitten old warden/teacher, the soft new one, the one you can take advantage of, the one you can't, and so on. Similarly there were prisoners who resisted the institution and fought it in all ways, those who played along with it and were the goody goodies, those who played along with it on the surface, but opposed it underneath, and so on. There were also strategies of resistance that applied to both: prisoners used a secret language, sometimes of special private words, but more often of nudges, winks, glances, and *doubles entendres* to communicate amongst themselves under the noses of and in resistance to the wardens/teachers. There was an oppositional subculture of the public areas of the prison, particularly the laundry where many of them worked, that paralleled the oppositional school subculture of the lavatories, the locker rooms, and special corners of the yard. And in both institutions there was a consistent attempt by the official culture to colonize and control these areas, which was resisted and resented by the inmates who struggled to keep them within their own cultural control.

Palmer (1986) found a group of 11- and 12-year-old girls who regularly reenacted the previous night's episode of *Prisoner* in the schoolyard, sometimes even coopting a friendly teacher to play one of the wardens:

ANNETTE (11): If we played *Prisoner*, well, Miss would be one of the officers, like, because she had the loudhailer and she used to scream at us through it.

INTERVIEWER: Did she watch *Prisoner*?

ANNETTE: I don't think so, but we'd tell her what to say.

INTERVIEWER: Which warden did you make her into?

ANNETTE: We made her one of the real bad ones, Officer Powell, she's a real baddie but she's all right now because there's a worse one than her, Miss Ferguson. (p. 111)

It is significant that the teacher, with her symbol of authority (the loudhailer), was cast as "a real baddie." The teacher's good-humored involvement in the game is a mark of her popularity, yet the girls' acceptance of this individual teacher coexisted with a resistance to the authority she represented. Palmer comments:

From the girls' description, it seems there was much good humour generated on both sides by the teacher's participation in such a way. Both children and teacher were acknowledging the disparity in their own positions in the school by playing it out but they were also entering into a kind of friendly conspiracy to laugh about it. (p. 111)

Prisoner provided Australian school students with a language, a set of cultural categories complete with connotations, value systems, and ideological inflection with which to think through their experience of school from their own position, to make a kind of sense of school that suited *their* social interests in that it enabled them to articulate their powerlessness and offered them positive ways of understanding it. These included a range of categorized and therefore usable conceptual strategies to adopt in understanding institutional and social power relations, conceptual strategies which ranged from the oppositional, through degrees of accommodation, to modes of acceptance. The children inserted the meanings of the program into their social experience of school in a way that informed both – the meanings of school and the meanings of *Prisoner* were each influenced by the other, and the fit between them ensured that each validated the other.

Turnbull (1984) has found that young girl fans of the program find in it meanings that they can use to produce a sense of subcultural identity and esteem for themselves. Images of strong, active women fighting the system, gaining minor victories (although finally succumbing to it), give them pleasure (in the resistance) and a means of articulating a discourse of resistance to the dominant ideology that paralleled the discourse (often called rebelliousness) that they used to make sense of their social existence. The contradictions and struggle between authority and resistance to it existed in both the program and their subjectivities, and the meanings that were activated and the pleasures that were gained were the ones that made social sense to the subordinate and the powerless.

School children have found and used a potential discourse of resistance in the program and, interestingly, a number of teachers have complained to the producers that the program teaches insubordination. Similarly, Radway (1984) has found that some women readers of romances have been able to be more assertive towards their husbands as a result of their reading. This may have resulted from the act of reading itself – it was something they did for themselves, in opposition to their ideological role of constantly caring for others and the home – or it may have resulted from their readings of the texts themselves. These readings saw the progress of the narrative as one of the feminization of the hero: at the start he was cruel, unfeeling, remote (a feminine view of masculinity), but by the end he had become sensitized enough to the heroine's finer feminine sensibility for him to be fit for her to marry.

There is some evidence that finding a discourse in a text that makes sense of one's experience of social powerlessness in a positive way is the vital first step towards being able to do something to change that powerlessness.

Hodge and Tripp's (1986) study of the ways that Australian Aboriginal children made sense of television is of significance here. They found that the children constructed a cultural category that included American blacks, American Indians, and themselves. This cultural category, a tool to think with, conceptualized the political and narrative powerlessness of non-whites in white society, and was used in making sense both of television and of social experience. A particularly popular program among these children was *Diff'rent Strokes*, whose leading character, an American black child adopted by a white family, they saw as Aboriginal. One can imagine the sort of sense they made of his small size, his eternal childishness, and the consistency with which he is "misunderstood" and set right by his white "father" and "elder sister," particularly when we remember that American Indians are part of the same cultural category.

What the Aboriginal readers were demonstrating was the ability of a subculture to make its own sense out of a text that clearly bears the dominant ideology. The discourses of powerlessness through which they lived their lives activated a set of meanings that resisted those preferred by the dominant ideology. When they supported and identified with American Indians in their fights against white cowboys, they knew both that their side was doomed to lose, and that they were being obtuse or awkward in reading a western in this way. Reading television in this way provided them with a means of articulating their experience of powerlessness in a white-dominated society and the ability to articulate one's experience is a necessary prerequisite for developing the will to change it.

Mattelart (1980), in his studies of the Third World reception of Hollywood television, comes to a similar conclusion:

> The messages of mass culture can be neutralized by the dominated classes who can produce their own antidotes by creating the sometimes contradictory seeds of a new culture. (p. 20)

Another example of the subcultural reading of a television program is provided by the way that *Dynasty* has become a cult show amongst gays in the USA (Schiff 1985). D&D parties (Dinner and *Dynasty*) are fashionable, and a gay bar in Los Angeles shows endless video-loops of catfights between Alexis and Krystle. The program's emphasis on high style, high fashion, and its portrayal of interpersonal relations as competitive point-scoring are all readily inserted by a gay subculture into the discourse of camp. The character of Alexis, played by Joan Collins, is "normally" seen as the apotheosis of the sexuality of the older woman, but gays may read her not as a representation of femininity, but rather as a destroyer of sexual difference: for this subculture, her style of dress with its broad shoulders and sometimes severe lines combines with her interpersonal aggression to deny traditional distinctions between masculinity and femininity, and her incorporation of masculine traits into a feminine body produces an inversion of the male gay that is equally subversive of dominant gender roles. This critical subversion of the ideology of the haute bourgeoisie which is a subtext to the preferred structure of the program provides the subculture with a means of articulating its own form of oppositional relationship to the dominant system.

Katz and Liebes (1984) found that different ethnic groups negotiated the interaction of *Dallas* with their own subcultures in ways that included misreadings of the text. A group of Arab viewers found it incompatible with their culture that Sue Ellen, having run away with her baby from her husband J. R., should go to her former lover's house, and instead they "read" into the program that she returned to her own father – an action more compatible with Arab culture. At other times the differences between the cultural values of *Dallas* and of the viewers were mobilized to support those of the viewers in opposition to the program's. A Moroccan Jew says:

71

I learned from this series to say "Happy is our lot, goodly is our fate" that we're Jewish. Everything about J. R. and his baby, who has maybe four or five fathers, who knows? The mother is Sue Ellen, of course, and the brother of Pam left, maybe he's the father ... I see they're almost all bastards. (p. 31)

□ Modes of reception

The study of culture must not be confined to the readings of texts, for the conditions of a text's reception necessarily become part of the meanings and pleasures it offers the viewer. Television ethnographers have begun to study the ways in which television is integrated with the culture of the home.

For television is essentially a domestic medium, the routines of viewing are part of the domestic routines by which home life is organized. Hobson (1982) went into the homes of viewers of the early evening soap opera *Crossroads*, watched it with the women and their families, and talked with them about the role the program played in their lives. Her observations enable us to trace a number of ways in which the program, as an example of television in general, is integrated into the routines of the home. One problem facing the housewives who were Hobson's main subjects was that *Crossroads* was screened at about the time of the family tea, and the preparation and serving of this was, in the culture of the homes she visited, part of women's work, part of the definition of gender roles and the meanings of gender difference. In this culture, then, it was impossible for the man to prepare the tea while the woman watched television. Some women organized tea to come either before or after *Crossroads*, but for others the clash seemed inevitable. Sometimes this was the result of a recalcitrant husband who insisted that his tea be served at the time he found convenient, sometimes the woman appeared not to question the need of her family to have tea at this time, she accepted her ideologically given position as nurturer/servant whose needs always took second place to those of her husband and children. The women evolved two coping strategies; one was to listen to the television in the living room as they worked in the kitchen, and the other was to have a black and white set in the kitchen for them to watch while they worked. In both cases the colored television in the living room was the cultural center, the kitchen one was secondary; and the women used to nip into the living room if there was anything that the sound track or the black and white drew their attention to. For those with black and white sets, this was most frequently the color of someone's clothes or hat, for television is an important part of the culture of fashion, as the producers of shows like *Dynasty* well know.

For these women, however much they may have wished television to occupy the primary place in their culture, it was, in fact, secondary, and its secondariness was part of the meaning of their subordinate position in the patriarchal family. For other women, however, such as those with more accommodating husbands, or those who lived alone, *Crossroads* was their primary cultural activity at its time of screening, and they watched it with undivided attention.

Palmer (1986) in her ethnographic study of how children interact with television reported similar findings. Children's reports on their television-watching showed how they integrated it into the household routine:

> In the afternoon I watch *Simon Townsend's Wonder World* and after that I watch *Matchmates* and then I just go and do something, maybe homework or something, and when I come back I watch *Family Feud* and then *The New Price Is Right*, and I watch some news and in that case I have to do the washing up and I watch *Sons and Daughters* and on Monday at 7.30 I watch *Hart to Hart* and after that I watch *Prisoner* and then go to bed.
>
> (p. 48)

She also found that children watched with a wide variety of modes of attention that varied from rapt, total absorption often with the child within a couple of feet of the screen, to a very loose "monitoring," when, for instance, a child would play cards with her/his back to the screen and would turn round to look only when something on the sound track (often laughter) caught his/her attention. Periods of rapt attention rarely lasted for more than ten minutes at a time, and the range of activities that children combined with their watching of television was remarkably wide. Palmer (1986: 63) lists twenty different common activities that range from doing homework, through building models or doing craft work, to singing, dancing, talking, jumping, and fighting. Watching with pets was very common, even the family goldfish which were repeatedly reported to share the children's viewing by swimming on the side of the tank nearest to the television set! While such studies do not tell us about the meanings that viewers make of television, they do show us how viewers incorporate television into their daily lives and are rarely dominated or controlled by it as so many of its critics would claim.

Television, to be popular, must not only contain meanings relevant to a wide variety of social groups, it must also be capable of being watched with different modes of attention, what Hartley (1984b) calls "regimes of watching." Viewers may watch television as a primary activity when they are "glued to the screen"; they may, like some of Hobson's housewives, reluctantly give it second place in their attention while they do something else; or they may have it on as background while they read the paper, converse, or do homework; it gains their full attention only when an item makes a strong and

73

successful bid for their interest. A 1985 study of British viewers by the IBA found that most people were doing something else while they were watching television – cuddling, knitting, talking to each other and to the television set, especially when alone in the room. Tulloch and Moran (1986) make the point well:

> To sit and watch a program like *A Country Practice* with a household is to be reminded what an intensely social activity television is. Viewers talk to each other while the program is in progress. They move in and out of the room in the course of doing household tasks or homework. The TV set and the program are just part of a general environment in which viewing occurs.   (p. 236)

Some may listen to it rather than watch – McQuail, Blumler, and Brown (1972) found that many women alone in the house during the day had the television on because the sound of its voices made them feel less lonely and Tulloch and Moran (1986) and Hobson (1982) have both shown how important this companionship is for the elderly. The next chapter will explore the effects that this variety of regimes of watching has upon the nature of the television text: for the moment we need to note that television is not the dominating monster it is often thought to be; viewers have considerable control, not only over its meanings, but over the role that it plays in their lives.

This is another way in which television differs from film, which has to cater for only a single mode of watching and does not have to compete for the viewer's attention. Screen theory's emphasis on the power of the text over the reader is more justifiable for cinema than for television, and the cinema audience may well be relatively more powerless than the television audience. Television is normally viewed within the domestic familiarity of the living room, which contrasts significantly with the public, impersonal place of cinema. In going out to cinema we tend to submit to its terms, to become subject to its discourse, but television comes to us, enters our cultural space, and becomes subject to our discourses. The living room as cultural space bears different meanings for different members of the family – a fulltime houseparent may watch daytime television as part of the culture of domestic labor, and nighttime television as part of the culture of family relationships, whereas a fulltime wage earner may insert television viewing into the culture of leisure. These different meanings of the cultural space of viewing result in different social discourses being brought to bear upon television, and thus in different readings of it.

But television's significance is not confined to the way it is watched, nor to the meanings that are found within it. Sometimes the act of watching television and of choosing what is watched can itself play an important role in the

74

culture of the home, which is, as we have seen, generally patriarchal. The part that television plays within this culture can vary according to the viewer's position towards this ideology. Hobson (1982) has shown us how housewives who accept their subordination in patriarchy allow their television interests only a secondary role. But other of Hobson's housewives are aware of and sometimes kick against patriarchal domination, and television can become part of their resistance. Many women knew that their husbands despised *Crossroads* and disliked their watching it. Watching it became for them a (minor) act of defiance, a claiming of a piece of feminine cultural territory within the masculine hegemony. Like Radway's (1984) romance readers, this creation of their own cultural space enabled a self-generated sense of feminine identity: the program became a piece of popular cultural capital (see chapter 1) that women possessed, but men did not. The women's sense of cultural possession of the program, that it was *their* culture, was profoundly outraged by changes made to it by the producers in 1981. These included changing its slot in the schedule, reducing it from four to three episodes a week, and, most emphatically of all, deciding to write out the main female character. This outrage was consistently expressed in terms of what right had *they* got to do this to *us*? And the *they* was seen as men and authority in general acting against the interests of women. *Crossroads*, in opposition to the "facts" of its production, was made into women's culture, by the women viewers themselves.

The program and the watching of it (for the two are inseparable) can constitute a piece of cultural capital for women. Sometimes this women's culture was expressed in direct opposition to that of men: *Crossroads* was often contrasted with the news, which either preceded or followed it in the flow of early evening scheduling. The news, with its murders, muggings, politics, and sport, was seen as men's concern – a finding supported by earlier work by Hobson (1980) in which she found that women frequently felt it their duty to keep the children quiet while their fathers watched the news. Watching *Crossroads* in the face of masculine disapproval, and understanding it in terms of its opposition to the masculine culture of the news, became an assertion of the woman's right to contribute to the culture of the home and even to control a part of it.

Television, then, plays a vital role in what Morley (1986) calls "the politics of the family." By this he refers to the patterns of power and resistance within the everyday culture of the home. The two main axes of this power are between parents and children, and men and women. Parents frequently use television as a means of discipline, particularly by depriving children of viewing as a means of punishment. Rogge (1987) records a typical instance which is met with an equally typical tactic of resistance. A single mother of three sometimes uses this form of discipline on her 6- and 11-year-old sons, "but then neither of them will talk to me. They've really got me where they want me. They know I don't like being on my own. I nearly always give in."

Parents and schoolteachers frequently feel it is their responsibility and right to "guide" children's viewing preferences – such guidance typically consists of an attempt to impose adult cultural tastes upon children and to denigrate children's cultural tastes. Power all too often operates under the mask of responsibility, and is as frequently exercised through sarcasm and scorn as through direct control or prohibition.

Hodge and Tripp (1986) give a useful insight into this adult power. They found that children learned quickly to distinguish between the different modalities of television's modes of representation (modality is the apparent distance between the text and the real). Cartoons are a mode of low modality, formulaic narratives such as *The A-Team* are almost as low, whereas the news, with its foregrounded "truth," operates in a far higher level of modality. In grammatical terms, cartoons and *The A-Team* operate in the conditional mode of the world of the "as if." News, on the other hand, operates in the indicative mode, the world that "is." By the age of 8 or 9 children had learned to distinguish between modalities and thus were able to cope easily with violence in cartoons and *The A-Team*: what they found hardest to handle was violence on the news, yet it was the news that parents and teachers wanted them to watch. Children's pleasure in cartoons and formulaic narratives is a source of worry to many parents who denigrate these tastes with a vaguely defined criticism that they are "bad" for children.

Similarly, men denigrate women's tastes in television (especially for soap opera), women's mode of watching (diffused rather than concentrated) (see Morley 1986 summarized in chapter 11), and women's talk about it, which men call "gossip" in opposition to their own talk about their programs which they typically refer to as "discussion" (Tulloch and Moran 1986). Some women have adopted this masculine value system and denigrate their own tastes ("Typical American trash, really, I love it" (Morley 1986: 72)) while others are more assertive of the value of their own cultural tastes. But whatever their orientation to this family power structure, the point remains that the meanings and pleasures that women find in soap operas and children in cartoons are inevitably inflected by their situation in the politics of the family, and part of the pleasure in viewing them lies in their felt defiance of masculine or parental power.

Similarly, the male's preference for news, documentary, sport, and realistic or "muscle" drama becomes translated into the "natural" superiority of these genres, which, in turn, allows the male to impose his viewing tastes upon the household, not because he is more powerful, but because the programs he prefers are innately "better." This also gives him the right to impose his viewing habits, generally those of undistracted attention, upon the rest of the household and to demand that the women and children refrain from talking while he is viewing (Morley 1986, Hobson 1980).

Television, with its already politicized pictures of the world, enters a context that is formed by, and subjected to, similar political lines of power and resistances. The intersection of its textual politics and the politics of its reception is a crucial point in its effectivities and functions in our culture.

☐ Gossip and oral culture

The word gossip is clearly from a phallocentric discourse: its connotations are of triviality and femininity, and it is opposed, by implication, to serious male talk. But these negative connotations can only get in the way of our understanding its role in television culture. It is a form of "social cement" (Geraghty 1981) which binds together characters and narrative strands in soap opera, binds viewers to each other as they gossip about the show, and establishes an active relationship between viewer and program. It is patriarchally wrong to see women's gossip about soap operas as evidence of their '2.5inability to tell fact from fiction: it is, rather, an active engagement with the

issues of the program and a desire to read them in a way that makes them relevant to the rest of their lives. As Katz and Liebes (1984) say, "it is clear from these examples that people are discussing and evaluating not only the issues of the Ewing family but the issues in their own lives" (p. 31). McQuail, Blumler, and Brown (1972) and others working with the uses and gratifications approach have shown how common it is for television to be used as something to talk about, whether at the factory tea break, at the suburban coffee morning, or in the schoolyard. As one of Palmer's (1986) subjects put it:

> You come back the next day and just say if you like it. "Oh, see when that happened" and so and so. You know, that's really the best part of it, about TV, kind of talking with your friends about it. Probably I think you probably enjoy it more then. (*Michael*, 12)   (pp. 92–3)

Uses and gratification theory and ethnography all too frequently assume that such a social use is in itself an adequate explanation, and they fail to ask further how gossip can be read back into the program, can activate certain of its meanings, and can become part of the critique of its values.

So much critical and theoretical attention has been devoted to the *mass* media in a *mass* society that we have tended to ignore the fact that our urbanized, institutionalized society facilitates oral communication at least as well as it does mass communication. We may have concentrated much of our leisure and entertainment into the home (see Garnham 1987, Hartley and O'Regan, 1987) but we attend large schools and universities, many of us work in large organizations, and most belong to or attend some sort of club or social organization. And we live in neighborhoods or communities. And in all of these social organizations we talk. Much of this talk is about the mass media and its cultural commodities and much of it is performing a similar cultural function to those commodities – that is, it is representing aspects of our social experience in such a way as to make that experience meaningful and pleasurable to us. These meanings, these pleasures are instrumental in constructing social relations and thus our sense of social identity.

Feminists (e.g. Hobson 1982, Brown 1987a, Brown and Barwick 1986) have begun to revaluate gossip as part of women's oral culture and to argue that it can be both creative and resistive to patriarchy. Tulloch and Moran (1986) also find positive value for women in gossip:

> arguably it is males' refusal to be open in their emotions, and to gossip, which is a major reason for their put down of soaps. They displace their own inadequacies onto the viewing habits of women. And in asserting the value of gossip and emotional release, women are insisting on their own adequacy, their own personal and social space, in the face of male dominated culture. (pp. 247–8)

The fact that men consistently denigrate gossip is at least a symptom that they recognize it as a cultural form that is outside their control. The difficulty of controlling oral culture and its potential as a site and means of resistance was more formally recognized in the history of English imperialism over Scotland, Ireland, and Wales: one of the first acts of the English conquerors was to outlaw the native language for they well knew that political control required linguistic control, and conversely, that political resistance depended upon a language of the oppressed with which to think and talk that resistance.

Oral culture is responsive to and is part of its immediate community. It resists centralization and the ideological control that goes with it, and it promotes cultural diversity. Like mass culture, it is highly conventional – talk and gossip are as clearly formulaic as any TV crime-buster series – but the conventions of talk vary as widely as the social situations or social group within which that talk operates. Teenage girl talk differs from male worker talk, lounge room talk differs from public bar talk, and the differences are in the conventions. When this talk is about television it works to activate and circulate meanings of the text that resonate with the cultural needs of that particular talk community.

Katz and Liebes (1984, 1985) in their study of ethnic audiences of *Dallas* found that during and after the programme, people discuss what they have seen, and come to collective understandings .... Viewers selectively perceive, interpret and evaluate the programme in terms of local cultures and personal experiences, selectively incorporating it into their minds and lives.

(1984: 28)

This incorporation of the program into local culture is an active, oral process that denies any overwhelming precedence to the Hollywood culture. The audiences participate in the meanings of the program in a way that the Hollywood moguls can neither foresee nor control.

For oral culture is active, participatory. Because the conventions are so well known and so closely related to the social situation of the community, all members of that community can participate more or less equally in the production and circulation of meanings: talk does not distinguish between producers and consumers.

In its interface with mass culture, oral culture necessarily brings its activeness to that process by which the viewer becomes the producer of meanings. An important part of a mass-produced text's ability to appeal to a wide diversity of audiences is the ease with which its conventions can be made to interact productively with the conventions of the speech community within which it is circulating.

Thus Geraghty (1981), Brown (1987a), and others have shown how the conventions of daytime soap opera (its "nowness," its concern with relationships and reactions, the real-seemingness of its characters) enable it to interact fruitfully and creatively with women's gossip.

Katz and Liebes (1984, 1985) found that part of the appeal of *Dallas* to non-American audiences was the way that it was so easily incorporated, via gossip, into local, oral culture. They conclude that

the feeling of intimacy with the characters ... has a "gossipy" quality which seems to facilitate an easy transition to discussion of oneself and one's close associates. It is likely that the continuous and indeterminate flow of the programme, from week to week, in the family salon invites viewers to invest themselves in fantasy, thought and discussion.

(1984: 32)

What Katz and Liebes (1985: 188) call "conversations with significant others" help viewers select "frames for interpreting the programme and, possibly, incorporating it into their lives" (1985: 188). Talk plays a crucial role in "the social dynamics of meaning-making" (Katz and Liebes 1984: 28). As Tulloch and Moran (1986) put it, "this process of watching aloud is important because it enables the viewer to go beyond his or her individuality and call on group reactions, group knowledge" (p. 244).

Hobson (1982) has shown how the viewers of *Crossroads* were overwhelmingly concerned with the program's realisticness: they had an internalized set of social norms that enabled them to evaluate how "real" an incident, a reaction, or a piece of dialogue appeared to be, and the more real, the better. The norms themselves and their application to the program were influenced by gossip. Talking about television is a process of bringing out the meanings that "work" for a particular audience group, which then, in turn, functions to activate those meanings in the next viewing. In this way solitary viewing can be experienced as group viewing, because the viewer knows well that other members of her/his group are viewing at the same time. Gossip works actively in two ways: it constructs audience-driven meanings and it constructs audience communities within which those meanings circulate.

The "trekkies" (the fans of *Star Trek*) are a particularly active and creative TV audience (see Jenkins 1986). They publish a number of newsletters in which fans imagine the continuing lives of the characters in the serial. Some of these imaginings have grown to novel length and there are even soft-porn novels of Spock and his sex life in circulation. Those privately produced and circulated publications are explicit and extreme manifestations of the audience activity in which viewers, particularly of serials, write future "scripts" in their heads and then check these scripts against the broadcast ones. They are also gossip which has had to revert to the typewriter in order to overcome the problems of a geographically dispersed audience community. Commercially published soap opera magazines serve a similar function: they promote and circulate gossip within a community that is defined not geographically but by a commonality of taste deriving from a shared social situation.

Children, too, have a dynamic oral culture that interacts with the culture of television. They frequently incorporate television into their games, songs, and slang, and, indeed, use television as the raw material out of which to create new games and new songs. All of this suggests that a folk, oral culture still lives despite the dislocations of mass society, and that television is not only readily incorporable into this, but that it is actually essential to its survival. For television provides a common symbolic experience and a common discourse, a set of shared formal conventions that are so important to a folk culture. And an oral or folk culture provides the television viewer with a set of reading relations that are essentially participatory and active, and that recognize only minimal differentiation between performer and audience or producer and consumer.

☐ The social determinations of meanings

Meanings are determined socially: that is, they are constructed out of the conjuncture of the text with the socially situated reader. This does not mean that a reader's social position mechanistically produces meanings for him or her in a way that would parallel the authoritarian way that texts used to be thought to work. The word "determine" does not refer to such a mechanistic, singular, cause and effect process; rather it means to delimit or set the boundaries. It would be ridiculous to suggest that all members of the working class or all women would construct identical meanings that were determined directly by their social situation. However, it would be equally ridiculous to suggest that there is no such thing as a working-class reading or a feminine reading. The boundaries of working-class experience or of female experience leave plenty of room for different inflections, for any one person is subjected to a wide variety of social determinations. So, to take an example, a Catholic trade unionist working in a Detroit car plant will inflect working-class social experience quite differently from, say, a Protestant, "nonpolitical," agricultural worker in Wisconsin. The range of inflections of female social experience in a patriarchy is probably even wider, and in the last chapter we looked at some of the variety of social forces that work to develop a social subjectivity. The argument that people's subjectivities, their consciousness of self, and their social relations are produced socially rather than genetically or naturally, does not mean that all people are clones of each other, the mass products of an identical social mold. The social histories of people in societies as diverse as western capitalist democracies are constructed out of such a variety of social experiences and social forces as to provide for almost as much individual difference as any natural gene bank. A theory of social determination not only leaves room for individual and other differences, it emphasizes them: but it also emphasizes that the significant differences are produced socially rather then genetically, and that these differences exist within and against a framework of similarity.

This diversity of social histories necessarily involves contradictions within the subject. As Morley (1986) puts it:

> the same man may be simultaneously a productive worker, a trade union member, a supporter of the Social Democratic Party, a consumer, a racist, a home owner, a wife beater and a Christian. (p. 42).

Morley takes pains to point out that these contradictory subject positions are not all equivalently effective, but that some will be more powerful than others, and some dependent on others. His account of how these different social positions, intersecting in a historical (though hypothetical) viewer, can produce contradictory readings of the same program is so clear and exemplary that I can do no better than quote it at length:

> Perhaps this issue can be made clearer if we take a hypothetical white male working-class shop steward (identified in the *Nationwide* project) and follow him home, and look at how he might react to another *Nationwide*

81

programme, this time in his home context. First, it would seem likely that in his domestic context, away from the supportive/regulative mores of the group of fellow shop stewards with whom he viewed the "News" tape in the *Nationwide* interview, the intensity of his "oppositional" readings will be likely to diminish. But let us also look at how he might respond to a few items in this hypothetical *Nationwide* on different topics. So, his working-class position has led him to be involved in trade union discourses and thus, despite the weaker frame supplied by the domestic context, he may well still produce an oppositional reading of the first item on the latest round of redundancies. However, his working-class position has also tied him to a particular form of housing in the inner city, which has, since the war, been transformed before his eyes culturally by Asian immigrants, and the National Front come closest to expressing his local chauvinist fears about the transformation of "his" area; so he is inclined to racism when he hears on the news of black youth street crimes – that is to say, he is getting close to a dominant reading at this point. But then again his own experience of life in an inner city area inclines him to believe the police are no angels. So when the next item on the programme turns out to be on the Brixton riots he produces a negotiated reading, suspicious both of black youth and also of the police. By now he tires of *Nationwide*, and switches over to a situation comedy in which the man and woman occupy traditional positions, and his insertion within a working-class culture of masculinity inclines him to make a dominant reading of the programme.   (pp. 42–3)

The ability of what Grossberg (forthcoming) has called "the nomadic subjectivity" to produce meanings that span the whole range from the dominant to the oppositional is evidence of the activity of the viewer in producing meanings and of the social determinations that underlie this activity. Negotiating meanings with the television text is a discursive, and therefore social, process, and not an individualistic one, but it still allows the socially situated viewer an active, semi-controlling role in it. Morley comments on his hypothetical viewer:

He is indeed a "subject crossed by a number of discourses", but it is he, the particular person (who represents a specific combination of/intersection of such discourses), who makes the readings, not the discourses which "speak" to him in any simple sense. Rather, they provide him with the cultural repertoire of resources with which he works.   (p.43)

The production of meaning from a text follows much the same process as the construction of subjectivity within society. The reader produces meanings that derive from the intersection of his/her social history with the social forces structured into the text. The moment of reading is when the discourses of the reader meet the discourses of the text. When these discourses bear different interests reading becomes a reconciliation of this conflict. For MacCabe and early screen theorists, this reconciliation involved the surrender of the social interests of the reader to those of the text. For Hodge and Tripp (1986), however, exactly the opposite is the case. Their studies "constitute a compelling argument for the primacy of general social relations in developing a reading of television, rather than the other way about" (p. 158).

This is because social relationships carry "immediate rewards and sanctions" (p. 158) which make them much more powerful in their effectivity than any television program. Children, as well as adults, are aware of the gap between television's representations and reality, a gap that does not appear to exist in the experience of social relations. The effectivity of social relationships in the construction of subjectivity and meanings is greater than that of television to the extent that these social relationships appear more "real." "We must be prepared to find that non-television meanings are powerful enough to swamp television meanings" (Hodge and Tripp 1986: 144).

These "non-television meanings," that is, those that derive from the discourses of the reader rather than those of the text, are ones that are frequently promoted and circulated orally. If the television program fails to allow space for these non-television meanings to be generated from it, it is unlikely to be popular. Morley (1980a) found that black women, for example, simply rejected *Nationwide* because it held nothing for them: it failed to provoke them to produce meanings and failed to provide the spaces within which such meanings could be inflected to represent their social interests.

To be popular with a diversity of audiences television must both provoke its readers to the production of meanings and pleasures, and must provide the textual space for these meanings and pleasures to be articulated with the social interests of the readers. Readers will only produce meanings from, and find pleasures in, a television program if it allows for this articulation of their interests. The textual and intertextual characteristics by which this is achieved form the subject matter of the next two chapters.

Chapter 6

Activated texts

The last chapter argued two main propositions: that the television audience is composed of a wide variety of groups and is not a homogeneous mass; and that these groups actively read television in order to produce from it meanings that connect with their social experience. These propositions entail the corollary that the television text is a potential of meanings capable of being viewed with a variety of modes of attention by a variety of viewers. To be popular, then, television must be both polysemic and flexible. In this chapter I shall characterize the television text as a state of tension between forces of *closure*, which attempt to close down its potential of meanings in favor of its preferred ones, and forces of *openness*, which enable its variety of viewers to negotiate an appropriate variety of meanings. The last chapter drew attention to the social forces that worked to open the text up to this process of negotiation: in this one I shall explore the main textual devices that constitute this openness.

This requires a flexible definition of the television text. At one level there is no problem: the primary television text is that pattern of signifiers on the screen and in the airwaves at any one time. But no text is simply a pattern of signifiers: a text is a bearer of meanings, and relating signifiers to meanings is not just a matter of supplying them with appropriate signifieds. Rather, they identify and limit the arena within which the meanings may be found. A fictional image of a white hero shooting a Hispanic villain can never mean anything outside those terms. But within those terms there is considerable space for the negotiation of meaning: the reader can bring left- or right-wing politics to bear, racist or nonracist ideologies, television "knowledges" either of previous episodes of the same series and thus the accumulated "meanings" of the hero, or of other similar series and thus of a generic TV hero and victims or villains. Or readers may, consciously or unconsciously, bring to bear extra-generic television meanings – a news item about US action in Nicaragua, for example, may well form part of the meanings of our hypothetical, but not untypical, incident.

These television knowledges are not confined to television itself. There is a whole publicity industry producing secondary texts, writing about television in a wide variety of forms – journalistic criticism, gossip about the stars, specialist magazines for fans (particularly of soap opera), "novelizations" of the television scripts (e.g. ones of *Dr Who*, or *The A-Team*), advertisements, posters, and television promos. These may be secondary texts, but they can be read back into the primary text, the transmitted image.

There is also a third level of text – the readings that people make of television, the talk and gossip they produce: these too are part of this web of intertextual relations that must be taken into account when we wish to study television as a circulator of meanings in the culture.

☐ The polysemy of the television text

But we have to start somewhere. I propose to continue the close analysis of the two scenes from *Hart to Hart* that opened chapter 1. Our initial reading showed how the dominant ideology is structured into the text and, by implication, how the text establishes the boundaries of the arena within which the struggle for meaning can occur. We must now extend the analysis to reveal some of the textual devices which open it up to polysemic readings, which therefore work against the attempted ideological closure, and which make it accessible to, and popular with, its variety of audiences.

☐ IRONY

One of these devices is irony. The classic and simple definition of irony is a statement that appears to say one thing while actually meaning another.

Thus when the villain says, "Well maybe a few good investments and we can pitch the whole bloody business. But we are going to need a bit more for our retirement fund." his words are treated by the text ironically. The ECU of his face, the heavy irony in his English accent, and the fact that the pretty American villainess has just characterized his attitude as greed combine to lead the viewer not to take his words at face value. We "know" that he is talking about crime and not a pension fund. In other words, we know that this is irony, and that the unstated meanings take precedence over the stated ones. But our spectatorial confidence may not be as secure as this account suggests. For the position of omniscience granted us by the irony in this realist text may be challenged by the social discourses brought to bear on it. A subordinate non-white or non-American, whether in the USA or the rest of the world, could read this to be a subversive use of the discourse and ethics of capitalism which turns the system back on itself.

The irony brings together the discourses of capitalist economics with those of race and of crime, and this collision of discourses cannot be totally controlled by the text or by the dominant ideology. It could be read to mean that the only way in which a male member of a subordinate race or class can participate in the validated activities of patriarchal capitalism (looking after his woman and providing for their old age) is by what the dominant class calls "crime." Such a reading would shift the responsibility for the crime away from the (evil) individual and place it firmly onto the social system, and thus make a sense servicing the interests of an oppositional subculture by contesting the dominant sense proposed by the irony.

Irony, as a rhetorical device, is always polysemic and is always open to apparently "perverse" readings because it necessarily works by simultaneously opposing meanings against each other. Screen theory, like the preferred reading one, would place these meanings in a hierarchical relationship with each other – we "know" that the dominant one (this man is evil) takes precedence over, and is used to explain, the manifest "meaning" of the words (he is behaving responsibly). In this case irony prefers one meaning over the other, and is seen to work in the same way as the perfect camera viewpoint does: it gives the reader/spectator privileged knowledge; we understand the villain's words better than he does, we have a privileged insight into him, and our understanding is complete and adequate. Irony is, in this reading, always part of MacCabe's (1981a) "hierarchy of discourses" that construct for the reader this position of "dominant specularity." But the text cannot enforce its preferred meaning. An oppositional reader may well activate those meanings clustered around "this-man-is-behaving-responsibly." This shift of the moral judgment of the irony away from the individual towards the social system reverses the politics of the meaning. Irony can never be totally controlled by the structure of the text: it always leaves semiotic space for some readers to exploit.

There is irony, too, in the way that the heroine assumes a southern accent to respond to a compliment: "Oh, that's the cutest thing you've ever said to me, sugar." The patriarchal meaning of this is borne by its reference to the traditional myth of the southern belle as the most contentedly and severely subordinate of all female stereotypes; the irony lies in the tension between our liberated, northern heroine adopting this role and the self-aware, parodic way in which she does it. This could be read as foregrounding the gender politics of the myth as she triggers it: in which case the irony would use the discourse of the northern liberated woman to comment critically upon the myth of the southern belle. This appears to be the preferred reading, but a sexual chauvinist could well reverse the preference and read her ironic tone of voice as a form of sexual playfulness that would give the "subordinate" discourse precedence over the preferred, "liberated" one.

☐ METAPHOR

The heroine's ironic response is to a compliment couched in metaphorical terms. Like irony, metaphor necessarily involves two discourses, for it always describes one thing in terms of something else. Again, a hierarchical relationship between these two discourses can be preferred, but it can never be enforced. The metaphor that explains a woman's attractiveness to a man in terms of bees, honey, and flowers obviously works to ground a patriarchal view of gender relations in nature and thus, literally, to naturalize it. But the metaphor is spoken in an exaggerated tone of voice that draws attention to its metaphorical nature and thus its artificiality. It could well work to demystify the conventions by which men and women are socialized into relating to each other in our society, and could therefore be read as a critical comment on the ideology inscribed in the practice.

The collision of discourses in irony and metaphor produces an explosion of meaning that can never be totally controlled by the text and forced into a unified sense producing a unified and singular position for the reading subject. The contradictions are always left reverberating enough for sub-cultures to negotiate their own inflections of meaning.

☐ JOKES

Jokes, like irony, like metaphor, work through a collision of discourses. The last chapter has shown how the window/porthole/laundromat joke attempts to give the masculine technical discourse hierarchical precedence over the feminine domestic one: it wants us to laugh at the inadequacy of the woman. But its offensiveness to women can be read as a parodic display of patriarchy at work, or even as a comment on the inability of patriarchy to cope with the changing definitions of gender. However hard it may try, the text can never finally control the meanings that may be generated when the discourse of patriarchal control collides with that of feminine liberation.

☐ CONTRADICTION

Contradiction, literally "speaking against," must be adequately accounted for in any theory of television's popularity in a heterogeneous society, for contradictions are another agent of polysemy. MacCabe (1981a) argues that two of the defining characteristics of bourgeois realism are its inability to treat the real as contradictory, and the work of its metadiscourse in resolving any low-level contradictions in the text. His account does at least show us that contradiction is an issue in both "the real" and the text, or rather, in the understanding of both.

Ideology, as theorized by Althusser, works to iron out contradictions between its subjects' real and imaginary social relations. It constructs a "consensus" around the point of view of the bourgeoisie and excludes the consciousness of class conflict. Conflict of interest can only be expressed through *contradiction*, speaking against, so the repression of contradictions in "the real" is a reactionary ideological practice for it mobilizes a consensus around the status quo and thus militates against social change.

Textual and reading strategies are similarly ideological and work in a similar way. Textual strategies (such as that of MacCabe's "metadiscourse") that propose a unitary, final "truth" of the text work by resolving contradictions and thus deny the force for social change, or at least social interrogation, that is embedded in them. A reading strategy that cooperates with this textual strategy is similarly reactionary: its acceptance of a final "true" meaning of the text can only be achieved by the adoption of the satisfied reactionary reading position of "dominant specularity" (MacCabe 1981a).

Conversely, more radical social and textual theories seek to expose the work of the dominant ideology in naturalizing a bourgeois resolution of contradictions, and work to recover and reactivate them. This need not be a conscious theoretical project. Hodge and Tripp's (1986) school children activated the contradictions in *Prisoner* and used them to "speak against" their subordination by the school system. If texts that bear the dominant ideology are to be popular amongst those who are oppressed or subordinated by that ideology, they must contain contradictions, however repressed, that oppositional readers can activate to serve their cultural interests. Without them, the text could be popular only amongst those who accommodate themselves more or less comfortably with the dominant ideology.

Kellner (1982) also sees contradictions as central to television's ability to appeal to a diversity of social groups. His contradictions work on a larger scale, for they are to be found between different programs: where they occur within a program they are resolved by the narrative working through MacCabe's metadiscourse:

> Television mythologies often attempt to resolve social contradictions. For instance, the cop show *Starsky and Hutch* deals with the fundamental American contradiction between the need for conformity and individual initiative, between working in a corporate hierarchy and being an individual. Starsky and Hutch are at once conventional and hip; they do police work and wear flashy clothes *and* have lots of good times. They show that it is possible to fit into society and not lose one's individuality. The series mythically resolves contradictions between the work ethic and the pleasure ethic, between duty and enjoyment. Television mythology speciously resolves conflicts to enable individuals to adjust. (p. 400)

Newcomb (1984) turns to the theories of Bakhtin (1981) to discuss television's multivocality, its collage of discourses which must necessarily include contradictory ones. Bakhtin's distinction between a "heteroglot" text, that is, one composed of many voices, and a "monoglot" one which is singular in its discourse and view of the world, fits well the theory of Barthes (1975a), who suggests that all narratives are composed of an interweaving of voices that cannot finally be structured into any controlling hierarchy (see chapter 8 and 15). As a society contains many voices all striving to be heard over the others, so too must texts that circulate popularly in that society.

Bakhtin (1981) explains heteroglossia in terms that see it as working equally effectively in both society and texts; the heteroglossia of society is structured in the discourse:

> Bakhtin's basic scenario for modelling variety is two actual people talking to each other in a specific dialogue at a particular time and in a particular place. But these persons would not confront each other as sovereign egos capable of sending messages to each other through the kind of uncluttered space envisioned by the artists who illustrate most receiver-sender models of communication. Rather, each of the two persons would be a consciousness at a specific point in the history of defining itself through the choice it has made – out of all the possible existing languages available to it at that moment – of a discourse to transcribe its intention *in this specific exchange*.
>
> (p. xx, in Newcomb 1984: 40)

Bakhtin is careful to set this heteroglossia within a context of power relations. Each social group relates differently to the linguistic community, and each is in a constant struggle to draw words and meanings into its own subculture in order to reaccent them for its own purposes. The languages of those with social power attempt to extend their control, and the languages of the subordinate try to resist, negotiate, or evade that power.

A single voice, or monoglossia, is one that attempts to exert control from the center and to minimize the disruptive and vitalizing differences between groups. Heteroglossia not only results from a diversity of voices emanating from a diversity of social positions, it also helps to maintain this diversity and its resistance to the homogenization of social control.

> [Heteroglossia is] that which ensures the primacy of context over text ... all utterances are heteroglot in that they are functions of a matrix of forces practically impossible to recoup, and therefore impossible to resolve. Heteroglossia is as close a conceptualization as is possible of that locus where centripetal and centrifugal forces collide.
>
> (Bakhtin 1981: 276)

Heteroglossia, polysemy, and contradictions are interconnected concepts for they are all ways in which social differences and inequalities are represented textually. As society consists of a structured system of different, unequal, and often conflicting groups, so its popular texts will exhibit a similar structured multiplicity of voices and meanings often in conflict with each other. It is the heteroglossia of television that allows its texts to engage in dialogic relationships with its viewers.

"Dialogic" is another term from Bakhtin that refers to the fact that any use of language necessarily involves a dialogue between historically and socially situated people. Language, and that includes television, cannot be a one-way medium. The last chapter has shown how viewers, differently situated socially, enter into a "dialogue" with the television program, contributing their point of view, their voice, to the exchange of meaning.

Volosinov (1973) (who was part of the same group as Bakhtin, if not actually the same person) uses the term "multiaccentuality" to refer to the dialogic aspect of language. All language can be spoken in different accents, that is, it can be inflected differently according to the social context in which it is used and the social situation of the people using it. *Dallas* need not speak only with the accent of capitalism; in dialogue with a Marxist or a feminist, for example, it can be spoken with a radical accent that criticizes capitalist or patriarchal values (see Ang 1985) and for Moroccan Jews it said clearly that money did not bring happiness (Katz and Liebes 1985). Similarly, the physical/racial characteristics of the villain in the *Hart to Hart* segment may not "speak" only with a WASP accent, but may be inflected to voice the concerns and viewpoint of subordinated ethnic minorities.

The structure of the television text and its ideological role in a capitalist society may well try hard to iron out and resolve the contradictions within it, but, paradoxically, its popularity within that society depends upon its failure to achieve this end successfully.

☐ EXCESS

The characteristics of excess have been widely noted in recent criticism, particularly by feminist writers on film and television. Excess can take two forms, both of which are polysemic. The first is *excess as hyperbole*, which is a specific textual device, a form of exaggeration which may approach the self-knowingness of "camp" as in *Dynasty* or self-parody as in Madonna's music videos. The other is a more general *semiotic excess* which is a characteristic of all television, not just of particular programs.

When the heroine of *Hart to Hart* dresses up as bait for the criminals, she deliberately wears excessive jewelry. This is *excess as hyperbole*, and works partly to convey class-based meanings – lower-class tastelessness is excessive, middle-class taste is restrained, or so the dominant discourse would have us believe. But its function does not stop here. Excessive jewelry draws attention to the role of jewelry in patriarchy and interrogates it.

Similarly, the exaggerated chivalry of the hero as he says "they may not be able to see the honey for the flowers" and the exaggerated southern accent of the heroine as she replies can both be read as excessive. Their excess enables them to carry contradictory meanings: there is a straight meaning which is borne by the face value of the words and fits the dominant ideology, and there is an excess of meaning left over once this dominant meaning has been made that is available for viewers to use to undercut the straight meaning. The compliment and response can be seen as an example of "natural" gender relations in patriarchy, or as a parodic exposure of the artificiality of the conventions that govern those relations and therefore of the ideology inscribed in them.

Excess as hyperbole works through a double articulation which is capable of bearing both the dominant ideology and a simultaneous critique of it, and opens up an equivalent dual subject position for the reader. The reader can both enjoy the compliment and response and at the same time be (slightly) critical of her/himself for doing so. Soap operas are often derided for their excess, yet it is precisely this characteristic that allows the complex reading positions assumed by many fans. These fans treat the operas as if they were real and sometimes relate to their characters as though they were their own family. Yet they know what they are doing, they know that their pleasure in reading soap opera as real life is illusory and that they are, according to their more normal standards, being somewhat silly in doing so. The viewer of soaps can be simultaneously naive and knowing just as can the hero of *Hart to Hart* as he exaggerates the chivalry of his compliment.

Excess allows for a subversive, or at least parodic, subtext to run counter to the main text and both "texts" can be read and enjoyed simultaneously by the viewer, and his/her disunited subjectivity.

Semiotic excess functions similarly, but differs from hyperbolic excess in that it is not a specific textual device, but a characteristic of television in general: there is always too much meaning on television to be controllable by the dominant ideology. There are always traces of competing or resisting discourses available for alternative readings. As Hartley (1983), comparing television with the press, points out:

On television the more complex modes of representation generate an even greater excess of meaningfulness, since TV signifies by colour, motion, sound and time as well as by pictures, words and composition. All these are variously affected by their internal juxtapositions and their external relations with discourses and social relations off-screen. It is hardly

91

surprising, then, to find television itself characterized by a will to limit its own excess, to settle its significations into established, taken for granted, common senses, which viewers can be disciplined to identify *with*. Disciplining is done partly by television's conventionalised codes of composition, lighting, movement, narrative, genre, etc., and partly by "external" limits such as those professional, legal and other exclusion devices which limit who and what gets on air.

However, I would argue that television can never succeed in its will to limit its own excesses of meaningfulness. (pp. 75–6)

This "excess of meaningfulness" can be clearly traced in the compliment and response in our extract from *Hart to Hart*. Here a number of codes are juxtaposed in a variety of associative relations that can therefore produce a variety of meanings for different audiences. Thus a male chauvinist could associate the make-up, the jewelry (not seen as excessive), and the bees-honey-flowers metaphor in a mutually supportive relationship that would then deny the irony of the compliment and its response, and would read the exaggerated southern accent as sexual playfulness. An anti-patriarch, on the other hand, might activate the contradictions between the codes, such as those between the excess of the jewelry, the normalcy of the make-up, and the way that both of these are in association with an assumed southern accent, to foreground their ideological origin, and the amount of ideological labor that is required to make them fit together well enough to deny their mutual contradictions. Such a reading would also comment critically on the pleasure felt by the sexist with which his/her ideological labor is rewarded. The point to make here is that the conjunction of these multiple codes and textual devices generates far more meaningfulness than the text can control. And this is typical of television. As Hartley (1983) puts it:

Television's signifying practices are *necessarily* contradictory – they must produce more than they can police. Concomitantly, for the viewer, the discipline of the "preferred reading" must be disrupted continuously by the presence of the very ambiguities it is produced out of.

It seems then that the signifying *practice* of mainstream, broadcast network television is not so much to exploit as to control television's semiotic potential. (pp. 76–7)

In the dialogue about the porthole, the heroine says, "I know they are supposed to be charming, but they always remind me of a laundromat." The preferred reading, as we saw earlier, may well be working to defuse any potential threat that a female detective might pose to masculine domination by showing her having to translate the technical discourse of portholes into the domestic one of windows and laundromats. But in this comment she distances herself from the traditional, sentimental feminine view of portholes as romantic; this distance may well be great enough, for some readers, to resist her textually preferred recuperation into patriarchy. Enough of the modern feminine discourse escapes what Hartley calls the "policing" of meaning by patriarchy to disrupt the smooth surface of the preferred reading. When the heroine's dismissive tone of voice is taken into account as well, the disruptive reading is strengthened so that the joke could mean, to some viewers, that women are not the sentimental fools that they are made out to be, and that there is no need for them to join in men's games of using technical jargon in order to prove it. This sort of disruptive reading is not only made possible by the polysemy of the television text, it is made necessary by the diversity of the audiences amongst whom television must be popular.

The television text is, like all texts, the site of a struggle for meaning. The structure of the text typically tries to limit its meanings to ones that promote the dominant ideology, but the polysemy sets up forces that oppose this control. The hegemony of the text is never total, but always has to struggle to impose itself against that diversity of meanings that the diversity of readers will produce. But this polysemy is not anarchic and unstructured: the meanings within the text are structured by the differential distribution of textual power in the same way that social groups are related according to the differential distribution of social power. All meanings are not equal, nor equally easily activated, but all exist in relations of subordination or opposition to the dominant meanings proposed by the text.

Interestingly, television's economics, which demand that it can be made popular by a wide variety of social groups, work against its apparent ability to exert ideological control over the passive viewer. The fears of the pessimistic Marxism that characterizes in different ways both the Frankfurt School and the screen theorists are contradicted by this culturalist and ethnographic approach to the understanding of television. So, too, are the fears of the moralists, such as Mary Whitehouse or the Rev. Fred Nile: television's excess of meaningfulness may account for their terror of its effects, but their terror is misplaced for it is based upon a fallacious model of the audience as passive and helpless before this semiotic power, rather than one of active viewers exploiting this excess for their own purposes. The power of the people to make *their* culture out of the offerings of the culture industry is greater than either of these schools of thought realized, and so too is their power to reject those offerings of the culture industry which do not offer them that opportunity. It is the audiences who make a program popular, not the producers.

☐ Open, writerly texts

Television's need to be popular in a society composed of a variety of groups with different, often conflicting interests, requires its texts to be what Eco (1979) calls "open." By this he means texts that do not attempt to close off alternative meanings and narrow their focus to one, easily attainable meaning, but rather ones that are open to a richness and complexity of readings that can never be singular. The open text resists closure, whether this closure be exerted by the dominant ideology working through its discursive structure or by the author exerting his or her authority over the reader. Eco goes on to argue that open texts are generally associated with literature and highbrow, or minority, tastes, whereas the mass media characteristically produce closed texts. This would seem to contradict his earlier assertion (Eco 1972) that aberrant decodings are the norm in mass communication, and is certainly contradicted by the studies of the culturalists and the ethnographers. Nevertheless the concepts of open and closed texts are useful, particularly when we ally them with the notion of a struggle for meaning. We can then characterize the television text as a site of struggle between the dominant ideology working to produce a closed text by closing off the opportunities it offers for resistive readings, and the diversity of audiences who, if they are to make the text popular, are constantly working to open it up to their readings.

Barthes's (1975a) categorization of texts into the readerly and the writerly has some similarities with Eco's into the closed and open. A readerly text is one that approximates to what MacCabe calls a "classic realist text," that is, one which "reads" easily, does not foreground its own nature as discourse, and appears to promote a singular meaning which is not that of the text, but of the real. As Silverman (1983) says:

> The readerly text thus attempts to conceal all traces of itself as a factory within which a particular social reality is produced through standard representations and dominant signifying practices. (p. 244)

The writerly text, on the other hand, is multiple and full of contradictions, it foregrounds its own nature as discourse and resists coherence or unity. None of its codes is granted priority over others, it refuses a hierarchy of discourses. The readerly text is a closed one, the writerly text an open one. Silverman (1983) describes the writerly text as one that replaces the concepts of "product" and "structure" with those of "process" and "segmentation." Segmentation is one of the basic principles of the television text (see below) and works to fragment its unity and destroy its transparency: it works against the classic realist, or readerly, text. In *S/Z* Barthes segments Balzac's novella *Sarrasine* into its smallest units or "lexias," sometimes a single word, sometimes a phrase, rarely more than a sentence. This segmentation forces the

94

lexias to reveal their cultural construction, their encodedness, and denies them the luxury of appearing "real" or natural. Barthes's reading of *Sarrasine* is an elaboration of the way that television has to be read by many of its viewers. The writerly text, which the television text often is and always can be, requires us, its readers, to participate in the production of meaning and thus of our own subjectivities, it requires us to speak rather than be spoken and to subordinate the moment of production to the moment of reception.

□ Producerly texts

While television exhibits many of the characteristics of open or writerly texts, it also differs from them in one fundamental characteristic: television is popular, whereas open, writerly texts (in the way that Eco and Barthes originally theorized them) are typically avant-garde, highbrow ones with minority appeal. Television, as a popular medium, needs to be thought of as "producerly." A producerly text combines the televisual characteristics of a writerly text with the easy accessibility of the readerly. Unlike the writerly avant-garde text, television does not work with an authorial voice that uses unfamiliar discourse in order to draw attention to its discursivity. The avant-garde author-artist will shock the reader into recognition of the text's discursive structure and will require the reader to learn new discursive competencies in order to participate with it in a writerly way in the production of meaning and pleasure. The producerly text, on the other hand, relies on discursive competencies that the viewer already possesses, but requires that they are used in a self-interested, productive way: the producerly text can, therefore, be popular in a way that the writerly text cannot.

Similarly, the producerly text shows many of the characteristics that Kaplan (1983b) calls for in the radical text (see chapter 3): it draws attention to its own textuality, it does not produce a singular reading subject but one that is involved in the process of representation rather than a victim of it, it plays with the difference between the representation and the real as a producerly equivalent of the writerly mixing of documentary and fictional modes, and it replaces the pleasures of identification and familiarity with more cognitive pleasures of participation and production. But it does not do this in a so-called "radical" way: it does not emphasize differences between itself and more familiar modes of representation, it does not address itself to a minority, alienated group in society. Rather it treats its readers as members of a semiotic democracy, already equipped with the discursive competencies to make meanings and motivated by pleasure to want to participate in the process.

Understanding television as a producerly text logically requires us to pluralize the term and speak only of its *texts* which are produced by the viewers at the moments of viewing, or of its *textuality*, the more abstract semiotic potential from which these *texts* are produced. This distinction between television's textuality and its texts derives from Barthes's (1977b) between a *work* and a *text*. A work of literature is a lifeless object, a fixed pattern of signifiers on the pages of a book: this only becomes a text when the book is opened up and read. A work is potentially many texts, a text is a specific realization of that potential produced by the reader.

The producerly text, then, needs to be understood as a category that need not be determined only by the structure of the work, but one that can be entered by the strategy of reading. Thus chapter 1 treated the episode of *Hart to Hart* on its own terms as a readerly text, but earlier in this chapter we brought different reading strategies to bear that activated its polysemic potential and treated it more producerly. The "writer" does not put meaning into the text, but rather assembles a multitude of voices within it, what Bakhtin (1981) calls heteroglossia. These voices cannot finally be pinned down in a "hierarchy of discourses," for different readers can "listen" more or less attentively to different voices. The reader makes his or her text out of this "weaving of voices" by a process that is fundamentally similar to that of the writer when s/he created the work out of the multitude of voices available in the culture.

Television's "nowness" invites the viewer to adopt a producerly stance towards the text, sometimes almost literally. Brunsdon (1984) tells how she, as a soap opera fan, "writes" in advance the script for the soap opera *Brookside*:

> At the moment, I don't really think that Sheila Grant is going to have the baby that she is pregnant with. My reasons are partly generic – I know that a very high proportion of soap opera pregnancies come to little more than a few months' story. They are partly what I experience as "intuitive" – she is in her forties, she has already got three children, the house isn't big enough. Partly cynical – she's the only character of child-bearing age on the Close who wouldn't have an abortion (Heather, Karen, Michelle (?)) or hasn't already got young children (Marie), so she's the only one that pregnancy will be a big issue for. If I'm right, what I don't know is how she is not going to have it. So my pleasure (rather unpleasantly, in this case) is in how my prediction comes true. (p. 83)

Here the viewer assumes the role of author and sets her "script" against the one to be broadcast in the future. This "script production" is remarkably similar to the actual scriptwriting process in that both are writing processes which draw upon the same knowledge of the conventions of soap opera in general and the structure of character relationships within this one in particular. They also share a sense of what would be "realistic" in a way that conflates textual knowledge with social knowledge. This sort of "writing" is only made possible because of television's sense of happening in the present in the same time scale as that of its viewers. The future of a television serial appears to be "unwritten," like the real future, but unlike that in a book or film, whose readers know that the end has already been written and will eventually be revealed to them.

The suspense in television, its resolution of uncertainty, engages the viewer more intensely because its enigmas appear to be unresolved and the viewer is invited to experience their resolution, not merely to learn of it. Sometimes this engagement can be so strong as to lead the viewer to attempt to intervene in the actual scriptwriting. Tulloch and Moran (1986) found that fans of *A Country Practice* frequently wrote to the producers attempting to influence future scripts. One fan, for example, having heard gossip that Vicky was going to die on her honeymoon, wrote desperately trying to prevent the script being written. Her arguments share the same sort of knowledge of viewers' pleasures and identifications that the professional scriptwriters need to work with:

> I am 14 and a regular viewer of *A Country Practice* and I have heard that Vicky whilst on her honeymoon, is to be killed. If this is true I think you will lose many viewers because the younger members of the cast are the main reason why many of the viewers watch it. Even more, Vicky and Simon have attracted viewers.
>
> If Vicky does die I believe the ratings for *A.C.P.* will drop dramatically and you will lose viewers and there will be no way you will be able to find a replacement for Vicky.
>
> For the sake of *A.C.P.* and Channel 7 I hope that this is not true. If this is true I hope I am not too late in forwarding this important letter.
>
> (p. 232)

The viewer engagement entailed by television's "nowness" is obviously exploited by news, by sport, and by quiz shows. Quiz and game shows go to great lengths to disguise the fact that they are prerecorded, and the winners are known, in order to give the viewers the pleasures of engaging with the uncertainty, of predicting and then experiencing its resolution.

Television producers recognize how important this "writing" by the viewer is. Tulloch and Moran (1986) quote one who has a more respectful and, I would argue, more accurate, view of the audiences than those interviewed by Gitlin (1983) and quoted in chapter 4. "Anticipation is a very important thing for television viewers. Television ... needs to allow people to be smarter than the scriptwriters." (p. 200).

This "writing" by the viewer is frequently part of the gossip discussed in the last chapter, and is encouraged by the fanzines that we will discuss in the next.

Television has in the past been treated by most critics as a readerly or closed text. This approach fails to account not only for many of its textual characteristics, but also for its various modes of reception and its heterogeneous audiences. While we can certainly see in it forces of closure, these are met by the opposing desires of its audiences to exploit its writerly potential by making their "texts" out of its "work."

This same struggle between openness and closure can be seen in the larger structure of the television text, as well as at the micro level of our reading of the *Hart to Hart* extract. Two opposing ways of organizing texts and therefore meanings are relevant here. The first is one based upon logic and cause and effect. This is essentially a strategy of closure because it attempts to specify relations between incidents or elements in a narrative according to universal laws of logic that are the same for everyone and therefore make (literally) *common* sense. Classic realism is a prime example of this principle in practice: in it all actions have both a cause and a consequence, all narratives start with a disruption to the status quo which is then worked through to a resolution that completes (or closes off) the chain of incidents and leaves both the narrative and the viewer in a state of final equilibrium. There are no unexplained irrelevancies in a classic realist text, everything is logically related to everything else, and everything contributes to the sense of the narrative. Realism's construction of a web of rationally explicable connections between all its elements lies behind its self-presentation as the natural, common-sense way of making sense of the world in a scientific, empiricist, rationalist society such as contemporary western society. It shares with science the attempt to close off the meanings of the world to a unified, universal set and to exclude as "unrealistic" or "unscientific" those aspects of experience that disrupt or defy the schema. Realism and empiricism are both agents of ideological closure, but neither is totally effective.

The second organizing principle is one based upon the laws of association rather than those of cause and effect. This is a much more "open" principle for it allows of a far greater variety of associative relations and thus meanings to be made. It is also more typical of the workings of the subconscious than the conscious mind, and thus works differently, not to say disruptively, to the discipline of reason and logic. Earlier in this chapter we noted some of the textual devices (irony, metaphor, jokes, contradictions) which create the possibility for resistive readings: all of these work by the laws of association, and, as we saw, they are unable to specify with any final authority the relations that the reader should make between their different elements or discourses. The reader of an associative text is less "disciplined" than the reader of a logical text. Of course, no text is either purely associative or purely logical, all texts contain both principles and the tension between them is part of the textual struggle between openness and closure, between domination and resistance. Television exhibits the contradictions betwen these conflicting principles more starkly than any other medium. As we saw in chapter 2, its typical mode is realism, which is a logical way of organizing our representation of the world; yet, as Ellis (1982) and Williams (1974) have pointed out, its typical way of organizing its texts at the macro level is essentially associative. Williams uses the term "flow" to express this principle, Ellis the term "segmentation," and the difference between the two words indicates the difference between the two approaches to what is essentially the same principle, that of association.

☐ Segmentation and flow

When Williams talks about the television experience as being one of "flow" he means that television is a continuous succession of images which follows no laws of logic or cause and effect, but which constitutes the cultural experience of "watching television." He glosses the phrase by contrasting it to the way we normally specify the title of a book or a film; books and films are specific texts, television is a generalized textual experience. Marc (1984) makes a similar point. Summarizing a two-year research program by an audience research firm he writes that "the viewer does not turn on the set so much to view this or that program as to fulfill a desire 'to watch television'." He quotes: "Most of us simply snap on the set rather than select a show. The first five minutes are spent *prospecting* channels, looking for gripping images" (p. 31).

The concept of flow suggests two main characteristics of television, both of which contribute to its textual openness. The first is this associative sequence of images in which any realistic sequence within films or programs is constantly interrupted by commercials, by news breaks, by promos. Williams, used to the more organically organized literary work and to the less interrupted flow of British television, was initially confused by his first experience of American televisual flow:

One night in Miami, still dazed from a week on an Atlantic liner, I began watching a film and at first had some difficulty in adjusting to a much greater frequency of commercial "breaks". Yet this was a minor problem compared to what eventually happened. Two other films, which were due to be shown on the same channel on other nights, began to be inserted as trailers. A crime in San Francisco (the subject of the original film) began to operate in an extraordinary counterpoint not only with the deodorant and cereal commercials but with a romance in Paris and the eruption of a prehistoric monster who laid waste New York. I can still not be sure what I took from that whole flow. I believe I registered some incidents as happening in the wrong film, and some characters in the commercials as involved in the film episodes, in what came to seem – for all the occasional bizarre disparities – a single irresponsible flow of images and feelings.

(1974: 91–2)

Williams's use of the word "irresponsible" seems to derive from his literary desire for a named author to be responsible for a text, and for this responsibility to be exercised in the production of a coherent, unified text. Of course, no individual is responsible for television's flow in this sense, but that does not mean that the flow is random or unstructured. Indeed, Williams goes on to provide two levels of analysis of this flow in order to uncover its structure. His first level he calls a "long-range analysis of sequence and flow" (pp. 97–8) which consists of a discussion of an evening's typical schedules for six channels. His analysis is relatively superficial. Apart from some generalizations about homogeneity and contrast he has little to say about how the scheduling policy does, in fact, act as an "author" at this level of flow, and, unlike most literary authors, has an explicit and stated intention – to build an identifiable audience which can then be "sold" to advertisers. This institutional, anonymous author, of course, knows all too well the limits of his or her authority – the viewer is free to construct his or her own flow by switching between channels, and though "channel loyalty" exists, it is only a tendency and is never total.

Williams's "medium-range analysis of flow and 'sequence'" (pp. 100–4) is more interesting. He lists forty consecutive segments of a news program including its commercials and promos for programs later in the evening. He notes, for example, the lack of explicit connections between a news report about false claims in drug advertising and two drug commercials later on in the bulletin. He points to a similar lack of connection between promos for a western film and news stories about the Indian protest action at Wounded Knee, and between news stories about a CIA agent being released from China and American soldiers being released from "tiger-cages" in Vietnam. His regret of this lack of explicit or intentional connections in what he calls "undiscriminating sequence" is evidence not only of his literary background, but also of his lack of sympathy with the nature of television and the reading relations it sets up with its audiences. But he does discern under this sequence

a remarkably consistent set of cultural relationships: a flow of consumable reports and products, in which the elements of speed, variety and miscellaneity can be seen as organising: the real bearers of value. (p. 105)

What he does not see is that the lack of connections opens the text up – the relationship between the Wounded Knee item and the promo for the western, for instance, can be read from a progressive or a reactionary position. The textual contradictions reflect contradictory positions in society about the "problem" of the American Indians and their relationship to white power.

Budd, Craig, and Steinman (1985) also find a deep structural coherence underlying apparently disconnected segments of television's flow, and their analysis inevitably "closes" the text down to its ideological, commercial meaning. They analyze the advertisements inserted into an episode of *Fantasy Island* and trace clear links between the first ad of each commercial break and the preceding narrative sequence. For instance, a narrative sequence dealing with a mother's concern for her child's happiness is immediately followed by a commercial for a cereal which makes children happy. Similarly, the sequence in which a mother perceives a problem is followed by a commercial for an ointment which solves an itching problem, and a sequence in which the mother reunites the family across generations is followed by two commercials, one of which shows how Cream of Wheat reunites old friends and generations, and the other in which A.T.&T. does the same. They conclude that

> commercials respond fairly directly to the problems, desires and fantasies articulated in the program's narrative by promising gratification through products. (p.297)

The links they describe may well be there, but they are links of association, not of cause and effect, and some of them, for instance the second, are contradictory rather than complementary.

Because sequence and flow are organized according to associative rather than logical relations, the connections are not made explicitly in the text, but are devolved to the viewer where their associative nature will allow them to be made subconsciously. These connections will then not necessarily work to unify the segments of the text (as Williams wishes them to) but may leave the contradictions between segments active and unresolved. Textual unity is an agent of ideological closure, and resisting that unification resists that closure.

The other characteristic suggested by the word "flow" is that television should be continuous and should not end. It is commonplace in the USA for television to be broadcast twenty-four hours a day, but this is still comparatively unusual elsewhere, where there is often pressure from the public (and the broadcasters) to extend the hours of transmission. This does not necessarily mean that people want to watch twenty-four hours a day, but rather that they wish to decide for themselves when to stop watching, and not to have that decision made for them by government regulation or by the economic concerns of the networks.

Altman (1986) relates the extent of the flow of television to its economic context and usefully reminds us that flow promotes and is exploited by the commercial interests of television. By disguising the boundaries between programs, it disguises potential switch-off points:

> Provisionally, I would suggest the following hypothesis: flow replaces discrete programming to the extent that 1) competition for spectators is allowed to govern the broadcast situation, and 2) television revenues increase with increased viewing. (p. 40)

In support of this he argues that television programming is most discrete in eastern bloc countries, but that in quasi-state controlled, quasi-independent systems, such as those of France and Britain, a measure of flow appears in the scheduling, whereas network US television is dominated by a heavily promoted flow of images. US public cable channels, on the other hand, approximate more to the British and French situations.

In the USA two sorts of strategy have evolved to promote flow and encourage channel loyalty, one of scheduling, and one of promotion. Scheduling strategy designs the sequence and choice of programs in an attempt to build and hold a large prime-time audience whose demographics are desired by advertisers. It will typically use a strong "lead-in" program to begin prime time and attract the audience that must then be held. Then two alternative, or alternating, strategies are used. "Tent-poling" consists of placing a strong, popular program at the peak of prime time and "hanging" less popular ones on either side of it. "Hammocking" consists of suspending a weaker or newer program between two strong, well-established ones. Both strategies, as their metaphorical names suggest, aim to tie programs together into an unbroken flow and to produce equivalently unbroken viewing in the audience. This scheduling strategy is then supported by the promotional, in which "promos" for programs later in the evening are inserted early into the flow, so that later programs are tied in to earlier ones. Similarly, programs are consistently advertised in journals such as *TV Guide* as linked pairs, threes, or groups. So *O'Hara*, 8.00 p.m., and *Spenser for Hire*, 9.00 p.m., share the same *TV Guide* advertisement under the headline "Top Guns" (April 6–10, 1987), and in the same issue CBS takes a page to advertise its Monday night's flow of women's sitcoms, *Kate and Allie*, 7.00 p.m., *My Sister Sam*, 7.30 p.m., *Newhart*, 8.00 p.m. and *Designing Women*, 8.30 p.m.

Such an account of the economic purpose of televisual flow should not blind us to its textual characteristics. It is effective in the economic sphere only because its textuality appeals to popular tastes and modes of viewing.

Though Williams does not use the word "segment," his analysis reveals how segmented the television flow is. Ellis (1982) argues that it is characteristic of television to broadcast its text in relatively discrete segments, "small, sequential unities of images and sounds whose maximum duration seems to be about five minutes" (p. 112). These segments are organized into groups like news stories, commercials, or scenes of a narrative, and the flow occurs across these segments. These segments typically follow each other with no necessary connections, and indeed, Ellis argues, news and current affairs programs have made a virtue of this necessity by deliberately mixing items. Title sequences frequently exploit this segmentation by editing together shots from the forthcoming or past programs in a rapid, highly enigmatic way. Music video is another example of exaggerated segmentation. Even drama series and serials, where the narrative requires the principles of logic and cause and effect, may be segmented into short scenes with logical links omitted. The switching between one narrative strand and another in multi-narrative programs such as soap operas is frequently rapid and unmotivated.

Segmentation is more characteristic of open or writerly texts than of closed or readerly ones. Allen (1985) finds soap opera's abrupt changes from plotline to plotline a device that opens the text up and requires an active reader:

> The mere syntagmatic juxtaposition of two apparently unrelated scenes represents a paradigmatic indeterminacy for the reader: could the relationship between them be more than sequential? (p. 80)

This "indeterminacy" is, of course, a general effect of segmentation and is not unique to soap operas, though it is emphasized in them. Indeed, Allen's final question could equally well be asked of the "syntagmatic juxtaposition" in the news of the "apparently unrelated" stories of a "strike" and of rising unemployment (see chapter 15). Ellis (1982) agrees that the disruptive breaks between segments outweigh any attempts of continuity or consequence to unify the text. Syntagmatic links are agents of closure (which is why realistic narrative insists on proper consequence rather than mere sequence), and their absence opens up "syntagmatic gaps" through which the "reader inserts himself or herself into the text" (Allen 1985: 78).

Larger versions of these gaps occur between episodes, and in these the viewer "enters the text" in the imaginative and creative way that we traced earlier in this chapter and in chapter 5. These gaps quite literally make the soap opera a producerly text, for they invite the reader to "write in" their absences, and the invitation is readily accepted by many viewers, of whom Palmer's (1986) subjects are typical:

> [About *Fame*] We usually get together and start talking about it, 'cause it's really good and you remember what happened, and you wonder what's going to happen next in it. (*Clara*, 11) (p. 101)

> We could both tell each other about it if we missed any of the TV and we could both think of what is going to happen if it is continued. (*Philippa*, 8) (p. 101)

Advertisers, with their powerful economic motive, have been concerned to exploit this producerly activity of television audiences. Martin Buckland, an executive with USP Needham, Melbourne, says:

> In techniques and style, there is a trend towards advertisements in which the viewer is asked to complete the circle: the message is implied rather than stated, and it is up to the public to take the final step in understanding. This has come about because of increasing audience sophistication – largely as a result of growing up with television.
>
> (quoted in Hewitt 1986: 14)

An ad for men's toiletries by Manege exemplifies this:

□ *Visual*	□ *Voice-over*
ECU of bottle – woman's hand – rubbing it on man's jaw, hand slipping down man's chest, playing with the button on his denim jacket.	When a woman puts Manege on a man he knows that the more she puts on . . . (long pause) . . . the more life will take off.

The long pause invites the viewer to "complete the circle," to write "she" instead of "life." The "newly written" viewer-script, which says what the official one dare not, exploits the polysemy of language in its pun, for it means simultaneously "the more of his clothes she takes off" (supporting the visual message), "the more of her clothes she takes off" (the scandalous, unspeakable message), and "the more she 'flies high'" (as in the verbal message). The writing by the viewer exceeds that of the official script, for it contains three, as opposed to two, patterns of meaning and it implicates the viewer into the process of making meanings for the product. Obviously the advertiser hopes that this implication will engage the desires of the viewer and transfer them to the product. But, as I shall argue in chapters 13 and 16, the viewers' pleasures of making meanings, of "writing," are not necessarily transferred to the interests of the advertiser: many more viewers gain pleasure from advertisements than buy the products being promoted.

Segmentation allows another form of "writing" by the active viewer – zapping. Zapping consists of flicking through the channels watching snatches of each, and moving on as soon as attention or pleasure is lost. Commercial breaks often trigger the finger on the channel switcher and the US networks plan their schedules so that their ad breaks occur at the same time in an attempt to ensure both that their audience watches the ads which provide the networks' income and that they "hold" their audience through the ads. The advent of cable has nullified any effectiveness this strategy may have had. The television viewer can watch a program under roughly similar conditions to the watching of a film, or a televisually literate viewer (and many younger viewers are particularly literate) can watch two programs simultaneously by zapping back and forth between them, using his or her televisual literacy to fill in the enlarged syntagmatic gaps produced by the practice which Palmer (1986: 79) calls "systematic switching" in order to distinguish it from the more random channel searches of zapping.

Zapping allows the viewer to construct a viewing experience of fragments, a postmodern collage of images whose pleasures lie in their discontinuity, their juxtapositions, and their contradictions. This is segmentation taken to the extreme of fragmentation and makes of television the most open producerly text for it evades all attempts at closure. It is a form of scratch video that produces an individualized television text out of its mass-produced works.

The television text, then, is composed of a rapid succession of compressed, vivid segments where the principle of logic and cause and effect is subordinated to that of association and consequence to sequence. Flow, with its connotations of a languid river, is perhaps an unfortunate metaphor: the movement of the television text is discontinuous, interrupted, and segmented. Its attempts at closure, at a unitary meaning, or a unified viewing subject, are constantly subjected to fracturing forces.

□ Television and oral culture

Television's distinctive textual characteristics, quite different from those of literature or film, have derived from and are inserted into a popular culture in which orality plays a central role. Television is so often treated as an inferior cultural medium with inferior textual characteristics because our culture is one that validates the literary, or rather the literate, and consequently de-values the oral. Fiske and Hartley (1978) list some of the main differences between oral and literate modes of communication:

□ *Oral modes*	□ *Literate modes*
dramatic	narrative
episodic	sequential
mosaic	linear
dynamic	static
active	artifact
concrete	abstract
ephemeral	permanent
social	individual

105

metaphorical	metonymic
rhetorical	logical
dialectical	univocal/"consistent"

The list of oral characteristics needs to be extended to include "nowness," a sense of the future that goes with an "unwritten" text, and a direct, personalized address and its production of a textual or cultural *experience*, rather than of separate, labeled works of art.

The formal characteristics of television are essentially those of oral rather than literate modes of communication. This does not mean that television is an oral culture, but that its popularity is due, in part, to the ease with which its programs can be inserted into those forms of oral culture which have survived in a mass, industrialized society.

Ong (1982) suggests that an "electronic" society produces a form of secondary orality which is based upon and derived from literacy, rather than vice versa:

> with telephone, radio, television and various kinds of sound tape, electronic technology has brought us into the age of "secondary orality". This new orality has striking resemblances to the old in its participatory mystique, its fostering of a communal sense, its concentration on the present moment, and even its use of formulas (Ong 1971, 284–303; 1977, 16–49, 305–41). But it is essentially a more deliberate and self-conscious orality, based permanently on the use of writing and print, which are essential for the manufacture and operation of the equipment and for its use as well. (p. 136)

Ong rightly emphasizes the participatory nature of this "secondary orality" but overemphasizes its dependence upon the written word. The orality of television is not just a spoken version of a literate culture: its textual forms, not just its "spokenness," are oral, and, more significantly, it is *treated* as oral culture by many of its viewers. They enter into a "dialogue" with it, they gossip about it, they shift and shape its meanings and pleasures.

Oral culture is embedded in everyday life unlike writing which produces an abstract knowledge that is disengaged from immediate social experience:

> for an oral culture learning or knowing means achieving close, empathetic, communal identification with the known (Havelock 1963, 145–6), "getting on with it". Writing separates the knower from the known and thus sets up conditions for "objectivity", in the sense of personal disengagement or distancing.

(Ong 1982: 45–6)

The "knowing" or "learning" offered by *Dallas* or *Prisoner* is deeply embedded in the social context of their reception and use. The "knowledge" is essentially oral. Its meanings are determined more by the contexts of its readings than by the central system of television and can thus take an oppositional stance with little sense of strain. As Bakhtin (1981) argues, oral culture, especially in literate societies, is typically associated with subversive or scandalous movements and stances. It is the essentially oral forms of television that allow it to be embedded so firmly in the social-cultural life of its viewers and that enable such an active, participatory, selective set of reading relations.

This means that television is able to play in industrial societies a similar role to that played by folk culture in more homogeneous ones. This is not to romanticize television, nor to homogenize it, for television is clearly not "of the folk." Yet the meanings made from it are readily incorporated into the cultural lives of various social formations in such a way that they work as folk culture. Seal (1986) lists four criteria for defining a folk culture and it is remarkable how closely watching and talking about television can meet them. They are:

1. Folklore defines and identifies the membership of a group for its members, often in opposition to other groups.
2. Folklore is transmitted informally, either orally or by example, and consequently does not distinguish clearly between transmitters and receivers.
3. Folklore operates outside established social institutions such as the church, the educational system or the media, although it can interact with them and traverse them.
4 There is no standard version of a folk text – it exists only as part of a process.

There may be a broadcast version of a television program, but the text that a particular subculture may make of it exists only as part of the cultural process of that audience: the school students' *Prisoner* is part of their process of making sense of their experience of subordination and of their resistive stance to it.

Television's openness, its textual contradictions and instability, enable it to be readily incorporated into the oral culture of many and diverse groups in many and diverse ways so that, while it may not in its broadcast mode be a form of folklore, it is at least able to serve folkloric functions for some of its audiences. Its popularity among its diversity of audiences depends upon its ability to be easily and differently incorporated into a variety of subcultures: popularity, audience activity, and polysemy are mutually entailed and interdependent concepts.

Chapter 7

Intertextuality

The theory of intertextuality proposes that any one text is necessarily read in relationship to others and that a range of textual knowledges is brought to bear upon it. These relationships do not take the form of specific allusions from one text to another and there is no need for readers to be familiar with specific or the same texts to read intertextually. Intertextuality exists rather in the space *between* texts. Madonna's music video *Material Girl* provides us with a case in point: it is a parody of Marilyn Monroe's song and dance number "Diamonds are a Girl's Best Friend" in the movie *Gentlemen Prefer Blondes:* such an allusion to a specific text is not an example of intertextuality for its effectiveness depends upon specific, not generalized, textual knowledge – a knowledge that, incidentally, many of Madonna's young girl fans in 1985 were unlikely to possess. The video's intertextuality refers rather to our culture's image bank of the sexy blonde star who plays with men's desire for her and turns it to her advantage. It is an elusive image, similar to Barthes's notion of myth, to which Madonna and Marilyn Monroe contribute equally and from which they draw equally. The meanings of *Material Girl* depend upon its *allusion* to *Gentlemen Prefer Blondes* and upon its intertextuality with *all* texts that contribute to and draw upon the meaning of "the blonde" in our culture. Intertextual knowledges pre-orient the reader to exploit television's polysemy by activating the text in certain ways, that is, by making some meanings rather than others. Studying a text's intertextual relations can provide us with valuable clues to the readings that a particular culture or subculture is likely to produce from it.

We can envisage these intertextual relations on two dimensions, the horizontal and the vertical. Horizontal relations are those between primary texts that are more or less explicitly linked, usually along the axes of genre, character, or content. Vertical intertextuality is that between a primary text, such as a television program or series, and other texts of a different type that refer explicitly to it. These may be secondary texts such as studio publicity, journalistic features, or criticism, or tertiary texts produced by the viewers themselves in the form of letters to the press or, more importantly, of gossip and conversation.

☐ Horizontal intertextuality

The most influential and widely discussed form of horizontal intertextuality is that of genre, and it is this that we will concentrate on first. But there are other axes of horizontal intertextuality such as character: B. A., for instance, one of the characters of the adventure series *The A-Team*, is also a hero of a cartoon series, and the actor who plays him, Mr T, not only introduces the cartoon series but also appears on television as a wrestler or a guest on talk shows. The meaning of Mr T/B. A. (for the character and actor are almost indistinguishable) does not reside in any one of his screen appearances but in the intertextuality which is the aggregate of all and an essential part of the reading of any one. Of course, different viewers will have different intertextual aggregates of Mr T/B. A. according to the variations in their intertextual experience of him. Adult viewers of *The A-Team* may well not see the cartoon series and so "their" B. A. will differ from that of their children who do watch it. Madonna is similarly a web of intertextual meanings crossing media boundaries, "she" is a sign formed by television, film, records, the press, and the publicity industry.

Williams's (1974) analysis of television's *flow* has shown how intertextual relations of content can easily cross genre boundaries: the meaning of a traditional western is intertextually inflected by its juxtaposition with a news item about American Indians protesting their place in a white-dominated society. Adventure films taking place in unspecified Third World countries run by corrupt regimes relate all too readily with news reports from Africa or Latin America. But despite the ease with which intertextual relations cross genre boundaries, genre still organizes intertextual relations in particularly influential ways.

☐ Genre

Genre is a cultural practice that attempts to structure some order into the wide range of texts and meanings that circulate in our culture for the convenience of both producers and audiences. Television programs appear to fall "obviously" into clear generic categories – cop shows, soap operas, sitcoms, hospital dramas, quiz and game shows, and so on. Television is a highly "generic" medium with comparatively few one-off programs falling outside established generic categories. Even single dramas typically have their generic characteristics emphasized: on British television, for example, they are screened under generic titles such as *Play for Today* whose title sequence consists of a rapid montage of stills from previous plays in the series – a sort of intertextual memory jogger.

109

Thinking of television generically requires us to prioritize the similarities between programs rather than their individual differences. The conventions shared between different programs or series in a genre are often disparaged by being referred to as "a formula," and popular art is then labeled "formula art."

Cawelti (1970) opposes formula art to art with invented or original structures:

Like the distinction between convention and invention, the distinction between formula and structure can be envisaged as a continuum between two poles; one pole is that of a completely conventional structure of conventions – an episode of the Lone Ranger or one of the Tarzan books comes close to this pole; the other end of the continuum is a completely original structure which orders inventions – *Finnegans Wake* is perhaps the ultimate example. (p. 29)

The distinction is not just between the poles of convention and invention, but between highbrow and lowbrow art with all the value judgments that those metaphors imply. Highbrow, elitist works of art are typically valued for their unique qualities, and a whole critical practice is devoted to detailing and praising these elements that differentiate one particular work of art from others, for it is in its uniqueness that its value is believed to reside. Understanding works of art generically, however, locates their value in what they have in common, for their shared conventions form links not only with other texts in the genre, but also between text and audiences, text and producers, and producers and audiences. Generic conventions are so important in television because they are a prime way of both understanding and constructing this triangular relationship between producer, text, and audience.

Conventions are the structural elements of genre that are shared between producers and audiences. They embody the crucial ideological concerns of the time in which they are popular and are central to the pleasures a genre offers its audience. Conventions are social and ideological. A formula, on the other hand, is an industrial and economic translation of conventions that is essential to the efficient production of popular cultural commodities and should not be evaluated by aesthetic criteria that dismiss it as mere lack of imagination. Getting the right formula that transforms the right conventions into a popular art form is no easy task, but given the high cost of cultural production and the unpredictability of the cultural marketplace, formula art is an integral part of the culture industries and needs to be investigated, not dismissed.

Feuer (1987) suggests there are three main strategies for constructing generic categories. The first is the *aesthetic*, which confines itself to textual characteristics. The second she calls the *ritual*, which sees genre as a conventional repeated "exchange between industry and audience, an exchange

110

through which a culture speaks to itself." Generic conventions allow the negotiation of shared cultural concerns and values and locate genres firmly within their social context. The third approach she calls *ideological* and this is her most problematic one. At one level, this view of genre accounts for the way that genres can be called upon to deliver audiences to advertisers, and structure the dominant ideology into their conventions. More productively, however, Feuer suggests that the meanings of programs for viewers are influenced, even manipulated, by the genres they are fitted into.

The least productive is the aesthetic or textual:

> Genres are not to be seen as forms of textual codifications, but as systems of orientations, expectations and conventions that circulate between industry, text and subject.
>
> (Neale 1981: 6)

Genres are intertextual or even pre-textual, for they form the network of industrial, ideological, and institutional conventions that are common to both producer and audiences out of which arise both the producer's program and the audiences' readings. As Kerr (1981: 73) points out, genres predetermine texts and readings.

The difficulty with a purely textual definition of genre is that it tends to fix characteristics within genre boundaries in a way that rarely fits any specific instance. The characteristics of the crime thriller listed by Kerr (1981) are a good distillation of the genre, but any one crime thriller is unlikely to exhibit all of them, and is equally likely to include others:

> Briefly the realist crime thriller is comprised of a network of conventional practices including a teleological and formulaic narrative structure (an equilibrium posed, fractured by villainy and recovered by heroism); credible characterisation (a family allegory peopled by coherent, plausibly motivated, racial, sexual and class stereotypes, cruder in the background than the foreground); identifiable iconographic elements (as illustrated, for example, by the discussion in both studies of the imagery of the title sequence, emphasising costume, decor and the tools of the hero's trade); milieu (the use of "authentic" locations, the contrast between class settings, etc.); and finally the film and video conventions for the construction of these fictions (conventions of framing, shooting, lighting, editing, sound recording, composing, narrating, plotting, casting, acting, writing and directing). (p. 74)

A genre seen textually should be defined as a shifting provisional set of characteristics which is modified as each new example is produced. Any one program will bear the main characteristics of its genre, but is likely to include some from others: ascribing it to one genre or another involves deciding which set of characteristics are the most important. *Hill Street Blues* and *Cagney and Lacey* are either cop shows with characteristics of soap opera, or vice versa. *Remington Steele* and *Scarecrow and Mrs King* are cop shows with characteristics of the sitcom, *Miami Vice* a cop show with characteristics of music video. Each new show shifts genre boundaries and develops definitions. There is an intergeneric network of conventions with various points of convergence that form the foci but not the boundaries of the various genres when defined textually.

The difficulty of tying down the textual dimension of genre leads us to predict that a greater value will lie in the ritual approach which spans the realms of the producers/distributors and of the audiences; here genre acts as an agreed code that links the two. For the producers its advantages are primarily economic. The market response to a cultural commodity is notoriously hard to predict, and updating or modifying a previously successful genre can minimize this unpredictability. Genres rise and fall in popularity as popular taste shifts with social and historical changes. The rise of Reaganism and the rehabilitation of the US experience in Vietnam has modified the cop show and reasserted its popularity. Not only do many shows have heroes who learned their ideologically validated skills in Vietnam (e.g. *Magnum p.i., The A-Team, Simon and Simon*) but the narratives continually reenact the right of those in control of "The Law" to impose that law upon others. When this law is related to Lacan's "Law of the Father," the links between Reaganism, masculinity, the exercise of social power, and the form of the genre in the 1980s become clearer (see chapter 11):

> *Miami Vice* and its moment in American TV history comes at the end of a decade of attempts to reconstruct the credibility of male institutional authority from the vacuum created by Vietnam – a process of reconstruction that has, in a sense, been concomitant with the rewriting of the history of that war.
>
> (Ross 1986: 150)

Genres are popular when their conventions bear a close relationship to the dominant ideology of the time.

The overlap between the ritual and ideological approaches to drama should not lead us to the view that changes in sociocultural conditions produce changes in generic conventions directly. The industry plays a vital mediating role in identifying potential shifts in the culture and "testing" them with a new inflection of a genre. Feuer (1987) gives a good account of how MTM Enterprises in the 1970s produced sitcoms that picked up and developed cultural concerns with shifting definitions of femininity, and produced shows like *The Mary Tyler Moore Show, Rhoda,* and *The Bob Newhart Show.*

This higher profile given to the rights of women also began to influence cop shows, and modified the genre with the introduction of female cop heroines (*Charlie's Angels, Police Woman*), and the male/female hero couple of *MacMillan and Wife:* the masculine control of the Law was joined by more feminine values, but by the 1980s, the swing to the right and the reassertion of masculinity began to stress the contradictions more clearly.

These contradictions occasionally resulted in shows like *Cagney and Lacey* where they were dealt with seriously as a mainspring of the drama, but more often in shows that dealt with them humorously like *Remington Steele* or *Scarecrow and Mrs King.* The ideological contradictions between the rise of feminism and the reassertion of masculine power required the mixing of genres (cop show with soap opera or cop show with sitcom): the genre mix was also a gender mix – cop shows are a mainly masculine genre, sitcoms and soap operas are more feminine. (See chapters 10 and 11.)

This market-driven desire to predict and produce popularity lies behind scheduling practice as well. By a careful mix of genres – news, soap opera, cop shows, and sitcoms – the scheduler hopes to build an audience for the network or channel that is of maximum size and that contains the right mix of social groups to be sold to advertisers.

The scheduling of *Cagney and Lacey* provides a good example not only of its ability to build an audience, but also to affect meanings and popularity by influencing a show's generic affiliations. When CBS scheduled *Cagney and Lacey* after *Magnum* on a Thursday evening, it rated poorly. But when rescheduled on a Monday to follow *Scarecrow and Mrs King, Kate and Allie* and *Newhart* it topped the ratings. Monday became known as "women's night" and *Cagney and Lacey* was shifted away from the masculine generic relations with *Magnum* and towards more feminine ones. Because *Cagney and Lacey* shows a particularly even mix of generic characteristics, its prime genre was in some doubt, and so scheduling was able to tip the balance away from masculine cop show towards soap opera or woman's show. The cultural practices of producers and audiences are finally more influential than textual characteristics in determining genre.

A more extreme example of genre-shifting is given by Jenkins (1986) in his study of the fans of *Star Trek.* The numerous fan clubs consist mainly of women who run a whole secondary publication industry of newsletters and fanzines, and Jenkins finds ample evidence in these publications that the fans have changed *Star Trek's* genre to that of the romance. The popularity of the show for its female fans is centered around the personal, especially romantic, relationships of the spaceship's crew and the women fans were explicitly critical of the way that the masculine generic conventions of science fiction neglected this feminine focus. Reascribing the genre of a text is a tactic of popular reading that takes pleasure in its ability to evade or redirect the cultural strategy that serves the interests of the dominant economic or gender power structures.

Shows are conventionally marketed to networks and advertisers, and presented to reviewers and the public, as new inflections of a popular genre. Genre serves the dual needs of a commodity: on the one hand standardization and familiarity, and on the other, product differentiation.

But the work of genre is more than economic, it is cultural as well, and this is another aspect of Feuer's (1987) ideological approach. Genre spells out to the audience the range of pleasures it might expect and thus regulates and activates memory of similar texts and the expectations of this one.

For Davies (1978/9) genre knowledge is crucial to the pleasure of the mystery/thriller/adventure film, for it works to compensate for potential unpleasures in the plot structure:

> The mystery/thriller/adventure plot works through otherness. We have less knowledge and control as the narrative progresses and the mystery is compounded with further mystery. Why, then, are we not deeply disturbed by such a narrative pattern? . . . In such plots the reader finds generic rather than psychological points of reference. The disturbing effect of mystery and suspense is balanced by a confidence in the inevitability of genre. (p. 62)

Genre works to promote and organize intertextual relations, particularly amongst primary texts.

It also works within the practice of reading. Neale (1981) argues that it limits and conditions the audience response, and works to contain the possibilities of reading. Genre is part of the textual strategies by which television attempts to control its polysemic potential. As Hartley (1985) puts it:

> Audiences' different potential pleasures are channeled and disciplined by genres, which operate by producing recognition of the already known set of responses and rules of engagement. Audiences aren't supposed to judge a western for not being musical enough, a musical for not being very horrific, or a sitcom for not being sufficiently erotic.
>
> Such is the "contract" of genre. It entails a loss of freedom of desire and demand in order to achieve efficiency and properly labeled packaging.
> (p. 18)

Genre is a means of constructing both the audience and the reading subject: its work in the economic domain is paralleled by its work in the domain of culture; that is, its work in influencing which meanings of a program are preferred by, or proffered to, which audiences. It does this by preferring some intertextual relations and their associated meanings over others and in so far as the relations it prefers are those proposed by the industry, its work is likely to be reactionary. Reading the progressive meanings of *Hill Street Blues* or *Cagney and Lacey* requires the reader to distance them from their apparent genre of cop show, and to read them as a contradictory mix of the masculine and feminine, of the cop show and soap opera, of bourgeois realism and social realism.

□ Inescapable intertextuality

Generically driven intertextuality is finally constraining and does little to open the text up to the reader: similarly, it does little to advance our understanding of the inevitability of intertextuality, of the intertextual as the prime site of culture. This is the view proposed by Barthes (1975a) who argues that intertextual relations are so pervasive that our culture consists of a complex web of intertextuality, in which all texts refer finally to each other and not to reality. None of the five codes that structure all narratives and our understanding of them refer to "the real" or relate the narrative to it (see chapter 8). For Barthes "the real" is never accessible in its own terms, and is therefore not part of the study of meaning or of narrative. He replaces the notion of the real with that of culture's construction of the real, which can be found only in cultural products (such as texts) and not in reality itself. Every text, in this theory, refers not to reality but to all the other texts in a culture for the sense that it makes, even if this sense is a sense of reality. Codes are the bridges between texts that enable this constant intertextual interplay to take place. For Barthes, then, the knowledge of reality, and therefore, for practical purposes, reality itself, is intertextual: it exists only in the interrelations between all that a culture has written, spoken, visualized about it. In this sense, all texts refer to "what has been written, i.e. to the Book (of culture, of life, of life as culture), it (the code) makes the text into a prospectus of this book" (pp. 20–1). In this view, a television program can only be understood by its relationship to other television programs, not by any relationship to the real. So a representation of a car chase only makes sense in relation to all the others we have seen – after all, we are unlikely to have experienced one in reality, and if we did, we would, according to this model, make sense of it by turning it into another text, which we would also understand intertextually, in terms of what we have seen so often on our screens. There is then a cultural knowledge of the concept "car chase" that any one text is a prospectus for, and that is used by the viewer to decode it, and by the producer to encode it.

There is, according to Barthes, an adequate but limited number of such cultural knowledges, which he usually identifies by verbal nouns, because they are forms of action. Examples of these are "The Kidnapping," "The Meeting," "The Seduction," and so on. Each narrative is a rewriting of these already written "knowledges" of the culture and each text makes sense only in so far as it rewrites and re-presents them for us. Literary and high art critics, who set a high value on originality and creativity, may be offended by this theory, but those of us concerned with as conventional and repetitious a medium as television, should find it more readily acceptable.

Barthes was interested exclusively in literature as he developed his theory, and literature differs from television in that it is, in general, explicitly fictional. It is provocative, then, to apply these ideas to "factual" television, such as news. This would explain our understanding of a news item not in terms of its relation to the "real event" but as a prospectus of the already written (and thus already read) "Book." So a news item of politicians meeting a dignitary at an airport is encoded and decoded according to our cultural knowledge of "The Greeting." An earthquake, a fire, and a famine are similarly understood as specific transformations of "The Disaster" with all its connotations of the fragility of culture's control over nature. The intertextuality of news is not merely generic (in which all "economic" stories refer to each other) but is also more broadly cultural: news, as a narrative, refers to all other narratives and their knowledges. Representation, then, becomes a rewriting, rather than a specific response to a specific event or to an original, creative "idea."

Stuart Hall (1986) has noted that the twentieth century's massive development of the means of reproducing and circulating images has pushed representation into the center of the cultural arena. The nineteenth-century's empiricist concern with the reproduction of the real has receded as the real has faded behind the imperative, incessant images of our culture. Images are clearer, more impressive than the reality they claim to represent, but they are also fragmented, contradictory and exhibit a vast variety that questions the unity of the world of experience. Images are made and read in relation to other images and the real is read as an image. Television commercials are not "about" products, but are images of desire and pleasure that overwhelm the product they are attached to. TV news is a mosaic of images of elite persons, horrific nature, and human violence. TV sport is a kaleidoscope of images of muscle, of skill, of pain. The images are what matter, they exist in their own flickering domain and never come to rest in a firm anchorage in the real. Postmodernism posits the rejection of meaning in its affirmation of the image as signifier with no final signified; images exist in an infinite chain of intertextuality.

This denial of a final meaning for images has similarities with the deconstructionists' reading of Derrida: the infinitely receding signified reduces language to a free play of signifiers that denies the possibility of any fixed or final meaning. What is welcome in these views is their emphasis upon the instability of symbolic systems and the absence of a final authoritative "meaning" against which the "correctness" or "truth" of specific readings can be judged. What is unproductive, however, is the belief in the impossibility of a meaning, because meaning is necessarily infinitely elusive and thus the search for it is misdirected. To counteract this we need to shift our focus from the text to its moments of reading; points of stability and anchored meanings (however temporary) are to be found not in the text itself, but in its reading by a socially and historically situated viewer. Such a meaning is, of course, not fixed in a universal, empirical "reality," but in the social situation of the viewer. Different readings may stabilize texts differently and momentarily, but they do achieve moments of stability, moments of meaning.

☐ Vertical intertextuality: reading the secondary text

Denying any final textual meaning anchored in reality is only pushing the notion of polysemy to its extreme. It is part of the same view of the text which stresses its inability to police or fix its own meanings. Polysemy works through textual devices which admit of a variety of readings. This variety is not anarchic, but is delimited by the structure of the text, and the readings that comprise it are always made in relation to those preferred by the text itself. Because television is institutional art with a strong economic motive, this preferred reading will normally bear the dominant ideology, and the relation of any one subculture's reading to the preferred reading reproduces the relation of that subculture to the dominant ideology. Reading relations and social relations reproduce each other.

Chapter 5 has shown some of the ways in which the social situation of viewers influences the readings they make of television, and thus how they mobilize its polysemy to serve their cultural interests. Mobilizing its polysemy involves activating one set of meanings rather than any of the others, or responding to some contradictions rather than others. This selection is rarely a conscious or intentional process, but it is none the less an active one, so the phrase "activating a set of meanings" is apt. But besides being polysemic, the television text has leaky boundaries, and viewers bring to bear on it not only their material social existence, but also their cultural experience of other texts into which it leaks.

Vertical intertextuality consists of a primary text's relations with other texts which refer specifically to it. These secondary texts, such as criticism or publicity, work to promote the circulation of selected meanings of the primary text. The tertiary texts are the final, crucial stage of this circulation, for they occur at the level of the viewer and his/her social relations. Studying them gives us access to the meanings that are in circulation at any one time.

This vertical intertextuality works not only to provide the analyst with evidence of how television's polysemic potential is specifically mobilized, but also to serve as an agent of this mobilization for the viewer. As Hodge and Tripp (1986) say:

> Discourse about television is itself a social force. It is a major site of the mediation of television meanings, a site where television meanings fuse with other meanings into a new text to form a major interface with the world of action and belief. (p. 143)

An essential element of television is its intertextuality with what is written and spoken about it.

Secondary texts play a significant role in influencing which of television's meanings may be activated in any one reading. Television's pervasiveness in our culture is not due simply to the fact that so much of it is broadcast and that watching it is our most popular leisure activity, but because it pervades so much of the rest of our cultural life – newspapers, magazines, advertisements, conversations, radio, or style of dress, of make-up, of dance steps. All of these enter intertextual relations with television. It is important to talk about their relations with television, and not to describe them as spin-offs from it, for the influence is two-way. Their meanings are read back into television, just as productively as television determines theirs.

To illustrate this I wish to concentrate on the role played by journalistic writing about television. It may be helpful to imagine examples of this writing arranged on a scale whose two ends represent the producers' interests and the viewers' interests. At the producers' end lie program publicity and articles heavily dependent on studio press releases. At the viewers' end, there is independent criticism which seeks to serve the interests of the viewer, either by helping him or her to choose and discriminate, or by providing a response to a program to confirm or challenge his or hers. Somewhere in the middle come the fan magazines that purport to be independent of the studios, but obviously rely on studio press releases and cooperation for their material and access to the players for interviews. Studio gossip, commentary, interviews in magazines whose main subject matter is other than television will also fall somewhere towards the middle of the scale.

Bennett (1982, 1983b) and Bennett and Woollacott (1987) have theorized the role that secondary texts from the producers' end of the scale play in helping to promote certain readings of the primary text. In their case, the primary text was that intertextual phenomenon, James Bond. They show how promotional material has inflected the meanings of Bond differently in the different periods of his popularity. Their emphasis diverges slightly from ours, because their interest lies in how the dominant or preferred readings can change over time, whereas ours, more appropriate to the transience of television than to the more permanent forms of novel and film, is concerned with how the primary text can simultaneously give rise to different readings,

118

corresponding to the different audience groups. But their work still shows how secondary texts can activate the primary text in different ways. Thus, in the late 1950s and early 1960s, Bond was seen as the Cold War warrior – the publicity and bookjackets foregrounded guns and paraphernalia of spying – but a decade later Bond became the definer of the new sexuality. In this period the publicity for the films and novels emphasized the Bond girl, and the important enigma of the narrative became if, or how, Bond would win the girl rather than defeat the villain. Bond, at this time, liberated the bachelor from the ideal of marriage, and the girl liberated the new woman from the restriction of sexuality to marriage.

Criticism and publicity are, according to Bennett, an ideological system of bids and counterbids for the meanings of texts: they act as textual shifters for "Bond," who has no stable set of meanings discernible in the primary texts themselves. One of the most influential of these secondary texts was Sean Connery himself (the star of the early Bond films), whose "real" biography and opinions were read into the primary texts to flesh out the character of the fictional Bond. We will discuss the notion of character more fully in chapter 9, but it is important to note here how much attention these secondary texts devote to the lives and opinions of the actors and actresses who play the characters in television drama, and how these real-life biographies are mobilized to make the fictional characters appear more real.

The concern of Hobson's (1982) subjects with the realisticness of *Crossroads* focused primarily on the believability of the characters and their actions or reactions. Ang's (1985) viewers of *Dallas* expressed a similar concern in their evaluation of various characters' "genuineness." The way that viewers relate to characters is not as straightforward as the "cultural dope" fallacy would have us believe, and will be discussed in more detail in chapter 9, but it is certainly a common desire of viewers that characters should appear "real." So it is no surprise to find in soap opera fanzines, for example, photographs that are ambiguously of the player or the character, as though the two were indistinguishable. In Figure 7.1 (a), for example, it is not clear if the photographs are of the actors or of their characters. The codes of dress, expression, and make-up are ambivalent; only the code of the camera indicates that these images are probably of the actors. Actors, who are "real" people, conventionally acknowledge the presence of the camera and therefore of the spectator, by looking at the lens, characters rarely do. (This convention, like all others, is never inviolable: Figure 7.1 (b) shows characters acknowledging the still camera as they would never acknowledge the television one.) But the headline contradicts the camera code: it is, after all, the characters and not the actors who live in Pine Valley.

This promotion of a reading strategy that plays with the boundary between the fictional and the real occurs in the words of these secondary texts as well:

Figure 7.1 Ambiguous photographs: actors or characters?

**Michael Knight and Steve Caffrey
meet in a head-on heartthrob collision!**

(a)

Photographs are ambiguously of the character or of the player. In (a), the dress, settings, and headline suggest they are of the character, but the caption and the look at the camera suggest the opposite. In (b), the photograph is more clearly of the characters, yet they look at the camera as though they were "real" people. Merging player with character is another instance of having fun with the boundary between the fictional and the real.

(b)

120

It seems odd, doesn't it, that one day a Hardy boy would end up marrying a Vulcan? It's not really as strange as it sounds, but it is entirely true! Handsome Parker Stevenson, the evil and dirty Joel McCarthy of *Falcon Crest*, has found happiness in the arms of an alien. The ex-Hardy boy (he starred with Shaun Cassidy) met his wife-to-be while she was filming the feature *Star Trek: the Wrath of Khan*.

(Daytime/Nighttime Soap Stars No. 7, February 1985: 75)

The language slips easily, with no sense of strain, between that of representation, which separates player from character – "starred," "filming" – and that which identifies player with character – "a Hardy boy marrying a Vulcan," "Parker Stevenson, the evil and dirty Joel McCarthy." *Daytimers* (May 1985) carried an article "written" by the character about the player, which is only carrying to its logical extreme the common practice of having the player talk about his or her character as if it were a real person. This sort of secondary text, according to Bennett (1983b), constructs "a series of micro-narratives in which the 'real' biographies, views and values of the stars fill out, but are also filled out by, the character of the hero (or heroine)" (p. 216). We must be careful not to let the "cultural dope" fallacy lead us to believe that the soap fans are incapable of distinguishing between character and player: the jokey tone of the piece about the Hardy boy marrying a Vulcan is typical, and indicates that this is an intentional illusion, a conspiracy entered into by viewer and journalist in order to increase the pleasure of the program. A similar sense of self-delusion lies behind the photographs and their headlines of Figure 7.1.

This deliberate self-delusion is fun: it involves playing with the boundary between the representation and the real, and playing with the duality of the viewers' reading position as it switches between involvement and detachment. Both Hobson (1982) and Ang (1985) found this to be a common reading strategy which allowed viewers to enjoy the pleasure of the illusion without surrendering themselves totally to it.

The nature of television as representation is never lost sight of despite the deliberate denial. These secondary texts are equally concerned to celebrate the hard work and the professionalism of the actors and actresses. They frequently take the reader on to the set to show how the program is made, they frequently trace the personal history of the actor or actors through a number of different roles in different soap operas, and they frequently draw attention to the acting skills required to produce this illusion of the real (see Figure 7.2).

These secondary texts, then, are no more univocal than the primary ones. Though they promote a realistic reading of television, they are shot through with clear references to television as a system of representation. When we are reminded which character a particular player plays the tone is factual and

Figure 7.2 Representation and the real

acting — is in the *reacting* As evidenced by the plethora of hammy crowd reaction scenes in movies and television, only a select few can carry off a silent response to a line or situation with subtlety and honesty. It not only calls for acting of the highest caliber; it requires crackerjack directing.

Which is what David Pressman pulled off on ONE LIFE TO LIVE following the death of Tim Siegel (Tom Berenger) in the mid-1970's. At that time in the show, it was always expected that Dr. Jim Craig (the late, great Nat Polen) would come through the waiting room doors and say at the end of a Friday episode, "I'm sorry, Larry (or whoever). There was nothing we could do." On this particular occasion — thank goodness — the stock line was obliterated. Jim walked into the waiting room where his wife Anna (Doris Belack) and their best friend, Tim's mother Eileen (Alice Hirson) were sitting. Without a word of dialogue, Polen looked at Doris Belack, Ms. Belack uttered a quiet gasp at the realization of what that look meant, and Alice Hirson fell weepingly into Doris Belack's arms. It would be interesting to find out if the late head writer Gordon Russell had purposely omitted the spoken words, or if there had been scripted lines which were dropped in rehearsal. Either way, it was a superbly crafted moment on a show which has been consistently well-acted.

DAVID SELBY
We know, we know, David Selby was made up to look slightly strange as Quentin Collins on DARK SHADOWS, but we just couldn't resist. Don't you think he looks a bit more handsome as FALCON CREST's urbane but unprincipled Richard Channing?

What is going on here is work on the set of DAYS OF OUR LIVES. Actors usually arrive in Salem around 7:00 a.m. Blocking and rehearsal don't start much later, and the actual taping usually begins around 2:30 in the afternoon. That should give you some idea of how long these days can go.

Outside, it's rainy and cold, but inside this world of make-believe — a windowless studio (as all studios are) with four or five lighted sets that will be where the action takes place today — the mood is cheery and energetic. That's not surprising.

As they rehearse their words, Don tells Marlena how upset he is with her. Calmly, Marlena informs him that Stefano kidnapped her children. "You better sit down," Alice tells Don. He starts to sit, but Alice, or rather Frances, out of character, says, "Not there." The crew laughs.

Josh is one of the great leading men in daytime. He loves women, not just the sex. He takes control, embraces well, and has an inner choreographic ability in a love scene.

The pleasure of treating the representation as the real depends upon a knowing self-delusion. The soap opera press consistently foregrounds the act of representation and encourages its readers to distinguish the fictional from the real even as it pretends to deny the difference.

objective in contrast to the excessiveness of the language when the fictional is treated as though it were the real. These magazines encourage the reader to enter into the delusion of realism not just to increase the pleasure of that delusion, but also to increase the activeness and sense of control that go with it. The article that was headed by Figure 7.1 begins:

Competition. It's something *All My Children*'s Michael Knight and Steve Caffrey have been locked into for over a year now. On-screen their popular characters, playboy Tad Martin and man-about-town Andrew Preston, are in hot pursuit of the same Pine Valley cutie – Dottie Thornton. Off-screen Michael and Steve were recently vying for the same daytime Emmy award . . . .

But when you get down to basics, just which one of these *AMC* heroes is really the hottest guy in town? Perhaps an indepth look at both these fine actors and what makes them tick can help you decide.

(*Daytime TV,* November 1985: 16)

This is quite typical – the biographies of the actors, in real competition, are mobilized to authenticate the fictional competitiveness of the characters, so evaluating the sexiness of the character involves an in-depth study of the actor. There is also an attempt to mobilize the activity of the reader. These magazines abound with questions addressed to the reader asking his or her opinion on characters, on plotlines, or on incidents. Fans are asked both to evaluate and predict: "Will Shana's (Susan Kelly) love for Father Jim (Peter Davies) ruin any chance of happiness she may have with Mike (James Kilberd)?" (*Soap Opera Digest*, August 27, 1985: 71). These opinions are frequently formalized into polls, so that fans can compare their opinions with those of others. Thus the article about the rival *AMC* heroes quoted above ends with a ballot form so that every reader can contribute to answering the question "Who is the sexiest guy in Pine Valley?". Fans are encouraged both to "gossip" and to "write" their own scripts:

The identity of the mysterious priest (played by Ken Olin) in *Falcon Crest* next season is a secret, but we suspect he will turn out to be Julia's (Abby Dalton) illegitimate son. Think of the possibilities.

(*Soap Opera Digest*, August 27, 1985: 73)

Polls can be used to make this solitary imaginative activity into a collective public one and thus use it to help construct a sense of the community of viewers. These magazines do not create this activity, but they know it is there, encourage it, and give it a public status in their letter columns and polls in order to enhance the pleasures of the active viewer. They also enhance the producerly activity of the viewer, for the industrial producers do read them and do take account of them in their decisions about the development of plotlines.

☐ The tertiary text

This leads us on to the third level of the intertextuality of television. These are the texts that the viewers make themselves out of their responses, which circulate orally or in letters to the press, and which work to form a collective rather than an individual response. This is then read back into the program as a textual activator. These third-level texts form much of the data for the ethnographic study of audiences, they are "ethno-semiological data" (Katz and Liebes 1985: 189). They can be public, such as letters to the papers or the results of opinion polls, or private, such as the conversation between members of the family, or gossip between friends (see chapter 5). Or they can be somewhere in between such as the responses given to researchers like Morley (1980a), Hobson (1982), Ang (1985), Katz and Liebes (1984, 1985), Hodge and Tripp (1986), or Tulloch and Moran (1986). Studying them can give us insights into how the primary and secondary texts are read and circulated in the culture of the viewers.

The following letter gives us some clues as to how a *General Hospital* fan reads her favorite program:

> They are the shining stars of *General Hospital* and I couldn't imagine the show without them. On the other hand, when Luke and Laura left Port Charles, their departure seemed like the natural conclusion to a pair of previously beloved characters who, for whatever reason, had begun to fizzle out. I admit I missed Tony Geary and Genie Francis at first, but I'm glad they got out before their characters became such overpowering bores that we former fans would begin to despise them on sight. They had so many unreal adventures, what else was left for them to do or say? Holly and Robert, by comparison, have their feet planted firmly on the ground. We viewers can experience their true romance. Their chemistry is so right-on and their love scenes so believable that I really envy Emma Samms. I *never* wanted to step into Genie Francis' shoes! All she ever got was grief.
>
> (*Daytimers,* June 1985: 56)

This letter shows the familiar desire to see the fictional as real, a desire that both primary and secondary texts play on, and is an example of a tendency noted by both Hobson and Ang in which what is liked is seen as real, and what is disliked as unreal. But it also shows an awareness of the representational conventions of soap opera realism, that characters and stories have only so much life or interest in them, that they are, in other words, created to entertain the viewers rather than to represent the real in a transparent or objective way.

The pleasure of *General Hospital*, for this fan at least, is the pleasure of "implication" (see chapter 9), a controlled identification with characters that necessarily involves "believability" and "truth." The two words are almost interchangeable, but the criteria upon which their values are judged are not the objective ones of empiricism but the subjective ones of internalized norms of feeling and behavior. These norms derive primarily from the conventions of soap opera realism which require, for instance, that when a pair of characters begin to "fizzle out" their plotline should reach a "natural conclusion." These conventions produce an impression of "truth" resulting in a "believability" that may well be stronger than that produced by actual social experience, because the social norms are more clearly encoded in the conventions than in social experience. Where the conventions deviate from social experience is a point of possible interrogation of that experience, or of the norms, or of other, possibly more dominant and less "popular," values.

Ethnographic studies provide us with numerous examples of these tertiary texts, but ethnography typically tends to read these texts as responses, that is, as the *result* of viewing: it does not see them as being read back into the program and activating its meanings in a particular way. Any activity it finds in them, any ability to initiate consequences, is confined to social experience, not television. Yet the way that Hodge and Tripp's (1986) school children, for example, read *Prisoner* must have worked upon their continuous viewing of the program just as much as it did upon their experience of school, and Katz and Liebes (1984, 1985) found many examples of gossip helping viewers to activate certain meanings of *Dallas* in preference to others.

In a study of the cultural meanings of Madonna (Fiske 1987a), I used two sorts of tertiary texts as evidence of young girl fans' ability to make *their* subcultural meanings out of the primary text of Madonna herself. In a discussion between fans, one 14-year-old girl said:

> She's tarty and seductive ... but it looks alright when she does it, you know what I mean, if anyone else did it, it would look right tarty, a right tart you know, but with her it's OK, it's acceptable ... with anyone else it would be absolutely outrageous, it sounds silly, but it's OK with her, you know what I mean.

In this we can see her struggle to express her meanings of Madonna that contradict the dominant patriarchal ones of tartiness and to find ones "acceptable" to the girl fans, whose interests are clearly different from those of the dominant patriarchy, but who lack a formal language in which to express them: the texts of Madonna fill this lack for them.

125

A less direct tertiary text that serves the same purpose, is the words of other Madonna fans quoted in *Time* (May 27, 1985: 47):

She's sexy and she doesn't need men . . . she's kind of there all by herself

or

She gives us ideas. It's really women's lib, not being afraid of what guys think.

The contradictions in the primary texts of Madonna, her music videos, are expressed in the opposition between these fans' comments and that of *Playboy* (September 1985: 122) on behalf of its readers (a very different subcultural group):

Best of all, her onstage contortions and Boy Toy voice have put sopping sex where it belongs – front and center in the limelight.

☐ Intertextuality and polysemy

It is the polysemy of Madonna that allows her to appeal to such different audiences as young girls and *Playboy* readers, the first a resistive subculture, the second one that accommodates easily and exactly to the dominant patriarchal ideology. Intertextual criticism shows how the one primary text can be articulated (Hall 1986) with others, or with other cultural domains, to exploit its polysemy. Hall uses the term "articulation" in its dual senses of "speaking" and "linkage" (see below, chapter 14). When Madonna's primary texts are "linked" to the subordinate culture of young girls in patriarchy they "speak" quite differently from when they are "linked" with the sexist masculine culture of *Playboy*. Reading the secondary and tertiary texts can help us see how the primary text can be articulated into the general culture in different ways, by different readers in different subcultures.

The plurality of these meanings and articulations is not, of course, a structureless pluralism, but is tightly organized around textual and social power. The fact that *Dallas* has more meanings than Hollywood can control or any one audience group can activate, does not negate television's struggle to control its meanings, and prefer some over others. The preferred meanings in television are generally those that serve the interests of the dominant classes: other meanings are structured in relations of dominance-subordination to those preferred ones as the social groups that activate them are structured in a power relationship within the social system. The textual attempt to contain meaning is the semiotic equivalent of the exercise of social power over the diversity of subordinate social groups, and the semiotic power of the subordinate to make their own meanings is the equivalent of their ability to evade, oppose, or negotiate with this social power. Not only is the text polysemic in itself, but its multitude of intertextual relations increases its polysemic potential.

Chapter 8

Narrative

The narratives of the world are numberless. Narrative is first and foremost a prodigious variety of genres, themselves distributed amongst different substances – as though any material were fit to receive man's stories. Able to be carried by articulated language, spoken or written, fixed or moving images, gestures, and the ordered mixture of all these substances; narrative is present in myth, legend, fable, tale, novella, epic, history, tragedy, drama, comedy, mime, painting (think of Carpaccio's *Saint Ursula*), stained-glass windows, cinema, comics, news items, conversation. Moreover, under this almost infinite diversity of forms, narrative is present in every age, in every place, in every society; it begins with the very history of mankind and there nowhere is nor has been a people without narrative. All classes, all human groups, have their narratives, enjoyment of which is very often shared by men with different, even opposing, cultural backgrounds. Caring nothing for the division between good and bad literature, narrative is international, transhistorical, transcultural: it is simply there, like life itself.

(Barthes 1977a: 79, 1982: 251)

Narrative and language are two of the main cultural processes shared by all societies: they are "simply there, like life itself." Like language, narrative is a basic way of making sense of our experience of the real, and structuralists have argued that it shares many of language's properties, that it is structured along the twin axes of the paradigmatic and syntagmatic, that there may be a universal narrative structure, the equivalent of *langue*, of which specific narratives are the *paroles*, and that its signification necessarily works at denotative and connotative levels. Furthermore it is like language in that its denotative relationship with the real is illusory and its signifying ability derives from its systemic nature and its internarrative (intertextual) relations: that is, its categorizing and structuring processes signify not because of their operation upon reality, but because of their relationship to these processes in other narratives and other signifying forms.

Given that narrative is such a fundamental cultural process, it is not surprising that television is predominantly narrational in its mode. Television drama is obviously narrative, but so too is news; documentaries impose a narrative structure upon their subject matter; sport and quiz shows are presented in terms of character, conflict, and resolution. Many commercial and rock videos are mini-narratives; arguably only music lacks a narrative structure, and even that has similarities in its ability to structure time.

Narrative works as a sense-making mechanism primarily through two dimensions. The syntagmatic is the dimension upon which it links events rationally, according to the laws of cause and effect or to those of association. Whichever principle it employs, it links events together so as to make their relationship meaningful and therefore understandable. This refusal of randomness creates consequence out of sequence and in so doing provides the means of understanding that most elusive dimension – time. In the paradigmatic dimension, narrative takes character and settings and makes a nontemporal sense of them that serves as an additional unifying agency upon the syntagmatic chain of events. Narrative structure demonstrates that people and places are not anarchic and random, but *sensible*, and then combines the paradigmatic sense of places and people with the syntagmatic sense of events and time into a grand signifying pattern (Chatman 1978).

Lévi-Strauss finds a deep structure of meanings in mythic narratives that can only be grasped by taking characters, settings, and actions out of the syntagmatic flow, and by analyzing their paradigmatic relations of similarity and difference, usually in terms of binary oppositions. For him, the chain of events is surface structure and is thus less significant than the deep structure that he reveals beneath it. This deep structure is shared with other myths, other narratives, for Lévi-Strauss is finally interested only in narrative *langue*, not individual *paroles*.

Realistic narrative is, as was argued in chapter 2, the dominant mode of representation on television, but realistic narrative was developed essentially through the novel and film, and television realism departs significantly from a number of the conventions that are central to literary and cinema realism.

Words like "realistic" that are used to define and categorize narratives work on two dimensions. First they alert us to certain textual characteristics of the narrative: an episode of *Hart to Hart* is clearly generically different to the Eskimo myth of the capture of the south wind. But secondly, these words alert us also to reading strategies, which, as I will argue in the next chapter, are as ideologically driven as signifying practices. We can read *Hart to Hart* as a realist narrative or as contemporary urban myth. Reading it realistically requires us to give prime attention to such factors as the psychological realism of its characters and their individuality, and to the coherence of its specific chain of events and their believability according to the "natural" laws of cause and effect. In other words, we read it as a unique representation of unique individuals and events that is structured according to universal natural laws not cultural conventions.

Reading it structurally, however, requires us to focus on the conventions by which this sense of the real is established. It requires us to see that character acts primarily as a function of the plot; only then is it given individualizing characteristics as an ideological hook for the audience. Even these individualizing characteristics are best understood not in their uniqueness, but in terms of the overall structure of social values that are embodied in the structure of characters (hero + heroine + villain + villainess). Reading it mythically will lead us towards its "deeper" meaning. In Lévi-Straussian terms, each episode of a series would be a transformation of a common deep structure, which may well, finally, be shared with other series in the same genre. So *Hart to Hart* would share a deep structure with *Remington Steele*, *Scarecrow and Mrs King* and *MacMillan and Wife*, to name a few examples of the cop show with a male and female hero pair.

But the point to make at this stage is that labels such as "realistic" or "mythic" are not just descriptors of textual characteristics but are active: they promote particular reading strategies which activate particular meanings in the text.

□ Realism revisited

Classic realist narrative and its preferred reading strategy try to construct a self-contained, internally consistent world which is real-seeming. By this, I mean not that it is an objective reproduction of the real world, but that it appears to be, and this appearance is governed by the extent to which the common-sense conventions that structure our understanding of the real world appear adequate to decode the fictional world, that of the diegesis. Verisimilitude is based not on iconic representation, but upon replicating the conventions by which sense is made. It is thus an ideological practice. We approach the fictional world of realism with the same easy familiarity with which we approach the world of our social experience: the two worlds are equivalent in that they are open to the same ideological reading practices. But the disguised common sense upon which these practices rest masks the differences between the two worlds.

Realism imposes coherence and resolution upon a world that has neither. In a realist narrative, every detail makes sense, it contributes to that final overall understanding granted to the reader in his/her position of "dominant specularity" (MacCabe 1981a). This internal coherence requires that the diegetic world must appear self-sufficient and unbroken: everything that we need to know in order to understand it must be included, and anything that contradicts or disturbs this understanding must be excised. The diegetic world must not require the reader to turn beyond it to find the means to understand it, but it must, like the real world, appear to make its own sense according to the "laws of nature," not the conventions of culture.

These "laws of nature" are those of cause and effect, those of the psychology of human nature, and those of natural and physical science, and all are treated as universal laws that require exploration but not interrogation. Kuhn (1985) summarizes the features of the classic realist narrative thus:

1 linearity of cause and effect within an overall trajectory of enigma resolution
2 a high degree of narrative closure
3 a fictional world governed by spatial and temporal verisimilitude
4 centrality of the narrative agency of psychologically rounded characters.

(p. 216)

□ Structuralist approaches to narrative

Realism is a transparent mode that attempts to hide its nature as discourse. Structuralism and its developments are concerned to reveal and investigate the discursive nature of all cultural constructs, so structuralist theories of narrative have sought to explain the laws that govern its structure, not the accuracy of its representation of the real.

Early structuralism attempted to find a universal narrative structure, the equivalent of *langue*, and while this drive has now been spent it did provide some useful basic principles – particularly it showed us that narratives have much in common and need to be studied in terms of their relationship to others: a narrative, however realistic, is not a unique set of events whose only valid relationship is that of its verisimilitude to the real world.

□ Mythic narrative

One of the ways in which structuralism has sought to explain what a range of apparently diverse narratives have in common is through the concept of myth. Two writers have been most influential here, Lévi-Strauss, a structural anthropologist, and Barthes, a Marxist semiotician. Their two approaches have little in common except for their insistence that myth-making is a universal cultural process and that the deeper "truer" meanings of myths are not immediately apparent but can only be revealed by theoretical analysis.

For Lévi-Strauss myth is an anxiety-reducing mechanism that deals with unresolvable contradictions in a culture and provides imaginative ways of living with them. These contradictions are usually expressed in terms of binary oppositions, and form the deep structure of a number of apparently unrelated myths. These binary oppositions are large abstract generalizations such as good:evil, nature:culture, or humankind:gods. Myths work metaphorically to transform these oppositions into concrete representations by a process that Lévi-Strauss calls the "logic of the concrete." Thus in the western genre, culture:nature is transformed into indoors:outdoors and is structurally associated with values such as law and order:lawlessness, white: Indian, humane:inhumane, and so on. So a scene of Indians attacking a white homestead is a concrete metaphorical transformation of the opposition between nature and culture, and the narrative is an argument, via "the logic of the concrete," about the characteristics and consequences of this opposition.

In Lévi-Strauss's terms the deep structure of *Hart to Hart* can be modeled as in Figure 8.1.

Figure 8.1 The deep structure of *Hart to Hart*

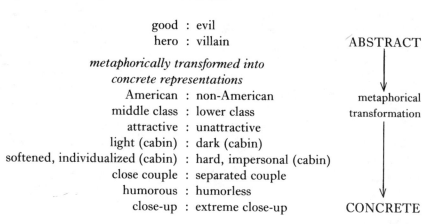

The opposed values are then given the narrative consequences of successful:unsuccessful. Alongside this is another deep structure:

masculine : feminine
active : passive
thinking : object of look
controller : controlled

Both these deep structures are evidence of cultural insecurity about the meanings and consequences of the opposed values: the myths do not solve this uncertainty (for example, that of gender difference) but they provide an imaginative structure by which the contradictions can be thought through:

the structure makes the contradictions conceptually and culturally capable of being handled and thus not dysfunctional.

Hartley (1982) analyzes in similar terms a news story about a dispute involving health service workers. The story concentrated on the effects of a withdrawal of labor upon hospital patients, particularly children. After analyzing the presentation of the story, Hartley concludes:

> This is not an industrial dispute at all. It is a political dispute between
>
> | children | : | public service workers |
> | government | : | strikers |
> | decent trade unionists | : | irresponsible minority |
> | us | : | them |
>
> (p. 127)

The gap between such clearly opposed categories often seems so stark as to be unbridgeable and the contradictions too violent to be coped with. In these cases, myth often produces a hero or heroine with characteristics from both categories. The hero thus has excessive meaning, extraordinary semiotic power, and acts as a mediator between the opposing concepts. In tribal myth such a figure is designated either sacred or taboo as a way of signifying or controlling his/her excess of meaning. Thus the heroes of many crime shows draw characteristics from both the value system of society and that of the criminals. They acquire the stature of heroic figures because of this excess of meaning. Additionally, in the mythic narrative, they act as mediators, as embodied resolutions of the conflict between the forces of order and those of disorder. Crockett and Tubbs, of *Miami Vice*, move literally between the worlds of the vice squad and the drug runners, and, in embodying certain values of both, they act mythically as mediators between both sides of the opposition. Their embodiment of the values and lifestyle of both demonstrates an imaginative way of coping with the conflict, which is a crucial mythic function, for the conflict itself can never be resolved. The "success" of the vice squad at the end of each episode is only temporary and in no way offers a permanent resolution of the conflict. It is only the hero figures of Crockett and Tubbs who demonstrate that society has ways of living with and coping with the opposition, even if not of resolving it.

For Lévi-Strauss, culture is a homogeneous concept: his theory does not admit that some classes may have different mythic needs from others, or that myths may work hegemonically. This may well be because his theories were derived from his work on tribal societies which are more easily conceived as homogeneous.

Barthes (1973), on the other hand, was concerned with the role of myth in industrialized capitalist societies marked by class conflict rather than homogeneity. His theory of myth, then, is very different from Lévi-Strauss's.

For Barthes myth works to naturalize and universalize the class interests of the bourgeoisie. It is not a narrative but an associative chain of concepts that works below the threshold of consciousness. The users of Lévi-Strauss's myths may not know the deeper meanings of them, but they do know that they are hearing or telling a myth: the user of Barthes's myths, on the other hand, is unaware even that he or she is handling a myth. Myths for Barthes are ideological and part of the power-class structure of capitalist societies.

Myths work to naturalize history. History is the accumulated social experience that has produced the divisions and differential power relations in our society, and thus forms an essential base for understanding that society. Myth overrides this. For instance, the *Hart to Hart* episode analyzed in chapter 1 is typical in having a villain with Hispanic features. This depends, in part, upon the white myth that Hispanics are devious, untrustworthy, and criminally inclined. The history of the white colonization and oppression of Latin America and the interracial relations it has produced are effaced in the myth. Crime statistics may well show that Hispanics in the USA are more likely to commit crimes than white middle-class Americans, but the myth finds the reason for this in their racial characteristics, not in the history of white oppression. The myth treats the belief that middle-class Anglo-Saxons are trustworthy, whereas swarthy lower-class males are not, as obvious common sense and natural. Similarly, the typical television practice of giving criminals working-class or ethnic accents is *not* a statement about the statistical probability that members of lower socioeconomic groups are more likely to turn to crime, because it does not require us to think through the relationships between social position and criminality. Rather it is a sign of a middle-class myth that denies the history of class relations and naturalizes the explanation of class differences into the "facts" of human nature.

Barthes believes that in capitalist societies all myth is bourgeois, that is, it always promotes the interests of the dominant classes by making the meanings that serve these interests appear natural and universal. Radical myth is impossible except in the limited sphere of politics where radicalism has achieved a degree of institutionalization and so can be taken for granted, and thus can work, within its own sphere, to naturalize the interests of the powerful. A left-wing myth of union solidarity is, therefore, possible, whereas a left-wing myth of, for instance, the family is not. Radical ways of understanding the family need to be conscious and rationally argued against the status quo: the only views that need no explanation or defense are those that have been naturalized or exnominated into common sense by the operation of myth. For Barthes then, *Hart to Hart* works mythically to promote the point of view of the white, male middle classes as the "natural" point from which to make sense of experience, and to disguise the sectional nature of this process by universalizing it.

Barthesian analysis can all too easily stop at the identification and naming of the bourgeois myths that are promoted by television. This shows an incomplete understanding of Barthes's theory, for he insists that myth is a form of speech, that it is a system by which meanings are made and circulated. The content of myths can change rapidly, but the mythologizing process is constant and universal. In this respect, he is similar to Lévi-Strauss who also found a universal cultural process in the way that mythic thought was structured. Barthes's exploration of this principle, however, is articulated in historically and culturally specific terms, particularly those of mid-twentieth-century capitalism, whereas Lévi-Strauss emphasizes his search for human universals. Mythic approaches to narrative are essentially paradigmatic in that they emphasize the cultural-ideological system that underlies the syntagmatic flow of the narrative.

□ Narrative structures

Propp's work (1968) provides the most extreme example of syntagmatic structuralist analysis. He analyzed one hundred Russian folk tales and found an identical narrative structure in each of them. He described this structure as a sequence of thirty-two narrative functions, divided into six sections. We can summarize them thus:

□ Preparation
1 A member of a family leaves home.
2 A prohibition or rule is imposed on the hero.
3 This prohibition/rule is broken.
4 The villain makes an attempt at reconnaissance.
5 The villain learns something about his victim.
6 The villain tries to deceive the victim to get possession of him or his belongings.
7 The victim unknowingly helps the villain by being deceived or influenced by the villain.

□ Complication
8 The villain harms a member of the family.
8a A member of the family lacks or desires something.
9 This lack or misfortune is made known; the hero is given a request or command, and he goes or is sent on a mission/quest.
10 The seeker (often the hero) plans action against the villain.

☐ Transference

11 The hero leaves home.
12 The hero is tested, attacked, interrogated, and, as a result, receives either a magical agent or a helper.
13 The hero reacts to the actions of the future donor.
14 The hero uses the magical agent.
15 The hero is transferred to the general location of the object of his mission/quest.

☐ Struggle

16 The hero and villain join in direct combat.
17 The hero is branded.
18 The villain is defeated.
19 The initial misfortune or lack is set right.

☐ Return

20 The hero returns.
21 The hero is pursued.
22 The hero is rescued from pursuit.
23 The hero arrives home or elsewhere and is not recognized.
24 A false hero makes false claims.
25 A difficult task is set for the hero.
26 The task is accomplished.

☐ Recognition

27 The hero is recognized.
28 The false hero/villain is exposed.
29 The false hero is transformed.
30 The villain is punished.
31 The hero is married and crowned.

Propp called these thirty-two narrative morphemes "functions" because he wanted to emphasize that what they *do* to advance the narrative is more important than what they *are*. The function of the magical agent, for example, can be performed by a cloak, a sword, or a purse. In television narrative this function may be performed by, for instance, the super-technological limbs of the *Six Million Dollar Man*, the computerized car of *Knight Rider*, or the (almost) superhuman mechanical ability of *The A-Team*.

The narrative functions are, according to Propp, always in the same sequence and they are common to all fairy tales, though not every tale will have every function.

Similarly, Propp's account of character is concerned only with what a character *does* in the narrative structure, not with whom he or she *is* as an individual. Character is defined in terms of a "sphere of action": thus the villain fights, opposes, or pursues the hero and commits acts of villainy. Different individual characters may perform the function (or character role) of villain at different times in the same narrative. This leads Propp to the conclusion that "the functions of characters are stable constant elements in a tale, independent of how and by whom they are fulfilled. They constitute the fundamental components of a tale."

There are eight "character roles" which are located in seven "spheres of action":

☐ Character Role	☐ Sphere of Action
1 Villain	Villainy, fighting, action
2 Donor (provider)	Giving magical agent or helper
3 Helper	Moves the hero, makes good a lack, rescues from pursuit, solves difficult tasks, transforms the hero.
4 The princess and her father	A sought-for person: assigns difficult tasks, brands, exposes, recognizes, punishes.
5 The dispatcher	Sends hero on quest/mission.
6 The hero (seeker or victim)	Departs on search, reacts to donor, attempts difficult tasks, marriage.
7 The false hero	Unfounded claims to hero's sphere of action

This morphology of functions and characters has been applied in detail to contemporary films and television (e.g. Wollen 1982, Silverstone 1981) and most popular television narratives conform more or less precisely to this structure. At times the conformity is astonishing in its precision. I tested the structure on an episode of *Bionic Woman* and found that the pre-title sequence conformed to "Preparation." "Complication" took the narrative to the next commercial break and so on. Some sections and functions are more emphasized in television narrative than others, for instance "Struggle" can be long and elaborate, "Return" and "Recognition" can be very rapid. Sometimes functions 16 to 19 are repeated to emphasize action and sometimes the functions of the false hero are very muted. But in general the structure underlies the typical television narrative with remarkable consistence.

The character roles, too, receive different degrees of emphasis. That of the princess (often a private eye's client, who may be male or female but is always comparatively powerless) is frequently performed by the same character as her father. The dispatcher is often the hero or a member of the hero team. The victim is one of the most multiple of these character roles whose function can be fulfilled by a character who elsewhere in the narrative plays the hero, the helper, the princess, the dispatcher, or any role that opposes that of the villain.

On the evidence of Propp and his successors, there appears to be something close to a universal structure of popular narrative (a narrative equivalent of *langue*) of which individual stories are transformations or *paroles*. The cultural specificity or ideology of a narrative lies in the way this deep structure is transformed into apparently different stories, that is, in which actions and individuals are chosen to perform the functions and character roles.

The possibility of a universal narrative structure raises some intractable theoretical problems. Lévi-Strauss was able to ground his universal principle of making meanings by binary oppositions in the working of the human brain and thus explain its universality. It is difficult to envisage the physiology of the human brain producing thirty-two functions in sequence. It is safer not to talk in terms of human universals, originating in human nature, but rather to seek the origins of a common structure in human society, for all humans live in social organizations. Narrative can then be seen as the means of articulating the profound and uncertain relationship of the individual with the social. Anthropologically, Propp's narrative schema tells the archetypal story of the young male's acceptance into maturity and society: marriage is the achievement of individual maturity and the insertion of that mature person into a network of social roles and obligations. *The A-Team,* as I will argue in chapter 11, enacts masculinity/maturity and its conflict/accommodation with social responsibility (*The A-Team* episodes follow Propp's structure particularly clearly and closely.)

In such an explanation of Propp's structure, the struggle between the hero and villain is a metaphorical transformation of that between the forces of order and those of disorder, good and evil, or culture and nature. Such a struggle is fundamental to all societies, and the narrative explores the role of human and social agents in it.

Todorov's (1977) model of narrative also emphasizes the social over the individual. For him, narrative begins with a state of equilibrium or social harmony. This is disrupted, usually by the action of a villain. The narrative charts the course of this disequilibrium and its final resolution in another, preferably enhanced or more stable, state of equilibrium. "The second equilibrium is similar to the first, but the two are never identical" (p.11). In Propp's schema, "Preparation" and "Complication" chart the forces of disruption that have disturbed the original harmony. "Transference" and "Struggle" chart the hero's fight against these forces: in this fight the hero embodies the social values that stabilize society. The villain embodies the forces of disruption and the conflict between them is the conflict between equilibrium and disequilibrium. "Return" and "Recognition" resolve the conflict and work to restore a new harmony. Narrative here is less the accommodation of the individual with the social, and more the exploration, within the social, of the opposing forces of stability and disruption. The ideological work of the narrative can, in this model, be discerned in two ways: the first is the comparison of the opening and closing states of equilibrium, and the second is in identifying what constitutes a force of disruption, and what a force of stability.

Todorov's model is particularly useful for its ability to explain news stories and to model news as the social narrative of the conflict between the social order and disruptive forces (see chapter 15). Todorov specifies two kinds of elements in narrative, a state (either of equilibrium or disequilibrium) and a passage from one state to another, usually through an event or chain of events. Newsworthy events, then, are those that disrupt or restore equilibrium. The state of equilibrium is not itself newsworthy and is never described except implicitly in its opposition to the state of disequilibrium which, typically, is described in detail. Here, the ideological work is at its clearest in the selection of *which* events are considered to disrupt or restore *which* equilibrium and in the description of what constitutes disequilibrium. Thus the event conventionally selected as a cause of an industrial dispute is an action of a worker or union, whereas the event selected to restore order is equally conventionally an act of management or government agency. In the narrative structure this puts unions into the role of villains and management into that of heroes. Similarly, the description of the disequilibrium will usually be in terms of the dispute's effect upon consumers, and rarely in terms of the hardships undergone by the striking unionists. This again serves to position the reader with the hero/victim (i.e. management-consumer) and in hostility to the villain (union). Bell (1983) shows how these character roles of hero-helper-victim-villain form the underlying structuring principle of drugs stories in the news media (see chapter 15).

This sort of model can also reveal simply the ideology at work in fictional stories. In the *Hart to Hart* episode analyzed in chapters 1 and 6 the disruptive event is the jewel theft, the restorative event is the catching of the thieves. Disruption and restoration occur at the level of individual or unique events, and thus the social system underlying the state of equilibrium is

139

shown as coping with disruption and therefore as adequate. Another version of the story, however, could present the disruptive event as an attempt by a member of a disadvantaged minority to provide for his wife and his retirement. In this case the restorative event could be the negotiation of a minimum wage and national pension rights! But that would be a very different story and a very different ideology.

Todorov's model does not imply that narrative in itself is either radical or reactionary. But in popular culture the narrative structure is likely to be used in favor of the status quo. In realist narrative the equilibrium is a reproduction of the values of the current social order that is rarely represented directly, but only indirectly in terms of its disruption. It is, therefore, mythologized into the taken-for-granted, the common-sense view of how things really are, which is necessarily supportive of the status quo. To present a critical view of the social order, it would be necessary to take it out of the realm of the taken-for-granted, to "nominate" it, to represent it directly and critically, and thus to demythologize it. Most television narrative does not do this.

If the narrative's originary state of equilibrium is assumed to be fair and good, then the forces of disruption (which include forces for social change) necessarily take the role of the villain and the restorative event is necessarily performed by the sociocentral hero who restores the status quo, or preferably an enhanced version of it. The "rewriting" of the *Hart to Hart* episode (above) posits an unjust state of equilibrium at the start in which stability is maintained only by the exercise of class and economic power. The representation of such an equilibrium in a bourgeois society could not be commonsensical: rather it would need to be explicitly represented in opposition to conventional representations and their furtherance of the dominant ideology. If an unacceptable state of equilibrium exists at the beginning of the narrative, then clearly the forces of disruption can play the hero role, and the restorative event produces a completely new equilibrium.

The conservative drive of the narrative structure may be undeniable, but its effectivity is far more open to doubt. It works to center the meanings within the dominant ideology and to close off alternative ones. But, as chapter 5 has shown, alternative and resistant readings are possible within and against any dominant textual structure. A textual structure is a hegemonic line of force that may, at any time, meet an equivalent line of resistance.

The structuralist accounts of narrative that we have looked at so far tend, through their emphasis on structure, to imply a unity within each narrative as well as between narratives. Barthes's early work "An Introduction to the Structural Analysis of Narrative" (1976) shares this concern with structure as a producer of meaning, but his later work *S/Z* ([1970] 1975) brings a completely different perspective to bear.

140

In *The Structural Analysis of Narrative* Barthes uses the close analogy between language and narrative to argue that narrative is open to the same sort of descriptive analysis as language, which can be achieved at different "levels of description" (Barthes 1977a: 85). Language can be described first at the level of phonemes and morphemes, then the description can move "up" a level to that of words, then to that of phrases, then to the sentence, the paragraph, and so on. Propp's functions are, according to his theory, the equivalent of morphemes – the smallest signifying units. Barthes takes this analysis a stage further by classifying the functions into different types, not by relating them syntagmatically.

His first level of classification is that between functions and indices. *Functions* are events that are strung together to form the sequence of the narrative. *Indices* are the constants that are involved in this sequence, but do not advance it – characters, settings, atmosphere, and so on. Functions are distributional and syntagmatic, whereas indices are integrational and paradigmatic. All narratives contain both, but in some the functions predominate and in others the indices. Thus folk tales are predominantly functional, psychological novels predominantly indicial. Popular television series, especially cop and adventure shows aimed at men and children, tend towards the functional, whereas serials, such as soap operas, often aimed at women, tend to put more stress on the indicial.

Functions are then subdivided into two types – *nuclei* (or *cardinal functions*) which are essential to the progress of the narrative, and *catalyzers* which "fill in" between the nuclei and could, logically, be dispensed with. This does not mean that they are redundant, but that they are not crucial to advancing the narrative. Instead they accelerate it or slow it down, they can summarize, anticipate, recall, or even mislead. Nuclei have antecedents and consequences, catalyzers do not. Thus in the *Hart to Hart* scene the heroine's putting on the ostentatious jewelry is a nucleus, it has the consequence of attracting the thieves. The hero's discussion of the robbery is a catalyzer, it summarizes and slows the narrative.

Indices are divided into *indices proper*, which are the narrative agents, atmosphere, mood, and *informants*, which identify or locate in time and space. We have looked already at the indices which indicate which two characters are playing the role of the hero, and which two the role of the villain. *Informants* are those functions that indicate the setting on a ship, the contemporary time period, the location in America. Informants are also called by Barthes "realism operators" and work to make the world of the narrative appear to relate closely to the "real" world of our experience. They perform the important ideological function of verisimilitude.

These functions are then, according to Barthes, structured into "sequences," as words are structured into phrases. A sequence is a "logical succession of

141

nuclei bound together by a relation of solidarity" which can be "named," usually by a verbal noun that describes action – Fraud, Betrayal, Seduction, Contract, Greeting, etc. The *Hart to Hart* scene is part of the sequence "Setting the Snare." These sequences or phrases can be combined into larger sequences or sentences and so on.

☐ Narrative codes

This attempt to provide a structural linguistics of narrative is useful in so far as it provides a vocabulary for the close analysis of narrative sequences: it is a micro-grammar. Barthes's later work *S/Z* (1975a) concentrates on the discourse of narrative, that is, its structure above the level of the sentence, and this has produced a more widely used model.

S/Z is a very detailed analysis of Balzac's short novel *Sarrasine* from which Barthes derives major conclusions about narrative in general. Unlike his earlier work, and that of Propp, Barthes's aim here is to reveal not a structure, but a "structuration," the process by which meaning is structured into narrative by the writer-reader, for if there is a universal in narrative it lies in this structuration in which the writer and reader engage on equal terms. Barthes's shift in emphasis is away from the formal structure of the text and towards the reading/writing process that creates meaning from that structure and its intertextual relations. For the structure of the text is, finally, an interweaving of voices which are shared by reader and writer and which cross the boundaries of the text itself to link it to other texts and to culture in general.

These voices are, according to Barthes, organized into five codes.

The *symbolic code* organizes the fundamental binary oppositions that are important in a particular culture. These include masculine:feminine, good:evil, nature:culture, and so on; they are the antitheses upon which the narrative is founded. This is the code that Lévi-Strauss would prioritize above all others.

The *semic code*, or the voice of the person, works in a similar way to construct the meaning of character, objects, or settings. Barthes concentrates on its operation in constructing character to explain the way it works. "Semes," or basic units of meaning in the text, are repeatedly attached to a proper name in order to create a character. They bear the meanings of speech, clothing, gesture, action, and are the means by which a "figure" is individualized into a "character." A "figure" is a cultural stereotype common to many narratives – "the distraught mother," "the misunderstood son," "the cruel king/father." These "figures" are similar to Propp's character roles in that they exist before and independent of any notion of the individual, but

142

they differ in that they are determined not by the needs of the narrative structure, but by the needs of the culture of which that narrative is a part. They are a Lévi-Straussian rather than a Proppian concept.

This "culture" works most directly, and paradoxically, through what Barthes calls the *referential code*. This is the code through which a text refers out beyond itself, but this reference is not, as in so many other theories (e.g. those of Jakobson and Peirce, see Fiske 1982), to "reality" in an objective, empirical sense, but rather to cultural knowledges. "The real" is the common stock of a culture as it is expressed in the "already written" knowledges of morality, politics, art, history, psychology, and so on. These knowledges, as they pervade the texts of our culture, constitute our sense of "life," of "reality." They are the commonplaces of a culture to which a writer refers or which s/he quotes, in order to produce a sense of reality. "Reality" is "the product of discourse" (O'Sullivan *et al.* 1983), and in so far as its knowledges are already written, "reality" is intertextual (see chapter 7).

The *code of actions* (the proairetic code) is similarly intertextual and is the one which relates most directly to Barthes's earlier structuralist endeavors. It suggests that we understand any action in a narrative by our experience of similar actions in other narratives, and that our narrative experience is an aggregation of details arranged in generic categories of actions – murder, rendezvous, theft, perilous mission, falling in love, etc.

Barthes's final code is the *hermeneutic*. This code sets and resolves the enigmas of the narrative and is motivated by the desire for closure and "truth." It controls the pace and style of the narrative by controlling the flow of information that is desired by the reader to solve the enigma or make good a lack. It first proposes the enigma or mystery, finally resolves it, but in between works by delaying our access to the desired information. It is thus the motor of the narrative. Barthes suggests that it works through ten morphemes which may occur simply, in any combination or in any order. Silverman (1983) summarizes them as "thematization, proposal of the enigma, formulation of the enigma, request for an answer, snare, equivocation, jamming, suspended answer, partial answer and disclosure" (p. 257).

Barthes's achievement in *S/Z* was to destabilize the notions of text and reader so that neither is seen as an entity or essence, but rather as interdependent processes by which meanings are constructed and circulated, and by which, paradoxically, "reality" is created. The text works in two dimensions, the intra-textual and the intertextual. As Johnston (1985) explains:

The various ... devices identified in *S/Z* as forming the intra-textual system illustrate the highly crafted and selective nature of the procedures through which the realist world is built up. On the other hand, the work depends upon a set of external relationships, its position within a grid of

143

other cultural texts; its *intertextuality*. Realism, Barthes argues, "consists not in copying the real, but in copying a depicted copy of the real" (*S/Z* pp. 54–6). (p. 239)

Barthes's description of the writerly narrative as a "limited plurality" echoes Morley's (1980a) description of a text as "structured polysemy" and both are attempting to model how a text can allow for a multiplicity of meanings within boundaries that its structure sets. For Morley, the motor of polysemy is the diversity of social situations of the text's readers which produces the multiplicity of discourses they bring to bear on the text. For Barthes, the "limited plurality" of a text is a result of collapsing the role of the reader into that of the writer in the construction of a text from a work. A code is a bridge between texts, and meaning is encoded via intertextuality. Intertextuality is not a system of allusions between specific texts, or of references between one text and specified others: rather it is located in that space between texts to which all texts and readers/writers refer more or less equally, but which all activate differently.

Early structuralist accounts of narrative tended to see it as a closed system. Barthes in *S/Z* has demonstrated that even the most apparently closed narrative, a realist one with its closing reliance upon "truth to reality" as its final pleasure, is available to open, "writerly" readings and, indeed, requires them.

☐ Televisual narrative

Feuer (1986) argues that television has produced and developed distinctive forms of narrative that invite what I have called "producerly" relations with the text. The series and the serial, which she characterizes as television's dominant narrative forms, are, she argues, inherently more open texts that the one-off, completed, closed narratives typical of the novel and film.

The television serial, typified by the soap opera (see chapter 10), departs from traditional narrative structure in a number of ways, the most obvious being the way that its many plots never reach a point of closure, and its absence of any originary state of equilibrium from which they departed. But Feuer (1986) does point out that there is an unwritten and unachieved ideal of the stable, happy family against which all the disruptions are plotted.

She also makes the point that traditional narrative theories are better at describing "masculine" narrative, such as the cop/adventure show, than "feminine" narrative, such as the soap opera. Even so, the series, while reaching a resounding conclusion to each episode, never resolves the ongoing situation. The police force is engaged in a constant war against crime, *The A-Team* has a constant supply of "little people" who need its help because of the

144

limitations of the official agencies of law and order. Similarly Eaton (1981) argues that in television sitcoms, the comedy may be resolved each week, but the situation never is. The syntagmatic chain of events may reach a closure, but the paradigmatic oppositions of character and situation never can. It is a requirement of television's routine repetition that its stories can never be finally resolved and closed off. Similarly, chapter 15 argues that the conventional, repetitious nature of the news means that its stories, however formally they may be closed off, never really end: there will always be more terrorists, more political conferences, more murders, more disasters, more kittens in trees, tomorrow, next week, or next month. The narrative tension between equilibrium and disruption is always there.

Television's sense of time is unique in its feel of the present and its assumption of the future. In soap opera, the narrative time is a metaphorical equivalent of real time, and the audiences are constantly engaged in remembering the past, enjoying the present, and predicting the future. In series, the future may not be part of the diegetic world of the narrative, but it is inscribed into the institution of television itself: the characters may not act as though they will be back with us next week, but we, the viewers, know that they will. The sense of the future, of the existence of as yet unwritten events, is a specifically televisual characteristic, and one that works to resist narrative closure.

It also makes the hermeneutic code work differently. Television's "nowness" makes suspense seem real, not manufactured, and invites the viewer to "live" the experience of solving the enigma, rather than be told the process of its already achieved and recorded resolution. The story appears to be happening *now*, its future to be still unwritten. So in soap opera, in sport, in quiz shows, the hermeneutic code is more imperative, the engagement it requires is more "equal," for both narrative and viewer appear to be equally lacking in knowledge as they live through the enigma's resolution. This is a more engaged and empowering reading relation than that offered by the novel or by film.

Chapter 6 argued that the television text was typically segmented. Ellis (1982) says that an effect of this is succession, rather than consequence. The inevitable sequence of cause and effect that marks the progression of the traditional narrative to its point of resolution is constantly interrupted in television by advertisements, promos, spot announcements, and so on. The self-sufficiency of the single diegetic world of traditional realist narrative can never be maintained in television. On similar lines Feuer (1986) argues that television has three diegetic worlds that constantly intersect and interrupt each other – that of the television program, that of the ads and promos, and that of the viewing family.

These interruptions of the narrative that fracture its diegetic world are characteristic of the apparatus of television, that is, of its commercial mix of programs and advertisements and of its domestic mode of reception, which means that it may be watched either continuously or interruptedly, according to the way the viewer inserts it into her/his domestic routine. It is arguable that women's domestic routine is the most insistent and interruptive (see chapter 10) so the feminine narrative of the soap opera is least like the traditional closed narrative and most amenable to being viewed with differential modes of attention. Its diegetic world is not only fragmented into its multiple plots, but is interrupted by its advertisements in a way that Flitterman (1983) argues is unique. She suggests that the ads aimed at women and inserted in the daytime soaps are mini-narratives that bear an inverse relationship to the narrative structure of the programs. The ads are closed narratives that reach a successful, if temporary, closure. The problem of stained shirts, facial wrinkles, or muddy floors which disrupts the "normal" state of equilibrium (ideologically proposed as a state of perfect hygiene, beauty, and agelessness) is solved by the hero-product which restores an enhanced order. But, like the episodic sitcom, the resolution is temporary and fragile, and in no way touches the basic situation of dirt-bearing children/husbands or the passage of time/youth/beauty which constitutes the ongoing problems of the housewife. The ads, Flitterman argues, complement the program by providing a limited sense of achievement and satisfaction which is constantly deferred in the narrative of the program itself. But they do more than this, they frequently address the viewer directly, acknowledging the bridgeable gap between their diegetic world and that of the viewing housewife. They make explicit the sense of intimacy between the televisual world and that of the viewer in a way that breaks the self-containedness of television's diegesis by presenting it not as a separate world (like that of a film or a book) but as a part of the "real" world of the viewer. The viewer willingly enters into this illusion to increase her pleasure (see chapters 5 and 9) and in so doing interacts with the world of television in order to create a meaningful relationship between it and her world. She uses Barthes's referential and semic codes positively in order to construct bridges between her "life as culture" and the representational world on television. She is a writerly viewer of a writerly text.

Masculine narratives, such as *The A-Team,* also interact with their ads in a similar way, though here the relationship is reversed. The masculine program closes with successful achievement, but the ads often emphasize the means to that achievement rather than the achievement itself. Ads for cars and power tools emphasize the mechanical extensions of the masculine body, and beer ads promise male bonding and the "feel" of masculinity (see chapter 11). But the effect is the same, the ads mediate between the diegetic world of the program and the world of the viewer – they show that the diegetic world

146

is not complete within itself, but that its boundaries can be broken where it intersects with the "real" world of the viewer.

Recent masculine narratives, such as *Miami Vice* and, occasionally, *Hunter*, do not wait for the ads to fracture their diegetic world, but use pop songs in the sound track to relate out of the world of the narrative and into the cultural life of the viewer's previous experience of the song or, intertextually, to rock video or MTV (see chapter 13). The diegesis is fractured by emphasizing and exploiting the cultural work of Barthes's referential code.

The intertextuality of television which crosses diegetic worlds is typically more explicit than that of the novel or film. Feuer (1986) notes some examples of deliberate exploitation of this, such as when a trauma drama on teenage suicide is followed by a discussion program on the problem. Similarly *Threads*, a fictional telemovie on the effects of a nuclear war and the nuclear winter, was followed by expert comment by scientists and politicians on the "real world" problem. Commercially the interdiegetic references are exploited by inserting ads showing Krystle/Linda Evans extolling her brand of cosmetics in *Dynasty*, in which she is a major character. Ads in which sportsmen or sportswomen endorse a product are frequently inserted into sports broadcasts in which they are performing. A less intentional, but no less significant, Australian example occurred in a commercial break that contained a station identification for Channel Nine and a promo for *The Flying Doctors*, a program to be screened later in the evening. The promo previewed one of the plotlines which concerned the drama of a pregnant woman in a remote rural area needing the services of the Flying Doctors' team. Channel Nine's identification consisted of a rapid series of portraits of typical "real" West Australians, one of which showed a pregnant woman being helped into a "real" Flying Doctors' aircraft. This blurring of the distinctions between the fictional and real replicates the denial of genre differences between fiction, fact, and advertisement, and reduces the power of the text to construct a viewing subject position. The text can only suggest that the various diegetic worlds are related, not self-contained: it cannot specify the links that the viewer makes between them.

Television viewing is more interactive than either cinema spectating or novel reading and consequently its narratives are more open to negotiation. The segmented, fractured nature of television, its producerly texts, and its active audiences, come together to oppose any forces of closure within its narrative structures.

The structuralist theories of narrative I have outlined here have developed largely from studies of folk tales or legends: the more sophisticated narrative forms of some novels and films have given rise to different theories, in particular ones that stress the difference between story and discourse (Chatman 1978) or fabula and syuzhet (Bordwell 1985).

Narrative theory which is derived from folk tale, with its emphasis on common structures and conventions that relate directly to its social context, would seem more pertinent to a popular medium like television, with its simple, repeated structures. But folk tales developed in essentially homogeneous tribal societies, or in simple agrarian ones, whereas television narratives have to be popular in heterogeneous societies amongst audiences with different and often conflicting social interests and experiences. So television narrative must be more open and multiple than the singular folk narrative with its comparatively tight closure. Television narratives may embody the repetitious, straightforward structure of the folk tale, but they must be able to build into it contradictions that weaken its closure, and fragmentations that deny its unity.

Chapter 9

Character reading

Television is centrally concerned with the representation of people – its most typical image is a mid-shot or close-up of someone talking or reacting. Two- and three-shots establish identities, spatial relationships and location, and then the camera moves in on the individual. Even the news is personalized and news readers receive similar fan mail to that of soap opera stars.

The producers know the importance of character, too. About 80 per cent of prime-time US network television is fiction, and this is typically presented in terms of its leading characters. Series titles commonly are those of their leading characters (*Starsky and Hutch, T. J. Hooker, Magnum, Simon and Simon, Cagney and Lacey*, etc.) and studio publicity heavily promotes the shows in terms of their star personalities. The cover picture of *TV Guide* is almost invariably of the star or stars of one of the week's series. An interesting exception to this naming policy is provided by daytime and nighttime soap operas, whose titles stress place, family, or generalizations about social experience (*Dallas, Dynasty, Knots Landing, Days of Our Lives, The Young and the Restless*). Similarly, the police shows that appropriate elements of soap opera form appropriate their titling strategies too (*Hill Street Blues* [USA], *Cop Shop* [Australia], *Z Cars* [UK]).

But even though soap operas appear, by their titles at least, to deviate from television's typical strategy of inviting us to read drama through its characters, their fans and their industry of secondary texts (fanzines, feature articles in magazines, etc.) give character high priority. The difference in titling strategy between soap operas and other television drama is due rather, as we shall see in the next chapters, to the soaps' emphasis on a family or neighborhood of characters rather than an individual hero/ine, or hero/ine pair or team.

Character representation on television differs significantly from the cinema or theater, and this difference arises from two prime televisual characteristics: its series or serial form, and its "nowness" or "liveness." Television relies on regularity of scheduling to establish a routine. The commercial intentions of this are obvious – it gets people into the habit of viewing a particular program at a particular time each day or week, it allows for proper planning of production resources, it enables an audience to be predicted in advance and thus sold to advertisers, and so on. Thus production houses like producing series and serials. A series has the same lead characters in each episode, but each episode has a different story which is concluded. There is "dead time" between the episodes, with no memory from one to the other, and episodes can be screened or repeated in any order. The lead characters appear to have a life only in each episode, not between them, and do not grow or change as episode follows episode. Serials, on the other hand, have the same characters, but have continuous storylines, normally more than one, that continue from episode to episode. Their characters appear to live continuously between episodes, they grow and change with time, and have active "memories" of previous events. The next two chapters will explore in more detail the differences between series and serials and why one appeals to a primarily masculine audience and the other to a feminine. For the moment I wish to comment on their similarity, which lies in their constant use of the same characters and of their conflation of player with character.

The constant repetition of a character means that characters "live" in similar time scales to their audience. They have a past, a present, and a future that appear to exceed their textual existence, so that audience members are invited to relate to them in terms of familiarity and identification (a problematic term that will be examined more fully later in this chapter). TV characters have a future; they will return tomorrow, or next week, and the end of each episode has built into it the expectation of the next, either explicitly in serials or implicitly in series. This offers the viewer a quite different relationship to the character from that offered by film, where the end of the film is normally the end of the character. In this respect, popular cinema resembles television in its production of miniature series, which it calls "sequels" – *Rocky I, II, III,* and *IV, Mad Max I, II,* and *III, Rambo I* and *II,* the James Bond films, and so on.

Dyer (1979) has shown how traditional cinema stars bring the continuity of their presence to the various characters they play – the John Wayne western hero is almost the same from film to film despite the different "character" filling the hero role. But they are *stars* – the continuity lies in their "real life" presence, not in that of the characters they portray.

Langer (1981) makes the point that TV deals not with stars but with personalities – stars have a glamor that sets them apart from and above their fans: personalities have a familiarity that offers their fans a much more intimate, equal relationship. Classic Hollywood stars were bigger than their roles, and were remembered or promoted by their own names not those of their characters. Television personalities merge into their characters or are submerged by them. J. R. Ewing and Larry Hagman are almost indistinguishable. Tom Selleck is Magnum or Magnum is Tom Selleck. Mr T and

B. A. are so confused that some fans are uncertain which is the actor and which is the character. Where cinema produces series of films, and thus where it most closely resembles television, the same merging occurs – Silvester Stallone *is* Rocky, Clint Eastwood *is* Dirty Harry: the trend was started, as were so many, by the James Bond films – Sean Connery was more completely and complexly James Bond (see Bennett 1983b, and Bennett and Woollacott 1987) than almost any other star-character conflation.

The "realness" given to the character by its merging with the player, combined with its familiarity and its "nowness," give television characters a unique relationship with their fans. These characteristics also blur the difference between fact and fiction: Phil Donohue, Walter Cronkite, Robin Day, and all the hosts and hostesses of chat and game shows, the news readers, the reporters, and the commentators use their off-screen or real-life personalities to make their on-screen roles appear more "real" in precisely the same way that the players do in series and serials. Hobson (1982) has shown how the players in the English soap opera *Crossroads* choose their own costumes – costuming the character becomes the same as dressing themselves and their taste guarantees the authenticity of the character's appearance.

All this suggests that character portrayal on television works to deny the difference between the real and the representation in both the production and the reception processes. This view accords well with the theory of realism outlined in chapter 2 which argues that denying or disguising the difference between the real and its representation has a number of ideological effects. These effects stem from the way that "the real" is used to authenticate the representation which is thus granted an objective status – the real appears to exist in its own right and the representation is judged according to how closely it approximates to it: the representation is seen as reflective, not productive. Structuralism, with its emphasis on discourse, reverses this and uses the representation to question what is accepted as the real. In its explanation of representation and, as we shall trace in this chapter, in its reading strategies, structuralism thus opposes realism.

☐ Realist and structural approaches

When studying the representation and reception of character on television we can usefully begin by using theories of realism and structuralism as opposing polarities, which actually constitute different ideological reading strategies. (It is, by now, widely accepted that the production of images is an ideological process, but fewer recognize that "reading" is equally ideological.)

At one end of the scale, then, we have what I shall call the realistic theory of character, at the other the structural or discursive. Realism proposes that a character represents a real person. The text provides us with accurate and adequate metonymic pointers to the characteristics of the person being portrayed : we, the viewers, then call upon our life experience of understanding real people (for social experience also gives us only metonymic pointers of what someone is "really" like) to fill out these characteristics in our imagination so that we make the character into a "real" person whom we "know" and who has a "life" outside the text.

What Ang (1985) calls the "ideology of popular culture" invites us to evaluate this process in two ways. In literature or highbrow drama, it is the mark of the skill and art of the author to create such characters, the ones that E. M. Forster calls round, as opposed to flat. Chatman (1978) writes:

> We remember [round characters] as real people. They seem strangely familiar. Like real life friends and enemies it is hard to describe what they are exactly like. . . . Round characters function as open constructs, susceptible of further insight. Our "readings out" are not limited to the actual period of immediate contact with the text. The character may haunt us for days or years. (p. 132)

Bradley's (1904) work on Shakespeare's tragedies is often seen as the one that established and validated this tradition: in it he treats Shakespeare's heroes and heroines as if they were real people with independent lives outside the plays, and uses this psychological realism to prove Shakespeare's genius.

When this confusion between a character and a real person occurs, however, in forms that the ideology of popular culture devalues, such as soap opera, its effects are derided, not praised. The soap opera fans who fantasize characters into real people (sometimes to the extent of writing them letters) are derided for their stupidity while critics such as Chatman or Bradley are praised for their insight. In fact, the fans and the literary or dramatic critics both retain, even if in a suppressed form, the awareness of the difference between a character and a person: the illusion of realism is only as complete as we allow or wish it to be.

Using psychological realism as a way of understanding, responding to, and evaluating character portrayal is as widespread as it is and appears as natural and as commonsensical as it does, because it fits so well into the ideology of individualism with its insistence on the uniqueness and consistency of the self. Like realism, individualism sees the self as the prime site for unifying and making sense of experience; a unified sense of experience produces and is produced by a unified sense of the self. This self is unique and different from other selves: its origins are rarely examined but are assumed to be natural, or biological, rather than social. The uniqueness and naturalness of the human body are often used as a disguised metaphor to authenticate the uniqueness of the self. Thus the unique physical characteristics and biographies of actors and actresses are used to authenticate the unique "selves" of the characters they portray. This foregrounding of the self pushes the social or political dimension into the background, which is why this form of classic realism is often criticized for its tendency to depoliticize social issues and to resolve them through individualization. Thus, the problem of a socially deprived childhood can be "solved" by a happy marriage: the solution is found in the realm of the individual whereas the problem is located in the social. Individualism diverts attention away from any questioning of the social system, for individual "solutions" to social problems are always possible, and this, when coupled with the belief in the primacy of the self, fits with and underpins the role of realism in naturalizing bourgeois ideology.

In contrast to realism, structuralism and discourse theory focus on the mode and means of representation. In this approach character is seen as a textual device, constructed, like other textual devices, from discourse. On television the physical presence of the player is used, not to authenticate the individual self, but to embody (literally) discourse and ideology. In the structuralist inflection of this position, a character cannot be understood as an individual existing in his or her own right, but only as a series of textual (and intertextual) relations. The most obvious of these are the relationships with other characters. Sue Ellen in *Dallas* can only be understood in terms of her subjection to J. R. and in her relationship to Pamela and Pamela's loving relationship to Bobby. Sue Ellen is defined in part by her relationship of similarity and difference to Pamela – both are women married to markedly patriarchal Ewings, but both exhibit different feminine characteristics within the patriarchal paradigm: one is what the other is not and the meanings of one are explicable only in terms of the meanings of the other. The fans studied by Ang (1985) are aware of this – though they try to describe each woman as an individual, they constantly fall back on her difference from the other, they veer between realist and discursive reading strategies:

Pamela: a nice girl (I find her a woman of character: she can be nice, but nasty too). Sue Ellen: has had bad luck with J. R., but she makes up for it by being a flirt. I don't like her much. And she's too sharp-tongued. (*Letter 3*)

Why do I watch *Dallas* every Tuesday? Mainly because of Pamela and that wonderful love between her and Bobby. When I see those two I feel warmth radiating from them. . . . I also find the relationship between Miss Ellie and Jock nice, but I'm scarcely interested at all in J. R. and Sue Ellen. (*Letter 8*)

Sue Ellen: just *fantastic*, tremendous how that woman acts, the movements of her mouth, hands, etc. That woman really enters into her role, looking for love, snobbish, in short a real woman. Pamela: a Barbie doll with no feelings, comes over as false and unsympathetic (a waxen robot). (*Letter 12*)

Sue Ellen is definitely my favourite. She has a psychologically believable character. As she is, I am myself to a lesser degree ("knocking one's head against a wall once too often") and I want to be [attractive]. ... Pamela pouts, and is too sweet. (*Letter 17*) (p.124)

The idea of character as a discursive, textual structure fits with the notion of the subject rather than the self. The subject is itself a social and discursive structure, which contains contradictions as our social experience contains them. These contradictions may be suppressed, but they are never resolved, and are always there waiting to be reactivated. Realism, with its narrative closure and stress on the unity of the self, works to deny contradictions in both the text and the reading subject: discourse theory and later developments of structuralism, on the other hand, work to exploit these contradictions and activate them. This discursive view of character also sees character as having a sociopolitical dimension: thus Sue Ellen's drinking can be read as a metaphor, or displaced articulation, of women's helplessness in the face of their subordination in patriarchy: it is less an insight into her personality than a textual expression of her powerlessness in the face of J. R.'s sexual and economic politics. Of course, the text can be read either way, or both ways, Sue Ellen's drinking can be either an insight into her character or an enacted metaphor of feminine helplessness in the face of patriarchal power, or both: the point is that it is the reader and his or her ideology of reading that activates either the individual psychological reading, or the discursive socio-political one, or both in varying proportions of emphasis.

Realism invites us to read character psychologistically as the representation of a unique individual: this invitation is likely to be accepted by those who accommodate themselves comfortably to the dominant ideology and the individualism that is so central to it. But those who are positioned more oppositionally are more likely to read character discursively, as an embodiment of social values and their functions in the narrative. Discursive reading strategies discourage identification and promote a Brechtian critical alienation between viewer and character (see below). Discursive readings emphasize the social, realistic readings the individual: discursive readings are thus more radical, realistic ones more reactionary. The conventions by which character is represented on television are open enough to allow either reading strategy, or a combination of or alternation between them, according to the political orientation of the viewer.

☐ **Reading character from the primary text**

These different reading strategies and the ideologies that underlie them will become clearer with an analysis of four scenes from a double episode of *Cagney and Lacey*. The main plot concerns Lacey's possible breast cancer and her reactions to it, the main subplot is about the disappearance of an 8-year-old boy and the ability of his black single parent, Mrs Taggart, to care for him adequately. Scenes 1 and 2 in the transcript were separated in the program from 3 and 4 by a commercial break, news headlines, and three other scenes lasting a total of six minutes:

☐ Scene 1

Mrs Taggart's kitchen, she is pouring a cup of tea for Lacey.

LACEY: We'll have fliers made up with that picture you gave us of Kevin – the uniformed officers are going to hand that out, plus we also put his name and description in the national computer file. Thanks. (*She takes cup.*)

TAGGART: I walked all over the neighborhood yesterday. I walked for blocks.

LACEY: I know, it's a hopeless feeling.

TAGGART: Why would he want to do something like this to me? You know I missed two days out of work already and I talked to my supervisor and she tells me that I might not have a job to come back to.

CAGNEY: (*enters with portable radio-cassette player.*) Mrs Taggart, did you buy this for your son?

TAGGART: Doesn't belong to Kevin, he doesn't have anything like that.

CAGNEY: I found it stashed way under his bed. Where d'you think he got the money to pay for it?

TAGGART: So what are you trying to say, he stole it? My son doesn't steal.

LACEY: Nobody says he did, ma'am. Would you excuse us, we have to go apply for that warrant, and the office closes at five o'clock. C'mon Christine. We'll be in touch.

(*They leave.*)

☐ Scene 2

The stairs outside Mrs Taggart's apartment.

CAGNEY: You heard her, she's more worried about her job.

LACEY: She's not thinking straight, her kid's been missing 23 hours.

CAGNEY: Maybe he wouldn't have if she'd taken better care of him.

155

LACEY: Easy to say.

CAGNEY: Oh Mary Beth, we know she hit him at least once, she leaves him alone for hours every day . . . .

(*They leave the building and walk down the street.*)

LACEY: So what are you saying? He ran away? If that's true, then how come he didn't take his brand new radio? Now I was a latch-key kid myself before they called it that – my father took off, my mother had to go to work each day, I was by myself every day after school when I was 8. I didn't turn into a thief and I didn't run away from home.

CAGNEY: That's completely different, Mary Beth.

LACEY: Why? Because I'm white?

CAGNEY: No, and you know I didn't mean that. And I want to give you something here. It's the name and telephone number of a doctor . . .

LACEY: Oh.

CAGNEY: . . . the one I told you about. Mary Beth, he's a cancer specialist and I think you should see him now. . . . Listen to me, I know you're frightened, I'll go with you if you want me to. . . . Mary Beth, will you talk to me?

LACEY: Talk?

CAGNEY: Yes.

LACEY: You want to talk about how we feel in case maybe I have breast cancer . . . OK . . . in case maybe I have breast cancer. You go first. . . . Thanks for the chat, Christine. It's best if only one of us applies for the warrant, so I'll go down town and you find out whether or not the fliers are ready.

(*She walks off leaving Cagney.*)

CAGNEY: (*Shouts down the street after her.*) It doesn't matter how I feel about it, it matters how you feel.

(*Two passing black youths turn and look at her.*)

☐ Scene 3

Mrs Taggart's kitchen.

TAGGART: So that's it. That's all you're going to do to try to find him.

LACEY: Believe me, Mrs Taggart, if we could be doing anything else we'd be doing it.

TAGGART: It's been almost three days. I guess you don't send cops out there to look for a low income child.

LACEY: Ma'am, even if we had the personnel, we don't know where else to look for him. He could be anywhere.

TAGGART: Look, if he was rich and white I tell you where he'd be. He'd be home because you'd move heaven and earth to try to find him.

CAGNEY: Hey lady, I'm getting real tired of your attitude. We're doing everything we can, we've got nothing else to go on. Nobody knows where your son goes or what . . . .

LACEY: Chris

CAGNEY: . . . he does after school . . . .

TAGGART: So what are you trying to say to me, you think I neglect him?

CAGNEY: I just don't understand how you could leave a child . . . .

TAGGART: No, you're damn right you don't understand. You make a nice salary paid you by the City, you can afford a babysitter or private day care. I make 80 cents above minimum wage and I take home less than $130 a week and I got a choice, right, big choice, I can either pay for day care or pay my rent.

LACEY: Mrs Taggart, there's City agencies that . . . .

TAGGART: Ah. Charity. Welfare. The ADC and food stamps is the same as I make for 40 hours . . . I didn't want Kevin to grow up on handouts, so I went out and got myself trained and I got a job so he could see somebody standing on their own two feet. And what did it get me? People going around here telling me I'm a bad mother because I don't want to stay home on welfare. Well, you ask yourself, lady, what would you do if you were me?

□ Scene 4

The steps outside Mrs Taggart's apartment building.

CAGNEY: Perfect end to a perfect day.

LACEY: What do you expect? She's in a hell of a bind trying to do it all by herself everyday.

CAGNEY: Come on, everyone's got problems. It shouldn't matter to you . . . .

(*A young girl runs past, chased by a boy.*) Whoa, look out!

LACEY: (*grabs the boy by the lapels and shakes him violently.*) Hey, you leave her alone!

CAGNEY: Mary Beth!

Let us use the discursive reading strategy first. Hamon (1977), quoted in Frow (1986), defines character as

157

a bundle of relations of similarity, opposition, hierarchy and disposition (its distribution) which it enters into, on the plane of the signifier and signified, successively and/or simultaneously, with other characters or elements of the work.

The relations of similarity, in this case those of gender, nation, place, time, and age, form the social frame that is not called into question by the narrative but rather forms the common ideological ground upon which the differences play out their oppositions in the narrative.

Frow goes on to explain that the signified of character is constituted not only by repetition, accumulation, and transformation, but also by its oppositional relation to other characters.

There are three women in these scenes. Two of them are the constant characters in the series who have accumulated, by repetition, a set of character traits with which the regular viewer is familiar. So Cagney's spatial distance as she stands apart from Lacey and Taggart is easily read as her coldness, aloofness, whereas Lacey's physical proximity to Taggart is read as her characteristic of warmth. Taggart, on the other hand, is a construction of this episode, so she has more limited and less marked character traits, and those that she has are general rather than individualized ones like the distraught mother, the economically deprived, the single parent, the black. She is what Barthes (1975a) calls a figure rather than a character, that is, an embodiment of already encoded cultural "semes" (in this case "the woman victim," "the robbed mother") upon which the more individualizing semes of character are overlaid.

Table 9.1 models the relations of opposition and similarity among the women (the parenthesized characteristics for Taggart are textually unmarked and thus relatively unsignifying: they are the semes that, if marked, would help to lift her from figure to character).

What is striking about this list is the preponderance of traits that are not derived from the nature of the individual, but are social, political, or economic in origin. And, in the case of Taggart, with its absence of accumulation and repetition, they are almost exclusively so. This discursive or structuralist reading strategy reveals how easily character in TV drama may be read not as the representation of psychologically layered and motivated individuals but as a metonymic representation of social positions and the values embodied in them. These values are deeply encoded in the "symbolic codes" (Barthes 1975a) of the culture, the codes that organize our understandings around such fundamental oppositions as male:female, married:single, or family: career. These are the thematic equivalent of the pre-psychological, cultural codings that Barthes calls "figure." They are transformed first when they acquire social and political values and then when they are given the trappings of individualization that Barthes calls "character." This surface is what the psychologistic, realistic reading strategy reads. The discursive reading, how-

Table 9.1 *The value structure of characters*

Character trait	Cagney	Lacey	Taggart
Similarities			
Gender	Female	Female	Female
Nation	US	US	US
Place	Urban (NY)	Urban (NY)	Urban (NY)
Time	Now	Now	Now
Age	Prime (plus)	Prime (plus)	Prime (plus)
Differences			
Social			
Race	White	White (ethnic)	Black
Class	Middle	Lower	Lowest
Home	Trendy	Traditional	Ghetto (not slum)
Money	Comfortable	Tight	Poor
Professional			
Type of job	Potential detective sergeant	Detective	Secretary
Job motivation	Ambition	Satisfaction	Self-sufficiency
Job reward	Career	Duty/Service	Money
Socio-Sexual			
Type of woman	Modern	Traditional	Victim
Marital status	Single	Married	Separated
Love status	Not yet	In love	Lost
Parental status	No children	Children	Lost child
Physical			
Body	Slim	Pudgy	(Slim)
Hair	Blonde	Brunette	(Black)
Face	Pretty	Homely	(Pretty)
Personal Style			
of Dressing	Mannish–trendy	Motherly–frumpish	(Female)
of Caring	Tough, soft-centered	Soft, tough-centered	Emotional, incompetent
Interpersonal	Detached	Involved	(Proud)
	Analytical	Experimental	(Emotional)
	Judgemental	Sympathetic	(Dependent)
Name	Tough, masculine	Soft, feminine	Down to earth

ever, passes through this attractive surface to see character as an embodiment of abstract social and political values, and conflict between characters as an enactment of social conflict.

The character traits of Cagney, Lacey, and Taggart call for some kind of categorization, but resist it. There is a difference between social markers of character difference such as race, class, marital status, and more psychologi-cally presented ones such as the one I have called "style of caring" in order not to foreground too strongly its psychologistic dimension. There is also a potential category of physical appearance and mannerisms. There are a number of problems that occur with any categorizing system. The choice of categories is never self-evident, nor is the ascription of a defined unit to its appropriate category: for instance, "attitude to work" can be, depending on the strategy of the reader, a psychological trait or a social one. Psychologically, Cagney's ambition can be seen as a function of her character, but discursively, it is read as the political reaction of a woman to patriarchal subordination. But even when a categorization has been completed, however arbitrarily, we are still no further towards understanding the relationship between the categories, for meaning derives from relationship, not from essences. For instance, do we read Cagney's marital status as an effect of her career ambitions, or a cause of them? And how do both relate to her physical characteristics?

The categories and their relationships are not inherent in the text, but are ways of thinking; they are meaning-making processes of the reader, not part of the physical structure of the text, and explanation for them must be sought in the social relations of reading.

The discursive theory of understanding of character is polysemic, because texts are. A character is a paradigmatic set of values that are related through structures of similarity and difference to other characters: character is a conjuncture of social discourses held in a metaphorical relationship to notions of individuality and embodied in the appearance and mannerisms of an individual actor or actress. Character, then, is an embodied ideology, and is used to make sense of the world by the relations of discourses and ideology that it embodies.

The realistic reading of character, on the other hand, proposes that the world is made sense of through the perceptual and cognitive processes of the individual (originally the character as individual, but finally the individual viewer). Actions and events are what happen to individuals and what individuals do, and making sense of them is essentially finding a coherence into which to unify them. Unifying means closing off alternatives and finding "the" (satisfactory) meaning.

So, in this strategy, the connections between scenes 1 and 2 would be made "psychologically," within the coherence and constancy of the characters. Lacey's inability to deal with Taggart's social and parental problem is part of the "explanation" of her inability to come to terms with her own physical problem and similarly, Cagney's critical view of Taggart's personal responsibility for her plight "explains" her harsh determination to make Lacey aware of her personal responsibility to act. Cagney's misjudgment of Taggart can be explained in personal terms – because she is single, well off, and not a parent she cannot empathize with Taggart's position in the way that Lacey can. The text cannot tell us how to activate it, the difference in reading derives from a difference of critical and ideological practice.

The discursive reading of character looks also towards its unifying power, but accounts for this differently. These two pairs of scenes are related internally and with each other because Cagney and Lacey are in each, and it is their common presence that relates the sociopolitical crisis of the black, single mother and her delinquent child in a ghetto to the gender-political crisis of the working mother-wife with breast cancer.

Character still relates actions and events, but not internally. Rather it provides a framework of values by which to make sense of them, it provides the means of making sense rather than the site of that sense. The apparently unrelated events in scenes 1 and 2 are, in fact, related by the consistent frame of values provided by the character structure of the three women involved. Thus the two blacks who, at the end of Scene 2 look in amazement as Cagney shouts her concern for Lacey are not just local color, or what Barthes (1977a) calls "realism operators," but invite us to make sense of Lacey's terror of breast cancer by a set of values which include masculine:feminine, white: black, advantaged:disadvantaged, and which, through their blackness, relate to Taggart. Using the same set of values as a means of coherence enables us to see a significant relationship between Taggart's physical health but economic, social, and marital sickness and Lacey's physical sickness but economic, social, and marital health. Taggart's blackness and poverty enter a relationship with Lacey's physical sickness that is mutually validating.

Breast cancer and possible mastectomy are physical signs of the victimization of women in patriarchy; Taggart's powerlessness is a social sign of the same victimization. Each is a metaphor for the other. Tyne Daly, who plays Lacey, is well aware of this connection:

> When Daly first learned from the scriptwriters that she would have to play a cancerous Lacey, she was upset.
>
> "I didn't want to see the victimization of Mary Beth," she says. "I signed on to play the hero not the victim. And sort of as a general rule of thumb, I don't want to play victims. I'm not mad for women-in-jeopardy as an art form."
>
> She says the show's writers thought the breast cancer story line was "so juicy. I wish it wasn't so juicy. I just wish it wasn't juicy anymore in our society to see women threatened. ... I'm weary of that, not only as an actress but as an American citizen."
>
> (*USA Today*, February 11, 1985: D3)

This sense-making relationship between the physical and social victimization of women operates only when character is read as a discursive construct: it is not part of the perceptual and cognitive life of the characters for it forms no part of the sense that they make of their experience. Rather it is sense that is made when the discourses by which the reader makes sense of her/his social experience are used to "read" the text, and thus to read the characters as part of that text. The discourses (of gender, race, economics, health) that make sense of the incidents and settings also make sense of the characters.

The characters unify disparate actions not through their personal experience of them, but through their discursive structure as an embodiment of an abstract value system by which sense is made of the incidents. For Barthes (1977a) "characters form a necessary plane of description outside of which the slightest reported 'actions' cease to be intelligible" (p. 105). The characters not only unify scenes within an episode, but episodes within the series, they are the "character" of the series in so far as they bear its distinctive features, its ideological practice, and are the main agents for "hailing" and then interpellating the prospective audience. It is characters who turn settings into actions and events, and in so doing operationalize the ideological values of settings into the conflicts and closures of the plot. Figure 9.1 models this broad relationship between settings, values, and characters.

Figure 9.1 Settings, values, and characters

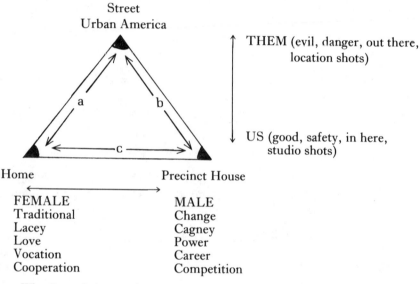

FEMALE	MALE
Traditional	Change
Lacey	Cagney
Love	Power
Vocation	Career
Cooperation	Competition

a = What Lacey brings to the street.
b = What Cagney brings to the street.
a & b = The success of the pair in mediating between top and bottom.
c = What the "new" woman brings to the worlds of work and home.
Cagney/Lacey as a relationship mediate between left and right.

In terms as general as these, of course, characters cannot be seen as individualized persons: here their function as producers of an identity or "character" for the series is paramount, and what we need to stress here is that this character is composed of contradictions and differences. How fully the characters of Cagney and Lacey perform their function as mediators between these contradictions is open to question. No episode ever resolves the horizontal or vertical oppositions into a final closure – they are always left reverberating, active, and ready for next week. So the sense of unity between our four scenes is not a closed unity, but one that depends upon the same paradigmatic set of opposed values to provide the ideological frame within which the possible meanings are negotiated.

This openness of values allows us to read Lacey's homeliness in terms of Cagney's refusal to marry and ambition to succeed in her career: in this discourse of the new career woman, her traditional family-centered values may be read as old-fashioned or reactionary. Conversely, in the "new" family discourse where the wife has a "better" job than the husband, but the marriage is still happy for both, Cagney's careerism may be seen to have been bought at too high a price. The text does not resolve the contradiction, nor center the reading subject in one discourse or the other. The reader is neither necessarily centered, nor unified, but can occupy both reading positions simultaneously because her or his subjectivity may well (by the late 1980s) have been formed by experiencing both the home-centered and the career-centered discourses as ways of making sense of social experience: these discourses may well have worked consecutively as one replaced the other – probably the career-centered one replaced the home-centered one as means of making sense of feminine priorities. But the earlier one, and the ideology it articulated, will not have been wiped out completely, but merely overlaid by the newer one. The traces of the value systems and ideologies we once held are still there contradicting the newer ones that our changed social experience has brought, and the two will exist simultaneously in the reading subject. A feminist may well find pleasure in the patriarchal representations of women in *Dallas*, and may be well aware of the contradictions, the disunity in her subjectivity that this entails. One of Ang's (1985) subjects wrote to her:

> Why does a person watch *Dallas* and in my case, why does a serious intelligent feminist like watching *Dallas*? It releases primitive feelings in me, I go dizzy, hate, love, loathe, feel disgusted, condemn and often dash away a tear. Personally I keep aloof from Mills and Boon, but I'm ready to play truant from evening school for *Dallas*. . . . My leisure reading consists 90 per cent of feminist books, but when I'm watching *Dallas* with my girl friend and Pamela comes down the stairs wearing a low-necked dress, then we shout wildly: just look at that slut, the way she prances around, she ought to be called Prancela. Bobby is a decent chap, like my eldest brother, and Jock is like my father, so I can hate them intensely too. I can stand Sue Ellen, neurotic as she is, and J. R. laughs just like Wiegel [a Dutch right-wing politician] and that has me jumping with rage. Lucy is too beautiful to be true and I don't find Miss Ellie all that marvellous since her breast operation. . . . I like to let it all hang out, a sort of group therapy, mostly together with friends.
>
> (*Letter 24*, p. 99–100)

Similarly a left-wing viewer writes:

Dallas ... God, don't talk to me about it. I'm just hooked on it! But you wouldn't believe the number of people who say to me, "Oh, I thought you were against capitalism?" I am, but *Dallas* is just so tremendously exaggerated, it has nothing to do with capitalists any more, it's just sheer artistry to make up such nonsense.

(*Letter 25*, p. 96)

Both these subjects have a struggle to reconcile within themselves the contradictions in the reading process and the disunity of the subject position they adopt towards the text. It is significant that they both try to find a unity that reconciles the contradictions and that it is the "excessiveness" of the program that allows them to occupy apparently contradictory subject positions simultaneously. Their position as social subjects differs from the reading subject proposed by the text, but the readers appear capable of occupying both positions though not without a struggle.

☐ Reading character: the secondary texts

The secondary texts can show us how these reading strategies can be activated to make a particular sense of the character. Much of the emotional impact of the episode of *Cagney and Lacey* we are studying comes from Lacey's reactions to her possible breast cancer. In the ideology of individualism and in the conventions of realism, the body is seen as a powerful metaphor for the self, so powerful, in fact, that its metaphorical nature is disguised or forgotten. Thus breast cancer may be seen as a threat to the self – Lacey cries to her husband, "They're going to cut *me* up!" (emphasis mine) – but it can also be read as a metaphor of women's victimization in patriarchy, part of the textual conventions which allow women to be given strong, central roles only when they are neurotic or victimized. Tyne Daly, quoted above, is well aware of these conventions. The female breast is a particularly powerful symbol in patriarchy because it represents both sides of woman, the mother and the whore: the bearer of man's children and the arouser of his lusts. Its power can be mobilized by either the discursive, or the realistic, reading strategy depending on the ideology of the reader. It is not surprising, given the interconnections of individualism and realism with patriarchal capitalism, that many of the secondary texts promote the individualistic, realistic reading strategy. *People* (February 11, 1985) gives an account of the shooting of this episode:

Visiting Tyne Daly in her trailer is like entering a sickroom. For a week she has been living with the certainty of impending doom. "Tyne is a very intellectual actress," says Barney Rosenzweig, the executive producer. As a method actress, she internalizes the problems and attitudes of her role, and hangs on to them with a terrier's tenaciousness, making them her own for as long as she needs them. "Before this episode started," Sharon Gless says, "Tyne came to me and said, 'Now listen, however I treat you, don't take it personally. I have cancer.' She feels that she is living with this disease. Because we know her and we love her, we're gentle right now. She's quite fragile." (p. 95)

Acting is as much an ideological practice as reading is. "Method" acting is characteristic of a bourgeois ideology that emphasizes the individual: Brechtian acting styles, however, minimize individualism and stress the social and political dimension of character, and are thus typical of a left-wing or more radical ideological stance. It is not surprising, then, that method acting is a characteristically American school, in that it minimizes the difference between character and player, mobilizes the psychology of the player to construct a real-seeming psychological existence for the character, and in so doing makes the body of the player deny the textuality of the character:

Mary Beth Lacey transmits the pain through her face, her eyes, her walk, her voice, every patch of her body except, perhaps, her hair. For a week now she has known she has cancer, and the awful truth has redefined her life. It has likewise possessed and remade the life of Tyne Daly, the woman whose body she shares. At the C & L studios in East Los Angeles, Mary Beth has just finished taping a scene in which she tries to submerge her anxiety about the lump in her breast while counselling a woman whose 8-year-old son has become involved with drug dealers. It is Mary Beth, not Tyne Daly, who makes her way back to the star's trailer during a break in the taping.

(*People*, February 11, 1985: 94)

The language is interesting here, for at one point it suggests that the character constructs the actress: "It has likewise possessed and remade the life of Tyne Daly, the woman whose body she shares." The body becomes the metaphorical container of the equal identities of Mary Beth Lacey and Tyne Daly, the site of their complete identification.

Thorburn (1982) promotes the same ideological view of acting although from an aesthetic position:

The television-actor (*sic*) creates and controls the meaning of what we see on the screen. ... Television has always challenged the actor. ... Its elaborate, enforced obedience to various formulas for plot and characterization virtually require him to recover from within himself and from his broadly stereotyped assignment nuances of gesture, inflection and movement that will at least hint at individual or idiosyncratic qualities. (p. 534)

Secondary texts act, as Bennett (1983b) puts it, as "cultural operators" which bear directly on those (primary) texts and preorientate their reading by culturally activating them in particular ways." But these "cultural operators" do not originate, but typify, the dominant reading practice. We do not need to have read either *People* or Thorburn in order to read the character of Lacey/Daly in the way they propose, for both the dominant reading strategy and the article in *People* are products and producers of the same dominant ideology. Therefore, similar reading strategies are promoted even in papers with as widely differing readerships as *The New York Times*, *MS*, and *People*. *The New York Times* (April 3, 1984) quotes Daly regretting the cancellation of an early series of the show: "The character hadn't stopped talking to me." *MS* (April 1984) quotes her on resuming taping after a break: "Mary Beth Lacey was still inside of her. 'I remember this woman,' she found herself thinking when she walked onto the set the first day." Characterizing the show as an example of a particular genre can also work as a cultural operator, for, as we saw in chapter 7, genres also activate reading strategies. The way that television journalists ascribe *Cagney and Lacey* variously to "cop shows" or "women's shows" will activate different readings. Scheduling works similarly as well. The show rated badly when scheduled at 9.00 p.m. after *Magnum p.i.* which implied a generic classification as "action drama" show, but when moved to 10.00 p.m. on a Monday, with that generic ascription of "adult" or "women's" show, it topped the ratings (though admittedly in a period of reruns).

The methodological point here is that Bennett's notion of "cultural operators" which activate the text in various ways gives us a useful way of watching reading strategies at work.

Most of these secondary texts promote readings that support the dominant ideology. There are, however, a few examples that activate more politically interrogative readings of the show and its characters. Thus *TV Guide* tells us that Barney Rosenzweig, the producer, was reading a feminist book when the idea for the series struck him:

> Having just met the very modern woman who was eventually to become his wife, Barney Rosenzweig was playing consciousness catchup by reading *From Reverence to Rape*, Molly Haskell's analysis of women in film. In the book he came upon the notion that "never in the history of Hollywood movies or television have two women related to each other like Newman and Redford in *Butch Cassidy and the Sundance Kid*." It sounded like a good idea, and Cagney and Lacey was the result.
>
> (February 16, 1985: 26)

Both Sharon Gless and Tyne Daly are aware of the political importance of the show for women, though it is significant that the media typically place the evidence of this awareness in quotation marks, so that it appears to be simply the opinion of an individual. This contrasts markedly with the way that the more bourgeois readings are given a superior position in the "hierarchy of discourses" (MacCabe 1981a) by not being ascribed to a named individual and thus being treated as "common sense." The bourgeois voice is, once again, exnominated. So the political importance of the show to women is nowhere stated objectively in the "common sense" discourse of journalism, but is always attributed to a named, usually female, individual. Thus Sharon Gless is quoted:

> "We were told a lot was riding on the success of the show," Gless says. "That's why we felt badly when it was cancelled – for television, for the future of women in television."
>
> (Washington Post, April 23, 1984)

A more incisive political awareness was shown by Tyne Daly on learning that Lacey was to suffer from breast cancer (quoted above). Her wish that "it wasn't juicy anymore in our society to see women threatened. . . . I'm weary of that, not only as an actress but as an American citizen," preorients the reader to equate the political victimization of women in patriarchy with Lacey's physical victimization by breast cancer.

Sharon Gless, too, is aware of the way that different gender politics can produce different readings of Cagney's character/Gless's body. When she took over the role of Cagney,

> the press didn't make her job any easier, badgering her about whether she would bring more "sexiness" to the show. "That bothered me a lot because it suggested there was no *femininity* on the show before her. I made sure to make her a real strong lady."
>
> (Washington Post, April 23, 1984)

Gless's lexical shift from "sexiness" through *"femininity"* to "a real strong lady" is a discursive shift and therefore has a sociopolitical dimension. "Sexiness" is from an explicitly patriarchal discourse, "femininity" is from a discourse that attempts to naturalize gender construction and difference in terms of the status quo and is therefore implicitly patriarchal, whereas "real strong lady" is from a discourse that consciously opposes and exposes both the explicit and implicit patriarchy of "sexiness" and "femininity."

But not all the secondary texts promote a political reading of the program. Indeed, many show how it is possible to "read against" its potentially interrogative politics, and negotiate its meanings back into the dominant ideology by labeling it "feminist" and so providing it with a nominated, and thus containable, relationship to the dominant ideology. The *Examiner* quotes Martin Kove, who plays the parodically macho Victor Isbecki: "It's really a feminist show that makes all the men look like wimps or stupid or just plain bad . . . it's appalling how many times I've been emasculated on the show." The article is headlined "Cagney and Lacey Are Shaming the Men of America" and ends with the fear of a (male) psychotherapist that the show "could alter the view that the rest of the world has about the US" (April 2, 1985).

The relationship between the gender politics of character and the broader social politics of the show is only rarely mentioned, and then sneeringly: *Penthouse* calls it a cop show for the "socially correct" (March 1985), and *Vogue* writes:

> The two detectives roam New York City saying, "Aaahhh kiss off!" and "Button it, will ya?" as they fight crime. But the crime they fight is not ordinary crime. It's socially significant crime. Specifically, it's crime relating to woman. . . . Cagney and Lacey, ace detectives bucking the prejudices of male cops, are really just TV's updated packaging for that old feminist anathema: the "woman's picture."
>
> (August 1984)

The political similarity of the readers of *Vogue* and *Penthouse* is obviously greater than their gender difference. Reading crime politically instead of individually is part of the same reading strategy as the discursive reading of character, and is motivated by the same ideological stance in the viewer. It is in the interests of the status quo to read character as the representation of a real person rather than as a bundle of social discourses and crime as individually, rather than socially, motivated because this allows the social system to escape interrogation, and allows for an individual solution to a social problem. In this case, Taggart's love for her son "solves" the problem of poor, black, single mothers and denies the need to question the system in which they struggle to survive.

Dyer (1981) makes the point well when he claims that the psychologistic theory of character representation is essentially bourgeois:

> The peculiarities of the bourgeois conception of the individual/character are, first, that the stress on particularity and uniqueness tends to bar, or render inferior, representation of either collectivity and the masses or the typical person/character (types being relegated to a merely functional role in promoting the central character); and second, that the concern with interior motivation reinforces a model of history and social process in which explanation is rooted in the individual conscience and capacity rather than in collective and/or structural aspects of social life.
>
> (p. 242)

□ Identification, implication, and ideology

The ideologically dominant reading and acting strategies are those of realism. They work to suppress the sociopolitical meanings of the text in favor of the individualistic, and in so doing promote a particular relationship of the viewer to the text. This relationship is often called "identification." Brecht, in his theories on theater, was among the first to point out that the identification of audience with performer was a reading relation of capitalism. He sought to fracture this with a style of writing, acting, and production that was designed to alienate audience from performance. The alienated audience was one that was aware of the performance as an arbitrary construction of the real, of the difference between players and characters, and was therefore aware that the people and incidents on stage were there to perform social and ideological actions that could only be understood in terms of their relationship to the dominant ideology. Alienation produced a thinking, interrogative, socially aware audience.

On the other hand, identification as a relationship of audience to performance disguised the arbitrarily constructed nature of the performance and encouraged the audience to *experience* the representation as though it were the real, and, in particular, to see characters as individually real people. This blurring of the distinction between the representation and the real disguised the fact that people and incidents were on stage to perform ideologically determined actions and made them appear as innocent, objective reflections of reality. It made them appear products of nature, not of culture. Identification encouraged the audience to share the experiences and emotions of the characters and thus produced a feeling audience, not a thinking one, an accepting not an interrogative one, and one that understood incidents and actions through individual experience rather than through a sociopolitical framework. Identification, for Brecht, was, like the realism that promoted it, always an agent of the status quo.

Such an account may foreground the importance of how an audience relates to represented characters, but it oversimplifies the complexity of the phenomenon. In order to think through some of its implications, I propose to discuss it under the three headings of psychological identification, implication, and ideology.

□ PSYCHOLOGICAL IDENTIFICATION

Identification for Freud was the projection of personal characteristics onto an external body or object in order to understand them better. It was a psychological practice engaged in by the subject for the subject's own benefit, from a motivation buried in the subconscious. When applied to television it implies both an understanding of the viewer as a unified individual and of character as the representation of an equivalent real and unified individual. The two are merged, by this mechanism of projection, into each other in an act of reading that is the equivalent of method acting. The projection of the viewer into the character appears to be involuntary, as though he or she is seduced by the attractiveness of the text to submerge his or her own identity into that of a fictional character. Central to this process is a kind of wish fulfillment, for the seducing character is claimed to embody many of the unsatisfied desires (e.g. for glamor, wealth, success) of the viewer.

These desires are ambiguously individual or social in origin and are assumed to be central to the appeal of the program for most, if not all, of its audience. Identification then becomes a process of imaginative wish fulfillment which can be, and is, criticized from at least two points of view. The moralists criticize it on the grounds that it is mere escapism, and in encouraging people to imagine a better existence for themselves discourages them from working to achieve it in reality. At the other end of the spectrum, the ideologists argue that identification is the process whereby the values of the dominant ideology are naturalized into the desires, almost the instincts, of the individual, and are thus endlessly reproduced and perpetuated.

The reward for identification is pleasure. This is not just the ideologically derived pleasure of seeing one's values and those of the dominant ideology constantly revalidated, but one that involves a greater sense of control of the relationship between viewer and character.

Many viewers report that one of the main sources of the pleasure of television is the opportunities it offers to identify with certain characters, to share their emotions and experiences:

> But *Dallas* could really happen. . . . For example, I can sit very happy and fascinated watching someone like Sue Ellen. That woman can really get round us, with her problems and troubles. She is really human. I could be someone like that too. In a manner of speaking. (Ang 1985:44)

This sort of identification enables a viewer to enter the character's skin in a way that is impossible with real people for characters are never fully represented in the text – they are metonyms that invite the viewer to fill in the rest. But viewers "know" at some level that characters are not real, and that identifying with them is a form of intentional self-delusion. The thrown-away phrase, "in a manner of speaking," is evidence that this viewer, at least, is aware of what she is doing as she "identifies" with Sue Ellen. This process can also be creative, or imaginative, particularly when it involves a projection of the self into what the character will do in the future or might have done had things been different. This projection frequently takes the form of the

170

viewer imagining how he or she would have behaved had they been in a character's shoes at a particular moment, an active identification that has the reader sharing the role of writer, for reading creates sense in a way that parallels the act of writing: "I try to find more and more in the various characters. After each shocking event I try to imagine what they'll do" (Ang 1985: 50). This sort of identification is quite different from that in which the viewer's identity is "lost" in the character. It is active and involves the viewer in completing the meaning of character or incident from his or her knowledge of him- or herself. The viewer is less a subject of the dominant ideology and more in control of the process of identification and thus of his or her own meanings. This is approaching what I shall call later on "implication." Hobson (1982: 133–5) gives further examples of viewers contributing to the meaning of a particular incident by projecting themselves into the characters involved. She comments approvingly on two of her subjects' reactions to a fictional incident:

> I think this is a wonderful example of the supremacy of the audience's own perception of the reality of the programme. It is so firmly based in the women's own feelings of what they might do in the same situation as Diane.   (p. 134)

Ang (1985) quotes one of her subjects who is equally deserving of Hobson's approval:

> I think it's marvellous to project myself into *Dallas* and in my mind to give J. R. a good hiding when he's just pulled off yet another dirty trick, or admire Miss Ellie because she always tries to see the best in everyone, or to bring it out in them.   (p. 25)

This active engagement of the viewer in bringing her own life experience to the reading of the character is quite different to the view that the character or the program overwhelms the helpless viewer with its real-seemingness, so that he or she is rendered incapable of distinguishing between representation and reality.

Of course, stories abound of viewers treating characters as if they were real people. Typical is one example from *Crossroads*, quoted by Hobson (1982):

> Kathy Staff, who plays Miss Luke, talked about this aspect of the letters which she receives:
>
> KS: There are people who realize that you are an actress and are doing a job, then you do get the others that really believe in you as a character and they write to you as Doris Luke. For instance, when, a couple of years ago, Benny was had up – well, the police were looking for Benny

for murder and it wasn't Benny at all. Of course it was the manager of the garage that pushed the girl down and then whipped off and Benny came in and found her. And I mean, the letters I got telling me what happened, "You go, Miss Luke, you go to the police and tell them, I saw it on my television. It wasn't Benny at all." And I mean they really believed it and they were writing to me as Benny's best friend, and like a mother character, to get him out of trouble.   (p. 145)

This sort of "deluded" behaviour is widely believed to be common, if not typical, and apparent instances of it are frequently quoted in the press and in conversation. But what is significant is that none of Hobson's nor Ang's subjects reported being duped by the representation in this naive way. Rather they played games with its relationship to the real. Hobson (1982) tells of overhearing four old people treating gossip about their real families in the same terms as gossip about soap opera characters, as though there were no distinction. She comments:

Yet from the conversation it was obvious that the speakers were playing a game with the series. They did not actually believe that the characters existed, they were simply sharing a fantastic interest in the characters outside the serial.   (p. 125)

Ang (1985) comes to a similar conclusion. One of her subjects explains the pleasure she gets from *Dallas*:

The reason I like watching it is that it's nice to get dizzy on their problems. And you know all along that everything will turn out all right. In fact it's a flight from reality. I myself am a realistic person and I know that reality is different. Sometimes too I really enjoy having a good old cry with them. And why not? In this way my other bottled-up emotions find an outlet.   (p. 49)

Ang comments:

The "flight" into a fictional fantasy world is not so much a denial of reality as playing with it. A game that allows one to place the limits of the fictional and the real under discussion, to make them fluid, and in that game an imaginary participation in the fictional world is experienced as pleasurable.   (p. 49)

So the viewers of *Crossroads* who reportedly wrote to the actress Kathy Staff as though she were the character Miss Luke may not have been duped by the realism of the character portrayal, or by the ideological work of secondary texts, but may well have been contributing to their own pleasure by *deciding* to believe in the representation as though it were the real. Tulloch and Moran (1986) comment on a similar fan's letter:

It's impossible to tell from such a letter whether the writer accepts Vicky, Terence, Simon and so on as real people or whether he (*sic*) is deliberately and consciously revelling in the open-endedness of the serial.   (p. 227)

The letter appeared to treat the characters as though they were real, yet the writer signed it "A most devoted fan for all time (especially Penny Cook and Grant Dodwell)." Penny Cook and Grant Dodwell play Vicky and Simon, so it would appear that the writer was aware of the self-delusion involved in this pleasurable identification. Consistently, when fans talk as if they believed in the reality of the characters they give some indication that they know that they are participating in their own self-delusion:

> M: Well, I mean Jill had her ups and downs, didn't she, and so did Meg, and whatsit with her kiddie who she wants from America, I mean that can happen in real life, can't it. To me it's things in there that can happen in real life. It's not fiction to me. To me it's a real family story.
> DH: Now, when you say that, you don't mean you think they're real, do you?
> M: No, they portray that and they do it well.
>
> (Hobson 1982: 122)

The effectivity of the realism in the primary text and of the reading strategies promoted by the secondary texts is never total: if it works, it works because the viewer decides to go along with it in order to increase his or her viewing pleasure. But this cooperation with the realist text involves a dual positioning of the reader, for it involves a simultaneous awareness of the deception of realism that is willingly submitted to.

☐ IMPLICATION

Total identification, in which the viewer is lost in the represented character or world, rarely, if ever, occurs. What is more typical is what Brown (1987a), after Davies (1984b), calls "implication." Brown summarizes Davies:

> once "hooked," people vacillate between their need to know, or the pleasure of anticipation, and an *implication* with characters which is more complicated than identification. An implicatory reading would imply that an audience chooses a reading position which recognizes discursive possibilities.   (pp. 18–19)

One of Davies's subjects gives an example of the viewer's power to implicate herself with, or extricate herself from, the fictional character:

> Part of me is inside Linda – it feels rude when she takes off her stockings – it feels lovely when they kiss – but when she gets slapped I'm right back in our sitting room.   (pp. 90–1)

173

Similarly, in an article on *The Man-ipulators*, that is, women who induce men to do what they want them to, a soap fanzine writes:

a quick survey reveals we wish we could be more like the man-ipulators *only* when they're successfully pulling some man's strings. When they're getting the tough end of life, when their schemes fail and they're out in the blowing snow, we don't feel that much envy or admiration.

(Daytimers, June 1984b)

Ang's (1985: 106–8) subjects showed a similar simultaneous involvement with, and detachment from, *Dallas*. So rather than talking of implication it may well be more productive to talk of *implication-extrication* as a double relationship of the reader with the text.

Implication-extrication is closely connected with pleasure and unpleasure, with liking and disliking, and with the real and the unreal. Both Hobson's and Ang's subjects judged characters on how real they seemed, but revealed that the characters they liked appeared more real than those they disliked. The "real" characters were the ones they identified with: Ang (1985: 30–1) also reports that her subjects were detached from the characters they disliked, and were therefore more inclined to read them as embodiments of socio-political values. Different viewers "liked" different characters and thus found different characters to be "genuine" or "real." The real-seemingness of the character results from the viewer's projection of her/his own "real" self into the character in the process of identification. This process is motivated by the viewer's "liking" for the character, so identification, liking, and real-seemingness are all integral parts of the same reading process.

Students from ethnic minorities who see the *Hart to Hart* extract analyzed in chapter 1 are always quicker than whites to recognize the non-American status of the villain. This recognition could well be the first stage of their implication in his situation and their pleasure in finding in his "crime" an articulation of their own alienation from dominant white values.

Davies (1984b) argues that even implication with a painful situation or an unlikeable character can be a source of pleasure in that it can make the real situation of the viewer seem better by comparison:

The splitting of "identification" into vicarious satisfaction in the "good bits" (and the illusion of power) on the one hand, and into self-sustaining comparisons in the "bad bits" (and the reality of powerlessness) on the other, happens virtually instantaneously.

A viewer implicates him- or herself with a character when that character is in a similar social situation or embodies similar values to the viewer, and when this implication offers the reward of pleasure. But it is always accompanied by the knowledge that implication is a willing act of the viewer and

174

that extrication is instantly possible. Using the term "implication-extrication" foregrounds the viewer's activity and will: the *choice* of implicating oneself or not is an important source of the pleasure of implication: being induced by a text to make a fool of oneself can bring pleasure to few, if any.

The simultaneous or sequential processes of implication and extrication are reading relations that activate the contradictions in a text and that never totally lose sight of its textuality. They allow space for the viewer to read character and incident as bearers of social value, and thus to negotiate readings that relate to his or her social position.

Seiter *et al.* (1987) have revealed an important socio-economic dimension to this process. Some of the working-class soap opera fans in their study were able to find points of identification on the personal level with the middle-class, professional characters in their daytime soap operas, but were simultaneously aware of the class, and particularly the economic, differences between them and their own social situation.

> The experience of working-class women clearly conflicts in substantial ways with the soap opera's representation of a "woman's problem," problems some women identified as upper or middle class.
>
> (Seiter *et al.* 1987: 28)

Similarly, Katz and Liebes's study (1985, 1987) shows that non-American ethnic groups viewing *Dallas* can frequently find the pleasures of identification with the Ewings in the domain of kinship, while simultaneously distancing themselves from the Ewings as bearers of Americanness.

Much of the pleasure of television viewing derives from this complex viewing position in which the viewer is simultaneously self-implicated in, and self-extricated from, the text. The viewer's choice of certain points of identification does not preclude the ability to achieve an actively critical distance from other points, and these dual relationships with the text can be engaged in simultaneously. There is no pleasure in being "duped" by the text into a helpless viewer, but there is considerable pleasure in selectively viewing the text for points of identification and distance, in controlling one's relationship with the represented characters in the light of one's own social and psychological context.

Brown (1986), in her study of how women gossip about soap operas, identifies three main ways in which they talk about character and emphasizes how the same viewer can slip easily from one to the other. The first is one that sees character clearly as a mode of representation: it typically involves talk about how soaps are produced, goings-on on the set, and evaluations of the standard of acting. In the second category, the boundary between the real and the representation becomes fluid, and characters or players are talked about as though they were equally real or equally fictional. But the characters

175

still live, however really or fictionally, in the separate diegetic world of the soap opera. The third type of talk broke this separation: in it the characters were gossiped about as though they were part of the world of the viewer.

Such oral meanings exist only in the intimacy of personal relationships between viewers and in the deliberate reproduction of this intimacy in the willed identification of viewer with character. Gossip is not only evidence of a reading strategy, it is the means by which that strategy is put into practice to enhance the pleasure of the viewer.

Katz and Liebes (1984) report similar differences in their subjects' assessment of the "reality" of *Dallas*, but in their case the differences were between groups, not between different readings in the same group:

> Thus some groups will "gossip" about the characters as if they were real people, analyzing their motivations in everyday terms. At the other extreme, certain groups will discuss attributes or actions as "functions" in a dramatic formula, groping, as critics do, towards a definition of the genre to which *Dallas* belongs. (p. 29)

But the point remains, the reading strategies are part of the ideological practice of viewing: they are not a function of the text alone.

The secondary texts, not surprisingly in view of their function as published gossip, exhibit the same three ways of talking about characters as did Brown's subjects (see chapter 7). They also made the first two types of gossip possible by providing information about production processes, and biographies of players. This sort of material cannot, obviously, be part of the primary texts themselves but is an important part of their reception for many viewers. In the generation and circulation of the meanings of television within an oral culture, it is often difficult, and perhaps pointless, to decide which of the primary, secondary, or tertiary texts has the greatest effect. It is the viewer who is the site of this intertextuality and who determines the form it should take in any one instance.

☐ IDEOLOGICAL IDENTIFICATION

Reading is a socially determined activity, and the viewer must not be understood as a free-floating individual, but as a subject in ideology. Althusser (1979) argues strongly the need for a popular drama (and by extension television) that is not constrained by the dominating notion of the individual self, either in the portrayal of character or in the consciousness of the viewer or theater spectator. Such a domination, he argues, disguises the ideological relation of people to their social experience:

> This relation is necessarily latent in so far as it cannot be exhaustively thematized by any "character" without ruining the whole critical project:

that is why, even if it is implied by the action as a whole, by the existence and movements of all the characters, it is their deep meaning, beyond their consciousness – and thus hidden from them; visible to the spectator in so far as it is invisible to the actors – and therefore visible to the spectator in the mode of a perception which is not given, has to be discerned, conquered and drawn from the shadow which initially envelops it, and yet produced it. (pp. 145–6)

One way to perceive this relation which constitutes the political dimension of the text is by a reading strategy which understands "the existence and movements of all the characters" rather than by an identification with any one or more of them. This can be seen in the discursive relationship between Cagney, Lacey, and Taggart (see Table 9.1). It is this structure which is "visible to the spectator" but "invisible to the actors" and which has to be "discerned" by a discursive reading strategy which can draw it from the "shadow" of realism and into the light of day. This structural mix of ideological, social, and personal values is the textual equivalent of the reading subject that does not reflect the unity of the self but the diversity of social experience, and which therefore discourages any identification between a unified spectator and an individualized character. Althusser (1979) rejects as inadequate this process of identification by which the viewer-spectator projects himself or herself onto a character, particularly the hero:

But it must be said that the phenomena of projection, sublimation, etc., that can be observed, described and defined in controlled psychological situations cannot by themselves account for complex behaviour as specific as that of the spectator-attending-a-performance. This behaviour is primarily social and cultural-aesthetic, and as such it is also ideological. . . . If the consciousness cannot be reduced to a purely psychological consciousness, if it is a social, cultural and ideological consciousness, we cannot think its relation to the performance solely in the form of a psychological identification. Indeed, before (psychologically) identifying itself with the hero, the spectatorial consciousness recognizes itself in the ideological content of the play, and in the forms characteristic of this content. Before becoming the occasion for an identification (an identification with self in the species of another), the performance is, fundamentally, the occasion for a cultural and ideological recognition. (p. 149)

Althusser refuses to accept psychological identification as an adequate account of audience activity, but he recognizes how strongly it is promoted as a reading strategy for an audience whose "ideological and social relations of reading" (Bennett 1983b) are so much a practice of the ideology of individualism as ours are. But even within this ideology, it is more productive to

177

use a notion of multiple identification, which at least can allow for a dis-unified spectating self. Any one spectator may find in her/himself a number of points of relationship with that structure of ideological-social-personal values that is Cagney-Lacey-Taggart.

By implication-extrication the viewer can selectively identify with, or insert him/herself into, this structure of characters, and maintain some control of the process and therefore of the meanings while doing so.

Althusser (1979) stresses that any psychologistic identification, whether multiple or not, must be preceded by an ideological identification. In the four scenes of *Cagney and Lacey*, this identification would not be made between the individual viewer and one or more of the characters represented: but would rather be an equally pleasurable identification at the level of discourse. This is an identification with the discursive structure of the text that recognizes that its play of similarity and difference along the axes of nation, race, class, gender, power, work, etc., fits with the discursive structure of the reading subject. The pleasure depends not on agreement with the sense that is made, but on the agreement with the *way* that it is made, with the adequacy of our discourses and their cultural categories as a means of ordering our perception of both text and world.

Character in a realistic drama is a complex form of representation for it is constructed from one direction by the text and the narrative, and from the other by the body and performance of the player. Reading character requires the viewer to negotiate with great delicacy that boundary between the representation and the real and the ideological relationship between them. This negotiation must be conducted in two modes, the relationship between the real world of the player and the represented one of the character, and that between the real world of the viewer and the combined real-represented world of the player-character. In this chapter I have outlined some of the means by which the viewer conducts these negotiations, the alternate or alternative reading strategies, and the variety of forms of identification or alienation that are both available and adopted. Players can also use acting strategies and forms of identification that are the equivalent of those available to the viewers, for their role in the representation of character is the mirror image of the viewers'. Both maintain a relatively unstable balance between the modes of representation or reading that I have called the realistic or the discursive, the individualistic or the sociopolitical. Making sense of character is a precarious and skillful reading process that requires highly developed cultural competencies which enable viewers to control their relationships to the text so as to maximize the pleasure they can generate from it.

Chapter 10

Gendered television: femininity

The viewer's power to make the meanings that suit his or her social experience is not, of course, unlimited. Texts seek to prefer certain meanings, and while offering space for open or resistive readings, simultaneously attempt to limit that space to varying degrees. Some texts are more open than others, and this openness is controlled by different textual strategies. Adding these formal characteristics of texts to their manifestly different subject matter enables us to see some connections between the variety of television's programs and the diversity of its audiences. Put simply, different programs are designed (usually fairly successfully) to attract different audiences.

In these next two chapters I wish to explore some of the strategies by which television copes with, and helps to produce, a crucial categorization of its viewers into masculine and feminine subjects. Mellencamp (1985) traces this back to the 1950s, where she finds the origin of "the 'gender base' of television, with sport and news shows for men, cooking and fashion shows for women, and 'kidvid' for children" (p. 31). Television's techniques for gendering its audience have grown more sophisticated, and nowhere more so than in its development of gender-specific narrative forms. In this chapter I propose to look at soap opera as a feminine narrative, in the next to study the action series as a masculine narrative, and to draw from both the parameters of gender definition that we may use to understand the engendering work of other television genres.

☐ Soap opera form

Brown (1987) lists eight generic characteristics of soap operas:

1. serial form which resists narrative closure
2. multiple characters and plots
3. use of time which parallels actual time and implies that the action continues to take place whether we watch it or not
4. abrupt segmentation between parts
5. emphasis on dialogue, problem solving, and intimate conversation

6. male characters who are "sensitive men"
7. female characters who are often professional and otherwise powerful in the world outside the home
8. the home, or some other place which functions as a home, as the setting for the show.   (p.4)

Each of these characteristics merits considerable discussion, particularly if and why they constitute a feminine aesthetic. I wish to concentrate on the first two characteristics, that is, soap opera's ongoing, serial form with its consequent lack of narrative closure, and the multiplicity of its plots. As we saw in chapter 8, traditional realist narratives are constructed to have a beginning, a middle, and an end, but soap opera realism works through an infinitely extended middle. Traditional narrative begins with a state of equilibrium which is disturbed: the plot traces the effects of this disturbance through to the final resolution, which restores a new and possibly different equilibrium. Comparing the states of equilibrium with which it begins and ends and specifying the nature of the threat of disturbance is a good way of identifying the ideological thrust of a story. The end of such a narrative is the point of both narrative closure and ideological closure. The narrative resolves the questions it posed, makes good its lacks and deficiencies, and defuses its threats. The resolutions of these disturbances prefer a particular ideological reading of its events, settings, and characters. For the aim of realist narrative is to make sense of the world, and the pleasure it offers derives from the apparent comprehensiveness of this sense. This comprehensiveness is evaluated according to relation to the ideologies of the reader, and through them, to the dominant ideology of the culture. So a narrative with no ending lacks one of the formal points at which ideological closure is most powerfully exerted. Of course, individual plotlines can end, often with the departure or death of the characters central to them, but such endings have none of the sense of finality of novel or film endings. Departed characters can, and do, return, and even apparently dead characters can return to life and the program – four did so within two years on *Days of Our Lives*! But even without physical presence, the departed characters live on in the memory and gossip both of those that remain, and of their viewers.

□ Disruption

This infinitely extended middle means that soap operas are never in a state of equilibrium, but their world is one of perpetual disturbance and threat. The equilibrium of a happy, stable family is constantly there in the background, but is never achieved. Even a soap opera marriage, and marriages are ritual high points to be greatly savored, is not the same as a marriage in a traditional romance in which the couple are expected to live happily ever after. All soap opera marriages have within them the seeds of their own destruction. On one level the fans know that this is because a happy, unthreatened marriage is boring and incapable of producing good plotlines. But these generic conventions have not grown from some formalist ideal world of "good plotlines": they have a social base. Marriage is not a point of narrative and ideological closure because soap operas interrogate it as they celebrate it. Building the threat into the celebration opens marriage up to readings other than those preferred by patriarchy. This double evaluation is generic to soap opera, and is part of the reason for its openness. A wife's extra-marital sex, for instance, is evaluated both patriarchally as unfaithfulness, but also, more resistingly, as a woman's independence and right to her own sexuality. Such affairs often spring from the man's, or the marriage's, inability to satisfy her. A wife's "unfaithfulness," then, is capable of being read by both masculine and feminine value systems simultaneously.

As Seiter *et al.* (1987) found in their study of soap opera fans,

> women openly and enthusiastically admitted their delight in following soap operas as stories of female transgressions which destroy the ideological nucleus of the text: the priority and sacredness of the family.   (p. 27)

Two of the women to whom they talked expressed their pleasure in seeing marriage disrupted and one went so far as to use this in a playful, but actual, challenge to the power of her husband as it is inscribed in the conventions of marriage:

> SW: But there's lots of times when you want the person to dump the husband and go on with this . . . .
> JS: Oh Bruce [her husband] gets so angry with me when I'm watching the show and they're married and I'm all for the affair. (*Laughter.*) It's like, it's like (*voice changed*) "I don't like this. I don't know about you." (*Laughter.*) Dump him.   (p. 27)

The dominant ideology is inscribed in the status quo, and soap operas offer their subordinated women viewers the pleasure of seeing this status quo in a constant state of disruption. Disruption without resolution produces openness in the text. It can be read dominantly (patriarchally): such readings would produce fans who return to their more "normal" marriages with a sense of relief. But disruption can also serve to interrogate the status quo. As we shall see in our discussion of soap opera characters, the powerful women who disrupt men's power are both loved and hated, their actions praised and condemned.

The marital relationship is not the only one being simultaneously affirmed and questioned. One of the commonest plot themes is that of family ties and relationships. This concern to clarify relationships within the disrupted and unstable family may be seen as "women's matters," that is, as a domain where patriarchy grants women a position of some power. But if it is, its representation and the pleasure it offers overspill these ideological constraints. The ability to understand, facilitate, and control relationships is often shown as a source of women's power, used disruptively by the bitches and more constructively by the matriarchs. Men are often shown as deficient in these abilities and knowledges, and cause many problems by this masculine lack. This set of abilities and knowledges, normally devalued by patriarchy, is given a high valuation and legitimation in soap operas, and can serve as a source of self-esteem for the fans and as an assertion of women's values against the place assigned to them in patriarchy.

This concern with relationships often manifests itself in an extreme form in the theme of incest. Exploring the boundaries of permitted sexual and family relationships in this way may work not only to clarify those boundaries, but also to interrogate them and the system that established them. If Lévi-Strauss's theory of kinship systems is accepted, the incest taboo is an agent of patriarchy, for it defines which women can, or cannot, be given in marriage to which men. Central to it is the construction of women as objects of exchange, and of the kinship system as being patriarchally determined. Freud's Oedipus theory is concerned with a similar area, and offers an equally patriarchal explanation of sexuality, desire, and effect upon family relationships. The commonness of incest as a topic in soap operas, and its absence from more "masculine" television genres, suggests, at the very least, that women find more pleasure in interrogating the boundaries that it assumes, and thus in interrogating the system that has set them in place.

☐ Deferment and process

Disruption is not the only effect of the infinitely extended "middle"; deferment is an equally important characteristic. As Modleski (1982: 88) puts it, soap opera "by placing ever more complex obstacles between desire and fulfilment, makes anticipation of an end an end in itself." A soap opera narrative strand has no climax to close it off, no point at which it is seen to have finished: indeed, the outcome of most plotlines is relatively unimportant, and often not really in doubt. What matters is the process that people have to go through to achieve it. As Brunsdon (1984) argues, the pleasure in soap opera lies in seeing how the events occur rather than in the events themselves. Indeed, the soap opera press often summarizes future plotlines: the reader knows the events before they occur, her interest lies in how the characters behave and feel as they react to the events. Each event always has consequences, final outcomes are indefinitely deferred, and narrative climax is rarely reached. Instead there is a succession of obstacles and problems to be overcome and the narrative interest centers on people's feelings and reactions as they live through a constant series of disruptions and difficulties. No solutions are final, smooth patches are never free from the sense of impending disasters. The triumphs are small-scale and temporary, but frequent. They provide a mundane, almost routine, set of satisfactions of desire (what Barthes 1975b would call *"plaisir"* [see chapter 12]), but the final climactic *jouissance* (Barthes 1975b) of desire satisfied is constantly deferred. Indeed, the mini-climaxes complicate as much as they resolve. This might well be seen as hegemony at work: the soap operas teach women by example to forgo the real, final satisfaction of desire in favor of a series of unreal, minor pleasures. These minor pleasures "buy" the viewers, and win their apparently willing consent to the system that subordinates them. Women, this argument runs, harm themselves as a class by their pleasure as individuals.

But this endless deferment need not be seen simply as a textual transformation of women's powerlessness in patriarchy. It can be seen more positively as an articulation of a specific feminine definition of desire and pleasure that is contrasted with the masculine pleasure of the final success (see chapter 11). The emphasis on the process rather than the product, on pleasure as ongoing and cyclical rather than climactic and final, is constitutive of a feminine subjectivity in so far as it opposes masculine pleasures and rewards. This feminine subjectivity and the pleasures which reward and legitimate it are not bound to be understood according to their dominant construction as inferior to their masculine counterparts. Indeed, soap opera narratives consistently validate these feminine principles as a source of legitimate pleasure within and against patriarchy.

Deferment and process are enacted in talk and facial expression. The sound track of soap operas is full of words, and the screen is full of close-ups of faces. The camera lingers on the telling expression, giving the viewers time not just to experience the emotion of the character, but to imagine what constitutes that emotion. Porter (1977: 786) suggests that "a face in close-up is what before the age of film only a lover or a mother saw."

Close-ups are, according to Modleski (1982: 99–100), an important mode of representation in feminine culture for a number of reasons. They provide training in the feminine skills of "reading people," and are the means of exercising the feminine ability to understand the gap between what is meant and what is said. Language is used by men to exert control over the meanings of the world but women question its effectivity in this, and find pleasure in the knowledges that escape it. Close-ups also encourage women's desire to be implicated with the lives of the characters on the screen, a desire that is also satisfied by the comparatively slow movement of soap opera plots which allow reactions and feelings to be savored and dwelt on. As Brown (1987a) says, "soaps allow us to linger, like the pleasure of a long conversation with an old friend." Feuer (1984) suggests that the acting style of soaps is excessive and exaggerates the hyperintensity of each emotional confrontation. Editing conventions work in the same way:

> Following and exaggerating a convention of daytime soaps, *Dallas* and *Dynasty* typically hold a shot on screen for at least a "beat" after the dialogue has ended. . . . [This] leaves a residue of emotional intensity just prior to a scene change or commercial break. (pp. 10–11)

An event, however momentous or climactic, is never significant for itself, but rather for the reactions it will cause and the effects it will have. Events originate or reactivate plots instead of closing them.

☐ Sexuality and empowerment

As Davies (1984a) argues, soap opera sexuality is concerned with seduction and emotion rather than, as masculine sexuality is, with achievement and climax. If a woman's body and sexuality are all that patriarchy allows her, then, according to Davies, soaps show her how to use them as a weapon against men. It has been pointed out (e.g. by Geraghty 1981) that soaps show and celebrate the sexuality of the middle-aged woman, and thus articulate what is repressed elsewhere on television as in the culture generally. In the prime-time soaps the sexual power of the middle-aged woman goes hand in hand with her economic power in a significant reversal of conventional gender ascription. For in patriarchy, economic and sexual power have been closely interdependent characteristics of masculinity, but when reversed into femininity they undergo a necessary change of function from possession to control. The traditional patriarchal equation of possession of goods with possession of women is so commonly represented as to need no elaboration; we simply need to point out that it is a *state* to be achieved. Control, however, is a *process* that needs constant struggle to exercise it, it is ongoing, never finally achievable, and is thus an appropriate result of the feminization of the linking of sexual with economic power. The powerful women in soap opera never achieve a settled state of power, but are in a continual process of struggle to exercise control over themselves and others.

There is some evidence, too, of a similar feminization of a normally masculine pleasure, that of pornography. All soaps are highly sexual, and

184

Figure 10.1 Sex in the soaps and their press

The photographs of the hunks and their bodies approximate to a female pornography, an erotic fantasy that the soaps apparently arouse (in some), but leave to the press to satisfy. The real excitement derives from erotic relationships where the fantasies are less ego-centered, more other-directed, and more feminine.

Remember when Jack and his sexy stepmom, Jill, were a steamy duo? "I loved working with Deborah Adair. She was my favorite," says Terry. In fact, the two stars are still pals off-screen.

SOAP'S SEXIEST GUYS! PHOTO ALBUM!
24 Daytime Stars!
COLOR PIN-UPS!
PETER RECKELL
Centerfold!

...AND THE RIGHT TARZAN FOR TINA

☐ She may be a very nasty young lady, but Tina Lord is also a sexy one! So why isn't she involved in a steamy love affair? Bad, bad Brad Vernon might be her equal. Or does she deserve someone more evil, like Clay Monroe. Then again, she's had her eye on Clint Buchanan. Tell us who you think is Tina's perfect match. **TV**

. And if anyone can call Robert and Holly's steamy, sexy reunion scene in the swimming pool in Mexico anything but hot they must be watching the wrong show! By contrast, Luke and Laura's reunion scene two weeks later was not only cool and sedate, but downright boring!

Dear Daytimers:
I've heard that *General Hospital* will be bringing back Luke and Laura and I sure hope it's true. Since they left Port Charles there's been no heavy duty sex at all! Tony Geary and Genie Francis were really hot together, but since then we've been stuck with Mr. and Mrs. Scorpio. They might look pretty, but those two have all the steam and sizzle of wet kleenex. The show has lost its chemistry.

Dear Daytimers:
In you March issue D.V. of Philadelphia wrote a letter that stated that her old man has more "fire" than cool, cold Tristan Rogers and that Emma Samms is so cool she might freeze to death. To the above statement, my friends and co-workers would like to say that if Tristan and Emma are "cool and cold" then cool and cold are indeed beautiful. We adore them just as they are, whatever it might be called.
As far as her statement about them having all the "steam and sizzle of wet kleenex," we happen to think they have just the *right* amount of steam, sizzle, charisma, sex appeal, class and style to suit us.

many women use terms more conventionally applied to male pornography to describe their reaction to them (see Figure 10.1). The soap opera press frequently emphasize sexuality, most commonly either in a discussion of love scenes or in descriptions and photographs of the male hunks. Letters to these magazines evidence the sexual readings that some women make of the programs. It is possible, then, to see soap operas as pornography for some women. The response to the male "hunk" is a fantasy that appears very similar to the masculine pornographic fantasy, involving a fantasized identification with a sex object of the opposite sex, but there are crucial differences. The sexuality of the "hunk" is not always confined to his body, but is often contextualized into his relationships and interpersonal style. Similarly, the erotic turn-on of the love scenes is consistently described as resulting from the representation of a relationship, not the body of an individual. Brown (1987a) argues that the sexuality of soaps is "not constructed around the male gaze, but it is heard and spoken." It is thus part of a relationship between people, and it is relationships, rather than the body of the male, that are the source of the erotic pleasure offered by soaps.

Women's view of masculinity, as evidenced in soap operas, differs markedly from that produced from the masculine audience (see next chapter). The "good" male in the daytime soaps is caring, nurturing, and verbal. He is prone to making comments like "I don't care about material wealth or professional success, all I care about is us and our relationship." He will talk about feelings and people and rarely expresses his masculinity in direct action. Of course he is still decisive, he still has masculine power, but that power is given a "feminine" inflection. This produces different gender roles and relationships:

> Women and men in the soap operas are probably more equal than in any other form of art or drama or in any area of real life. By playing down men's domination over women (and children) the soaps and the game shows make the family palatable. On daytime TV the family is not a hierarchy, starting with the father and ending with the youngest girl, but an intimate group of people, connected to each other intimately through ties of love and kinship.
>
> (Lopate 1977: 50–1, in Hartley 1985: 23)

The "macho" characteristics of goal centeredness, assertiveness, and the morality of the strongest that identify the hero in masculine television, tend here to be characteristics of the villain. It is not surprising that, in women's culture, feminized men should be seen positively while the masculine men are more associated with villainy, but the reversal is not a simple one. The villains are typically very good-looking, and are often featured in the press as desirable "hunks"; they are loved and hated, admired and despised. Similarly, the good, feminized men, particularly the younger ones, typically have

186

the strong good looks associated with conventional heterosexual masculinity. It is rare to find sensitive, feminized looks (with their possible threat of homosexuality) going with the sensitivity of the character.

This opens their sexuality up to different readings. Their sensitivity and their passion are shown in their relationships with other characters. But their macho looks invite a fantasy relationship with some viewers at least. The primary texts concentrate on the relationship, whereas the secondary texts often emphasize the physical, compensating for the soaps' refusal to sexualize the body of the male in a feminized inflection of voyeurism. The soap opera press, however, has no such inhibitions. The commonest pin-up photograph is a close-up of the face, but there are frequent ones of male soap actors posed with bare torsos in traditional beefcake style (see Figure 10.1) which seem to invite a feminine equivalent of the masculine pornographic fantasy. It may be argued that such appropriations do at least make a "masculine" pleasure available for women, in addition to the more feminine eroticism of the represented relationship, but they do nothing to question that pleasure, nor to suggest alternatives to it.

Brown (1987a), on the other hand, argues that soaps are positive and empowering in the way they handle sexuality and sexual pleasure:

> Thus the image of the body as sexual currency is absent, but the spoken discourse of the power of the female body to create is given crucial importance. There is no need to reiterate here the number of pregnancies, the importance attached to paternity and sometimes to maternity or the large number of sexual liaisons between characters in soap operas. However, contrary to the discourse which places the pregnant woman as powerless over natural events, often women in soaps use pregnancy as power over the father of the unborn child. The father will usually marry the mother of his child, whether or not he loves her (or whether or not the pregnancy is real), thereby achieving the woman's felt need to be taken care of in the only way that is available to her in the dominant system. Women characters, then, use their bodies to achieve their own ends.　　(pp. 19–20)

A woman's sexuality does not, in soap opera, result in her objectification for the male. Rather it is a positive source of pleasure in a relationship, or a means of her empowerment in a patriarchal world. The woman's power to influence and control the male can never be finally achieved but is constantly in process. It is a form of power not legitimated by the dominant ideology, and can thus exist only in the continuous struggle to exercise it. A man's "conquest" of a woman, his possession of her, may be said to have been achieved at the moment of sexual climax: a woman's control over a man, however, has no such final achievement. The emphasis on seduction and on its continuous pleasure and power is appropriate to a contemporary feminine subjectivity, for that subjectivity has necessarily been formed through a constant experience of powerlessness and subordination.

Davies (1984a) goes on to show how advertisements in soap opera magazines lend support to the theory that women's bodies and sexuality are the main means open to them to achieve power in a patriarchy. The commonest type of advertisement is for products to improve the sexual power of the female body – losing weight, enlarging breasts, improving skin or hair, shaping buttocks – the list is limited only by the parts of the female body that can be constituted as a problem for a product to solve. These advertisements are obviously patriarchal capitalism exploiting the lack of self-esteem that the system produces in women, but they are not just that. They exist alongside another category of ads which also play on women's desire to improve their situation and thus their power in society. These are for courses to improve their qualifications, for ideas to start and run a business from home, or even for lucky charms. These magazines are for women in whom patriarchy has produced a low self-esteem but who have a desire for the social power that is denied them but which they claim is rightfully theirs. The advertisements capitalize on this with a range of exploitative products: the soap operas themselves, however, show how such a power may be achieved by feminine values rather than the products of patriarchal capitalism.

But this desire for feminine power is never simple, because it is a desire born in patriarchy and must contain those contradictions within it. An article in *Daytimers*, June 1985, with the title "Those Man-ipulators: Doncha Love Women Who Control Their Men?", explores these contradictory pleasures:

> These are a few of the man-ipulators, those women who control men and often make them look foolish.
>   Women who control their man.
>   Women who control *all* men.
>   Women we wish we could be more like.
>   Or do we?
>   Do we really want to control the men in our lives? Do we actually desire they do what we want, how we want and when we want? Do we truly yearn for their complete obedience under any and all circumstances? . . .
>   Do we, as average women, really want all this control?
>   You're damn right we do.
>   And that's why we probably admire those man-ipulators we see on the tube. Admire and fantasize about being as man-ipulative as they are.
>   Still . . . a contradiction. Don't we mutter at the TV set when witnessing a man-ipulator man-ipulating, "I sure hope she gets what's coming to her!"?

The subordination of women in patriarchy is challenged by the power of their man-ipulation, but reasserted in the acceptance of the punishment that is its apparently inevitable final outcome. The contradictory appeal of these character roles and viewing positions produces the contradictory process of implication-extrication of the viewing relations.

> With these autopsies of the man-ipulators, it's hard to imagine anyone feeling envy for them. But we often do feel a twinge of admiration and a quick survey reveals we wish we could be more like the man-ipulators *only* when they're successfully pulling some man's strings. When they're getting the tough end of life, when their schemes fail and they're out in the blowing snow, we don't feel that much envy or admiration.
>
> Still . . . to control the men in our lives does sound like it would be fun – if only for a while.
>
> *Daytimers* June 1985

The process of implication-extrication is here described sequentially, though, as we have seen (chapter 9), it is more characteristically and complexly simultaneous. This double articulation of a reading position challenges the power of the text to propagate the dominant ideology via its construction of a unified reading subject. The pleasure of implication with the character when she is exerting power may well be stronger than that of extrication when she is being punished. The difference in what Freud calls "affect," in the intensity of the experience, may well be great enough to prevent the ideological effectivity of the punishment.

For instance, *Charlie's Angels*, first screened in the early 1970s, featured three beautiful women detectives in an agency run by "Charlie," who was never seen, but only heard on the intercom as a controlling male voice. Each week the women would solve the case, even if they "needed" masculine help from Charlie's agent, Bosney, and, after the narrative climax, would always return to the agency and the control of Charlie's voice. Patriarchy was deeply inscribed in the series, particularly by this masculine closure of each episode and in the voyeuristic camera work on the three heroines. But it was challenged by the aggressiveness and success of the women detectives, and, as mentioned earlier, many women have reported to me that their pleasure in this was strong enough to overwhelm the patriarchal frame and block the effectivity of the ideological closure.

Neither *Charlie's Angels* nor the soap opera "*man-ipulators*" is a feminine text in an essentialist sense. They are historically and culturally produced, which means that the feminine readings they offer are within and against patriarchy. The struggle of women viewers to create a feminine space within patriarchy is paralleled by the struggle in these texts between feminine pleasure and power on the one hand, and patriarchal control on the other.

Kuhn (1984) traces a similar duality which she terms that between mastery and masochism. The pleasure of mastery is provided not only by the frequent representation of strong women, but also by the power of the feminine spectator to "solve" the enigmas of the plots. Masochism, however, is a spectating position or pleasure produced by "for ever anticipating an endlessly held off resolution" (Kuhn 1984: 27). Women's (and men's) suffering is as central a theme as women's power. Kuhn goes on to suggest that the mix of mastery and masochism produces in the viewer an "interplay between masculine and feminine subject positions." Her account is largely psychoanalytic: a more culturally inflected one might explain this interplay as an example of the process of implication-extrication or of the doubly articulated reading position that women have learned to adopt.

Modleski's (1982) account of the soap opera villainess reveals similar contradictions. She argues that the villainess is a negative image of the viewer's ideal self, which is constructed by the soaps as the ideal mother, able to sympathize with and understand all the members of her (and the soap opera's) extended family. Such a mother role is, of course, specific to the patriarchal family, for it denies the mother any claims on herself, and requires her to find her satisfaction in helping her children to come to terms with and resolve their multiple difficulties. She is other-directed and decentered.

Modleski's account derives from textual and psychoanalytic analysis and thus can identify only the ideological thrust of the text, but we can be chary of assuming its effectiveness in all situations. Seiter *et al.* (1987), for instance, found that many of their subjects explicitly rejected this textually constructed role:

> While this position [the Ideal Mother] was partially taken up by some of our middle-class, educated informants, it was also consciously resisted and vehemently rejected by most of the women we interviewed, especially by working-class women.
> (p. 24)

The villainess turns traditional feminine characteristics (which are often seen as weaknesses ensuring her subordination) into a source of strength. She uses pregnancy (real or alleged) as a weapon, she uses her insight into people to manipulate them, and she uses her sexuality for her own ends, not for masculine pleasure. She reverses male and female roles (which probably explains why Alexis in *Dynasty* is popular with the gay community) and, above all, she embodies the female desire for power which is both produced and frustrated by the social relations of patriarchy. The final control that the villainess strives for is, Modleski argues (p. 97), control not over men, but over feminine passivity.

Seiter *et al.* (1987) found clear evidence of the appeal of the strong villainess for women chafing against their subjection in patriarchy:

> All of these women commented on their preference of strong villainesses: the younger respondents expressed their pleasure in and admiration for the

powerful female characters which were also discussed in terms of trans-
gressing the boundaries of a traditional pattern of resistance for women
within patriarchy:

LD: Yeah, they van be very vicious (*laughs*) the females can be very
 vicious.
JS: Seems like females have more of an impact than the males and they
 have such a mm . . . conniving . .
SW: brain! Yeah! (*Laughter.*)
LD: They're sneaky!!! Yeah!
SW: They use their brain more (*laughter*) instead of their body! They
 manipulate, you know! (pp. 25–6)

But there was little evidence of any hatred for the villainess, rather the
respondents despised the woman who suffered despite her middle-class privi-
leges, a character type they called the "whiner," or "the wimpy woman" (pp.
24–5).

But, in the portrayal of the villainess, soap operas set these "positive"
feminine characteristics in a framework of moral disapproval, and follow
them at work through a repeated narrative structure that denies their ultimate
success. The woman viewer loves and hates the villainess, sides with her, and
desires her downfall. The contradictions in the text and its reading position
reflect the contradictions inherent in the attempt to assert feminine values
within and against a patriarchal society.

The text cannot and does not resolve these contradictions. It can be argued
that devalued representations of feminine control leave patriarchy unchallenged, so that the villainess acts as a mere safety valve for feminine anger, or
as a mere fantasy of feminine power. But

> if the villainess never succeeds, if, in accordance with the spectators'
> conflicting desires, she is doomed to eternal repetition, then she obviously
> never permanently fails either. . . . And if the villainess constantly
> suffers because she is always foiled, we should remember that she suffers
> no more than the good characters, who don't even try to interfere with
> their fates.
>
> (Modleski 1982: 98)

The contradictions in the villainess that enable her to bear meanings that
variously justify or challenge female powerlessness are typical of the openness
of soap opera texts. Representations of marriage and the family are shot
through with similar contradictions. Neither is ever stable, both are constantly in turmoil, threatened by incessant disruptive forces that stem largely
from individuals' desires or deficiencies. The difficulty experienced by such

191

dominant institutions as marriage and the family in coping with people's desires and behavior is clearly not an unequivocal assertion of their value, but sets them up, rather, as a site of contestation within which personal conflict can acquire a sociopolitical dimension. The ideal of a happy marriage and a stable family may never be explicitly attacked, but it is brought into question by the apparent impossibility of achieving it.

□ Excess

We have noted (chapter 6) that excess is a characteristic of television in general that works to open the text to alternative readings. Feuer (1984) reviews a number of critical accounts of melodrama (Mulvey and Halliday 1972, Bourget 1977/8, Willeman 1978, Elsaesser 1973, Nowell-Smith 1977, Mulvey 1977–8, Kleinhans 1978) which argue that what I have called hyperbolic excess is especially significant in the ideology of melodrama for its ability to open up "a textual space which may be read against the seemingly hegemonic surface" (Feuer 1984: 8). Feuer argues that melodrama (and soap operas are the prime televisual example of the genre) produces two texts. The first or main text is that preferred by the dominant ideology, and is accessible at the superficial, "obvious" level. The second text, however, is made available by the "excess" which overspills the control of the main text and subverts the dominant ideology.

Brown (1987a) in her discussion of Showalter (1985b) also raises the notion of a double text, but relates it specifically to feminine culture. She argues that women in patriarchy necessarily learn to use a double-voiced discourse which allows them to participate in both the dominant discourse (Showalter's "male crescent") and a feminine discourse which Showalter calls "the wild zone." The "male crescent" is where ideological control is asserted, the "wild zone" where meanings escape that control and where (almost) anything can happen. Melodramatic excess constitutes this wild zone in soap opera. Hodge and Tripp's (1986) ethnographic work provides some evidence in support of this. They found that girls tended to identify with both male and female hero figures on television, whereas boys identified with male heroes only. The girls were learning early to handle a "double-voiced discourse": the boys felt no such necessity and thus developed a much more limited discursive repertoire.

Mulvey (1977–8) also finds some positive value in medodrama's excess and suggests that it can work to activate ideological contradictions in notions of the home and family. But, she goes on to argue, it finally functions as a "safety valve" whose effect is hegemonic. Feuer (1984) disagrees with this, arguing that the excess of television melodramas gives them, at least, a radical potential:

The emergence of the melodramatic serial in the 1980s represents a *radical* response to and expression of cultural contradictions. Whether that response is interpreted to the Right or to the Left is not a question the texts themselves can answer. (p. 16)

Feuer is concerned mainly with prime-time soaps, but argues that her conclusions are equally applicable to the daytime ones. Excess may be comparatively easy to theorize, but it is not always easy to operationalize the theory and apply it to a specific example. Anna's misadventures in *Days of Our Lives* provide a typical example of excess. She has been away for five years, and on her return we learn that she has been kidnapped and held captive in a boat where she had been drugged, probably forced into prostitution, starved nearly to death and whipped so that her back is still scarred. She has multiple sclerosis and is offering Roman, her husband, a divorce so that he will be free to marry Marlene, the woman he fell in love with during her absence. On her return, she is nearly arrested by Roman, a policeman, for unknowingly having thousands of dollars hidden in a false compartment in her suitcase. Such a catalogue of signs of woman-as-victim may seem to push excess into the ludicrous, but we learn of the details slowly over a number of scenes and episodes. The process of revelation builds horror and sympathy which cannot be confined to masochistic identification with the suffering of the woman-victim, but can overspill into an awareness of the male power that produces the victimization. The extent to which Anna's sufferings exceed the victimization more normally experienced by women in patriarchy opens up a gap that can work in a number of ways. Logically, it would appear that it could produce the ideological closure of realism, but for the fan, this does not happen. It could equally well lead to demystification of those norms of victimization which are usually naturalized and unnoticed, but which excess foregrounds, thus revealing their patriarchal arbitrariness.

The text itself cannot resolve these doubts. Excess does not necessarily lead to subversive or interrogative readings: it allows for an overspill of meaning that escapes ideological control and that makes alternative readings possible.

Feuer (1984) has similar doubts about whether the visual opulence of *Dallas* and *Dynasty* works as a form of subversive excess. She points out that the characters exceed the norms of their viewers both morally and economically, but argues that this excess is not finally subversive because the text itself gives no indication that it is to be used as a countertext. However, such a textual indicator may not be necessary.

Brunsdon (1981) argues that watching a soap successfully demands a degree of cultural capital constituted by the knowledge of this particular serial as well as the conventions of the genre. She also argues that the subject position offered by the text may not match the position of the viewer as a "social subject," and that in such a case the viewer may not accept the subject position produced by the text. The contradictions between the social discourses that constitute the viewer as "social subject" and those in the text that constitute her as "reading subject" may well be used to interrogate the norms of the text. The extent by which *Dallas* exceeds the moral and economic norms of its viewers may just as well put those norms under question as reinforce them; indeed, it may do both simultaneously. The desire for material wealth may be stimulated at the same time as the realization that it will not bring the happiness or satisfaction it promises. The norms of family morality may be upheld as the pleasure and necessity of breaking them is experienced.

☐ Plenitude and polysemy

Soap operas are characterized by a multiplicity of characters and plotlines, and this plenitude opens them up to a variety of readings and reading positions. Thorburn (1982) emphasizes the effect of this "multiplicity principle" in opening the text up: because of it, "familiar character-types and situations become more suggestive and less imprisoning" (p. 539). The "populations" of daytime soaps can number as many as forty, which produces what Allen (1985) refers to as paradigmatic complexity. The characters in this population are read (see chapter 9) both as individuals offering opportunities for identification, and as bearers of social or moral values. The network of relationships by which a reader understands "who a character is" is immensely complex and impossible for the narrative structure to control, and its complexity resists the sort of structural analysis we were able to perform on Cagney, Lacey, and Taggart in chapter 9. Allen argues that soap opera's repetitiousness, its syntagmatic redundancy of repeated talk about the same events or relationships by different characters in different situations, is more than just a means of bringing up to date a viewer who missed a particular episode: it is, for the regular viewer, an invoking of the paradigmatic network. He concludes that "to the experienced reader, however, soap opera's distinctive networks of character relationships open up major sources of signifying potential that are simply unreadable to the naive reader" (p. 71).

On the syntagmatic dimension, the multiplicity of plotlines allows a variety of topics to be introduced and explored from a variety of positions. "Progressive" subjects, such as abortion, test-tube babies, or interracial marriage can be introduced and explored through the different experiences of a number of characters. The viewer of soap opera is never allowed a stable reading position: no sooner has she understood and empathized with one character's reaction to an event than the focus changes and she is required to shift her experiential knowledge to that embodied by another. All sides of an issue can be explored and evaluated from a variety of social points of view, and, in contrast to the masculine narrative investigated in the next chapter, no point of view, no evaluative norm, is given clear hierarchical precedence over any other.

Allen (1985) suggests that this anti-hierarchical openness has been developed over time by television soap operas. Early examples had an extra-diegetic narrator whose disappearance not only produced a greater sense of verisimilitude, but also refused any "perspectival hierarchy." He argues that though there is an "underlying normative perspective," new normative positions can be explored:

> the soap opera's textual openness allows it to colonize new normative territory at little cost – in the process opening up spaces for new groups of readers. New characters and situations can be introduced in an attempt to attract new audience members, but since the new narrative strands are positioned alongside other, more "traditional" ones, there is little risk of alienating existing viewers.   (p. 175)

The absence of closure prevents these contradictions being resolved, and allows the juxtaposition of traditional values with new ones to be read either progressively or conservatively. The multiplicity of plots allows the soap opera to offer a variety of pleasures and identifications to a variety of viewers. A plotline that seems silly is compensated for by one that is enjoyed, and the soap opera press is full of viewers' opinions about which plotlines are "silly" and which "enjoyable" or "believable." The marked lack of consensus amongst these opinions is evidence of soap opera's ability to appeal to a variety of audiences. The obvious economic advantage to the producers of this narrative plenitude does not prevent the resulting polysemy and openness being activated in the cultural interests of the audiences (see chapter 16).

☐ The feminine as decentered

A defining characteristic of soap opera is its denial of a unified reading position and of a coherent meaning of the text. Its texts and its reading subjects are decentered. Chodorow (1974: 44) suggests that the feminine subjectivity is less centered than the masculine. Its lack of center produces an insecure boundary to the feminine ego:

> in any given society, feminine personality comes to define itself in relation and connection to other people more than masculine personality does (in

195

psychoanalytic terms, women are less individuated than men; they have more flexible ego boundaries). Moreover, issues of dependency are handled and experienced differently by men and women. For boys and men, both individuation and dependency issues become tied up with the sense of masculinity, or masculine identity. For girls and women, by contrast, issues of femininity, or feminine identity, are not problematic in the same way. The structural situation of child rearing, reinforced by female and male role training, produces those differences, which are replicated and reproduced in the sexual sociology of adult life.

(quoted in Brown 1986)

Whether this is an inherent, natural difference between females and males or a socially produced one is a subject of considerable debate. What is not at issue, however, is that the cultural formations of patriarchy constantly reproduce and revalidate these differences, and soap operas work more explicitly than most art forms to connect with women's decentered subjectivity, their social relations in patriarchy, and the structure of texts that are popular with them.

The decenteredness of the soap opera form with its multiple reading positions is argued by theorists such as Modleski (1982) to be the textual equivalent of woman's role in the patriarchal family. Here she is decentered, finding her identity only in her relationships with children and husband, constantly reconstituting herself to accommodate the changing demands of these relationships.

Similarly, the constant repetition of plot themes (Wiebel 1977, in Modleski 1982, lists eight as the most frequent) and the inevitability of their outcomes can be seen as a formal equivalent of the domestic routine imposed upon housewives. In this view the multiplicity of characters and plots is equivalent to the multiplicity of simultaneous tasks that make up housework. The frequent interruptions of the television text (of one plotline by another, of program by commercial) are the textual equivalent of the constant interruptions of housework, and the lack of narrative closure parallels the unending nature of housework.

The difference between women's and men's modes of viewing in the family follows a similar pattern. Morley (1986) has shown how women typically view while doing something else, often housework, while men tend to view more concentratedly. Feminine work, feminine viewing practices, and feminine texts combine to produce decentered, flexible, multifocused feminine subjectivities. All of these elements are contrasted with male work, masculine texts, and a masculine subjectivity.

These accounts may well clarify the relation among textual characteristics, women's social roles, and their decentered subjectivity. But what is problematic is the effect of this relationship. It can be argued that these

196

are the devices of masculine hegemony, working to naturalize patriarchy in the feminine subjects who suffer from it. Alternatively, it can be argued, as Modleski (1982) does, that these are the characteristics of a feminine aesthetic. They constitute not an oppositional feminist culture, but a feminine culture that asserts the value of feminine characteristics and pleasures within and against patriarchy. Lovell (1980) makes a similar point about popular entertainment in general and soap opera in particular:

> Some of the pleasures of entertainment will be readily mobilised for domination. Others may be more intractable. Among the latter will be those expressing the hopes and aspirations of the dominated which are thwarted under patriarchy. To be sure, these will be deeply embedded alongside the contradictory sensibilities of domination. . . . But their expression and development in however contradictory a manner within popular culture ensures that they remain alive and available for different mobilisations and articulations. (p. 49)

In negotiating a feminine terrain where feminine meanings can be made and circulated, they keep patriarchy under constant interrogation, they legitimate feminine values and thus produce self-esteem for the women who live by them. They provide, in short, the means for a feminine culture that pragmatically is the only sort possible because it takes account of current social relations. It is a feminine culture in constant struggle to establish and extend itself within and against a dominant patriarchy. While it may not challenge that patriarchal domination in any direct or radical way, at the very least it constantly whittles away at patriarchy's power to subject women and at best it provides both a masculine-free zone from which a direct challenge may be mounted and the self-esteem that such a challenge would require.

Chapter 11

Gendered television:

masculinity

Masculinity is as much a cultural construct as femininity but its different relationship to patriarchy produces different textual constructions and reading practices. Shows like *The A-Team*, which cater for largely male audiences, have less need to produce a *double text* that allows for oppositional or resistive meanings to be circulated. Their texts are structured to produce greater narrative and ideological closure, and there is little evidence that this closure needs to be resisted by a significant number of audience groups. The more typical reading strategy is likely to be one of negotiation, as male subcultures, situated differently in the social system, seek to accommodate their social situation with the dominant ideology. Masculine texts appear to be less polysemic than feminine ones because masculinity's relationship to patriarchy is less resistive than femininity's.

This is not to say that men do not experience problems with patriarchy's construction of masculinity: they certainly do, and the popularity of programs like *The A-Team* depends, to a greater or lesser extent, on the degree to which they offer meanings that are of use in coming to terms with the differences between the experiences of men in their various social positions and the ideological construction of masculinity which is offered as the way to make sense of those experiences.

☐ The structure of the masculine *A-Team*

The A-Team and masculinity, then, are both cultural constructs working to set up meanings according to a structure of similarities and differences. The A-Team consists of four men (there was originally a woman in the team but she was written out after the first season). They are Vietnam veterans, members of a crack commando unit wrongly accused of a war crime. They escaped and operate now, outside the official law, helping powerless but worthy people to defend themselves against criminal and evil forces in areas

198

where the official system of law and order is ineffective. Each of the "clients" has to meet two criteria – they must be able to pay, and they must have the initiative and determination to find the A-Team. There is certainly no socialist motivation of helping the weak as a class – only those who exhibit the competitive, individualistic, and economic motivations appropriate to capitalism.

The team is led by Hannibal Smith (played by George Peppard), a man in late middle age, sardonic, a master of disguise, physically fit, who is prone to lighting a phallic cigar at moments of achievement and satisfaction. His second in command is Templeton "Face" Peck (Dirk Benedict), a good-looking, charming man, good at adopting a variety of social roles in order to con his way into social groups and situations. His weakness is women: he often falls for female clients and has to be torn away from the arms of a pretty girl at the end of an episode. B. A. Barracus (played by Mr T) is the "muscle" of the team. He is a huge black with a Mohican haircut who wears large quantities of gold chains around his neck and bangles on his wrists. He is the driver of the team's van, their engineering and explosives expert. The final member is "Howlin' Mad" Murdock (Dwight Schultz), who lives in a mental hospital (presumably as a result of the Vietnam trauma) from which he has to be sprung for each mission. His mental instability is often manifest in childish behavior and expressions, but he is an expert helicopter pilot and a good back-up driver.

The structure of similarities and differences underlying the A-Team and masculinity can be modeled as shown in Figure 11.1.

Figure 11.1 Structure of masculinity in *The A-Team*

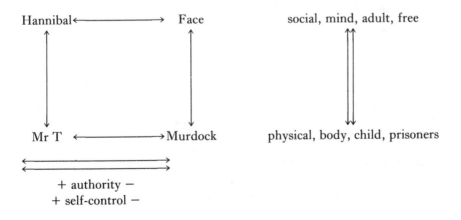

The team as a whole can be seen as a composite structure embodying those contradictions of masculinity that problematize it for men living in patriarchy. Let us analyze this structure in some detail to reveal how it works as a structure of masculinity.

One aspect of masculinity in our culture is its connection with maturity. "Be a man" is a frequent admonition to young boys that requires them to behave more maturely than their physical age. Many popular narratives dramatize the "boundary rituals" whereby a youth crosses into manhood. In *The A-Team*, the diachronic process of maturation is presented synchronically. Murdock, unsocialized and somewhat wild, represents the infant instinctual male. B. A. Barracus is the young boy's fantasy of masculinity as physical strength (including its mechanical extension into guns, cars, and machinery). B. A. is particularly popular with boys at the age at which they have learnt that their masculinity requires them to be dominant, but who have neither the physical strength nor the social position to meet this requirement.

Hannibal and Face, on the other hand, represent adult masculinity. Their power is exercised more by social means than physical; they plan and scheme whereas Murdock and B. A. act. They are the brains of the Murdock-B. A. body. Hannibal is the more mature and has the authority of his experience and ability to plan successfully. Face is the young adult, who imposes his will on others by social means such as charm or role playing, but whose romantic weakness shows a partial loss of self-control that makes him "younger" than Hannibal and closer to Murdock. He is close to the boundary between the adolescent and the mature adult. Hannibal, on the other hand, is the mature father figure. Hannibal's self-control is authenticated by the frequent press accounts of George Peppard's previous reputation as a hard-drinking hell-raiser: a "Murdockian" wildness that had to be controlled before he could be allowed to play Hannibal Smith.

Hannibal, as leader of the team, exhibits most of our culture's constructs of masculinity. As Shere Hite (1981) discovered, in her survey of what men thought masculinity consisted of, "a man should be self-assured, unafraid, in control and autonomous or selfsufficient, not dependent". Other qualities that emerged were those of leadership, the ability to take charge, and dependability. Root (1984: 16) describes a similar study in which investigators

asked doctors, psychiatrists and social workers for definitions of "normal adults", "normal healthy men" and "normal healthy women". The lists in the first two categories, adults and men, were almost identical, with independence, self-reliance and resilience strongly featured. A "normal healthy woman", however, turned out to be almost the opposite of a "normal healthy person", and was described as vulnerable, dependent and in many ways childish.

Maturity and masculinity come together in a confident definition which masks a host of contradictions. In order to live up to it in capitalism men must undergo a complex set of experiences involving repressions, guilt, and contradictory feelings. These are centered on the roles of women and marriage, and the organization of work and society; and they involve the constant redefinition of masculine identity in a capitalist patriarchy. Some of the terms we will use to explore these areas are psychological ones, but the contradictions in the masculine psyche are largely socially produced and certainly reproduced in social conditions. In other words, they are not part of the nature of the male, but part of our social construction of masculinity.

The characteristics elicited by Hite are all expressions either of individualism or of power and control. But society frequently denies males the means to develop these qualities by placing them in institutions (such as work) which deny them the opportunity either to express their individuality or to exert any power or control. This is particularly true of men in lower socioeconomic groups and may well underlie the aggressiveness of much working-class "style" and the sexism of much working-class and lower-middle-class subculture. Because men's idea of masculinity can rarely be realized at work they have developed a masculine style for their leisure and social activities that consists of excessive signs of masculinity in an exaggerated and compensatory display. The same gap between the ideological ideal and social experience also explains the sexism and aggressiveness of much adolescent male style, for, like lower-class men, young boys are also denied the social means to exercise the power that our ideology tells them is the prerequisite of their masculinity.

Hero figures such as B. A., the Incredible Hulk, the Six Million Dollar Man, or Superman are popular among young boys whose bodies are not strong enough to grant them the power that is their ideological requirement, and who also occupy powerless social positions in the family and school. The physical strength of such heroes is frequently extended by cars, guns, and machinery. In this view B. A.'s mechanical and driving skills are extensions of his physical strength, and the cars in programs such as *The Dukes of Hazzard* or *Knight Rider* are part of the masculine identity of the heroes.

Lacan's theory of the mirror phase in which the infant sees in the mirror not a reflection of his or her real body-self, but of the imaginary one that has none of the deficiencies of the real, may account for this pleasure in part. But it can do so only if we inflect his theory socially as well as psychoanalytically: the gap between the imaginary and the real which desire strives to close is caused not just by the human condition, but by social conditions which ensure that the material experience of masculine subjects never measures up to their ideologically produced expectations. This gap, inevitably, is wider than men would wish, for our society denies most males adequate means of exercising the power upon which their masculinity apparently depends. Masculinity is thus socially and psychologically insecure; and its insecurity produces the need for its constant reachievement in shows like *The A-Team*. Like any ideology, patriarchy works through alibis, absences, and reductive misrepresentations to disguise the masculine insecurity upon which it is based.

Like most masculine texts, *The A-Team* works by writing out of its world three of the most significant cultural producers of the masculine identity — women, work, and marriage.

☐ The absence of women

Masculinity in patriarchal capitalism is shot through with contradictions and repressions. Freud argues that the male child gives up a sexual desire for his mother from fear of rivalry with the father and the threat of castration which this would bring. For, in psychoanalytic theory, one of an infant's first constructions of identity is that of gender, and male infants learn quickly that masculinity brings with it social power. But, in order to achieve this power, the boy has to reject his mother and suppress both his love for her and the feminine in himself in order to identify with the father and the power of the masculine. Easlea (1983) suggests that in many tribal societies this involves access to the power of "men's magic." We hardly need Lévi-Strauss to remind us that in our societies technology and science have replaced "magic," as the social manifestations of male power. For boys, guns and machinery are not just symbolic compensations for their lack of physical strength, nor ways of compensating for their envy of women's procreative power, they are their means of entry into the masculine. Chodorow (1978) explains the boy's entry into the world of male power more psychoanalytically:

> A boy gives up his mother in order to avoid punishment, but identifies with the father because he can then gain the benefits of being the one who gives punishment, of being masculine and superior. ... Compared to a girl's love for her father, a boy's Oedipal love for his mother, because it is an extension of the intense mother–infant unity, is more overwhelming and threatening for his ego and sense of (masculine) independence. ... This mother–son love threatens her husband and causes him to resent his son. The intensity of the Oedipal mother–son bond (and the father–son rivalry) thus causes its repression in the son. (p. 131)

Psychoanalytic theory tells us that the repression of the feminine in the male and the rejection of the mother with its subsequent Oedipal guilt are the

202

origins of the mass of contradictions and repressions that constitutes masculinity in patriarchy. It proposes that women, as embodiments of the feminine, threaten the masculine by bringing with them the male's guilt and fear of castration. Women stand for the repressed in the male and the devalued in patriarchal society, that is, the vulnerable, the sentimental, emotion, commitment, nurturing, caring. As Holloway puts it:

> [Women] have already been constructed in such a way that they manifest the [emotional] characteristics that men are suppressing. Likewise [women] experience themselves as wanting commitment and, materially, are more likely to be in a position of needing it, because this is how they have been positioned historically.
>
> (in Moye 1985: 51)

The repressed feminine is defined oppositionally to the foregrounded masculine, and Nelson (1985) has collected some of the semiotic areas upon which this gender difference is commonly constructed in our society:

masculine	:	feminine
active	:	passive
presence	:	absence
validated	:	excluded
success	:	failure
superior	:	inferior
primary	:	secondary
independent	:	dependent
unity	:	multiplicity
organized	:	scattered
intellect	:	imagination
logical	:	illogical
defined	:	undefined
dependable	:	capricious
head	:	heart
mind	:	body
subject	:	object
penis	:	vagina
firm	:	soft
sky	:	earth
day	:	night
air	:	water
form	:	matter
transcendence	:	inurement
culture	:	nature
logos	:	pathos

(quoted in Brown 1987b)

It is important to remember here that these characteristics are cultural constructs of masculinity and femininity and in no way form a set of natural differences between males and females, however much the physical differences between the sexes may be mobilized in an attempt to naturalize them. Despite "common sense," the greater strength of the male body is not a reason for the social power of the masculine; similarly the female's comparative weakness does not explain the "feminine" desire for commitment, nor does her ability to bear children necessarily produce the "feminine" qualities of nurturing and caring. Cultural constructs, however naturalized, are not produced by nature.

These oppositions are patriarchal ones for they carry the connotations derived from their history that the "masculine" characteristics are powerful and valued whereas the "feminine" ones are weaker and devalued. Our cultural development of masculine and feminine identities has built into it notions of male superiority.

These "inferior" and "weak" characteristics of the feminine are repressed in the masculine psyche and *exscribed* from the masculine narrative. Exscription, the opposite of inscription, is the process whereby a discourse writes out of itself topics that are ideologically or psychologically discomforting. The feminine is exscribed from the masculine discourse of *The A-Team* just as women are written out of the narrative.

Face is typical of many male heroes in so far as part of the narrative closure consists of him rejecting, however reluctantly, a woman for whom he has fallen. His sentiment is seen as a weakness that detracts from the masculine business of the A-Team, but his possession of this "weakness," and the constant need to conquer it, is a naturalized part of the masculine problem. Rejection of the woman is the narrative exscription of the feminine that is working hard to deny the contradictions in masculinity by reducing it to uncontradictory notions of power and independence. It also reduces the feminine, for women are represented solely as threats to masculinity. Their nurturing and their desire for intimacy (with its threat to masculine independence) are the repressed aspects of masculinity and must thus suffer reiterated narrative rejection. The exscription of the feminine is the narrative equivalent of the male's repression of his Oedipal guilt. The male hero's rejection of the woman at the end of the episode legitimates the rejection of the mother by affirming the masculine need for independence.

There is, of course, an inversion here between masculine ideology and male social reality: the social male desires both to possess the female and to live in a society in which both genders have their place. But the ideology of masculinity, at odds with its social materiality, demands a rejection at the level of representation.

Ross (1986) notes this inversion in a comparison of the primary and secondary texts of *Miami Vice*. The cover of *Us* magazine promotes a feature article on Don Johnson (who plays Crockett) thus: "A woman's love saves a tarnished golden boy from the vices of alcoholism, drugs and debauchery." The story tells how a stable love life has enabled a previously degenerate star to reform his life: the feminine is written in powerfully as a source of social and emotional stability for the actor (the social male). For the character (the ideological masculine), the opposite is the case, for in the narrative the "tarnished golden boy" can save others from "the vices of alcoholism, drugs and debauchery" only by rejecting the feminine. So the pilot episode shows Crockett in the process of divorcing his wife and all the usual narrative conventions save him from other women for the rest of the series. As Ross comments, "it is the public service of law and order that saves a man from the corrosive effects of heterosexual love" (p. 149).

The cover of *Us* signals a paradox here, for it headlines its feature story "The Sexiest Man on TV" which sets up Johnson/Crockett not only as an object of narcissistic identification for the male, but also as an object of desire for the female viewer. Males may find few contradictions in patriarchal representations of masculinity that separate it from the feminine. But females are taught to admire and desire that which rejects them in a typical piece of ideological double-talk.

There have been attempts recently to account for this paradox without putting women in the position of "cultural dopes." Neale (1983) has argued that cinema is starting to construct the masculine as spectacle, as the object of narcissistic identification for men and of erotic desire for women. Flitterman (1985) argues that *Magnum p.i.* has, over its run, gradually placed greater emphasis on the spectacle of the star, Tom Selleck, as an erotic object. She goes further than Neale in arguing that this is part of a feminization of the series which, by reading Selleck/Magnum's body as encoded in the same way as the lush, sensuous beauty of the Hawaiian scenery, opens up the series to nonpatriarchal pleasures for women. Morse (1983) also finds in television's display of male bodies, this time in sport, evidence that the apparent glorification of masculine prowess need not always be read in that way. There is a reading that allows women to objectify the male body and subordinate it to their desires. *Miami Vice* displays as much male flesh as female, if not more, and the narratives of *Magnum p.i.* are regularly interrupted by shots of Selleck/Magnum in the surf or on the beach, serving a narrative and ideological function that patriarchy conventionally reserves for shots of the female body (see chapter 12). The male bathing beauty is a modification of traditional representations of masculinity, albeit a problematic one.

☐ The absence of work and marriage

Work, in patriarchal capitalism, plays a central role in producing a masculine identity, but is not without its contradictions. For many men, if not most, the conditions of work are such that it subjects them and works to construct them as dependent and powerless. Yet it is upon the man's position as the bread-winner that his masculinity and power in the family depends. Men typically report (see Tolson 1977) that unpalatable work is made bearable only because it provides them with the satisfaction of providing for the family (and with the power that this brings). Patriarchal resistance to working wives is often strongest in classes and ethnic groups where the men have low status, low social power, and low incomes. The need for women to contribute to the family income is often economically strongest when ideologically most threatening as it appears to undercut the man's only remaining source of power.

But even men who are able to provide adequate income for their families do not escape the contradictions of masculinity. The "breadwinner" role may be a source of power, but it also forms a prison which denies masculine independence and freedom. The concept "breadwinner" contains within it the domains of work and of the family and the contradictions in both, for in it the masculine role is experienced as a constant vacillation between power and subjection, between freedom and restraint.

The A-Team is full of images of restraint and the masculine desire to break them. Mr T (who plays B. A.) wears gold chains and bangles as a reminder of the recent slavery of black people in America. This intended meaning is not, however, confined to its intention. The contradictions in having the symbols of slavery made in gold (the symbol of success) and multiplied excessively (see Figure 11.2) open them up to a variety of meanings negotiable by differently situated males within this dialogue between freedom and re-straint. The meanings of gold may be more important for whites than blacks, the weight and strength of the chains may be more important for some males, their stylishness for others, but all men are offered the opportunity to negotiate appropriate meanings for themselves within the semiotic excess generated by the conjuncture of gold, chains, style, physical strength, and blackness.

In the show's title sequence, B. A. bursts onto the screen by smashing through a door, and cars break through windows and walls. The voice-over tells us that the A-Team escaped from their army accusers in Vietnam. These images of male power breaking free are metaphors for masculinity's desire to break through the laws and the social constraints with which society tries to contain it.

Male sexuality is understood to have a "natural" wildness that is dangerous and in need of control. The tension between society as a system of artificial restraints and masculinity as naturally wild and imperative produces a set of contradictions that are embodied in Murdock. His wildness requires him to be locked up in an institution from which he has to be freed for special

Figure 11.2 Mr T

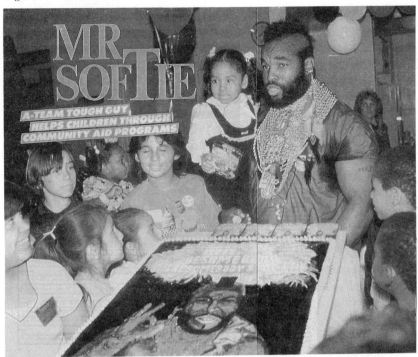

I am the 10th child of 12. Our mother brought us up on a meagre welfare cheque in one of Chicago's most crime-ridden housing projects. We had three meals a day: oatmeal, no meal and miss-a-meal!

Do you have a special message for the children of today?

Yes. Don't be giving your parents a hard time. I don't do drugs, I don't hang around, I don't smoke and I still listen to what my mother has to say.

I am a very active member of the Rev Hardy's Cosmopolitian Community Church. I often sing in the choir and frequently speak at meetings.

Back in '75 I was the highest-paid bodyguard of all time, because I did my job extra well. I have protected millionaires, preachers, politicians, judges, bankers and a list of superstars like Diana Ross, Michael Jackson, Muhammad Ali and Leon Spinks.

I really have a split personality, something like Dr Jekyll and Mr Hyde. I'm nice and kind — if you leave me alone. But if I'm crossed, then you asked for it!

Is your jewellery real?

Of course it's real! How dare you! It's valued at around $300,000 all up, and I'm adding to it every day. So by the time TV SOAP prints this interview, it will be worth even more.

Why do you wear so many gold chains?

They are a symbol of my great African ancestors, who were brought here as slaves in iron chains. I turned my chains into gold, so my statement is this: I wear gold chains instead of iron because I'm still a slave, but my price tag is higher.

Source: Fairfax Magazines, Sydney, Australia

projects, in just the same way as "real masculinity" can only be freed from its social control on special occasions. The social definition of Murdock as "insane" is contradicted by his value and success when integrated into the masculine structure of *The A-Team*, and yet his value to the team hinges on the fact that he needs to be locked up for most of the time. It is worth pointing out here the symbolic role of Crockett's pet alligator in the equally, but very differently, masculine show *Miami Vice*. The alligator (the wild primitive side of man) is kept chained up but occasionally breaks free to go on a rampage of destruction.

Masculinity is a paradox of power and discipline. The privilege of authority is bought by the discipline of duty and service. Man's achievement at work is in the service of his family, at war in the service of his nation, in sport in the service of his team or country. The A-Team has the privilege of action and power but only in the service of the weak, of those suffering injustice. As Tolson (1977) puts it:

> In the final analysis, "masculinity" is a kind of cultural bribe. A boy's social commitment is won at the price of his independence – for which he is offered the empty promise of "manhood". The very notion of "manhood" is internally paradoxical – offering a dream of fulfilment on condition that the boy submits to authority and convention. . . . This paradox points the way to work, which becomes a man's central experience. (p. 46)

In patriarchal capitalism masculinity is a problem structured around notions of power and service, freedom and discipline, individuation and dependency. This problem is constantly activated by the sexual sociology of adult life in the family, in the workplace, and in society at large, and it needs consistent symbolic solutions if masculinity is to appear in its own eyes as clearly defined as the men surveyed by Hite (1981) claimed that it was. The tension between power and discipline, freedom and restraint, authority exerted and submitted to, is built into the structure of *The A-Team* (see Figure 11.1) as it is into our cultural definition of masculinity.

The intertextual relations activate readings around these contradictions. Mr T has become almost indistinguishable from B. A. Barracus, partly because the appearance, dress, and style are identical in both "characters," and partly because of the exactness of the fit between the "real" Mr T as portrayed in the secondary texts, the fictional Mr T in the cartoon program named after him, and the fictional B. A. in *The A-Team*. (See Figure 11.2.)

It is widely reported that Mr T used to be a professional bodyguard, using his strength in the service of others. His strength is also contained and controlled by his strong religious and moral convictions. In the cartoon series he (ambiguously Mr T or B. A.) appears in a filmed insert at the start and finish of each adventure to point the moral, socially conforming message.

This insert is interesting for it not only makes vertical and horizontal intertextual relations more explicitly than is typical, but it also confuses modalities. Cartoons bear a "conditional" relationship to the sense of reality; they do not work in the indicative mode of realism which says "This is happening," but in the conditional mode – "This would (or could) happen if . . . ." Hodge and Tripp (1986) have shown how quickly young viewers of television learn to decode the various modal relationships between the representation and the real. They do not confuse the low modality of cartoons with the high modality of news. Henderson (1986) and Osborn (1984) have found that children recognize the comparatively low modality of *The A-Team*, they know that no one is hurt by the violence and that much of the action is "impossible." Low modality clearly invites fantasy, and Mr T's realistic, high-modality film inserts work to connect that fantasy to social reality.

Mr T's masculinity also works through his connection with sport. In the cartoon series he runs a gymnasium for children and teenagers who also accompany him on his adventures. The gym is where physical abilities are both built up and controlled. Similarly, Mr T also takes part in professional wrestling. This is the television spectacle where the social control over the natural wildness and aggression of masculinity is at its most fragile. The relative impotence of the referee (the metonym for social control) to prevent the carefully staged fights and rule breaking is a central part of the spectacle.

For just underneath all of Mr T's image as the protective, responsible male, lies "Howlin' Mad Murdock." He is quoted:

> I really have a split personality, something like Dr Jekyll and Mr Hyde. I'm nice and kind – if you leave me alone. But if I'm crossed, then you asked for it!
>
> (*Fame*, February 10, 1986:35)

He is as powerful a meaning generator as he is because he embodies so precariously the tension between the uncontrollable natural forces of masculinity and the opposing forces of society.

☐ *The A-Team* as achievement

Masculinity can never be taken for granted. Boys learn to prove it constantly in various forms of competition with each other. Tolson (1977) argues that for middle-class boys, this competitive proof is often channeled into school and sport. For working-class boys, who may find school values alien, masculinity is found in the peer group or gang. Maintaining their membership involves a constant performance of aggression and toughness typified by games of dares and challenges. Aggression is the basis of much working-class style, and of male youth style in general. Masculinity is performance. *The A-*

Team embodies elements of the middle-class team or social organization along with those of the aggressive working-class gang, which makes it semiotically accessible to a variety of differently situated males.

Men are cast into ceaseless work and action to prove their worth. The insecure base of masculinity means that it is constantly having to be reachieved particularly in the eyes of others. "Masculinity," then, is constructed as an agent of capitalism, because it both motivates the man to achieve in work, and keeps him a prisoner in work when he finds that his achievement is hollow, that it is for the benefit of others (his family or his boss), not for himself.

Capitalist ideology is equally well served by the idea that a man must be able to cope with any situation. Masculinity becomes almost a definition of the superhuman, so it becomes that which can never be achieved. Capitalism needs this gap between the material experience of men and the ideological construction of masculinity to keep men striving for more and more achievement in order to maintain the "naturalness" of the ideological concept of progress, which is so central to capitalism.

Achievement and successful performance (the primary definers of masculinity) are the fundamental requirements of capitalism. *The A-Team* and other television adventure shows play a vital part in the circulation and maintenance of these meanings of masculinity. Their requirement that each episode ends in success which is achieved by a constant display of masculine performance differentiates them sharply from the soap operas, and associates them with pornography.

☐ The phallus, the penis, and porn

Moye's (1985) account of pornography also stresses the role of performance. Pornography reduces masculinity to penile performance uncomplicated by any feminine notions of caring or intimacy. The objectification of the woman is another way of exscribing her femininity and difference from the male. As the myth of masculine total competence produces an ideology of the superman which the actual man can never achieve, so the actual penis can never, as Moye points out, measure up to the phallus. The phallus is a cultural construct: it bears a culture's meanings of masculinity and attempts to naturalize them by locating them in the physical sign of maleness – the penis. This use of the natural to disguise the arbitrariness of the cultural is argued by Lévi-Strauss to be common to all societies, even though the meanings of the cultural will vary from society to society.

The use of guns and vehicles (or other machinery) as what can be called "penile extenders" is an attempt to close the gap between the penis and the phallus, between the real and the imaginary, or the material and the ideological. They operate in Lacan's world of the imaginary where actual male performance is unified with the ideology of masculinity and the gap between them is erased. They attempt to deny the masculine insecurity, whether we understand this as psychological (e.g. Oedipal guilt and the suppression of the feminine) or social (e.g. the denial of social power to some working-class men or to those of "devalued" races, or the lack of physical and social power in boys).

Male performance in *The A-Team*, as in *Magnum*, as in *Starsky and Hutch* and the rest of the genre, is always effective, and always ideologically sanctioned. It is not always socially sanctioned, however. *The A-Team* are on the run from the military police, and other detective heroes frequently operate outside, or in conflict with, official law enforcement agencies. Even policemen, such as Starsky and Hutch, are in constant conflict with their superiors and the bureaucracy of their institutions.

This is hardly surprising, for society is, as we have argued, in conflict with the freedom and wildness of masculinity. It is equally in conflict with that closely connected ideology of individualism. So the institutional agencies of society often become the ideological enemy. In *M.A.S.H.* the real enemy of Hawkeye and his friends is not the North Koreans, but the army as a bureaucratic institution. Excessive bureaucracy is a common sign, in capitalist popular culture, of Communism. Capitalism as such is never named in this culture: rather it lurks beneath more acceptable concepts such as freedom and democracy and is aligned with such naturalized concepts as the individual. Thus James Bond defeats the villain because he is a free individual, able to think quickly and respond flexibly. The villain, on the other hand, loses despite his wealth, his technological strength, and his manpower because he is so bureaucratic and "programmed" that he is outwitted by Bond. He is a prisoner of his social organization, Bond is free. Hence Bond is an embodiment of capitalism (called free democracy), the villain an embodiment of Communism (or, at least, of the west's popular construction of it).

The set of oppositions that structures this relationship is

> individual : society
> freedom : constraint
> natural : artificial
> true : false
> good : evil.

It can be transformed equally well into

> the private eye : the police/legal system
> the A-Team : the military police
> democracy : communism
> Hawkeye : the army.

What interests here, of course, is how the values on the lefthand side of the structure become incorporated into masculinity, whereas those on the right are manifestations of the problems and oppositions that masculinity faces in society.

The way our ideology merges its construction of the masculine with that of the individual and the natural underlies Dyer's (1985) argument that the penis-weapon absolves man from responsibility for any harm caused in the exercise of his power. The natural wildness of masculinity (typified most impressively and frighteningly by the image of Murdock with a machine gun) requires social control or channeling into the ideals of service and responsibility. B. A. and Murdock need the social control of Hannibal Smith. When a male hero kills, he has a psychological alibi that parallels the social and moral alibi provided by the plot.

It can also be argued that the alibi of the penis-weapon can be used to justify men's sexual power over women and, finally, rape. The typical patriarchal and capitalist strategy of blaming the victim is only the reverse of the same coin.

The heroine-in-jeopardy and the woman-as-victim are products of the same patriarchal ideology. The heroine-in-jeopardy corresponds to the repressed side of masculinity, whose repression and weakness are thus narratively justified. But also, according to Dyer, in her role as woman-as-victim, she legitimates male revenge for the threat she poses to masculinity and for the guilt she inspires. But, paradoxically, the male still has to save her. Dyer (1985) demonstrates how, at the points of maximum danger or terror for the heroine, the camera typically positions the spectator as rapist/terrorizer, whereas the narrative positions him or her with the hero as savior. The male is thus doubly positioned as oppressor/rapist and savior which is a parallel paradox to the much more commonly recognized one of woman as virgin and whore.

The contradictions between the social and the physical in *The A-Team* are those between the male as oppressor and as savior. The successful performance does not work simply to close the gap between the penis and the phallus, but to enact the contradictions between oppressing and protecting. The same qualities that enable the male to save the female are those that enable him to oppress (and rape) her. Popular narratives and social conditions are shot through with the same contradictions. The uneasiness of the resolutions that popular narratives achieve is evidenced by the need for them to be constantly reachieved night after night in prime-time television.

☐ Male bonding and the hero team

The exscription of women leads to a male bonding which is a close relationship protected from the threat of intimacy. The bond of the A-Team, of

Magnum and his co-heroes, is goal-oriented, not relationship-oriented. The relationship is there to serve a common goal, not the needs of the relationship itself; it depends on action not on feeling. The need to depend on others is there, but it is externalized onto a goal, not internalized into a basic need of the male. The closeness of the ensuing relationship does not, therefore, threaten masculine independence, and the justification of this intimacy by the external goal means that the relationship can contain homosexual desire and pleasure without either the guilt or the unmanning that typify representations of the homosexual in a heterosexual ideology.

Starsky and Hutch exhibited many signs of a homosexual relationship, but their physical and emotional intimacy was not, in itself, a source of satisfaction and pleasure to them. Their fulfillment came from the goals that their relationship enabled them to achieve, not from the relationship itself.

Chodorow (1978) suggests that the way that males and females are brought up in our society teaches males to find their identity in goals and achievements and females to find theirs in relationships with other people. Goals are more singular than people and tend to be more clearly prioritized, thus males develop a more centered subjectivity than do females. Thus masculine narrative tends to deal more with singular goals and achievements, feminine narrative more with people and relationships. The multiple plots and multiplicity of characters in soaps are reflective of a feminine subjectivity and productive of a feminine pleasure. Conversely, the singular or clearly prioritized plot structure of masculine narratives is characteristic of a masculine subjectivity and productive of a masculine pleasure.

But the avoidance of intimacy places the male in a terrible isolation, hence his need for a goal-oriented, nonthreatening male bonding. The team hides the insecurity of the individual without threatening his independence. No man, despite the myth, can be totally competent, unless he has "magic" abilities (Superman, the Six Million Dollar Man), but the hero team can mold individual competencies into something approaching total competence. The A-Team closes the gap between the penis and the phallus.

But the hero team does more than embody the need for male bonding that our construction of gender definition and difference has produced. It also provides the viewers with multiple points of entry for their identification with the hero.

For those whose sense of masculinity seems to be best achieved through physical or mechanical power, through an aggressive style, B. A. will provide the point of entry. Those whose sense of masculine identity depends more upon leadership and planning, probably different in social situation and age, will find their means of identification in Hannibal. Similarly, Face and Murdock provide other ways of prioritizing the concepts and abilities that constitute masculinity for differently situated males. Elsewhere (Fiske 1987a)

I have shown how the hero team of *Magnum p.i.* works similarly, with, briefly, T. C., the black, embodying physical and mechanical power, Higgins, the majordomo, embodying social constraint and responsibility, and Magnum himself, embodying freedom, individualism, leadership, and power in the service of the weak.

These hero teams, or hero pairs, are always hierarchical with a distinct leader. They embody power relations which appear to be so crucial to masculinity within their own structure. This power differential is frequently expressed in racial difference. The teams often include a black, who almost inevitably is the driver – Mr T, T. C., or Mark in *Ironside*; Starsky, the urban Jew, was the driver for the brainier, college-educated Hutchinson who "happened" to be blond and Aryan. Such mixed-race hero pairs have long roots in cultural history and include the Lone Ranger and Tonto, Captain Ahab and Queequeg, and Huck Finn and Jim. In more recent series, such as *Miami Vice*, the power differential of the mixed-race pair is less marked, though the race difference is still there. The more feminine drama of *Cagney and Lacey* presents a much more equal partnership, though Cagney is both middle-class and blonde Anglo-Saxon, whereas Lacey is working-class and from an Italian family. In our society power is distributed along axes of gender, class, and race, and the correspondence between the domains acts to naturalize the status quo, and the close relationship within which that power is exercised works to minimize gender, class, and racial differences in a display of social cohesion. But despite these unifying forces in the text, the contradictions between the more and the less powerful still exist, as they do in society, and the hero teams are open to this sort of reading. Those denied power by their social position are the more likely to activate these sorts of readings, and the secondary texts frequently cater for them.

The off-screen disagreements between George Peppard, who plays Hannibal, and Mr T, who plays B. A., were widely reported in the press in 1985 and 1986. They worked intertextually to activate the power differences in the primary text, and to act as realism operators that blurred the distinction between the representation and the real by mobilizing an account of the (apparently) real to authenticate the represented relationship. Mr T, in one incident, complained excessively about the service on a ship on which the team were filming. George Peppard tried to calm him down, and the argument escalated. In it, Peppard was playing the father role and Mr T that of the willful child bucking against discipline and social restraint. The power differential between father and son and its consequent tension is rarely as explicit as this in the fictional A-Team, but is there as a subtext available to young or black readers whose social interests would be served by activating it.

□ Gender and narrative form

Brown's (1987a) characteristics of soap operas form a useful framework for comparing masculine drama such as *The A-Team* and feminine drama such as soap opera.

1   Soap operas not only lack *narrative closure*, but appear to actively avoid it; *The A-Team*, on the other hand, has to close the team's narrative in each episode. Of course, this closure is not as final as that of a book or a film, for we know that the same characters will return next week in a similar adventure and the contradictions embodied in the structure of the team remain unresolved.

None the less they must achieve their objective, usually in a climax designed to display masculine performance. The word "climax" is significant for it has both a sexual and a narrative application. Dyer (1985) suggests that this is no coincidence, and argues that the emphasis on the climax and resolution in masculine narrative parallels the importance given to the climax in masculine sexuality.

2   Soap operas emphasize the process of *problem solving, intimate conversation, and the feelings* that people undergo. *The A-Team* emphasizes action, dialogue is minimal and often curt (for curtness connotes masculinity). Determination to succeed replaces feelings, mechanical ingenuity replaces insight into people, and success in problem solving replaces the process. Dyer (1985) suggests that in masculine sexuality and narrative, seduction and foreplay are means to an end; whereas in the feminine they are sources of pleasure in their own right. They involve, in both narrative and sexuality, the feminine values of intimacy and caring.

A simple, if not simplistic, summary of this position would be that feminine sexuality and narrative emphasize the process over the end product, whereas the masculine gives the product priority over the process. Chodorow, quoted by Modleski (1982: 99), suggests that the differences between male and female work in our society reproduce the same structure. Men's work is product-oriented, women's housework (and their lower paid wage work) is a repetitive, endless process. Work patterns, narrative form, and the meanings given to gender difference are all constructs of the same patriarchal culture so it is not surprising that they are based on the same structural play of similarity and difference. Their effectivity in gender politics derives from their relative autonomy within an overdetermined system: that is, work, narrative, and sexuality appear to be separate cultural domains, but in fact they are all subject to the same patriarchal overdetermination so that they all tell the same story. This correspondence between apparently autonomous domains makes the "story" appear natural, and not a cultural product, so it becomes all too easy to accept that these gender differences derive from the physical differences between male and female. This, of course, is what patriarchy desires for it naturalizes male domination and renders it apparently unchallengeable.

Davies (1984b) argues that the prime sexual pleasure offered by soap operas is that of the process of seduction, not its success. This fits well with Modleski's (1982) belief that soap opera pleasure derives from the constant deferment of a goal, from the experience of obstacle after obstacle to the fulfillment of desire.

Shows like *Cagney and Lacey* and *Hill Street Blues* are interesting mixtures of masculine and feminine form. In *Cagney and Lacey* the masculine "end" of the narrative is often neglected in favor of a feminine emphasis on the process by which that end is achieved. In one episode concerning pornography the narrative apparently posed masculine questions: will the two female detectives succeed in convincing the "male" police force and legal system that pornography is not a victimless crime but that all who are involved in it are its victims? Will they also bring a successful conviction against the producer/distributor of pornographic films? Their case hinged on the evidence of a woman star/victim of his films. She was reluctant to testify against him because she would lose her only source of income. In the final scene she entered the precinct and met Cagney and Lacey: the episode ends with close-ups of the three women smiling in their solidarity, their awareness of their common interests as women. The enigma of the narrative has been shifted from the masculine – "Will they nail the pornographer?" – to the feminine – "By what means can women learn to identify and act on their common interests in patriarchy?"

The state of equilibrium with which the episode opens is one that bears the norms of a society that disapproves of pornography and the exploitation of women while remaining patriarchal, but the one on which it finishes leaves the pornography problem unresolved and, instead, shows the women's realization that in such a world they must stand together. The mismatch between the two states derives from the program's mix of masculine and feminine forms.

Part of the representation of the state of equilibrium of the masculine narrative is a jokey scene which turns out to be the enigma of the feminine narrative. In it Cagney and Lacey's car breaks down. Cagney tries to fix it, but fails and loudly dreads the arrival of the police mechanic and his inevitable sexist remarks about women's mechanical incompetence. While they are waiting for him they investigate a shot (which turns out to be part of the filming of a pornographic movie). On their return, they find the legs of the mechanic sticking out from under their car. The mechanic slides out, they see that she is female, and Cagney's face registers the conflicting emotions of relief and disbelief. On seeing that the cops are women, the mechanic raises her eyebrows in masculine disdain and sneers, "It figures!" The scene, of course, is no joke, but sets up the complexities and contradictions of femaleness and femininity within patriarchy. It establishes the enigma of the feminine narrative – can women achieve solidarity? – and sets up the equilibrium of a society in which patriarchal hegemony is largely successful: women like the mechanic underwrite the system by succeeding in it, though their success is only possible through the adoption of masculine habits of thought. This ensures that women are kept divided from each other and thus unable to recognize their gender-class interests.

In the investigation, as in the opening of the episode, this feminine narrative plays second fiddle to the masculine one, but the end of the episode reverses this priority, leaving the masculine unresolved and the feminine at a moment of politically progressive recognition. The progressive end is achieved only by denying the closure of the "main" narrative. We never learn if the pornographer is found guilty, or even if he is brought to trial: we learn only of the process through which women recognize their gender-class interests. Similarly, the episode in which Cagney brings a sexual harassment action against a male superior ends without our knowing if her action is successful. The final shot is of another policewoman coming forward to testify against him despite her previous reluctance to do so.

3   Soap operas have *multiple characters and plots*, while *The A-Team* and other masculine narratives have a single plot, or a clearly defined hierarchy of main and subplots. Soap operas can have up to forty characters, of whom a dozen or more may be important. Masculine narratives usually have a single hero or a tightly knit hero pair or hero team. Soap operas encourage multiple identification and the ability to see an event from a number of different points of view or share a variety of people's reactions to the same incident. Masculine narratives are told from a more singular point of view, they produce a centered reading subject as opposed to the decentered reading subject that soap operas produce. Modleski (1982) summarizes the issue neatly:

> The classic (male) narrative film, is, as Laura Mulvey (1975) points out, structured "around a main controlling figure with whom the spectator can identify." Soap operas continually insist on the insignificance of the individual life. A viewer might at one moment be asked to identify with a woman finally reunited with her lover, only to have that identification broken in a moment of intensity and attention focused on the sufferings of the woman's rival.   (p. 91)

This can be linked to Chodorow's assertion that "feminine personality comes to define itself in relation and connection to other people more than masculine personality does. (In psychoanalytic terms, women are less individuated than men: they have more flexible ego boundaries.)"

To clarify my argument I have couched it in overly simple binary opposi-tions, but not all television is gendered along such clear genre lines. *Hill Street Blues*, for example, mixes both masculine and feminine characteris-tics, and as a result is a cop show that is popular with many women and, significantly, with progressive, if not radical, men.

The difference between centered and decentered reading subjects is partly explained by their different relations to the dominant ideology. Ideology works to produce a centered subject, and a centered subject is thus more likely to live through the practice of the dominant ideology. Conversely, a decentered subject is potentially resistive in that it provides for alternative or oppositional meanings.

Morley's (1986) work has shown the differences between male and female modes of viewing and it is instructive to link these with the differences between "masculine" and "feminine" narratives. The men in his sample of working-class and lower-middle-class London families tended to watch tele-vision with a singular concentration, hushing crying children and women who wanted to talk or engage in other distracting activities. Women, on the other hand, were nearly always doing something else while they watched; they talked, knitted, ironed, or folded clothes. They watched with a dis-persed attention that paralleled the dispersed narrative structure of the "feminine" genres.

This difference, of course, must not be seen as indicating essential differ-ences between men and women: rather it is a product of the politics and practices of the family in capitalism. For the male, the home is a place of leisure and relaxation that he has "earned" by his wage work outside. He can therefore indulge his pleasures in it undistractedly and guiltlessly. For the female, however, the home is the place of work, not leisure, and such leisure activities as watching television have to be fitted in with the unending flow of domestic duties. Housewives in a number of studies (Morley 1986, Seiter *et al.* 1987) report a feeling of guilt if they watch television while doing nothing else. On the other hand, women working outside the house feel no such "guilt" in watching their favorite programs in a "masculine" fashion (Seiter *et al.* 1987).

Similarly, homebound women will often use the video recorder to time-shift their programs to their "off duty" hours – usually very early or very late in the day or occasionally in mid-afternoon – when the rest of the family is not around. It is the presence of husband and children that determines these women's hours of work: in the family's absence they feel free to indulge themselves in their cultural pleasures undistractedly and guiltlessly (Morley 1986, Rogge 1987). The video recorder plays an important role in women's ability to avoid rather than confront male power, and to create spaces, however marginalized, for their own cultural pleasures.

218

4   We have argued above that television in general maintains a closer correspondence between its time and real time, than do films or books. But within television, soap operas *make this correspondence as close as possible*, whereas masculine narratives work to compress time. Their emphasis on achievement leads them to concertina the process to concentrate on the performance-climax that produces the result. They do not give the same impression that their characters are "living" in the gap between episodes, and contain little or no "memory" between one episode and any other. The masculine characters and narratives "live" in their moments of performance only, and in these moments time is manipulated to maximize the masculine performance.

Time is not only compressed to speed through the nonaction scenes, it is extended by slow motion to dwell on those of action/performance. So the shots of cars making huge leaps or overturning are always enhanced by low camera angles and slow motion which magnifies the power and the beauty of the performance. Slow motion is used in sport to celebrate and display the male body in action, to produce a sense of awe by making the physical performance appear beautiful. The male body in television sport does not consist merely of brutish muscularity, but is aestheticized and thus given positive ideological values (see chapter 13). So in action drama, slow motion is used to eroticize power, to extend the moment of climax.

In Hollywood's exposé of its own tricks of the trade, its conducted tours of Universal Studios, there is a "real-life" display by the A-Team, or rather by stand-ins for the "real" A-Team. Its intention is to glorify the team's prowess, but its effect is the opposite. The ramps from which cars fly through the air are less than a meter high, the leaps are completed almost as they begin, and viewed from above on the ranked seating, the whole performance is minimized. Without the masculinity intensifiers of slow motion, low camera angle, and celebratory editing, the climactic performance of the A-Team appears disappointingly ordinary.

5   *Segmentation* also is a characteristic of television in general, but it is more pronounced in soap operas than in masculine narratives. The abrupt switching from plot to plot is absent in the singular plotted narrative, where the segmentation is confined to rapid switches between scenes of the same plot. This segmentation follows more closely the "masculine" laws of cause and effect with their consequent narrative and ideological closure. The freer segmentation of soap opera, however, evokes the more open "feminine" laws of association. *Hill Street Blues* with its multiple plots and characters, its rapid switching from plot to plot, its sense that characters live between episodes, its "memory" from episode to episode combines many of the elements of soap opera with the action and achievement characteristic of masculine narrative. It is, significantly, one of the most popular cop shows with women.

6 and 7   In soap operas *major male characters are often sensitive men* and *major female characters tend to be professionals*, or otherwise powerful outside the home. In masculine narratives sensitivity is seen as a threat to masculinity and women are victims in need of male succor. Power is confined to the men, sensitivity to the women.

8   In soap operas *the setting is home* or a place which functions as home, a place where people meet, talk, and are established in their relationships. In masculine narrative the action is public, not domestic, it is visible and exterior for masculine success needs public acclaim and visibility. The issues it deals with are public ones of murder, money, power, terrorism, whereas soap operas deal with domestic issues of relationships and "women's issues" such as child abuse. Crime may be a regular ingredient of soap operas but it is not treated as a problem to be solved and cleared up, but rather as a source of reactions to be experienced and talked about.

Morley (1986) reports clear genre preferences between men and women. Men claim to prefer programs that increase their knowledge of the "world out there," and therefore of their power over it and their ability to act in it. The men in his study consistently expressed preferences for the national news, documentaries, and sport. When they liked fiction, they tended to like "realistic" fiction. Women, on the other hand, liked fictional programs, such as soaps, which were concerned with what Ang (1985) calls "emotional realism," sensitivity, and expressiveness, in contrast to the "empirical realism" preferred by men. One exception to this was women's strong preference for the local news, particularly of crime:

> *Crime Watch* – that's a good program to watch because it gives you some idea of what to look out for – what the kids should look out for as well. (Morley 1986: 73)

This finding is supported by Rogge's (1987) work in Germany. A single mother of three reported to him:

> Take the police report, for example. I think Irene should start to look at that, too . . . sometimes they've got to learn to take care.
> (Rogge 1987: 12–13)

Local news, and crime news, with its picture of the immediate outside world as a threat, is readily incorporated in the maternal caring role that women conventionally fill in our society's version of the family. The local news is the interface between the domestic and the public.

Masculine narratives use these characteristics to embody simple oppositions to mark gender difference:

```
sensitive : tough
domestic : professional
 private : public
 indoors : outdoors.
```

They then add *weak : strong* as an ideological value judgment to the structure. Feminine narratives refuse such clear value judgments. Similarly, they refuse to confine femininity to the lefthand side of the structure and masculinity to the right and thus deny the ability of such oppositions to construct meanings of gender. Masculine narratives clearly place masculinity on the right of the structure and femininity on the left; soap operas deny such a simple strategy of gender definition.

Ross (1987) suggests that this simplistic representation of masculinity is being modified in a way that softens "the contours of a traditional image of the redblooded male, competitive omnipotent, irredeemably sexist and emotionally illiterate" (p. 147).

This "softening" is occurring most markedly outside television, in fashion magazines, for example, but Ross argues that in *Miami Vice*, as in music video, television is beginning to modify its traditional representation of masculinity. On one level, the show is as traditionally masculine as any other cop show. Crockett and Tubbs are a typical hero team, whose differences supply each other's lack: both are tough, competitive, bonded in a male heterosexuality, and women are regularly exscribed from the narrative.

But against this, Ross argues, are signs of a new masculinity:

> As an expression of a genre soundly committed to delivering messages about social difference *Miami Vice* presents a metastatement about this generic imperative when, in its habitual confusion about the respective identities of undercover police, decoys, stool pigeons, and cops who have actually crossed the line, the central representational problem is the difficulty of exhibiting difference at all. In the case of Crockett and Tubbs, power is ascribed in the most superficial sartorial flourishes and in the obvious superiority of their good looks. (p. 152)

The idea that masculinity is expressed through surface appearance, through the language of pastel-shaded fashion, does not subvert the traditional masculinity of action, but brings to it a potentially contradictory, potentially "softening," dimension. *Miami Vice* shows the traditionally tough, bonded, masculine hero pair accommodating the newer, style-conscious, less differentiated masculinity without apparently giving up any of its established narrative terrain. But the contradictions are there, and they open the narrative up to pleasures other than those offered by *The A-Team*, the pleasures of style, look, and appearance that our culture has traditionally associated with the feminine. Similarly, the opening up of the male hero pair

221

to a male/female pair can be seen as traditional masculinity accommodating the new woman within its power structure, and attempting to extend the pleasures of a masculine narrative to female audiences.

The cop show genre, like all genres, modifies its conventions in a dialectical relationship with changes in social values. The extreme masculinity of *The A-Team* is challenged by the admission of feminine values, weakly in *Scarecrow and Mrs King* and *Hart to Hart*, but more strongly in *Remington Steele*, and very threateningly indeed in *Cagney and Lacey*. *Miami Vice's* challenge to the meanings of masculinity may be the most insidious and politically effective, because it occurs not at the level of *what* is represented, but *how* it is represented. The other shows may represent women performing "masculine" roles, but *Miami Vice* encodes masculinity differently. As *Cagney and Lacey* refuses (some of) the conventional encodings of the feminine, so *Miami Vice*, more explicitly, demands a change in the encodings of the masculine.

The close connection between genre and gender is evidence of the social construction of both. The psychological dimension of gender becomes a problem that requires narrative expression only when it meets our ideological practices and the gender roles they produce and maintain themselves in. There are important differences in the social meanings of masculinity and femininity in capitalism, and it is not surprising that these differences are transposed into textual differences between genres. The relationship between the social and the textual is never clear or singular and is certainly oversimplified to the point of distortion by the belief that the generic conventions by which gender is represented textually do nothing more than reproduce and maintain the social.

The crucial differences between cop adventure shows and soap operas are not to be found in their textual conventions, but rather in the reading relations they invite. Feminine genres, because they articulate the concerns of a gender whose interests are denied by the dominant ideology, must, if they are to be popular, be open enough to admit of a variety of oppositional, or, at least, resistive readings. The genre, then, has fewer attempts at closure or at centering the reading subject. Masculine genres, on the other hand, speak to audiences who are positioned quite differently to the dominant ideology, and whose reading strategy is more likely to be one of negotiation by which they seek to accommodate their social differences with patriarchy, rather than one of resistance.

In terms of class, race, or age, however, oppositional or resisting stances are more likely. The tension between Hannibal and B. A. is not always resolved in the terms favored by the power in their relationship, that is, it is not always the values of the white, older officer class that provide the point of resolution. Those to whom B. A. offers an articulation of their sense of social subordination may well find oppositional or resisting pleasures in the impossibility of ever subordinating totally such a powerful and intransigent figure as he. But the genre does not offer similar opportunities to interrogate the patriarchal values of masculinity. In the ideology of gender, its closure appears to be almost complete: in the ideologies of class, race, and age it offers much more open spaces within which to resist or evade its hegemonic thrust.

Chapter 12

Pleasure and play

Whatever the controversy about television's role in our culture, there is no doubt that people enjoy it, and that watching it is a major source of pleasure in our lives. This word "pleasure" occurs widely in recent critical writings and appears to be crucial to our understanding of popularity. But, like many widely used terms, it is remarkably difficult to pin down and define. It is also multidiscursive, that is, it means differently in different discourses.

Thus, the psychoanalytic use of the term tends to relate it with desire and places it as the main motivator of human action. Feminist work deriving from Lacan suggests that while masculine and feminine pleasures may be experienced differently in patriarchy, in general the origin of pleasure and unpleasure is located in the early psychic process common to all human infants, and its essential structure is laid down before social influences such as gender, class, race, education, or religion come into the picture. In psychoanalytic terms, the pleasure principle comes close to being a human universal.

Barthes (1975b), however, uses the word "*plaisir*" to refer to a pleasure which is essentially cultural in origin, and the more ecstatic "*jouissance*" to refer to a physical pleasure, located, like sexual orgasm, in the senses of the body rather than in the workings of the subconscious. "*Jouissance*" has similarities with Freud's "affect" in which the intensity of the experience is its important dimension.

Then there is a third discursive use, which is broadly social in emphasis. It seeks the meaning of pleasure in its relationship to the social structure and to the social practices of the subjects who experience it. While the first two uses look for essentially abstract and singular meanings, this third one tends towards more concrete and plural ones.

These three categories, the psychoanalytic, the physical, and the social, constantly leak into each other, and the pleasure or pleasures experienced at any one time are likely to include elements of all. The categories are, like all categories, explanatory strategies, they exist for a heuristic purpose, not in their own right. But while it is important to insist on the differences between them, it is equally important to point out that all of them depend, to a greater or lesser extent, on the relationship between pleasure and power. Broadly, the psychoanalytic view of pleasure sees it as the product of accommodation to the dominant ideology. According to Mulvey (1975), pleasure is the reward offered to the conforming spectator by patriarchal cinema: it is the prime hegemonic agent.

In both its other discourses, however, pleasure can be associated with resistance and subversion. For Barthes as for many of the postmodernists, pleasure can be the opposite of ideology, not, as for Mulvey, its reward.

☐ Psychoanalysis and pleasure

Mulvey (1975) in her influential article "Visual Pleasure and Narrative Cinema" turned for her theoretical base to Freud's theory of voyeurism – the pleasure and power of looking. She argues that the spectator of mainstream Hollywood cinema is positioned like the peeping Tom: the screen is like the window of the lighted room through which the invisible, unacknowledged voyeur looks. His (for voyeurism is a masculine pleasure) ability to see the secret, the private lives of others, gives the voyeur a power over them. This voyeuristic pleasure is produced by the masculine look at the female body, so the typical progress of Hollywood narrative is male action that advances the plot alternating with interruptions during which the female body is gazed at or possessed by the male protagonist. The male protagonist becomes the embodiment of the masculine spectator and the masculine "look" of the camera upon the pro-filmic event. The visual pleasure of looking at and possessing the female is a reward for successful male action in the preceding segment of narrative. This produces a masculine reading subject, even though the cinema audience may be composed of both males and females. In patriarchy, women can be constructed as masculine subjects and can consequently experience masculine pleasures. They, like men, can subject the female body to a masculine gaze.

Alongside the power of voyeurism goes the cinematic practice of the fetishization of the female. A fetish, according to Freud, is the overvaluation of a threat. The movie camera "worships" the female form to excess, as a way of defusing the castration threat and Oedipal guilt that the woman bears. This produces the cinematic fragmentation of the female body, as the camera worships, in close-up, the eyes, lips, thighs, hair, and almost any part of the female body.

For Mulvey, the pleasures produced by the satisfaction of the voyeuristic desire are perfectly aligned with the requirements of patriarchy and she comes close to constructing an unbreakable relationship among patriarchy, pleasure, and the natural differences between male and female. She appears to ground patriarchy in human nature and to explain the pleasure of cinema by treating patriarchal power as indistinguishable from the nature of human sexuality. As a feminist, she is thus led to a call for a destruction of pleasure as we currently experience it, and for its replacement by a new pleasure, the pleasure of defamiliarizing what is taken for granted and in producing a new way of seeing.

But mainstream pleasure results from finding the structures of infant sexuality reproduced in the structures of mainstream cinema, which leads the spectator to accommodate himself or herself to the dominant ideology, by adopting the textually produced subject position with all its subjection to the demands of patriarchy and of human sexuality. Pleasure is thus reactionary, for both the dominant ideology and Freudian explanations of sexuality work to naturalize the patriarchal status quo. Mulvey does, however, admit of the possibility of a radical pleasure, but does not elaborate in any detail how this may be produced.

Mulvey's argument may hold up well for cinema, but it translates less convincingly to television. The huge, bright cinema screen and the anonymous darkness of the auditorium reproduce much more precisely the situation of the peeping Tom than does the far less imperative television screen situated in the family living room in the middle of ordinary family life. Television is more interactive than voyeuristic. Its realism, which certainly has a voyeuristic dimension, is constantly fractured both by the segmentation of the television text and by its mode of reception. Its viewers, unlike cinema spectators, are not granted the same voyeuristic power over, and pleasure in, the image, just as they are less subjected to the positioning of the realist narrative.

While there are problems with applying Mulvey's theory of pleasure to television, it still has some explanatory power. The fragmentation of the female body into a fetish object is commonplace in commercials, particularly those for cosmetic products. The mobilization of masculine desire in the female viewer and the construction for her of a masculine reading position from which she can make sense of her own body through masculine eyes is an obvious economic strategy of the industry.

Similarly, there are numerous representations of the female body as an object of the masculine gaze and a producer of the voyeuristic power/ pleasure. The models that decorate the prizes in game shows, or that provide much of the "scenery" in shows like *Miami Vice* or *Mike Hammer*, are clear evidence of this voyeuristic pleasure at work. So, too, is television's tendency to confine women on the screen to the age of maximum sexuality and to physical types that conform to the patriarchal sense of attractiveness and normalcy for the women. Fat women, for instance, appear only rarely, as do pregnant women. In Australia, 1985, a female announcer/reporter was barred from appearing on screen when she was visibly pregnant. She invoked the law on sexual discrimination, won her case, and was allowed to introduce an opera. But the voyeuristic pleasure of the male requires an "available" woman, so that she can be possessed by the look: a pregnant woman, however sexually attractive, is not available for possession in the same way.

But this view of pleasure can only account for *some* of television's appeal. In particular, it allows for no possibility of resistance to the dominant ideology and no possibility of viewer-generated meanings, or at least, that there is no pleasure to be gained from these possibilities.

☐ Pleasure and social control

Barthes's (1975b) twofold notion of pleasure provides one way of addressing these difficulties. He uses the words *plaisir* and *jouissance* to distinguish between two different types of pleasure produced in the reading of a text. He stresses that pleasure, of either type, is not to be found in the text itself, but in its conjuncture with the reader; the theory is concerned not with what the text *is* but with what it *does*. He frequently uses the metaphor of the economy of the text, a metaphor that likens the generation and circulation of meanings and pleasures to the generation and circulation of wealth. The words or images in the text are exchanged for pleasure, the commodity that the reader buys is not a sense of the world, but pleasure in the processes of representing and figuring that world.

Freud, though not quoted directly by Barthes, is lurking just below the surface of his theory, firstly in Barthes's assumption that human beings always seek pleasure and avoid unpleasure, and secondly in his belief that pleasure in our society always produces two policemen – a political one and a psychoanalytic one. Pleasure is, in western societies, typically classed as an indulgence, the expression of selfishness, idleness, vanity and thus productive of guilt. The Church's constant attempt to curb the "pleasures" of the flesh was eagerly taken up by capitalism and transformed into the Protestant work ethic with its acceptance of only that pleasure which had been "earned" and which was used responsibly (i.e. to prepare the worker for more work). Bennett (1983a) has traced the ways in which the nineteenth-century middle classes attempted to control and channel the leisure of the emerging working class into ideologically acceptable forms.

The long tradition of attacks on television (preceded by attacks on comics and other popular forms) is part of this movement. The attacks use the discourses of morality, legality, or aesthetics in order to displace their actual origin in class-based social power. Television is immoral, the arguments typically run, because it shows extramarital sex, or it undermines law and order in its glorification of violence and crime, and it degrades people's ability to discriminate through its crudities, its crassness, and its appeal to the lowest common denominator. Similar arguments were used to ban the popular fairs and festivals in the nineteenth century (see Waites, Bennett, and Martin 1982) and stem from the same unvoiced fear that the pleasures of the subordinate classes are necessarily disruptive because they lie outside the control of the bourgeoisie. But class power is obviously open to contestation, so pleasure cannot be suppressed openly in the name of class: rather attempts to control it have to be seen to work through more universally accepted and thus less challengeable discourses such as those of morality, the law, or aesthetics.

Casting the popular as the degraded, the illegal, or the immoral justifies the policing action of the bourgeoisie in their constant attempts to devalue or curb it. It also legitimates Barthes's psychoanalytic policeman and the guilt through which he works. The histories of capitalism and of Christianity show how their fear of pleasure as disruptive, as hostile to their social power, produces the desire to subject it to moral, economic, and political control.

For Barthes pleasure is opposed to ideological control, though *plaisir* less so than *jouissance*. *Plaisir* is a mundane pleasure that is essentially confirming, particularly of one's sense of identity. It is a product of culture and the sense of identity produced by that culture. While Mulvey's (1975) masculine pleasure of mainstream cinema may be similar to *plaisir*, Barthes allows, in the way that Mulvey does not, for an oppositional pleasure. The pleasure experienced by more liberal or even radical viewers of *Hill Street Blues* or *Cagney and Lacey* is a form of *plaisir* to be found in confirming their social identity as one that opposes or at least interrogates dominant social values. Barthes gives comparatively little attention to *plaisir*, yet it is this more mundane, everyday sort of pleasure that is probably more typical of television. The conditions under which television is normally watched are not conducive to that intensity of experience which is necessary for *jouissance*. But *plaisir*, with its stronger political and social dimension, may be at least as progressive and interrogative a form of pleasure as *jouissance* whose roots seem to lie primarily in ideological evasion. *Plaisir*, too, is plural: the variety of social identities it confirms requires us to think of a diversity of *plaisirs*, whereas there is only one *jouissance*. And diversity is, itself, both an agency and an effect of resistance.

Jouissance is translated into English as bliss, ecstasy, or orgasm, and Barthes constantly uses sexual metaphors to explain it. It is a pleasure of the body, experienced through heightened sensualities that relate it to human nature, rather than culture. It is produced by the physical signifiers of the text – the "grain" that some singing voices have, but others, technically as perfect, lack. It is located in the body of the text and is responded to by the body of the reader – Barthes (1975b) uses words like flesh, throat, patina, voluptuousness, to describe it. It is, he says, an articulation of the body, not of meaning or of language:

> the language lined with flesh, a text where we can hear the grain of the throat, the patina of consonants, the voluptuousness of vowels, a whole carnal stereophony: the articulation of the body, of the tongue, not that of meaning, of language. A certain art of singing can give an idea of this local writing; but since melody is dead, we may find it more easily today at the cinema. In fact, it suffices that the cinema capture the sound of speech *close up* (this is, in fact, the generalized definition of the "grain" of writing) and make us hear in their materiality, their sensuality, the breath, the gutturals, the fleshiness of the lips, a whole presence of the human muzzle (that the voice, that writing, be as fresh, supple, lubricated, delicately granular and vibrant as an animal's muzzle) to succeed in shifting the signified a great distance and in throwing, so to speak, the anonymous body of the actor into my ear: it granulates, it crackles, it caresses, it grates, it cuts, it comes: that is bliss (*jouissance*).   (pp. 66–7)

Jouissance escapes the control of culture and of meaning by "distancing the signified" and thus foregrounding the signifier, particularly the way it is materialized (the grain, the breath of the voice, the fleshiness of the lips). It is found in the material body of the sign, in the sensuality of the body of the reader. In this way it is always erotic and its peak is properly described as orgasm.

Jouissance occurs at the moment of the breakdown of culture. "Neither culture nor its destruction is erotic: it is the seam between them, the fault, the flow, which becomes so" (Barthes 1975b: 7). Sexual orgasm is the moment when the body escapes culture, or, at least, makes that escape appear possible. The body and its sensualities oppose subjectivity, they provide a pleasure that is not to be found in the subject and its construction in culture by ideology.

The close-ups in soap opera may produce *jouissance*. The intense materiality of emotion in the magnified quiver of the mouth's corner, the narrowing of the eyes, the breathy wetness of the voice may produce tears in the viewer quite independent of, or even counter to, the narrative of what is said, of what is felt, and the way they work in the subjectivity. The loss is experienced in the body as the loss of subjectivity. (Ecstasy or orgasm can, of course, produce tears as an appropriate physical response.) "A good cry" which Brown (1987a) identifies as one of the pleasures of soap opera is not only the *plaisir* of expressing emotions and an identity which social life frequently represses, but often the *jouissance* of reading with the body, of establishing a presence that is outside culture, outside ideology, because it is not concerned with meaning (either of self or of the world) but with presence and intensity.

229

While the distinction between *plaisir* and *jouissance* is often difficult to make in practice, the importance of Barthes's theory lies in its shift of attention to readers in their differences away from the central, universal notions of pleasure deriving from a mix of psychoanalysis and ideology. Pleasure is decentralized and is part of the reading that creates a text out of a work (see chapter 6); central to it, then, is the sense that the reader has some control over the production of meaning.

Lovell (1983) offers an account of pleasure that has superficial similarities to Mulvey's because it is gender-specific, and to Barthes's, because it admits of resisting pleasures, but differs from both in its historical specificity which inserts it into patriarchal capitalism. She suggests that the clear division established by nineteenth-century capitalism between the public-political world of the man and the private-domestic world of the woman has resulted in the feminization of pleasure in the way it has been confined to private and personal life, while the world of "the serious" has been left to the masculine. But her earlier work (Lovell 1980) has shown how popular pleasures can be resistive, so we may argue that the privatization of pleasure allows for its articulation in the body and the senses, and its feminization allows it to be articulated with the culture of the repressed. Schwichtenburg (1986) insists that "it is important . . . to render pleasure out of bounds," for this sort of pleasure lies in the refusal of the social control inscribed in the "bounds." While there is clearly a pleasure in exerting social power, the popular pleasures of the subordinate are necessarily found in resisting, evading, or offending this power. Popular pleasures are those that empower the subordinate, and they thus offer political resistance, even if only momentarily and even if only in a limited terrain.

□ Pleasure, play, and control

Barthes (1977c) suggests that the pleasure of creating a text out of a work involves playing with the text, and he exploits the full polysemy of "play" in his ideas. Firstly, he says, the text has "play" in it, like a door whose hinges are loose. This "play" is exploited by the reader who "plays" the text as a musician plays a score: s/he interprets it, activates it, gives it a living presence. In doing this, the reader plays a text as one plays a game: s/he voluntarily accepts the rules of the text in order to participate in the practice that those rules make possible and pleasurable; the practice is, of course, the production of meanings and identities. In a text, as in a game, the rules are there to construct a space within which freedom and control of self are possible. Games and texts construct ordered worlds within which the players/readers can experience the pleasures of both freedom and control: in particular, for our purposes, playing the text involves the freedom of making and controlling meanings.

Freud draws our attention to the infant's "fort-da" game in which the child continually throws away a loved object only to demand its return. His explanation is that the game is enacting the disappearance and reappearance of the mother, and that in playing it the child is not only symbolizing his or her anxieties about the mother's return, but is also beginning to use symbols to control the meanings of his or her environment, and in so doing is exploring the relationship between the real and its representation.

Palmer (1986) provides many examples of children playing with television. At the simplest level, children enjoyed the control that the set gave them over the signifiers themselves – they played with the channel switches or tuning buttons to distort the image or make it disappear and reappear in a sort of electronic fort-da game. She comments on one, not untypical, pair: "Part of the delight of Amy and her brother seemed to come from playing out their mastery over the little box" (p. 58).

This empowering play with the mechanism of reproduction extended to playing with the representations themselves. Sometimes this took the form of fairly straightforward reenactment, as when girls in the schoolyard replayed scenes from the previous night's episode of *Prisoner*, but sometimes these reenactments were satirical – they were critical reformulations of representations of which the children disapproved. The fact that children explored their television shows from inside their experience of watching them instead of adopting the adult critical method of treating them as objects for analysis in no way invalidates the critical process in which they were engaged. Indeed, children's play may be more productive than adult criticism, for it can involve a remaking of the program to suit their social experience that is more creative than the dismissive negativity typical of so many adults. This "remaking" is a source of pleasure and power:

> Make-believe play and pretending is commonly associated with good feelings, with "interest and joy". Researchers have suggested that this is because play is a kind of "power transformation by which the child ... reconstitutes a miniature world which follows his or her rules" (Singer and Singer 1980:1). (Palmer 1986:113)

Similarly, Seal argues that children's games frequently explore the boundary between the symbolic and the real. The arguments between the child who plays according to the rules – "You're dead" – and the one who brings "reality" into it – "No I'm not – see I'm still breathing" – are arguments about who has the power to construct a representation of reality that is binding upon others.

231

This is fundamentally similar to the play of women viewers of soap opera that both Ang (1985) and Hobson (1982) report. The pleasure of these viewers in playing with the relationship between the representation and the real questions the power of the program to control the representational illusion and is a way of exercising control over their own viewing practices. Their active choice of whom to "identify" with (e.g. Sue Ellen or Pamela in *Dallas*) and their choice to identify or not in the process that I have called "implication-extrication" are both examples of exerting control through play.

The play may not in itself be resistive or subversive, but the control or empowerment that it entails produces a self-esteem in the subordinate that at least makes resistance or subversion possible. Radway (1984) has found that some women readers of romance novels reported that they chose to read the novels in the face of husbandly disapproval and found meanings in them that supported feminine values and criticized masculine ones. This choice and this validation of a subordinated value system gave them the self-confidence to assert themselves more strongly and to resist the patriarchal power of the male in the family.

Similarly, a study of young girl fans of Madonna (Fiske 1987a) showed that a major source of their pleasure was Madonna's control over her own image (or meaning) and the sense that this control could be devolved to them. They consistently saw Madonna as a woman who used the discourse of patriarchal sexuality to assert her control over that discourse and therefore over her own sexuality. Her sexuality was not represented in music video as a source of pleasure for men, but for herself and her girl fans. She used signs and images from a masculine discourse in order to assert her independence from men, from male approval, and therefore from that discourse. This was a particularly important source of pleasure for young girls because, as Williamson (1986) points out:

> she retains all the bravado and exhibitionism that most girls start off with until the onset of "womanhood" knocks it out of them. ... She does in public what most girls do in private, like a little girl in an adult world with no one to say "No". This gives an enormous sense of released energy, which is itself positive. ... And Madonna is never a victim, never passive, [her] persona is one of conscious ebullient confidence in her sexual image, utterly unembarrassed: this is the exact opposite of the sense of shame that poisons young girls' enjoyment of their own bodies from the moment they open a teenage magazine. (p. 47)

Madonna's music videos explore this boundary between the rules that conventionally govern the representation of sexuality in patriarchy and the sociosexual experience of young girls and their subcultural needs. They rapidly adopted the Madonna "look" which tore the signs of conventional female fashion (lacy gloves, ribbons, religious jewelry, peroxided hair, etc.) out of their original context and thus freed them from their original meanings. The meanings of the Madonna look, as of the Madonna videos, cannot be precisely specified. But that is precisely the point, the pleasure that they give is not the pleasure of *what* they say, but of their assertion of the right and the power of a severely subordinated subculture to make their own statements, their own meanings. Madonna's invitation to her girl fans to play with the conventions of patriarchy shows them that they are not necessarily subject to those conventions but can exercise some control over their relationship to patriarchy and thus over the sense of their identity.

Madonna's emphasis on style, on "the Madonna look," is a denial of meaning and of the ideology and power that it would bear. It is an assertion of the surface – the crucifix is a shape not a meaning – of the signifier, and of the ease with which the powerless can play with images/commodities to gain the power and pleasure of making their own personalized image-identity.

Rules have inscribed within them both the power they convey and its origin. Gilligan (1982) makes the point that men in patriarchy think and work through rules, because rules allow them to dominate: the women playing with the system of representation in soap opera are like children playing in that both subordinated "classes" are using play to question the rules that maintain their subordination. Rules, then, work in a similar way to ideology to maintain the power base in its current location. Like ideology, they emanate from a sociocentral source and attempt to construct social identities in relation to this sociocentrality.

But pleasure is not produced or experienced centrally: pleasure is decentered or centrifugal. So the school students' readings of *Prisoner* (chapter 5) were pleasurable because they were centered in their interests, were in their control, and because they resisted the centered, centripetal power that constantly worked to subject them. Many of the programs that are most popular with children are productive of this centrifugal pleasure that questions the rules and the central control of the system.

Barthes's shift from his earlier work where he saw ideology as central to the understanding of texts in culture (e.g. *Mythologies*) to his foregrounding of pleasure (e.g. *The Pleasure of the Text*) is a shift from the centripetal to the centrifugal. The centrifugal model of pleasure allows for a diversity of pleasures "around the circumference" and suggests a line of force in active opposition to the centripetal force that attempts to center control at a point of ideological and social unity. So Barthes moves away from seeking to explain a text by referring to its singular ideology towards the plurality of pleasures it can offer in its moments of reading. Pleasure may be *provoked* by the text, but it can only be *experienced* by the reader in the reading. It can thus differ from reader to reader, and even from reading to reading. Barthes suggests that any one reader reading any one text at different times may experience different pleasures, or none, at each reading. While this notion locates pleasure in the reader rather than the text and emphasizes difference rather than homogeneity, it does imply a randomness which is little help in explaining the process.

I would prefer to suggest that the variety of pleasures is a function of the variety of socially situated viewers. For those in easy accommodation with the dominant ideology, this pleasure will be conforming and reactionary, but it will still be experienced as self-generated: the subject will feel that he or she is voluntarily adopting a social position that happens to conform to the dominant ideology and is finding genuine pleasure in it. This, of course, is pleasure acting as the motor of hegemony.

But for those whose accommodation to the system is less complete, an essential component of pleasure must be an evasion, or at least a negotiation, of dominant ideological practice, the ability to shake oneself free from its constraints. This then opens up spaces for subcultures or groups to find their own pleasures in relationship to the ideology they are evading. Pleasure, in this subcultural role, helps to preserve and legitimate the heterogeneity of society and is thus properly seen as oppositional to the homogenizing force of ideology and can be summed up as the pleasure/power to be different. Television, like the society it serves, contains both tendencies in active contradiction.

☐ Pleasure and rule breaking

One of the pleasures of play is its ability to explore the relationships between rules and freedom. Rules are the means by which social control is exercised, and result in a social order that works to control the disruptive, anarchic forces of nature. Play enacts the opposition between freedom and control, between nature and culture.

Huizinga (1949) concludes that play, or the spirit of play, is essential to all cultural forms, including those of law, war, diplomacy, business, marriage, education, and the arts. The essence of play is that it is voluntary and therefore free, and that it creates order. The order that it creates is in the control of the players or, at least, is one voluntarily accepted by them, but the orderliness is never total, for it has built into it chanciness, the impossibility of knowing what will happen. The main structuring principle of play is the tension between social order and the "freedom" of anarchy or chance.

In sport this tension is as controlled as possible, technically by the referee and socially by the surrounding moral system of "responsibility" that centers sport into the dominant ideology. So "responsible" television coverage and commentary underpins the authority of the referee and the ideology of "fair play" which means playing both within the rules and the larger "spirit" of the game. But "popular" taste demands that television zoom in on the moments of rule-breaking, the fouls and fights, the professional "plays" that operate on or beyond the boundaries of the rules.

In *Rock 'n' Wrestling* (see chapter 13), for example, the impotence of the referee is a major part of the pleasure. The constant rule breaking of the wrestlers and their coaches indicates their refusal to accept the social roles imposed upon them. This can be read specifically, as the conflict between wild, "natural" masculinity and social control, or it can signify more generally the arbitrariness of rules and roles, and the "naturalness" of breaking or exceeding them. Similarly, in *TV Bloopers and Practical Jokes* what appears to be the "naturalness of the real" breaks through the roles and the rules of normal, conventional television. Both programs are playful and pleasurable in similar ways for they demonstrate that rule-governed systems are both arbitrary and fragile. Rules are one of the hegemonic forces through which the dominant try to win the consent of the subordinate to the control of their "unruliness." The pleasures of breaking rules or exposing their arbitrariness are resistive pleasures of the subordinate.

Many of the shows that give pleasure to children play with the limits of rule-governed systems. Shows like *Ripley's Believe It or Not*, or *Arthur C. Clarke's Mysterious World*, explore the wonders of nature that exist on or beyond the margin of rational scientific explanation. The shows demonstrate how nature itself keeps breaking through the rules that have been devised in order to understand and master it. Natural history documentaries, which are adult versions of these shows, are much less interrogative and skeptical of the rules. They tend to be either scientific and educational, in which case they exemplify science's power to explain and account for the wonders of nature, or they are unabashedly anthropomorphic, such as many of those produced by Walt Disney. In this case they either construct nature as a microcosm of the American suburbs, in which cute baby animals are protected and provided for by their hard-pressed parents until they are old enough to fend for themselves, or they make nature into something for human beings to wonder at, a wonder that celebrates an ingenious and intricate system of life on earth of which we are implicitly a part (see Turner 1985). In either case they are rule-bound, and their pleasures are ideologically conformist and celebratory, and available mainly to those who have accommodated, or are in the process of accommodating, themselves to the social system. This type of natural history program is frequently parentally approved viewing for children: *Ripley's Believe It or Not* is more likely to be parentally frowned upon but enjoyed by the children.

□ Empowering play

The play that produces this multiplicity of pleasures for the subordinate has a number of defining characteristics. First, it is structured according to rules and conventions that replicate, but often invert, those that operate in society. Unlike the rules of the social world, the rules of play are voluntarily adopted for they delimit the space within which the player can exercise control over meanings and events. Second, the player adopts a role of his or her choosing: even though the repertoire of roles may be limited, the sense of choice is far greater than in the adoption of the already written roles that society prepares for us. This voluntary adoption of player-chosen roles within player-chosen rules is liberating in that it inverts the process of social subjection. The player can implicate him- or herself into a role in play in a way that makes that role appear as "real" as the roles played in social life: the difference lies in the player's ability to implicate him/herself in, or extricate him/herself from, the role at will in an empowering and controlled movement between the world of play and the world of the social.

In so far as play is a representation of certain aspects of the social world, the power of play involves the power to play with the boundary between the representation and the real, to insert oneself into the process of representation so that one is not subjected by it, but, conversely, is empowered by it. The pleasures of play derive directly from the players' ability to exert control over rules, roles, and representations – those agencies that in the social are the agencies of subjection, but in play can be agents of liberation and empowerment. Play, for the subordinate, is an active, creative, resistive response to the conditions of their subordination: it maintains their sense of subcultural difference in the face of the incorporating forces of the dominant ideology. The pleasures of television are best understood not in terms of a homogeneous psychological model, but rather in those of a heterogeneous, sociocultural one.

In many ways play is a more productive concept than pleasure because it asserts its activity, its creativity. Play is active pleasure: it pushes rules to the limits and explores the consequences of breaking them; centralized pleasure is more conformist. Television may well produce both sorts of pleasure, but its typical one is the playful pleasure that derives from, and enacts, that source of all power for the subordinate, the power to be different.

□ Pleasure and textuality

Television's playfulness is a sign of its semiotic democracy, by which I mean its delegation of production of meanings and pleasures to its viewers. The reading relations that it invites are ones of greater or lesser equality. Its unwrittenness means that it does not set itself up as the *authority* (the pun between "author" and "authority" is far from accidental): it has no singular authorial voice proposing a singular way of looking at the world. The author role is delegated to, or at least shared with, its viewers. Television is a producerly text that invites a producerly set of reading relations: the production of meaning is shared between text and viewer so that television does not preserve its authorial power and privilege.

By foregrounding its authorial role and therefore its textuality, it offers the viewer access to its discursive practice. In sport and news, for instance, the discursive struggle of the author function that is involved in making sense of events as they happen is made visible and therefore accessible. Showing events, or rather representations of them, alongside their narrativization into commentary or news story, opens up the process of that narrativization, and the difference between it and the "live" events differently represented by the camera make the process of representation visible and thus part of the meanings and pleasures of the program.

In sport the authorial role is played by the commentators – but their "story" is told as the viewer watches the game "live." This "live" game is, of course, still mediated but it has a higher modality than the commentary, and any contradictions between the high modality of the (less written) game and the low modality of the commentator's story of the game invite the viewer to disagree, to produce his or her meanings (and one has only to watch a football game with a group of fans to see how eagerly this invitation is accepted). Television sport sets itself up to be disagreed with, its producerliness invites viewer-made meanings. This invitation to disagree can be part of the authorial function, as when two or more of the on-screen commentators/experts offer different "stories" of events in the game. More importantly, however, television's own discursive repertoire gives to the viewer authorial knowledge and the power to produce meanings that goes with it. The constant flow of background and statistical information, of replays from all angles and at all speeds, of diagrammatic explanations of tactics, all give the viewer the insider information that is normally the preserve and privilege of the author, to be released by him/her in controlled doses throughout the progress of the narrative. We don't need Foucault to tell us that knowledge and power are closely linked, though he was the first to propose that the matrix of knowledge/power/pleasure formed one of the most important forces in society. The sharing of authorial knowledge and authorial power is productive of pleasure.

In television news (as we shall see in chapter 15) the author role of the studio anchor is set in a similar relationship to the events represented in the actuality film or interviews as that of the sports commentators to the game. So when the "author" makes a "management sense" of an industrial dispute resulting in power cuts, but the union spokesperson on film says that it was management who switched off the lights (see chapter 15), the invitation to the viewer to disagree may be less explicit than in sport, but it is there none the less, and is an essential part of the pleasure of watching it. News, like sport, also uses electronic effects and graphics that draw attention to its own textuality, its own constructedness.

There is a similar trend, too, in the television shows that appear to be most "realistic," by which I mean the ones that are most similar to a novel or a film with their invisible authors. Cop and crime shows are increasingly fore-grounding their own textuality. In *Moonlighting*, perhaps the most sophisti-cated of them, the characters David and Maddy may suddenly walk off the set, or in their dialogue blame the writers for its shortcomings. In one episode, for example, Maddy is depressed and refuses to rise to David's teasing. When she asks why they have to argue, his reply is, "You know we always do, you watch the show on Tuesday nights." When caught in a locked hotel room with a corpse and a gun in his hand, David looks at the cops and says, "What a situation! Thank God I'm only an actor!" This self-reflexivity (which MacCabe and Kaplan list as a requirement of a radical text) has long been a staple of comedy: shows like *Saturday Night Live* (see Marc 1984), and *Monty Python's Flying Circus* depend upon their viewers' awareness of television's discursive practices for their humor. A more recent example of this textually deconstructive comedy is *The Young Ones*. In one episode of this, for instance, the following dialogue occurs:

RICK: (*looking out of the window*) Ah, here comes the postman.

VIV: Rick, you're so boring, why do you always tell us what's going to happen?

RICK: Because this is a studio show and they can't afford to use location shots.

Television's foregrounding of its own textuality is not always as explicit as here or in *Moonlighting*. In shows like *Miami Vice* and others that have been influenced by it, such as *Stingray*, or, to a lesser extent, *Hunter*, devices such as excessive stylishness, self-conscious camera work, unmotivated editing, and the occasional breaking of the 180° rule, bring its textuality forward as a source of pleasure in its own right. The mode of representation is made visible and thus the relationship between the representation and the real is brought into question.

Of course, the viewers were ahead of the producers in this. Hobson (1982) and Ang (1985) have both shown that much of the pleasure of the viewers of soap opera lies in playing with the boundary between the representation and the real. Their power to do this has been increased by the fan magazines and other secondary texts which give them an insider knowledge that is broadly similar to that given by television itself to the sports fan or the news viewer. This can, in some instances, double the textual pleasure by providing a "ghost text" like the ghost image on a poorly tuned television set. So the fan with the insider knowledge of the "real" relationship between, say, George Peppard and Mr T, can read the ghost image of this relationship as s/he watches Hannibal and B. A. interact on *The A-Team*. The presence of this ghost text, of course, draws attention, however mutedly, to the textuality of the representation.

Television's increasingly sophisticated viewers are demanding access to television's mode of representation. Their pleasure in television is not explained by the ease with which they can accommodate themselves to its ideologically produced meanings and subject positions. A better explanation of the pleasures of television lies in understanding it as a text of contestation which contains forces of closure and of openness and which allows viewers to make meanings that are subculturally pertinent to them, but which are made in resistance to the forces of closure in the text, just as their subcultural identity is maintained in resistance to the ideological forces of homogenization. But we need a theory of pleasure that goes beyond meanings and ideology, a theory of pleasure that centers on the power to make meanings rather than on the meanings that are made. This is the thrust of what I have called television's "semiotic democracy," its opening up of its discursive practice to the viewer. Television is a "producerly" medium: the work of the institutional producers of its programs requires the producerly work of the viewers and has only limited control over that work. The reading relations of a producerly text are essentially democratic, not autocratic ones. The discursive power to make meanings, to produce knowledges of the world, is a power that both program producers and producerly viewers have access to.

Television's foregrounding of its discursive repertoire, its demystification of its mode of representation, are the central characteristics of its producerliness. They require, and, more importantly, are required by, the active, sophisticated, and televisually literate viewer. They offer the viewer two sorts of producerly pleasures: the one is the pleasure of making subculturally pertinent meanings, but the more important one is the pleasure in the process of making meanings, that is, over and above any pleasure in the meanings that are made. The pleasure and the power of making meanings, of participating in the mode of representation, of playing with the semiotic process – these are some of the most significant and empowering pleasures that television has to offer.

Chapter 13

Carnival and style

In the last chapter I argued that popular pleasure necessarily contained elements of resistance. The ideological pleasure of recognition, by which the viewer recognizes and confirms his or her ideologically constructed subjectivity, is essentially a low level of pleasure, if, indeed, it is pleasurable at all. Comfort and pleasure do not necessarily go together. In this chapter I wish to explore ways in which some of the popular pleasures offered by television can evade, resist, or scandalize ideology and social control. This tendency can often be seen most clearly in "extreme" forms of television, such as wrestling or rock video, but I wish to show that these "extremities" are not actually untypical, but that the same tendencies can be found in shows like *Miami Vice* or in commercials.

The line of argument that I wish to follow to link such apparently disparate shows is one that centers on the role of the signifier, on the body, and on the surface. Its core is the notion that ideology works through the signifieds and the subjectivity to construct and control meanings of self and of social relations. This can be resisted on its own terms by producing counter-ideologies, counter-meanings that serve the interests of the subordinate rather than those of the dominant. But there is an alternative semiotic strategy of resistance or evasion that refuses to accept the terrain within which ideology works so well, and instead substitutes one that favors popular pleasures rather than social control. This terrain encompasses the signifier, the body, and physical sensation. These two opposing terrains can be related in terms of the following oppositions:

Ideology	:	*Popular pleasures*
signified	:	signifier
meanings	:	physical sensations
depth	:	surface
subjectivity	:	the body, physicality
responsibility	:	fun
sense	:	non-sense
unity	:	fragmentation
homogeneity	:	heterogeneity
THE TERRAIN OF CONTROL	:	THE TERRAIN OF RESISTANCE/REFUSAL

240

The term "resistance" is used in its literal sense, not in its more overtly political or even revolutionary one of attempting to overthrow the social system. Rather it refers to the refusal to accept the social identity proposed by the dominant ideology and the social control that goes with it. The refusal of ideology, of its meanings and control, may not of itself challenge the dominant social system but it does resist incorporation and it does maintain and strengthen a sense of social difference that is a prerequisite to any more direct social challenge. The opposition of popular pleasures to social control means that they always contain the potential for resistance or subversion: the fact that this subversive or resistive activity is semiotic or cultural rather than social or even military does not denude it of any effectivity. Sociopolitical systems depend finally upon cultural systems, which is to say that the meanings people make of their social relations and the pleasures that they seek serve in the last instance to stabilize or destabilize that social system. Meanings and pleasures have a general and dispersed social effectivity, though maybe not a direct and demonstrable social effect.

One of the crucial questions then is whose are the meanings, whose are the pleasures? Bakhtin (1968) approached this through his theory of carnival which he developed in order to account for the popularity of Rabelais. The physical excesses of Rabelais's world and their offensiveness to the established order echoed elements of the medieval carnival: both were concerned with bodily pleasure in opposition to morality, discipline, and social control. Television's sense of the body may be more muted than was Rabelais's, but the world of the carnival, as theorized by Bakhtin, can nevertheless provide some useful points of comparison with the popular pleasures that television offers.

The carnival, according to Bakhtin, was characterized by laughter, by excessiveness (particularly of the body and the bodily functions), by bad taste and offensiveness, and by degradation. Television is frequently accused of, or more rarely praised for, these same vices or virtues. The Rabelaisian moment and style were caused by a collision of two languages, the high, validated language of classical learning, and the low, vernacular language of the folk. A similar semiotic tension exists in television between its official, ideological language, and the vernacular, low languages it carries, though contains with difficulty, and that may collide healthily with its official voice. The carnivalesque is the result of this collision and is a testament to the power of the "low" to insist upon its rights to a place in the culture. The carnival constructs a "second world and a second life outside officialdom" (p. 6), a world without rank or social hierarchy.

> Carnival celebrated temporary liberation from the prevailing truth and from the established order: it marked the suspension of all hierarchical rank, privileges, norms and prohibitions. (p. 10)

241

Its function was to liberate, to allow a creative playful freedom,

> To consecrate inventive freedom ... to liberate from the prevailing point of view of the world, from conventions and established truths, from clichés, from all that is humdrum and universally accepted. (p. 34)

In carnival life is subject only to "the laws of its own freedom" (p. 7). Carnival is an exaggeration of play, the space for freedom and control that games offer is opened up even further by the weakening of the rules that contain it. Like play, carnival abides by certain rules that give it a pattern, but unlike play (whose rules tend to replicate the social), carnival inverts those rules and builds a world upside down, one structured according to the logic of the "inside out" that provides "a parody of the extracarnival life" (p. 7).

As we saw in the last chapter, many children's shows test the boundaries of the rules and show a world that escapes their control. Cartoons and comedies frequently invert "normal" relationships and show the adult as incompetent, unable to understand, and the children as superior in insight and ability. Alternatively "inverted" adults are constructed more sympathetically and are treated as honorary children. B. A. in *The A-Team* is a carnivalesque figure: he is an inverted adult, an honorary child, he is excessive, is all body, and verges on the grotesque. His blackness speaks the "low" language of carnival. He offers, in a muted form, to those who identify with him, the invitation to participate in the momentary liberation from the laws of social control, as, before him, did the grotesque green torso of *The Incredible Hulk*.

The practical jokes played on the stars in *TV Bloopers and Practical Jokes* and on the public in *Candid Camera* work according to the "logic of the inside out." They depend on rules which are inversions of the normal and which the players/spectators know but the "victims" do not. The *Candid Camera* lady who coasted a car without an engine into a filling station at the bottom of a hill and asked the attendant to check the oil and plugs was inverting the "prevailing truth," was escaping from "all that is humdrum and universally accepted."

Allowing the viewer to be "in the know" and to participate in the joke reverses the power relations involved in watching normal television, when it is the viewer who lacks knowledge which those on the screen possess and impart. There is a similarly empowering inversion of viewing relations in the practical jokes played on the stars in *TV Bloopers and Practical Jokes*: the viewer knows that the pratfall will come, the viewer knows the script in advance; it is the star, the performer, in the position of ignorance.

These moments contain other elements of the carnivalesque: "[The carnival] belongs to the borderline between art and life. In reality, it is life itself, but shaped according to a certain pattern of play" (p.7).

"Life" erupting through art, as stars forget their lines or get the giggles, or as sportsmen lose their tempers and break the rules, crosses that borderline between reality and representation in the same way as do the viewers of soap opera. The pleasure involved is carnivalesque, for it is the pleasure of the subordinate escaping from the rules and conventions that are the agents of social control.

Carnival is concerned with bodies, not the bodies of individuals, but with the "body principle," the materiality of life that underlies and precedes individuality, spirituality, and society. The stage prop that refuses to work, the door that intransigently refuses to open, reduces the individual performer to a body wrestling with an object: it is a representation of the level of materiality on which all are equal, which suspends the hierarchical rank and privilege that normally grants the star power over the viewer. The star reduced to helpless laughter is joined in laughter by the viewer and both become equal laughing bodies. The degradation of carnival is literally a bringing down of all to the equality of the body principle.

☐ *Rock 'n' Wrestling*

Rock 'n' Wrestling is a carnival of bodies, of rule-breaking, of grotesquerie, of degradation and spectacle. Barthes (1973) alerts us to the function of wrestling as a popular spectacle in terms that are remarkable similar to those used by Bakhtin to describe carnival. Both authors refer to the *commedia dell'arte* as an institutionalized form of popular spectacle that can act as an explanatory reference point. Both point to the centrality of the body, to excess, exaggeration, and grotesqueness. Both refer to the spectacle as an important principle, and to the way that wrestling or carnival exists on the borderline of art and not-art (or life).

Bakhtin (1968: 5, 11) finds three main cultural forms of folk carnival:

(1) ritual spectacles
(2) comic (verbal) compositions – inversions, parodies, travesties, humiliations, profanations, comic crownings and uncrownings
(3) various genres of Billingsgate – curses, oaths, popular blazons.

The spectacular involves an exaggeration of the pleasure of looking. It exaggerates the visible, magnifies and foregrounds the surface appearance, and refuses meaning or depth. When the object is pure spectacle it works only on the physical senses, the body of the spectator, not in the construction of a subject. Spectacle liberates from subjectivity. Its emphasis on excessive materiality foregrounds the body, not as a signifier of something else, but in its *presence*. Barthes argues that the physicality of the wrestlers *is* their

243

meaning: Thauvin does not stand for ignobility and evil, for his body, his gesture, his posture *are* ignobility and evil. All wrestlers in *Rock 'n' Wrestling* have excessive bodies and the rituals they perform are excessively physical – the forearm smash, the flying body slam, the hammer, the pile-driver are movements whose meaning is the clash of flesh on flesh: the forms they take emphasize the spectacular, the physical force, rather than their effectivity in "winning" the contest: the immobility of a wrestler in a hold is "the spectacle of suffering" (Barthes 1973: 20). For they are movements of ritual, not the skills of sport. As Barthes says, the function of a wrestler is not to win or lose, but "to go exactly through the motions which are expected of him" (p. 16). The humiliation and degradation of defeat exist only in the body and helpless flesh of the fallen wrestler, not in a structure of moral and social values that gives them "meaning." Hence the audience, and the "victor," are licensed to gloat over and glory in the crumpled body, and indeed the victor will frequently continue his attacks on and degradations of the vanquished body after he has been declared the winner, after the bout has officially ended. In defeat, "the wrestler's flesh is no longer anything but an unspeakable heap spread out on the floor, where it solicits relentless reviling and jubilation" (Barthes 1973: 21)

A bout between Andre the Giant and Big John Stud finished with Andre the "winner." King Kong Bundi, Big John's partner in "tag wrestling," tore into the ring, apparently in an uncontrollable rage. Big John suddenly grabbed Andre's legs, throwing him on to his back. Bundi, a gross figure with a bald head and wide expanses of smooth white flesh, then executed a number of body slams upon the Giant, brushing the helpless referee out of the way as he did so. The commentator was excitedly and joyfully screaming, "This is despicable, this is despicable . . . come on referee, do something even if it's wrong. There's no way the referee . . . no way he's going to stop King Kong Bundi, who's fouling Andre . . . he's obviously hurt, look at that sternum bone just sticking right out there!".

The (apparently) broken sternum bone of Andre the Giant became an object of spectacle, divorced from the real social world of moral values and law, its meaning was its appearance as a swelling on the huge chest of Andre that the camera zoomed in on, as it did in the subsequent interview.

Earlier in the bout, Big John Stud's manager had thrown him a huge pair of scissors with which he was threatening to cut Andre's hair. The two fought for the scissors, with Andre finally forcing Big John to let them go by sinking his teeth into the wrist of the hand holding them. The cold steel of the scissors against the sweating flesh of the wrestlers, the image of sharp teeth on yielding skin, all heightened the physicality of the contest, the plane of the body on which it occurred.

The carnival form of inversion and parody is equally clearly exhibited. As we noted in the last chapter, the main inversion is that between control and disruption. The rules of the "game" exist only to be broken, the referee only to be ignored.

A regular "character" on *Rock 'n' Wrestling* is "Lord Alfred Hayes" who provides one or two "updates" of information about wrestlers and the World Wrestling Federation. His name, his dress, and his accent all parody the traditional English aristocrat; he is a carnivalesque metaphor of social power and status who is there to be laughed at. The social rules that he embodies are to be broken at the same time as the information he imparts is accepted.

Rules organize the social and the everyday and control the sense we make of it, they determine not only behaviors and judgments, but also the social categories through which we make sense of the world. In carnival categories are broken as enthusiastically as rules: the wrestlers' managers fight as often as the wrestlers, wrestlers not officially involved join in the bouts, the ropes which separate the ring (the area of contest) from the audience are ignored and the fight spills into the audience who become participants, not only verbally (see below) but physically.

> Carnival does not know footlights, in the sense that it does not acknowledge any distinction between actors and spectators. .... Carnival is not a spectacle seen by the people: they live in it, and everyone participates because its very idea embraces all the people. (Bakhtin 1968: 7)

This participation ranges from the physical – raining (ineffective) blows on one wrestler, or helping the other to his feet – through the verbal – shouting encouragement and abuse or holding up placards – to the symbolic – waving manikin doll models of one's favorite wrestler, or wearing his image on T-shirts. The television camera plays on the crowd, who performs for it as much as do the wrestlers: the categorical distinction between spectacle and spectator is abolished, all participate spectacularly in this inverted, parodic world.

For wrestling is a parody of sport: it exaggerates certain elements of sport so that it can question both them and the values that they normally bear. In sport, teams or individuals start equal (see the next chapter) and separate out into winners and losers. In *Rock 'n' Wrestling* the *difference* is typically asserted at the beginning of the bout. Bouts often start with one wrestler (or a pair) already in the ring, dressed conventionally and minimally in shorts or tights, and given an everyday name such as Terry Gibbs. The camera then cuts to his opponent coming through the crowd, spectacularly dressed in carnivalesque costume and equipped with an outlandish name such as "Randy Macho Man Savage," "Giant Haystacks," "Junkyard Dog." The contest is between the normal and the abnormal, the everyday and the carnivalesque.

245

Rock 'n' Wrestling refuses "fairness." It is *unfair*. Nobody is given a "sporting chance" and anyone who attempts to "play fair" is taken advantage of and suffers as a result. Yet the commentators return us again and again to this rejected standard as a point from which to make sense of the action. The pleasure lies not in the fairness of the contest, but in the foul play which "exists only in its excessive signs" (Barthes 1973: 22).

Wrestling is a travesty of justice, or rather, justice is the embodiment of its possible and frequent transgression. "Natural" justice, enshrined in social law, is inverted; the deserving and the good lose more frequently than they win. It is the evil, the unfair, who triumph in a reversal of most dramatic conflict on television. There is a "grotesque realism" here that contrasts with the idealized "prevailing truth" of the social order: despite the official ideology, the experience of many of the subordinate is that the unfair and the ugly *do* prosper, and the "good" go to the wall.

In sport, the loser is not humiliated, or degraded, but in *Rock 'n' Wrestling* he is, excessively. Sport's respect for a "good loser" is part of its celebration of the winner, wrestling's "license" for the bad to win allows also the degradation and humiliation of the loser's body. Sport's almost religious respect granted to the human body and to the individual is here profaned, blasphemed against.

And this body is almost invariably the male body. Female wrestling occurs, though rarely on television. It is interesting to note that in its nontelevisual form in clubs and pubs it frequently exaggerates the humiliation and degradation even further by being held in wet slippery mud. In television sport the male body is glorified, its perfection, strength, and grace captured in close-up and slow motion. Morse (1983) suggests that slow motion, which is so characteristic of sport on television but used more rarely in *Rock 'n' Wrestling*, has the effect of making the male body appear larger in scale, and thus more powerful, and of presenting it as a perfection of almost spiritual beauty. She cites the Greek ideal of "kalagathon," in which the beautiful male body was linked to social and political power. Following Mulvey (1975), she suggests that there is a difference between the masculine gaze on active moving male bodies and upon passive female ones. She divides this masculine gaze upon the male into two – one is a scientific investigative look of the will to know, which is a sublimation of the voyeuristic look and produces a repressed homoerotic pleasure. The other derives its pleasure from the slow motion replays that produce the repetition that is associated with desire. The female spectator, however, is different. She is traditionally the uninvited observer (which presumably gives her the powerful position of the voyeur), but the televising of sport has, according to Morse, eroticized the male body so that it can become an object of feminine desire and pleasure. She wonders if there has been a significant shift in what she describes as sport's precarious balance between "play and display" (p. 45). In "play," the look upon the male body is transformed into an inquiry into the limits of human performance, in "display" the look has no such alibi. In this context she quotes a warning sounded by Stone (1971) that commercialization was transforming the inherently noble *game* into the inherently ignoble *spectacle*; she comments somewhat sardonically, "the surest sign of the degradation of sport into spectacle – as far as Stone was concerned – was the predominance of female spectators" (p. 45).

The "live" audience of *Rock 'n' Wrestling* includes many, often very participatory, female spectators (whose presence is catered for in the names of one tag wrestling pair, "Beefcake" and "Valentine") and it may well be that the construction of the male body as spectacle for the female viewer is more empowering than Morse allows. Her account of the pleasures offered by the display of the male body in televised sport leaves it aestheticized and eroticized, an object of admiration that can still appropriately bear the dominant ideology of patriarchy.

But in wrestling the male body is no object of beauty: it is grotesque. Bakhtin suggests that the grotesque is linked to a sense of earthy realism, indeed he talks about "grotesque realism." The realism of the grotesque is opposed to the "aesthetics of the beautiful" (p. 29) represented in sport's vision of the perfect body. The grotesque body is "contrary to the classic images of the finished, completed man" (p. 25); cleansed of, or liberated from, the social construction and evaluation of the body, it exists only in its materiality. The pleasure of the female viewer here is different from that theorized by Morse. Seeing masculine strength and power embodied in ugliness and engaged in evil sets up contradictory pleasures of attraction and repulsion. The excessiveness of this strength, in alliance with its ugliness, opens a space for oppositional and contradictory readings of masculinity: the grotesqueness of the bodies may embody the ugliness of patriarchy, an ugliness that is tempered with contradictory elements of attraction. There is a sense, too, in which this grotesqueness liberates the male viewer from the tyranny of the unattainably perfect male body that occupies so much of the "normal" television screen. Wrestling's carnival inverts televisual norms as successfully as social ones.

The third component of folk carnival is its "Billingsgate," its curses, oaths, imprecations. In *Rock 'n' Wrestling* these are both verbal and nonverbal, though the most emphatic are often the nonverbal, carried in what Barthes calls the "grandiloquence" (literally, the excessive speech) of gesture, of posture and the body. The wrestlers "swear" kinetically at each other, at the referee, at the spectators: the spectators similarly curse and cheer, hold up placards. The breaking of linguistic conventions is obviously "modified for

247

TV," in that actual obscenities and blasphemies are not permitted, but the process of bad mouthing, of insulting, is enthusiastically entered into. The interviews between the bouts consist largely of wrestlers lauding themselves and bad mouthing opponents. This "Billingsgate" is typically delivered, not to the interviewer, but direct to camera, involving the home viewer in the process as actively as the live audience. "Billingsgate" is oral, oppositional, participatory culture, making no distinction between performer and audience.

The carnivalesque parody of power and authority questions the way that power is exercised in the everyday world, and central to this irreverent questioning is its use of the body. Foucault has revealed in detail the ways in which western societies have made the body into the site where social power is most compellingly exerted. The body is where the power-bearing definitions of social and sexual normality are, literally, embodied, and is consequently the site of discipline and punishment for deviation from those norms. Dyer (1986) argues that our culture's obsession with making sense of the body is bourgeois ideology at work: the sexualization of the body, its aestheticization, and its signification of social norms and deviation, all work to disguise the fact that the body provides the essential labor of capitalism. It is the bodies of the majority that make the profits for the few:

> The problem of the body seems to me to be rooted in the justification of the capitalist system itself. The rhetoric of capitalism insists that it is capital that makes things happen; capital has the magic property of growing, stimulating. What this conceals is the fact that it is human labor and, in the last instance, the labor of the body, that makes things happen. The body is a "problem" because to recognize it fully would be to recognize it as the foundation of economic life; how we use and organize the capacities of our bodies is how we produce and reproduce life itself. (p. 135)

Sport's celebration of the body beautiful becomes a depoliticized celebration of physical labor in capitalism and aesthetics become the means by which the beauty of the male body is linked to social and political power in the ideal of "kalagathon." The sporting male body is, consequently, an active hegemonic agent for patriarchal capitalism, and as such fits neatly with sport's embodiment of our dominant ideology. The sporting values of fairness and equality for all its players, of respect for the loser and proper celebration of the winner, represent the dominant ideology by which democratic capitalism values itself.

The grotesque realism of the ugly, distorted body is therefore opposed semiotically and politically to the dominant. It is an appropriate means of articulating the social experience of many subordinated and oppressed groups in capitalism whose everyday sense of the social system is not one of fairness and equality: positioned as they are as "losers," the subordinated (whether by class, gender, or race) have little sense of being "respected" by the winners, nor do they necessarily feel admiration for the socially successful. The carnival is both a product and a celebration of the yawning gap between the interests and experiences of the dominant and the subordinated in white patriarchal capitalism.

Sport may be a hegemonic attempt to control the disruptive forces produced by this experiential gap, but in carnival these forces break that control. The carnivalesque, therefore, becomes the arena wherein repressed experiences can be symbolized in a way that articulates not only the meaning of the experience, but also the experience of the repression. If beauty has been harnessed as a metaphor for the socially dominant, then ugliness metaphorically expresses the experience and the essence of the subordinate. The grotesque is both what must be repressed and the impossibility of repressing it.

Bennett (1986) points out that Bakhtin did not see carnival merely as a set of transgressive rituals, but emphasized its positive aspects:

> The value of excess associated with carnival . . . formed part of an image of the people as a boundless, unstoppable material force, a vast self-regenerating and undifferentiated body surmounting all obstacles placed in its path.
>
> (p. 148)

It might be taking Bennett too far to suggest that he has given an accurate description of a television wrestler as a vast, self-regenerating, undifferentiated body surmounting all obstacles in its path, or even that the wrestler becomes the embodiment of the popular force which expresses itself in carnival. But we must not write carnival off as merely a safety valve that ultimately allows social control to work more effectively: rather it is a recognition of the strength and endurance of those oppositional, disruptive, popular forces.

In the postmodern world, style performs many of the functions of carnival. It is essentially liberating, acting as an empowering language for the subordinate. Its similarities to carnival lie in its insistence on the materiality of the signifier, in its excessiveness, its ability to offend good taste (bourgeois taste). While television may provide comparatively little of the carnivalesque, it is concerning itself more and more with the language of style. Fans who prefer *Dynasty* to *Dallas* often report that the preference is determined by *Dynasty*'s "style," *Miami Vice* shot to popularity on its "look," music video circulates compositions of style as the visual equivalent of the music.

Style is a participatory dimension. The Madonna "wanna bes" ("look-alikes") can join with her in constructing her look. *Miami Vice* cotton jackets in pastel shades priced at $20 appeared in the department stores only months after the show was first screened, an instant democratization of its expensively constructed look, and young fans used the slow button on their video recorders to analyze and learn an intricately choreographed handshake in one episode. This is participation for it allows the viewer to become spectacle rather than spectator, to experience the pleasure of "speaking," of constructing her/his own image/identity.

The pleasure style affords is not of the same intensity as *jouissance*, nor does it entail the loss of subjectivity. Rather it is a pleasure of control and empowerment, a carnivalesque concentration on the materiality of the signifiers and the consequent evasion of the subjectivity constructed by the more ideologically determined signifieds. This form of pleasure also questions the unity and coherence of the world. It occurs in isolated fragments of experience, with no history, with no cultural pattern. Ideology insists on an overall controlling pattern of sense: fragmenting sense into the senses reproduces the liberation of carnival. In these terms, music video is arguably the contemporary carnival on television.

☐ Style and music video

Morse (1986) has argued that MTV deals with the products of bourgeois capitalism – urban landscapes, fast cars, flashy, glitzy style, in a parade of consumerist images that relate it closely to television commercials. But counter to this runs the text of pleasure that consists of the fast cutting, the high visual gloss, the extreme camera angles and vertiginous movement that enable the signifiers to overwhelm the signifieds. The visual images often have no meaningful connection to the words of the lyric, but are cut to the beat of the music. When there are connections they are tenuous, open-ended, allowed for rather than stated. Style is a recycling of images that wrenches them out of the original context that enabled them to make sense and reduces them to free-floating signifiers whose only signification is that they are free, outside the control of normal sense and sense-making, and thus able to enter the world of pleasure where their materiality can work directly on the sensual eye, running the boundary between culture and nature, between ideology and its absence. Of course, their images are images of patriarchal capitalism, but they are also signifiers distanced from their ideological signifieds, exploring the boundary between sense and no sense, between freedom and control.

Madonna's music video *Into the Groove* is almost exclusively about style. The visual track consists of a series of shots from her film *Desperately Seeking Susan* which is essentially about women seeking control over their social identity in contemporary metropolitan culture. And one key to this identity is style, with its close associations with "lifestyle." A heavily deco-

250

rated black leather jacket of Madonna's streetwise character, Susan, is acquired by Roberta, a disillusioned yuppie wife, and acts as one of her identity shifters as she struggles to change her lifestyle. A shot of the back of this jacket opens the music video, and chromakeyed into the design is Madonna's boyfriend, and then Madonna herself. In one corner of the screen is a polaroid shot of a stylish model's face. The camera pulls back, and the wearer of the jacket half turns to reveal herself as Roberta, not Susan; the polaroid snap becomes the personal ad that sets up the quest for self of the film, the ad that is "Desperately Seeking Susan." This opening shot, lasting only seconds, calls up the intertextuality between film, video, record, and Madonna-as-sign in a collage of signs of style, identity, gender, control, and the opposition between the streetwise and the home-dominated. The chromakey not only literally inserts Madonna into her jacket's personalized emblems, merging identity and appearance, but it relocates the sign in the domain of the signifiers. The signifieds and their verisimilitude on which the television screen so frequently depends, are distanced: the electronic gadgetry of chromakey and special effects generator allows a free play with the signifiers, a construction of the hyperreal that exists only in this realm. The image on the screen is its own reality, it needs no resemblance to the real, no signified, upon which to base its pleasure.

Television's ability to play electronically with its signifiers, to construct what it likes out of them, subverts its normal realism and thus can be indulged only in limited licensed moments.

There are "serious" uses of this electronic flexibility, such as slow motion and split screen effects in sport, or graphic charts and diagrams in the news, which are there to enhance television's representation of the real, to give more knowledge and more "truth" than the camera alone is able to. But there are also more "frivolous" uses whose function is not to produce the pleasure of enhanced dominant specularity, but a more carnivalesque, liberated pleasure. These moments of licensed play with the signifiers occur most frequently in the three genres of television that are meant to be viewed more than once, and that have an explicitly commercial purpose: music video, title sequences, and commercials. Each of them has the economic function of selling a commodity – a record or film, a program or series, and a manufactured product or service. There are many stylistic similarities between the three, they are all (or can be) producerly texts that require creative work from the viewer who wishes to engage with them, and they are often produced by the same specialized production houses. The paradoxical link between explicit commercial intention and the apparent freedom of the producerly text is one that we will explore more fully in chapter 16, for the moment we need only to note that television's electronic ability to free itself from the tyranny of the "real" of the laws of physics and consequence, is allowed free play only in strictly licensed moments.

Max Headroom is an attempt to extend the conditions of this license. "He" is a computer-generated DJ/interviewer who is a parodic travesty of all the talking heads that fill the television screen. Actually, the basis of Max is an actor, Matt Frewer, who is fitted with a rubberized mask that is molded into a cartoon parody of his own face. This image is then "chromakeyed, frame grabbed, digitized, video edited and scratch mixed to attain Max's final plastic performance" (*National Times,* March 21/27, 1986: 12). The voice is treated in the same way. Then image and voice are made imperfect – the image jumps, the voice repeats itself in an electronic stutter – foregrounding the process of manufacture.

With *Max Headroom*, television, the electronic medium, is producing its own electronic "reality" and instead of hiding its process of construction is celebrating it. One of Max's creators, Annabel Jankel, claims that Max touches a chord with people who are cynical about television: "We've made our statement with Max, about TV and talking heads and the idea that reality isn't necessarily as it's represented on TV." In relation to everyday television, Max Headroom is a carnivalesque inversion, a liberation from the transparency fallacy and the ideology that it bears. He exists only in a two-dimensional intertextuality, in an infinite parodic play of signifiers, a spectacle, a travesty, an authorless work of street art.

Grace Jones is almost a Max Headroom, her body is turned into an image whose appearance becomes her reality. Her excessive length of limb and width of smile are located by the camera as though they were its own constructions, as, in a sense, they are, and in her video *Slave to the Rhythm* her image is electronically played with, distorted, fragmented, recombined in a total liberation from any confining idea of "who" she "really" is. Image and identity in this world are no longer fixed, but can be played with, constructed, and deconstructed.

So Madonna, in *Into the Groove,* plays with the construction of her own image. Many of the edits are marked by the flash of photographers' flash-bulbs, sometimes of her own camera as she takes a polaroid of herself, sometimes her (moving) image appears within the frame of a polaroid photograph. She constructs her own look in a grotesque bricolage that combines the crucifix with lacy underwear and men's suspenders with a pink see-through top. Like Max Headroom, she foregrounds the process of her construction, but moves beyond him in asserting her control over this process: she is not only the product but also the producer. She wrenches the crucifix out of its original discourse with its religious signifieds and asserts her right to use it as a signifier: similarly she demonstrates her control over the "language" of pornography (flesh, flimsy underwear, black leather) by using it nonpornographically for *her* pleasure, *her* identity, not those of men. Combining the crucifix with the signs of pornography is a carnivalesque profanity, but the new combination does not "mean" anything specific, all it signifies is her power over discourse, her ability to use the already written signifiers of patriarchal Christianity, and to tear them away from their signifieds so that she is not subjected by the discourse as she uses it. Her liberation from the signifieds is a moment of empowerment. Lewis (1987) finds in Tina Turner's high heels, short leather skirt, and excessively sexual movements a self-confident aggressiveness that asserts that she is using these signifiers of patriarchal sexuality for her own pleasure, to assert her own interests, her own strength. Contemporary urban style is empowering to the subordinate for it asserts their right to manipulate the signifiers of the dominant ideology in a way that frees them from that ideological practice and opens them up to subcultural and oppositional uses.

Madonna's music videos have a number of extreme close-ups of her face, her mouth, her eyes, her feet, her navel in a use of the code that more normally is one of the most objectionable bearers of patriarchy. This is the camera code that fragments and fetishizes the female body, turning any part of it into a depersonalized object of masculine desire. This is one of the codes of classic Hollywood cinema whose chauvinistic pleasure Mulvey (1975) condemns so roundly, but which has been enthusiastically adopted by advertising, particularly of cosmetics and fashion. Madonna's idiosyncratic sexualization of her own navel is a parody of this process that makes her a controlling part of it. In the same way, the extreme close-ups of her mouth or eyes in this video are in her control: she looks this way for the camera and requires the camera to look at her in this way. She turns herself into a spectacle and thus denies the spectator the empowered position of the voyeur. She does not subject herself to the voyeuristic gaze, but instead controls the conditions of the look. In acknowledging the construction of both her look and the presence of the viewer, she controls both the look and the looking: she is no object given meaning only by the masculine gaze – she is her own spectacle. There can be no voyeurs in spectacle; the normal power relations of looking are inverted, and, as in carnival, the looker and the looked-at participate equally in the process of looking and the making of meanings that it entails. The carnivalesque element of spectacle denies both class and gender subordination and thus refuses to acknowledge the social power of the discourse it uses.

Into the Groove is a collage of signs of Madonna's spectacular construction of her own image: one shot can serve as an example – an ECU of her mouth is recuperated into feminine discourse where it means differently from its more normal masculine discursive use. Brown (1987b) finds a similar feminine appropriation of masculine discourse in the commercial that Geraldine Ferraro and her daughters made for Pepsi. These appropriations, or excorporations, are typical of the way that contemporary style is fashioned. The subordinate, in a reversal of incorporation, steal the discourse of the dominant and use its signifiers for their own pleasures, their own identities.

One of the discourses that is most readily available for these appropriations is that of the commodity, so the language of style becomes a creative use or reuse of commodities that serves the interests of both the subordinate and the dominant. The glitzy, flashing images of the marketplace are not restricted to their economic function of providing profit for their producers, they are also capable of a pleasurable, empowering range of uses by the subordinate.

Music video has been called the first postmodern television (see Fiske 1986c, Tetzlaff 1986). Similarly *Miami Vice* has attracted the label of the first postmodern cop show (Ross 1986, 1987). Postmodernism emphasizes the fragmentary nature of images, their resistance to sense, the way that images are more imperative than the real and have displaced it in our experience. It refuses sense, refuses the notion of subjectivity as a site where sense is made, for sense-making is the ultimate subjecting process. Sense, common sense, is the prime agency where the social machine enters and destroys the individual, so, in rejecting sense, postmodernism is rejecting the social machine and its power to regulate our lives and thinking. For Baudrillard this rejecting of sense is the ultimate political act, and the only resistive one available to the powerless masses in late capitalism.

Postmodernism refuses categories and the judgments they contain: it denies distinctions between fine art, the mass media, vernacular subcultures, and it harnesses the new technologies to shatter these boundaries. It refuses neat generic differences, so that in music video, ads and programs are indistinguishable, and in *Miami Vice* narrative, commercial, music video, fashion parade all intermingle. As Wollen (1986) points out, music video is a special mix of ad and program, for the visuals act as an ad whereas the sound track is a sample of the commodity. He also comments that fashion events have taken on the style of music video: we can take this further by noting how music video provides the "atmosphere" in trendy boutiques, and how, in some, the clothes and style the boutique is offering are displayed in music video style on multiple screens around and outside the store. Coca Cola have been quick to sign Max up for a commercial, and "he" has already opened supermarkets and featured in a record and music video in total disregard for genre discipline. The postmodern style crosses genre boundaries as easily as those of gender or class.

Postmodern style asserts its ownership of all images. As Madonna steals lacy gloves and crucifixes, so postmodernism "plunders the image-bank and the word-hoard for the material of parody, pastiche and, in extreme cases, plagiarism" (Wollen 1986: 168). Music video plunders old films, newsreels, avant-garde art: it parodies romances, musicals, commercials. Nothing is inappropriate, all is appropriated, excorporated; the exclusive is included,

254

distinctions and categories dissolved into coequal fragments. The post-modern style produces the pleasures of the surface, of the body, of the liberation from the social, the contextual, and sense.

□ The pleasures of *Miami Vice*

There is a set of interconnections between music, the materiality of signifiers, and a liberating pleasure, that is common to *Rock 'n' Wrestling*, music video, commercials, and title sequences, though these connections may well be articulated differently. They come together, too, in the cop show *Miami Vice*.

One of the stylistic innovations of *Miami Vice* is the use of current top twenty pop songs accompanied by visuals of masculinity, of cruising the urban landscape, as interruptions in the narrative. Their style is typically borrowed from music video or from commercials, and as they rarely advance the narrative, or increase our understanding of the characters, plot, or setting, or provide any clues to the solving of the enigmas that drive the narrative, it is fair to assume that their function is purely pleasurable. A shot analysis of one such segment is given in Figure 13.1. It occurs in the narrative when Crockett and Tubbs, working undercover as usual, are preparing to meet the villains in a nightclub. It falls into two parts stylistically; Part A, *Preparation*, is shot in extreme close-up and its eighteen shots are solely of objects that are bearers of high-style, high-tech, commodified masculinity. Human hands appear, identifiable only by skin color as those of Crockett or Tubbs and only to handle the objects of style.

In Part B, *Transference*, the sound track continues, but the visual style shifts significantly and becomes more conventional. Their Ferrari is shown in nighttime streets in conventional locating shots (shots 19 and 24) that bracket a shot/reverse shot sequence of Crockett and Tubbs in conventional close-up inside the car. The segment ends with a series of quick cuts of nightclub flashing lights in which the camera moves rapidly from long shot to extreme close-up. The repeated shot/reverse shot sequence (shots 20–3) is longer than conventionally required to establish that Crockett and Tubbs are in the car and to personalize the Ferrari's movement. There is no dialogue to "time" the cuts, instead the pop song dictates the pace of the editing. Similarly, the move from long shot to extreme close-up in a rapid sequence of shots of the flashing lights not only connotes the speed of their arrival and the urgent, anxious "feel" of the club, but also illustrates the beat of the music.

The first part, *Preparation*, is theoretically more interesting. It does have a narrative "alibi" of showing the two men preparing for their night out, but the alibi is weak. The link between the previous scene, in which they

255

Figure 13.1 Analysis of a pop music segment in *Miami Vice*

Shot no.	Shot length (secs)	Description
5	2.2	White hands picking up aftershave bottle. Gun visible.
6	1.8	Front wheel of Ferrari at speed.
7	2.0	White hands pick up and flick through roll of banknotes.
8	4.6	Black hands pick up gold necklace and caress it in the fingers.
9	2.8	White hands pick up credit cards.
10	2.5	Shot over Ferrari hood, driving at speed.
11	2.5	Black hands rubbing aftershave into their palms.
12	2.6	White hands picking up aftershave bottle. Gun visible.
13	2.6	Black hands adjust tie knot, big ring visible on finger.
14	2.3	Hub-height shot of front wheel of Ferrari at speed looking forward, passing other traffic.
15	7.8	White hands caress magazine, insert it in gun, check it.
16	5.0	Black hands insert bullets into revolver chamber.
17	2.1	Hub-height shot of Ferrari at speed, looking forward, white-out in lights of approaching car.
18	4.8	White hands pick up and test high-tech radio.
Part B:	*'Transference'*	
19	7.6	Location shot of Ferrari driving along street.
20	3.0	Shot of Crockett in Ferrari.
21	2.5	Reverse shot of Tubbs in Ferrari.
22	2.5	Shot of Crockett in Ferrari.
23	4.4	Reverse shot of Tubbs in Ferrari.
24	9.8	Location shot of Ferrari driving along street.
25	1.2	Long shot of flashing nightclub lights.
26	1.0	Mid-shot of flashing nightclub lights.
27	1.2	Close-up of flashing nightclub lights.
28	1.0	Extreme close-up of flashing nightclub lights.

Words of lyric

Left home with a friend of mine
Gave two years and I don't know why
Now I'm happy all the time
I can't think and I feel inspired
A girl put me in a situation
I'm going through some permutation
Did you hear me tell the sport
Now you're gonna hear some more
I know a place where dreams get crushed
Hopes are smashed but that ain't much
Voluntary experimentation
I'm going through some permutation

discussed their plans with their boss, and the next one in the nightclub would be adequately achieved by the more conventional *Transference* sequence of Part B. The visual and editing styles also undermine the narrative alibi by disrupting the chronological sequence. The inserts of the Ferrari traveling at speed (shots 6, 10, 14, 17) break the narrative sequence for they are intercut with shots of the men's preparations before they reach the car. The extreme close-ups and the sumptuous lighting work to make the objects bearers of pleasure in their own right, not mere functions of the narrative.

Rather than advancing the narrative, the segment interrupts it. The pop song, a driving rap beat, disrupts the narrative: it is one-off, not part of the theme music that links the segments within the episode and the episodes within the series. It fractures the self-containedness of the diegetic world, making explicit the intertextual links with the viewers' earlier experience of the song: it also emphasizes the intertextual links of television with the world of pop music and with other cultural forms that express an anxious, urban lifestyle. This fragment within the narrative links with other fragments of viewers' cultural experience rather than with the rest of the narrative.

The black accent and beat of the song also disrupt the social centrality of Crockett and Tubbs: its accent is closer to that of the underworld they are meant to control than of the mainstream society they are meant to protect. By prizing them loose, even if only momentarily, from their ideological role, it makes their style and masculinity accessible to more than those who conform to the dominant value system.

These narrative interruptions share some similarities with the song and dance numbers in the classical Hollywood musical. Mellencamp (1977) argues that these self-sufficient fragments are "spectacles" that both mirror and disrupt the structure of the film. In their mirroring they work to support the dominant ideology and its pleasures, but in their disruption they are excessive, conscious of their own artifice, and thus open to interrogative readings. The excessive masculinity-as-image of this video insert, presented as a source of pleasure for its own sake, may interrogate the norms that have produced the conventions of masculinity-as-action, femininity-as-image. Mulvey (1975) suggests that in masculine narrative the action is normally interrupted by moments of pleasurable visual contemplation of the female body: here masculine style is handled by representational conventions normally reserved for the female body.

The effectivity of this, of course, is problematic. It may be that the masculine becomes both the object and the subject of the look, and the feminine is totally exscribed from the narrative. The excessive sartorial stylishness of Crockett and Tubbs, their inexhaustible wardrobe of pastel designer clothes, could equally well be argued to be a masculine appropriation of a feminine language and pleasure. Or it may be the reverse. It may set

257

up contradictions between the excessively macho behavior and speech of the pair and the feminized style of their clothes and of the video inserts that turn them into the bearers of the visual pleasure of others, the bearers of their own image.

But, like all contradictions, these work within and against similarities. Their speech may be macho and laconic, but it is stylish: it has the deadpan wit of the Chandleresque private eye or the film noir hero. Such speech works through an excess of style and a style that is readily accessible to all. One of the conventional characteristics of these heroes is that their speech is more stylish/witty than that of other characters. Foregrounded style in speech, dress, and commodity is a marker of the popular urban hero.

The voluptuous visuals are more typical of advertising than of television realism. Berger (1972) makes the point that color photography has replaced oil painting in its ability to connote possession. Oil paint and glossy color prints represent the tactile uniqueness of objects which positions the spectator as sole possessor of them. Not only do the close-ups produce an excess of the gaze – only personal possessions are experienced as intimately as this – but the visual excess is transcoded into the sense of touch, of the materiality of the objects; touching, grasping, pocketing works more imperatively even than sight to establish possession. The display of objects in shot 2, for instance, is for the owner only, the disembodied hands invite our bodies to fill the absence. The sensuous hands caressing the gold necklet in shot 8, and the feel of the gold wristlet as it drapes itself round the owner's wrist, the sensuality of flicking through the banknotes in shot 7, and the eroticism of loading, checking, and feeling the weight of the guns in the hands (shots 15 and 16) are the sensualities by which the body of the owner experiences the objects in their materiality.

Of course these objects are ideologically loaded: they bear all the meanings of high-style, high-tech, urban, urgent, affluent masculinity. The fast editing, pausing to linger only on the guns, bears the ideology of action, purposefulness, and power. As such, it promotes *plaisir*, a confirmation of a particular masculine identity in a consumerist society: an identity that is bought with commodities and displayed through style.

The Ferrari is the ultimate commodity, a powerful bearer of both pleasure and ideology. Cunneen (1985) shows that car theft is a class- and gender-specific crime – practiced by young working-class males. The car is more than a symbol of masculine power, of freedom, of mobility; driving it is the *practice* of those values, it is not a substitute for masculinity, but a means of achieving it, particularly for those whose socioeconomic position denies them other means.

But the Ferrari is also excessive. It is more car and more style than police officers normally need or have. Its excessiveness extends its meaning beyond

258

the ideological domain of masculinity and into that freer, less controlled one of style. Its expense may limit its actual accessibility, but its style is that of consumption for pleasure and this style is achievable through less exclusive commodities.

For in this world style is all and the style is double-voiced – the reclaimed beach bum of Crockett, one-time alcoholic with an aversion to socks, the streetcorner "dude" of Tubbs with his mixed racial origins and his up-to-the-minute dress and music. The style is of the low life become affluent: however Guccified the commodities, the manner of their use bears the accent of deviant, devalued, and oppositional voices.

For those whose social identities are not centered on the worlds of work or of home, for whom the breadwinner role is irrelevant, commodities become their access to masculinity. The meanings of commodities are moved out of their original economic domain into the more pleasurable one of style. The circulation of commodities in the marketplace is, in the economy of style, the circulation of meanings and identities. For those who reject or are rejected by the system of productive labor, consumption forms their social relations. In the economies of late capitalism leisure displaces labor, consumption displaces production, and commodities become the instruments of leisure, identity, and social relations. Commodities, distanced from their economic function and from their signifieds of capitalism, become the signifiers of a discourse of style that the subordinate can steal from the dominant and use to articulate their own oppositional pleasures, just as they can steal the cars for their own joyrides.

Chambers (1986) argues that contemporary metropolitan society produces a culture of the spectacle in which the realization of the "self" is not achieved in the depth of one's inner being, but on the surface, through style, through image, through "a series of theatrical gestures" (p. 11). The distinctive and the personalized (that is, the *stylish* construction of the individual) is achieved through a creative bricolage of the commodities in the marketplace. The self is a shifting transient identity, literally self-created. "The individual constructs her- or himself as the object of street art, as a public icon" (Chambers 1986: 11) and in this spectacle, the gaze is neither masculine nor feminine, for it is not the gaze of a stable subject upon a stable object: both subject and object construct themselves out of the traditional signs and positions of either gender. This culture signals the death of authenticity, of any underlying "true" meaning of gender or of anything else. Style is what it appears to be, appearance is the reality.

In Madonna's *Into the Groove* there is a shot of her and her boyfriend close to a customized van: her style, his style, and the van's decoration in gold swirls on black, form a perfect "public icon," the self as street art. The black and silver hatbox which features so strongly in both the video and the film

259

Desperately Seeking Susan "contains" Susan/Madonna's "self" – the objects from which she constructs her look.

Miami Vice, too, *is* its look. H.Greene details the attention given to "the look," the huge wardrobe of selected pastel clothes: "No earth tones, no reds, no rusts, no browns, no oranges, no maroons. When dressed in the appropriate style, an actor is 'viced out.'" Even the props are stylish: "Like everything else on the set, the metal detector and the tables had been repainted for the 'Miami Vice' look. They were now aqua and white" (*Times on Sunday*, August 31, 1986, p. 27). The look, the style, of *Miami Vice is* its character, its spectacle is the source of its pleasure.

This postmodern language of urban style is essentially democratic, for in it we are all experts, all artists. We use and consume signs that circulate in the realm of the habitual, the signs have no origin, no author, no authority. The pleasure that results is an empowering one for it is the pleasure/power of speaking rather than of being spoken.

These images of style in *Miami Vice*, in music video, title sequences, or commercials open the viewer to a postmodernist pleasure. The fast editing, the dislocation of narrative sequence, the disruption of the diegesis may produce the sensation of fragmentariness, of images remaining signifiers, of the signifieds being not sold, but swamped, by the sensualities, of the physical uniqueness of experience rather than its meaning. Images are neither the bearers of ideology, nor the representations of the real, but what Baudrillard calls "the hyperreal": the television image, the advertisement, the pop song become more "real" than "reality," their sensuous imperative is so strong that they *are* our experience, they are our pleasure. Denying the narrative domain of these objects dislocates them from the ideological one as well. The pleasure here is not in resisting ideology, nor in challenging it with a "better" one, but in evading it, in liberating oneself from it. The more powerfully the text proposes the reading subject as the possessing male, the greater is the pleasure of rejecting that position, of rejecting the sense of the images.

Foucault (1978) alerts us to the close relationship of pleasure and power. Just as there is pleasure in exerting power, so there is a pleasure "that kindles at having to evade this power . . . the pleasure of showing off, scandalizing or resisting" (p. 45). This pleasure in resisting and scandalizing the forces of social control lies not only in the style and look of the program, but also in the content of its narrative. Miami is the "scandalous" place where pleasure rules in opposition to the work ethic of traditional capitalism: the city is the representation of a pleasure-centered consumerist society. The pastels of its look bear this pleasure, partly through their difference from the grimy, inner-city look of *Hill Street Blues* or, less markedly, of *Cagney and Lacey*.

Consumerism that provides a language of style in which the subordinate can speak is pleasurable in its excorporation of capitalism, its ability to use the products of capitalism while rejecting the ideology they more normally bear. Ross (1987) argues that the "vice" in Miami is "bad" consumerism. Drugs, pornography are the commodities of pleasure, they are "the most consummate expression of exchange-value because they do not hide their lack of use-value." Flaunting the lack of use-value is "criminal" in capitalism. Commodities of pure pleasure, pure waste, question the norms of the commodity itself, and crack the alibi that late capitalism tries to establish for itself in the ideology of consumerism.

In this fragment the commodities of masculinity exist on that point of friction between "good" and "bad" consumerism. Their pleasure, their style is close to that of the bad, as Crockett and Tubbs are close to voicing the underworld they are meant to control. The voluptuousness of the objects liberates them from their "good" narrative function. Like the camera of the television commercial, the camera pleasures the viewer into the role of consumer, but what is consumed is their sensuality, their lack of meaning, their postmodern rejection of use and of ideology. The camera is a "bad" consumer.

But traces of good consumerism remain, the residue of their use-value lingers on in their signifieds and bears with it their ideological meanings. But once these meanings are achieved, the excess of the images allows a non-ideological pleasure located in the sensualities of the signifiers, in the feel of the gold chain as it drapes itself round the wrist, the touch of the fingers against the necklet, the weight of the gun in the hand. In this world pleasure is both a product of a consumerist society, and a means of interrogating it. Criminal values are consumerist values taken to excess, but not different in kind. The boundaries are blurred between the good and the bad, and the power of the dominant to control both behavior and meanings is called into question as pleasure and style produce a multivocality in which commodities can be anybody's speech and not just the bearers of a capitalist economy. It is a world of fragments whose pleasure lies in their fragmentation.

The show's title segment is a montage of pleasure and physical sensations. Unlike almost all other television title sequences, it contains no shots of the leading characters, nor of examples of the action they are typically engaged in: it produces instead the sense and sensations of Miami. It varies slightly from week to week, but the constant feature, which occupies almost half the time of the segments, is a set of four shots in which the camera skims at speed just over the surface of the ocean turning the waves and surf into dizzying blurred images, giving the ocean an apparently solid surface with no depth: the heightening of physical sensations produces disorientation, as with drugs. The secondary emphasis is on Miami as playground – shots of horse- and dog-racing, of yachting and windsurfing, and of sunbathing beside swimming pools. Then Miami is shown in its modernity and wealth – the high-rise

261

buildings of contemporary capitalism and high establishment commodities of numerous Rolls Royces. This capitalist playground exists in an exotic, beautiful setting, a place of sunsets, palm trees, and flamingos.

The editing is slow-paced to begin with, though the camera movement is fast, and builds up to a climax just before the end: over it all is the rapid, percussive, electronic theme music. The camera style emphasizes the sensualities of the objects and the sensations of the viewer, either through tight close-ups or by vertiginous swooping and circling. The title sequence, then, sets up the viewer to read for pleasure and style, rather than character and action.

Against this, of couse, the generic structure of the cops and robbers show struggles to maintain ideological and narrative control and to gather the fragments into its flow. But the disruptive pleasures are barely contained. However hard the narrative fights to close each episode with a resolution in which sense, control, and masculine closure are all achieved, the style, the music, the look, the interruptions of the narrative remain open, active, disruptive and linger on as the pleasures of *Miami Vice*.

☐ Commodified pleasure

The commodity is double-voiced and the marketplace circulates both meanings and money in parallel but separate economies (see chapter 16). Lewis (1985) shows how shopping malls offer the commodities that can be used to make the Madonna look so that the "Madonna wanna be" can construct her personalized version of the style. But the shopping malls are not only used for buying. Pressdec (cited in Fiske, Hodge, and Turner 1987) uses the term "proletarian shopping" to describe window-shopping when there is no intention to buy. He found that unemployed youths indulged in this practice in shopping malls as a way of consuming images and space, not commodities, consuming for *their* pleasure, not for the profit of the producers.

Commercials on television are particularly available for "proletarian shopping" and many a viewer has reported loving the commercial but hating the product. There is a wide range of styles of commercial upon television but many of the most expensive and most admired are those that approach music video. Typically these will be aimed at a young audience and will be advertising fast food, soft drinks, or young fashion. They offer a series of sensuous images of desire, of style, and of materiality. Paradoxically, the product often appears a minimal part of the message – Michael Jackson's ads for Pepsi and some of the ads for Levi jeans could almost be music video. The advertisers' purposes are fulfilled if a fraction of the viewers convert the pleasure they offer into purchases – but there are no statistics of the number of "proletarian shoppers" whose pleasure in the ads remains precisely that. Children, for instance, are very creative in rewriting commercial jingles into (usually scatological) new versions that they use in their playground games and oral culture (see chapter 16).

But for all this, commercials tend to be less open than music video: the contradictions between their shots are less shocking, their syntagmatic gaps less wide. The intention of the advertiser is to engage and channel the desires of the viewer, not to give them free play. Inevitably, then, there is an attempted closure around the product which is designed to aggregate the meanings and encapsulate the style. But the high production values, the glossy sensualities of the image, and the tight editing carry a stylistic pleasure of their own that is easily detached from the commodity on offer.

A Coca Cola ad that was Australian ad of the year in 1984 consisted of a succession of quick shots of beautiful young people playing with a huge inflatable Coke can on the beach and in the sea. The sound track was a soft pop version of the Coke song, "Coke is It." The screen was full of fun, of young beautiful bodies in constant movement, of the sensualities of close-ups of splashing water on tanned skin, of the smiling pleasure of the bodies' ability to dive, climb, fall, slide down the plastic Coke can into the sea: youth is physical sensation, liberated from any social or historical context with its constraints of social powerlessness, of subjection and control. The Coke bottle is part of this moment of bodily liberation: the camera and editing made it part of the body of youth. One shot of a girl's laughing body being pulled up out of the water by the huge revolving Coke can was cut to a bottle of Coke being pulled out of crushed ice in a perfect visual rhyme. A shot of a boy diving off the huge can was cut into a close-up of a girl drinking from a Coke bottle: the angle of the diver and the angle of the bottle matched perfectly: the diver's body moving through the air and into the water became the movement and the sensation of the Coke flowing through the bottle and into the mouth. The beach as a licensed space of freedom from the social, the body as freedom from ideology and control, fun as the pleasures of physicality, and youth as fun/body/beach, and Coke as youth: this is Coke's rhetoric of style, a carnival of excessive sensuality as an inversion of the everyday. "Coke is It," and "It" is the object which resists naming, which is presence, existence, but no meaning, a signifier with no signified, the body-principle, not the body that bears individuality and social meaning.

This popular glitzy style is television's version of the carnivalesque. Only in shows like *Monty Python's Flying Circus* or *The Young Ones* can television present the obscenely grotesque inversions of the normal that characterized Rabelais's world. Television's popular, postmodernist stylishness is more domestic in scale, its grotesqueries muted to mere bad taste, its concern with the body transformed into a concern with the surface. For broadcast television grants no license to indulge to excess in the bodily pleasures of eating, drinking, and sexuality: the license is to play with the surface of the body, to deny the interiority of self or of reality. But the parody, the travesty is still there. The Madonna look parodies consumerism, the *Miami Vice* look turns style into spectacle. This spectacle of television is not the grotesquerie of carnival (though *Rock 'n' Wrestling* approaches close to it), nor is it the panoramic spectacle of cinema, it is a street-scaled spectacle, dimensioned around and on the human body. It engages not the power-bearing, subjugating look of Mulvey's cinema, but a look of equals, for the looker participates in the spectacle, the looker can be the looked at. So the object of spectacle is not subjugated to the power of the look, but in constructing her/himself as a public icon is inviting, controlling, and participating in the pleasure of looking. The ambivalence of the word "look" points to the similarity between the "look" that is looked at and the "look" that does the looking. In television's carnival of style, the pleasures of "the look" are indistinguishably of both sorts: its look is participatory, it destroys the power difference between the object and subject of the gaze and produces empowering pleasures for the subordinate.

Chapter 14

Quizzical pleasures

American television has broadcast something over 300 different quiz and game shows, the majority in daytime, or, at least, outside prime time. But one or two frequently edge their way into prime time and into top ratings in most western countries. They are a major television genre, with their roots in radio, and before that in party and community games. Their grounding in oral culture gives them a vitality and a strongly interactive relationship with the viewers, but it also makes them one of the neglected and devalued forms: for so much of television criticism stems from a literary base and therefore foregrounds those televisual forms which appear to be most literary. Although, as we will see, there is a narrative structure underlying quiz shows, their basic structure lies in the nonliterary forms of game and rituals.

☐ Game and ritual

Lévi-Strauss distinguishes between games and rituals by defining games as cultural forms in which participants start out equal and finish differentiated into winners and losers, whereas rituals take differentiated groups and provide them with equalizing communal meanings or identities. Games move from similarity to difference, rituals from difference to similarity.

Quiz shows are primarily games, though there are important rituals particularly at the beginning and sometimes at the end. Thus *Sale of the Century* has the structure of ritual–game–ritual. At the beginning the contestants are introduced, their individual differences – names, family circumstances, occupations, and sometimes personal details such as likes and dislikes, hobbies, or ambitions – are given a ritual recitation that moves them from differentiated individuals to equal competitors. The common form in which the details are given overrides their individual differences. Then the game takes over when this equality is tested and found to be an equality of opportunity but not of ability. This gradually revealed inequality produces the winner who is then accorded a ritual of equality with the bearer of social power – the question-master – who takes him or her by the hand into the reserved part of the studio where the prizes are displayed in fetishistic splendor, and made the objects of a ritualistic celebration.

It is not difficult to see that this ritual–game–ritual is an enactment of capitalist ideology. Individuals are constructed as different but equal in opportunity. Differences of *natural* ability are discovered, and the reward is upward mobility into the realm of social power which "naturally" brings with it material and economic benefits. Similarly, as I have argued elsewhere (Fiske 1983), this structure of quiz shows reproduces the education system in western societies: in this, all students (supposedly) start equal: those with natural ability pass successively more discriminating tests (examinations) and emerge as the highly qualified few who are fitted (by nature, so the story goes) for the high-income jobs, and positions with high degrees of social power and influence. Such an ideology and its ritual/game performances grounds social or class differences in individual natural differences and thus naturalizes the class system.

Bourdieu (1980) in his theory of cultural capital has revealed the contradictions masked by such ideological formations. For Bourdieu the social role of culture is to classify people and thus underwrite a stratified society. He introduces the notion of cultural capital which is possessed by those who have taste and powers of discrimination. Discrimination and taste are both apparently natural abilities of the individual but are actually the products of a specific class and educational system. According to Bourdieu, culture, and the knowledge that is integral to it, are replacing economics as a means of differentiating classes. In late capitalism when many members of the subordinate classes are comparatively affluent, money loses its ability to mask class difference and culture moves in to fill the gap.

The educational system, for Bourdieu, is the main agency of cultural propagation. It is structured around a classifying process that is particularly effective because its classification proceeds under the widely accepted belief that education is unbiased and neutral, that it offers everyone the same opportunity. It pretends to measure and develop the natural talent of each individual while actually promoting middle-class values and rewarding middle-class students. Social differentiation is thus displaced into, and naturalized by, a notion of individual differences. "All are equal in front of the examination paper" is as widely believed a misrepresentation of social experience as is "Everyone has equal opportunities in democratic capitalism." Cultural capital, like economic capital, is presented as being equally available to all, but is actually confined to those with class power.

☐ Knowledge and power

Quiz shows use knowledge in the way that Bourdieu argues culture operates, that is, to separate out winners from losers and to ground the classification in individual or natural differences. But the knowledge that they use varies throughout the genre so much that we need to divide it into categories and refer to the overall concept as *knowledges*.

The type of knowledge that is most closely connected with the notion of power and cultural capital is the "factual," "academic" type used in shows such as *Sale of the Century*. This knowledge has an empirical base whose "facticity" masks its origin in, and maintenance of, a system of social power. It is contained in reference books, dictionaries, and encyclopedias, and reaches its most elitist manifestation in shows like *Mastermind*. In *Mastermind* contestants are first tested on their knowledge of a specialist area of their choice and then on more general knowledge. Specialisms vary from the traditionally academic (e.g. English Literature 1890–1904) to the eccentric (e.g. English Steam Engines in the 1880s), and the atmosphere is tense, quiet, and solemn, like that of an examination room. In the British version, the show is usually broadcast from a university; in Australia, the studio set is given the same hushed reverence. *Sale of the Century, Ford Super Quiz*, and *Jeopardy* are shows which inflect the knowledge in question towards a type of general knowledge, whose content is less determined by school learning, but whose form maintains all the authority and unchallengeableness of the school examination. It is, however, mixed here with a showbiz sense of fun, of glitter and excitement. The excitement and pleasure of the carnival is joined with the knowledge and discipline of the schoolroom in a set of contradictions that open the program up to a range of reading positions.

The star personality of the show combines these contradictions in himself (the role is invariably filled by a male): he is both the genial master of ceremonies and the stern (but fair) schoolmaster-examiner. Both roles are ones of control, but they come from very different cultural domains. The master of ceremonies role is directed more at the studio and home audiences, the schoolmaster at the contestants. In this role, he is the public guardian of this knowledge who controls access to it, and who uses his possession of it as a means of controlling the competitors and the progress of the game. It gives him the power of the high priest in the ritual.

There is another type of factual knowledge which is less academic, more everyday. In shows like *The New Price Is Right* the everyday knowledge of the prices of domestic and consumer goods is on trial: the winner is the one who best knows the values of a wide range of commodities. Similarly, *Wheel of Fortune* requires a general knowledge of words and popular sayings (it is based on the traditional parlor game of "Hangman"). Knowledge of this type is not gained through school or reading, but rather through common social experience and interaction: it is thus available to a wider range of people, it is democratic rather than elitist in temper.

But there is an entirely different category of knowledge that produces

267

entirely different sorts of shows. This is a knowledge that resides in the human or social rather than in the factual. It has no absolute right and wrong answers and thus cannot be possessed or guarded by an elite. It depends instead upon the ability to understand or "see into" people, either in general or as specific individuals.

Understanding people in general produces shows such as *Family Feud.* The winner here is the family who can predict the social norms, who knows best what most people are thinking. The questions take the form: "We asked a sample of one hundred people to name a job that requires people to get up early in the morning: what do you think they answered?" The contestants are scored according to how closely their answers conform to the norms established by the survey. The winner is finally the one who can most accurately predict the social consensus: the winner is, paradoxically, the most ordinary. This type of knowledge is, according to Mills and Rice (1982), politically opposed to the elitist one, it is more democratic, less divisive. It depends less upon "their" cultural capital and more upon "our" cultural experience, and the skills that gain access to it are not the formally taught skills of intellect and memory, but the human skills developed by social experience, the skills of understanding people.

Family Feud and *Play Your Cards Right* (another show based on this type of knowledge) are not played by individuals but by families or married couples, for this "democratic" social knowledge fits less well with individualism than does the more factual elitist knowledge.

But it can be given a more individualist inflection when it tests insight into, or knowledge of, a specific person. Shows based on this are ones like *Mr and Mrs, The Newlywed Game, Blankety Blank,* or *Perfect Match.* In *Mr and Mrs* or *The Newlywed Game* one spouse first answers a number of questions: the other, who has been in the soundproof booth, then has to guess what these answers were. The winners are those couples who "know" each other best as measured by their ability to guess the other's responses. In *Blankety Blank* the competitor has to guess the word that a panel of celebrities has associated with a given stimulus word or phrase. The winner is the competitor who guesses the word most frequently chosen by the celebrities. In *The Dating Game* a competitor has to choose a date from three unseen members of the opposite sex by their answers to his or her questions. The "winner" is the one who gets chosen, and the couple are then sent on a all-expenses-paid trip or date. *Perfect Match* is more complex, for there are three sorts of knowledge at work in it. The intuitive, personal knowledge or skill of the chooser in picking his or her "perfect match" is first tested against the more scientific, empiricist knowledge of the computer which selects, according to scientific principles and data, the "really" perfect match. If the scientific and human "knowledges" agree, that is, if the computer picks the same person as the chooser, the doubly validated couple are given an extra prize. These two sorts of knowledge – the scientific and the human-intuitive – are then put to the test of experience. Half the couples return to a later show to tell how they got on on their trip: the knowledge of actual experience is added to, and often set against, the other two knowledges.

Figure 14.1 The hierarchy of quiz shows

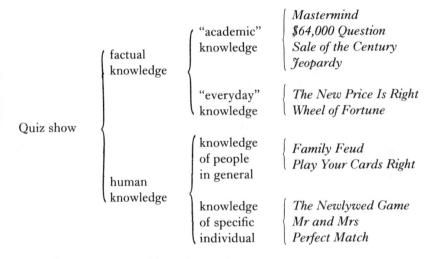

We can, then, categorize quiz shows according to their type of knowledge and its relation to social power, as shown in Figure 14.1. This produces a hierarchy of quiz shows – those at the top require an academic or specialist knowledge (*Mastermind, $64,000 Question*) that has a more popular inflection in "general knowledge" (*Sale of the Century, Jeopardy*). This category reproduces in game form the school system of students, teachers, examinations, and rewards – a point that will be developed in greater detail below. They tend to be prime time and to be watched and played by a greater proportion of men.

Further down the list, and the hierarchy, the shows tend to be screened in day-time or late afternoon, and are thus watched by audiences of predominantly women or women and children. As the "knowledge" becomes more democratized, so the popularity of the programs shifts towards those with less social power.

□ Luck

In all the shows, whatever the knowledge that is tested, there is an element of luck. In some, such as *Pick a Box,* luck is the motive force. In others, such as

Play Your Cards Right, the law of averages can be invoked to increase a competitor's chance of being "lucky" – in this case of guessing whether an unseen playing card is higher or lower than the revealed one. In shows such as *Mastermind,* luck is kept to a minimum, to the extent that each competitor chooses the topic for his or her "specialist" questions: in the second part of the show, when general knowledge questions, albeit esoteric ones, are asked, luck plays a slightly greater role.

Luck is often related to gambling – competitors stake points or dollars already won, in the hope of winning more. In *Sale of the Century* money won in the "luck" segments can override that won in the "knowledge" segments, so the overall winner can be the luckiest, not the cleverest.

Luck plays a vital role in the hegemonic structure of societies that are both competitive and democratic. The structure of such societies is necessarily hierarchical and elitist, they are like a pyramid with the mass of people at the bottom and very few at the top. Yet the dominant ideology insists that everyone has a chance to rise up through the class, economic, and power systems. The social system, not surprisingly, reproduces the educational system in its ideology of equal opportunity for everyone, so that those of natural talent will rise up through the structure, and the resulting class divisions will be able to present their inequalities as fair because they are based upon the "naturally" unequal distribution of talent amongst otherwise equal individuals. The corollary of this, of course, is that those who have not risen (by definition the majority) have failed to do so through their own "natural" deficiencies. Luck works to mitigate the harshness of this judgment, for luck provides an ideologically acceptable explanation of success or failure – (s)he is more successful than me because (s)he was luckier, not just because (s)he was cleverer. In a society that celebrates both the material rewards of wealth and the right of everyone to them, but limits the opportunities to acquire them to the minority, the appeal of gambling, of easy money, is hardly surprising.

The hegemonic function of luck is not just to minimize the personal sense of failure, but, more importantly, to demonstrate that the rewards of the system are, in fact, available to all, regardless of talent, class, gender, race, and so on. In the "rags to riches" story which is such a potent myth in capitalist societies and is manifest in the popular biographies of most stars of sport and entertainment, and of industrial stars such as Lee Iacocca, hard work and luck are interdependent elements: work and dedication which make the most of "natural" talents rely on the luck of being in the right place at the right time, or of a chance meeting with the right person, to provide the opportunities for that talent to flourish.

Vanna White, the hostess of the American version of *Wheel of Fortune,* is an embodiment of this myth. In 1986 she shot to celebrity status, a meteoric

270

rise that culminated in her photograph on the cover of *Newsweek*. This and other secondary texts provided viewers with biographical information that made her the living validation of the role of luck in our ideology. Her father, so the stories went, was a drunken, spouse-abusing Puerto Rican whom her mother divorced when Vanna was still an infant. From such a socially disadvantaged start she progressed to a number of undistinguished modeling jobs. Then she tried her luck in Hollywood, auditioned for the *Wheel of Fortune* role, and from cultural invisibility, became, almost overnight, a celebrity. The secondary texts consistently emphasized both her "ordinary" beginnings and her current success and lifestyle. Her story is the "true" enactment of the "fortune" (in its double sense of "luck" and "wealth") that the show symbolically offers. Vanna White is proof that this fortune is available to everyone (given a little bit of luck).

Huizinga (1949) suggests that games structure the tension between chance and rules, between the unpredictable and the predictable, the uncontrollable and the controllable. The games played by both children and television viewers are inevitably part of the same social system as the worlds of work and economics in their enactment of the centrality of luck.

While knowledge may be the socially validated way to power, influence, and material rewards, the elitism that is entailed by the competitiveness which both produces and proves its unequal distribution is given a democratic alibi by luck. But the alibi may not be simply hegemonic in its function. The generic characteristics of quiz shows are clearly effective bearers of capitalist and patriarchal ideologies; they can be articulated differently to provide pleasures and meanings that are less accommodating.

□ Commodities

The prizes are typically consumer goods or services, such as foreign tours or cruises. Sometimes money is the reward, and sometimes public respect and glory (*Mastermind,* for example, has no prizes or rewards for winners of the heats, and a discreet antique or work of art for the winner of the final). The commercial interests behind quiz shows, as behind so much of television, press to have their goods displayed to an audience of millions; for them quiz shows are the cheapest television commercial possible, and one that has the added bonus of presenting them as "sponsors" not as "advertisers." Quiz shows are often charged with encouraging materialism and with positioning the viewer, particularly the housewife, as a consumer. There is no doubt that this force is powerfully at work in them: we can see it in the glamorizing of the prizes and in the ecstatic excitement (almost *jouissance*!) of the winners and the studio audiences. There is a sense in which the prizes become the stars, and the visual climax of many a show is provided by the camera luxuriating amongst the glittering, brightly lit prizes.

Davies (1983) takes this even further. In a detailed analysis of the opening sequence of the Australian *Sale of the Century* he reveals how the representation of the star prize of the car may work subliminally on the viewer. The car revolves on a podium, surrounded by flashing lights, and the camera zooms in, not steadily, but in a series of jump cuts, until it finishes in a close-up of the radiator grille. The sequence is accompanied by a drumroll and frenzied applause and its effectivity is enhanced, according to Davies, by a form of subliminal perception. Each of the eleven jump cuts in the 3.6 second sequence is one-third of a second or eight frames. This editing rate of three shots per second falls within the frequency of stroboscopic effects which operate physiologically upon the brain.

Quiz shows, like advertising, are undoubtedly part of commodity capitalism, and use many of the similar cultural strategies. For instance, glamorous models are used to display the prizes and thus associate commodities with sexuality, thereby linking buying with sexual desire and satisfaction. Linking the domain of sexuality with that of economics is commonplace in our society. Shows like *Dallas* are no different from the commercials typically inserted into them in their equation of economic power with sexual power and attractiveness. Sexual competition, with its Darwinian explanation of the "natural" survival of the fittest, is easily mobilized to naturalize economic competition. The "natural" desirability of a beautiful woman, or man, is a metaphor for the capitalist desirability of the commodity with which she, or he, is associated. The person who is the object of sexual desire becomes objectified into the commodity so that both are purchased or won simultaneously. But the motivations of the producers of quiz shows that determine the main characteristics of the genre do not necessarily determine the ways that they are read or used by the viewers.

☐ The active audience

The first point to make is that quiz shows produce particularly active, participatory viewers. Their mini-narratives are structured around the hermeneutic code which poses and then resolves enigmas. But unlike typical narratives, quiz shows are not presented as enacted fiction, but as live events. The producers go to great pains to disguise the fact that all shows are prerecorded – five or six are typically taped in one recording session. Their "liveness" or "nowness" is crucial to their appeal for it positions the viewer as the equal of the characters in the narrative. The narrative appears unwritten, the resolution is as much a mystery to the characters as to the viewer, so the

272

text has less authority to impose itself. In the "unwritten" narrative occurring "now" suspense appears to be real, not manufactured and authorially controlled as in a novel or film, and thus the engagement of the reader is greater. The viewer of quiz shows, like that of soap opera, is positioned *actively* towards the text by its unwrittenness, its sense of a time span in which the present and future are equal for both characters and viewers.

The viewers are thus encouraged to compete with the performers, and, in *Perfect Match,* to set their insights against those of the competitors and to test their human knowledge against that of the computer and of "actual" experience, much as in soap operas they test their "scripts" against the ones actually broadcast.

But the activity of the audience does not in itself provide evidence that the commercial functions of quiz shows can be evaded or resisted. After all, advertisers too want an active audience because that is the audience which will most effectively incorporate the image of their product into its imagination. Williamson (1978), for example, has shown that many advertisements contain puns or puzzles for the reader to solve and in so doing to engage actively with the creation of meaning for the product. In this case, the audience activity is controlled as carefully as possible by the advertiser, but the effectivity of that control is still very limited. There are many more viewers who gain pleasure from a witty or punning advertisement than there are those who convert that pleasure into an actual purchase. Advertisements are seen, read, and enjoyed by millions of people who will never buy the commodity on offer.

Children, for instance, appropriate advertising jingles into their games, often subverting them by changing the words. Incorporated into children's culture, the advertising jingle bears very little, if any, of its original commercial meaning – probably not much more than nursery rhymes such as *Little Jack Horner* or *Georgie Porgie* retain their historical and political sense. The origin of a text neither guarantees nor determines its mode of reception, however powerful a party it may be in the process of negotiation. Viewers who participate in the pleasures of quiz shows are not necessarily incorporated into the consumerist ideology.

☐ Articulating quiz shows

Hall's (1986) theory of articulation is productive here. The word has two meanings, and his theory uses both of them equally and interdependently. To articulate is, in one sense, to speak and "speaking," we must remember, necessarily involves "response," it is a two-way process. So while quiz shows may articulate (speak) consumerism as they carry the voice of their producers, they may also, as I suggest below, articulate (speak) responses to that consumerism in accents that speak the interests of the consumer.

But articulating also means linking with a flexible movable point of contact as in a hinge, or as in the British name for a semitrailer – an articulated lorry. The first meaning of articulation directs our attention to the text, its production and reception, the second requires us to look at the way that the text (or the game of which it is an example) is linked to other cultural domains. Thus, when MTV is articulated with the record and music industry, its meanings are commercial and economic, but when it is articulated with the domain of youth, possibly with a drug-subculture, its glossy, rapid, consumerist images may articulate (speak) meanings of opposition or evasion.

The meanings of articulation leak into each other, for speech always occurs in a cultural domain that is related to others: it is never context-free. Hall's theory reminds us that the same speech, articulated to different domains, can mean quite differently and serve quite different social and political interests. The "multiple articulation" of quiz shows is a function both of their textual openness (their "unwrittenness," their use of excess and metaphor) and of the way they can be read in terms of their relationship with a number of cultural domains, particularly those of school, of the family, of shopping, of leisure, and of social relationships.

Quiz shows articulate with school in a number of ways. McQuail, Blumler, and Brown (1972) have found that viewers from higher socioeconomic groups (who are likely to be the better educated) use quiz shows to check and test their "academic" knowledge. Viewers from lower socioeconomic groups, however (likely to have had a shorter formal education), use the shows to "prove" to themselves that they are as clever as the contestants, and that their formally assessed academic performance is not a true measure of their ability.

Some used the shows as a basis for self-rating, with responses like "I imagined that I was on the program and doing well," or "I can compare myself with the experts." These self-ratings often produced the sort of self-esteem that the education system denied them: "I find I know more that I thought," or "I feel I have improved myself."

Its metaphorical relationship with school probably lies behind the *Sale of the Century*'s popularity with Australian school students (in 1983, it and *Prisoner* were the two most popular programs with school students). It offers metaphorical transformation of the school system which allows symbolic success to those who "fail" at school. Like all metaphors, the relationship between the representation and its referent operates on a interplay of similarity and difference. The similarity between the two is obvious: but the differences are equally important to the program's appeal. The school system, for example, sells itself to its students by promising that good work at school will provide a good job which in turn will provide the "good life." The

274

work has to be performed now, but the final reward is in the distant future. *Sale of the Century*, however, collapses the time gap – the rewards are instant – and in so doing squeezes the job out of the equation. Hall and Bennett have both noted how rarely productive labor is represented in capitalist popular culture: material rewards seem to follow directly and naturally from talent, or even good looks and social position, so that, in *Dynasty* or *Dallas*, physical beauty and wealth seem to be naturally and necessarily partners. The effacing of work from our screens, of course, effaces the fact that industrialized work benefits one class rather than another, and that its rewards are not necessarily related to the effort or time devoted to it. In this, *Sale of the Century* is operating as a typical capitalist text.

The fact that quiz shows are typically played by adults also inserts them easily into the mainstream of social values. It implies that the competitive testing of school is not confined to students, but continues into adult life. But this adult-child reversal may also be utilized as a source of pleasure for children; seeing adults subjected to the sort of disempowering process that they undergo regularly at school, being able to compete with adults on equal terms and seeing adults make mistakes and suffer immediate consequences from them are all ways in which children can find meanings that validate their interests, and that provide them with a source of self-esteem that their school experience frequently fails to. Sometimes this adult-child reversal takes the opposite form, for quiz shows also give children the opportunity to play adult roles, particularly those of teachers as Palmer (1986) discovered:

Quiz games were also popular in the playground:

ELIZABETH (8): At school sometimes I make some questions that are hard and I ask them to Anna and she thinks for a minute . . .

INTERVIEWER: What show is that?

ELIZABETH: *Matchmates, Sale of the Century, Ford Super Quiz*. The ones that I watch. (p. 107)

At other times this role reversal is done officially, as when teachers allow children to play the questionmaster role in classroom versions of television quiz shows.

Such an incorporation of the pleasure of quiz shows into the classroom may involve an element of accommodation to the social power system, but we oversimplify it and underestimate its effectivity if we allow accommodation to be its sole component. The interests of the dominant ideology are not necessarily well served by the empowerment of those subjected to it, nor by having its systems, when articulated with the domain of entertainment, read in alternative ways. This argument will be developed later, for the moment we need to note that the meanings of the text, when it is articulated with

275

education, can be mobilized in ways that affect the meaning of the educational domain and that reposition some students towards it.

For instance, *Sale of the Century* rewards speed of physical reflexes as much as knowledge (the first competitor to press the buzzer attempts to answer the question) which both opens up the class of "winners" and provides a face-saving alibi for the losers. It is also imbued with a sense of fun (which school, for many people, is not). When the game ends the losers add their consolation prizes to those they may have won during the progress of the game, and are encouraged to say how much fun they have had. In other words, they are encouraged to de-articulate the show from school, and re-articulate it to the domain of entertainment and leisure as a means of finding a positive meaning in their experience of losing. School has little chance of being re-articulated in other domains for those who are the "losers" in its system. The fields of knowledge that are used in *Sale of the Century* overlap with those of school – history, geography, literature, science, current affairs – but the show adds to them fields that are excluded from the official curriculum such as sport, popular music, and entertainment. These fields are given equal weight with the more academic ones, and are the fields in which the less academic viewers and competitors are more likely to have some expertise. The format of the show allows many, if not most, of its viewers to believe that they could have answered most of the questions. Teachers' introduction of quiz show formats into the classroom, particularly towards the end of school terms, is an apparent attempt to mobilize some of the values of entertainment and their power to democratize knowledge. This admits of an interrogation of the elitism of school-based definitions and use of knowledge and demonstrates, however implicitly, the validity of alternative knowledges.

A show that relies entirely on nonacademic and devalued knowledges is *The New Price Is Right*. Its skills are those associated with women, those of shopping and household management, skills which are often devalued or at least made invisible and confined to the private, domestic sphere. It is articulated not to education, but to consumerism. Of course it operates on one level as a national shop window for the commodity producers, and of course it trains women as enthusiastic consumers, but it contains also the elements of a countertext, one "written" by the consumers. In this show these skills are first of all made public and the person who uses them best is given a public acclaim that at times verges on the riotous.

Translating the womanly skills and knowledge out of the private sphere into the public gives them a status normally reserved for the masculine and prizes them loose from the domains in which they are devalued. The ecstatic public acclaim given by the studio audience to the winner is quite foreign to everyday housewifely experience, and is more or less explicitly contrasted with the taken-for-grantedness of such skills in their normal family setting.

The program is excessive: it produces an exaggerated sense of fun and of hectic pace. There are exaggerated expressions of elation or despair from competitors and audience, and an enormous amount of noise is generated. The excitement and frenzy separates the game off from "normal" shopping and shifts it towards the carnivalesque.

The carnival, as Bakhtin (1968) shows, is a time when the constraints of the everyday are evaded and its power relations temporarily reversed. Masters or mistresses become servants, and vice versa, the pleasures of the body, eating, drinking, and sexuality, are indulged to excess without guilt, and those who are normally subjected to a complex of power systems (economic, political, moral) are momentarily freed from their subjection. Carnival depends for its effect upon the recognition that the powerful and the subordinate have opposing interests, a recognition that ideology normally works hard to disguise and deny.

This carnival moment may be argued to be a safety valve that ultimately works to stabilize the status quo. But it is always potentially more than this: the pleasures that it produces can never be totally recuperated back into the system, they always produce a threat that puts social control at risk. (We noted in chapter 12 the way that those with social power have constantly mobilized notions of morality and law and order to erode and control the carnivalesque pleasures of the subordinate.)

The carnivalesque pleasures of *The New Price Is Right* are not those of total license, but they do derive from a reversal of the normal power relations between consumers and producers. The consumer is momentarily liberated from economic subjection: her knowledge of prices and value is no longer the product of her economic subjection to the system, derived from the need to make a limited amount of money go as far as possible. The release of the economic constraints which ensure her subordination allows shopping skills to become agents of empowerment. They become the means of beating the economic system and of turning it to the interests of those normally subordinated to it. *The New Price Is Right* is not just a shopper's wish-fulfilling fantasy, it is also an assertion that shoppers' interests are opposed to those of the producers and that the normal ideological practice of making the producers' interests appear identical to those of consumers is momentarily disrupted.

This sense of the carnivalesque articulates quiz shows with fun and entertainment. However powerful their metaphorical associations with school or domestic labor, they always have the trappings of showbiz – flashing lights, glitter, a stage and an audience, music, applause, and so on. School and shopping are part of the world of work, where the individual is subjected to external disciplines. The relationship of leisure to work is complex, but it always involves opposition: leisure is not-work. Whether leisure is supportive of work or contradictory to it is much more problematic and depends partly on the leisure activity that is chosen and partly on the pleasures gained from that activity. But leisure always appears to be something we *choose* to do, something that produces a sense of identity that is in our control. Of course the forces of capital latch on to this and industrialize it, so that leisure becomes a consumer activity. But their appropriation can never be total, for if it were it would destroy that which they are trying to appropriate: the industrialized or mass forms of leisure will necessarily bear capitalist ideology as will the industrialized forms of work, but the absence of economic necessity positions the subject quite differently. *Choosing* to answer questions or to shop for the fun of it is a carnivalesque, playful inversion of *having* to sit an examination or make the weekly trip to the grocery store. Articulating the forms of "work" with those of leisure may either defuse the opposition between the two and bind them into an ideological homogeneity, or it may activate those contradictions and thus maintain a set of oppositional meanings and subjectivities. Pleasure may be the bait on the hook of hegemony, but it is always more than this, it always involves an element that escapes the system of power.

The knowledge tested in *The New Price is Right,* despite its "ordinariness," is still firmly located in the domain of economic power. The prices and values are set by the commodity producers, not by the consumers, and the player is rewarded for her knowledge of *their* system. The shows that rely on what I have called "human" knowledge refuse this positioning. The knowledge that they validate is the knowledge of the people, of *us* as opposed to *them*. It invites us to articulate it to the world of the everyday, of "ordinary people." All quiz shows produce the pleasure of this particular articulation, for they all give "ordinary people" the role of "special people" – those on television. But in the "factual" knowledge shows, it is not their ordinariness that is tested and celebrated, but their "specialness," their ability to handle the knowledge of those with social power. The "human" knowledge shows, however, test and celebrate "ordinariness."

The concept of the ordinary is, of course, never defined by such shows, but is left open and available for a wide range of identifications. It is an open construct of "us" opposed to an equally generalized "them." Sometimes "they" are embodied in authority figures surrounded by encyclopedias, sometimes "they" are disembodied voices that decide if an answer is right or wrong. The compere and hostess mediate this boundary, they have access to the power and knowledge of "them," but display their ordinariness as a mark of affinity with "us."

Many of these shows, like *Blankety Blank,* mix stars, or special people, with the "ordinary" contestants, and what is displayed in the stars is not their glamor but their ordinariness. In *Blankety Blank* the contestants have to guess how a panel of celebrities will complete a given sequence of words. The winner is the ordinary person who is most like the celebrities. In *Family Feud* the winner is the family who is most like the social consensus. The devolution of knowledge to the ordinary people can go no further.

This is part of the same democratization that in the domain of politics has produced the doctrine of one person one vote, and the spread of opinion polls. But in politics, as in market research, the knowledge of what "ordinary people" are thinking is used in the interests of those with power: in *Family Feud* there can be no such appropriation of ordinary knowledge back in to the system. *Family Feud* is an expression of an oral popular culture, not a literate controlling one, and the knowledge that it tests is one best gained by ordinary interaction with ordinary people – an oral knowledge derived from social experience rather than a literate knowledge taught by social institutions.

One ordinary cultural domain to which the shows frequently invite articulation is that of the family. This articulation can take a number of forms. The shows have derived not only from the institutional "literate" experience of education, but also from the informal, "oral" tradition of family games, or parlor games as pre-television generations called them. Some of the televised versions are still played in this manner: McQuail, Blumler, and Brown (1972) found that the more educated viewers played the games with their families in front of the set. Family members would compete with each other and with the television competitors to answer the question first. Television became part of the oral culture of the family in a way that parallels the function of gossip in taking soap opera into the oral culture of women. Fiske and Hartley (1978) have shown how the compere and hostess play the role of the "jolly uncle and aunt" constructing the viewers into an extended family. In *Family Feud* some of the questions are answered not individually, but by the family as a consensus voice after a period of conferring.

But the articulation of the quiz show with family is not always supportive. In *The New Price Is Right* the housewife-competitor is freed from the demands of family shopping: the family here is not a source of fulfillment and pleasure, but an agent of constraint. Similarly, *Perfect Match* liberates sexuality from family morality and places it confidently and shamelessly in the realm of pleasure. The conventional romantic narrative which underlies the show – boy meets girl (or vice versa), boy wins girl (or vice versa) after a period of testing, and they are joined happily together – ends not in marriage, responsibility, and the acceptance of an adult social role – but in a weekend of pleasure.

Soap operas, once widely regarded as escapist pap, have been retheorized and their women audiences reinvestigated. These studies have revealed hitherto unsuspected values in the genre and in the cultural competencies of its viewers. Quiz shows share many characteristics with soap opera: they are widely devalued, they are excessive, they produce a high degree of viewer participation, they make visible and validate many of the normally invisible everyday life-skills of women, they are primarily a daytime genre though there are prime-time examples, and they appeal to the socially powerless. The recovery of soap operas and their audiences into cultural and political respectability is almost complete and thoroughly welcome: the same sort of re-examination of quiz shows and their audiences has hardly begun, but a similar recovery of the genre and its audiences is not only theoretically possible, but also, I would argue, both probable and politically desirable.

Chapter 15

News readings, news readers

News is a high-status television genre. Its claimed objectivity and independence from political or government agencies is argued to be essential for the workings of a democracy. Television companies applying for renewal of their licenses turn to their news and current affairs programs as evidence of their social responsibility. But the basic definition of news as factual information that its viewers need in order to be able to participate in their society gives us only half the story.

News is also a commodity. It is expensive to gather and distribute, and must produce an audience that is of the right size and composition to be sold to advertisers. In a cynical but productive phrase, news has been defined as "that which is printed on the back of advertisements." News has to be popular, it has to produce an audience. All television channels or networks use an early evening news program to lead into their prime-time schedules. This is designed to draw the male of the household into the TV audience. He is assumed to have just returned from work, finding his wife and children already watching the softer program preceding "his" news. Hobson (1980) has found that it is common for mothers to keep children quiet "while father watches the news," and in a later study (Hobson 1982) she found women who talked about "my" soap opera in contrast to "his" news. The national news is primarily masculine culture, though it often ends with a "softer" item that is intended to bring the female back into the audience. It is typically followed by a softer news magazine program, often of local as opposed to national interest, which is designed to appeal to women (see Morley 1986) and to consolidate the family audience in front of the set for the prime-time, prime-profit advertisements that are to be wedged apart by programs for the next two or three hours.

So what is this genre of news to which society and the schedulers attach such importance? It is one of the most complex and widely studied TV genres and one that mobilizes most effortlessly some of the key defining characteristics of the medium – "nowness," segmentation, repetition.

Most studies of television news concentrate on the institutional processes that produce it, or else use content analysis to reveal the categories of events that are deemed newsworthy and the proportionate time or space devoted to each. In this chapter I study news as discourse, that is, as a set of conventions that strive to control and limit the meanings of the events it conveys. Theories of news which foreground questions of accuracy, bias, or objectivity are based on an empiricist notion of reality that lies outside the theoretical framework of this book. These questions are, however, important not because they allow us to judge the quality of the news but because of the insight they can give into the professional ideology of the news makers.

News professionals in particular and broadcasters in general are keen to separate news from fiction, and to locate it firmly in the information side of the popular but leaky classification of television programs into the macro-genres of information and entertainment. The idea that television is a window on the world, now known as the "transparency fallacy," still survives, if anywhere, in TV newsrooms. Generic distinctions between information and entertainment or fact and fiction are crucial for the producers, for they describe different sorts of ethics, different definitions of responsible programming. For the viewers, too, this distinction marks a difference in reading relations, though I shall argue later that this is not as clearly cut as it first appears. But textually, there is not a lot of difference between television news and television series or serial drama. The fondness of television for docudramas is a sign of how easily its textual forms cross the generic boundaries between fact and fiction – and the public outcry that these docudramas frequently cause evidences the public's belief in the need to keep the genres distinct. In textual terms, the news may not be all that different from a soap opera, but there are very real differences in the way that the audiences and producers understand and approach the two genres.

The viewers studied by Tulloch and Moran (1986) not only kept the genres quite distinct but they politicized the distinction. The scheduling of the soap opera *A Country Practice* against *60 Minutes* on Sunday and *The World Around Us* on Monday split households along gender lines, with the males preferring the "factual" programs, and the females and children the soap. As Tulloch and Moran put it:

> All television programs yield knowledge and ideas about the world. Father, mother and girls don't dispute that. What is in dispute is what knowledge in what form ... Drama is concerned primarily with the private sphere, the emotional and the domestic ... News, current affairs and documentaries are more concerned with the public sphere.

> (1986: 239)

A similar gender-genre difference emerged elsewhere in their study; typical was the man who considered that the masculine "factual" programs stimulated "discussion," or "conversation," whereas the feminine soaps produced only "gossip" at the level of "what's happening to Vera in the next episode" (Tulloch and Moran 1986: 236).

This "common-sense" view, for all its gender politics, that what happens on the news is determined by fact, whereas what happens in a soap opera is determined by imagination, is a good enough place to start our investigation into the nature of television news. The news tells the story of the key events of the last twenty-four hours. This simple definition introduces the contradictions that we shall explore in this chapter. For events seem to be part of nature, whereas the telling of stories and the selection of the *key* events are clearly cultural activities. The first struggle of news is to impose the order of culture upon the polymorphous nature of "the real." The news text is engaged in a constant struggle to contain the multifarious events and their polysemic potential within its own conventions. For news is as conventional as any other form of television; its conventions are so powerful and so uninspected because the tyranny of the deadline requires the speed and efficiency that only conventions make possible. The type of stories, the forms that they will take, and the program structure into which they will be inserted are all determined long before any of the events of the day occur. During the forced withdrawal of Belgium from the (then) Belgian Congo, an American journalist landed at Lusaka airport and, on seeing a group of white women waiting for evacuation, rushed over to them with the classic question, "Has anyone here been raped, and speaks English?" His story had been "written" before landing, all he needed was a few local details.

The popularity of the news is determined largely by its generic characteristics which constitute the "strategies of containment" which attempt to control "reality." In this chapter I shall model television news as a constant struggle between these strategies and the disruptive forces that are characteristic of both "the reality" that news refers to and the social differences amongst its various audiences.

☐ The strategies of containment

The news's way of making sense of the real and of controlling its potentially anarchic polysemy follows those two familiar semiotic axes of the paradigmatic and the syntagmatic. The paradigmatic works through the processes of selection and categorization, the syntagmatic through combination and narrativization.

☐ Categorization

Galtung and Ruge (1973) suggest that for an event to be deemed newsworthy it should be recent, concern elite persons, be negative, and be surprising.

Recency demands that a newsworthy event should have occurred within the last twenty-four hours, and during that time things should have happened that can be seen as an origin and as a point of achievement or closure. There is little sense of continuous history in news, and few references to previous events. Even an ongoing story is divided into twenty-four hour self-contained segments: recency and segmentation are mutually supporting characteristics.

An event should concern elite persons. This means that the people in the news will all be familiar, if not individually, then at least in their social roles. Certain political, official, sporting, and entertainment people will be familiar in their own right. In other cases, the roles will be familiar even if the individuals filling them may vary – the trade unionist, the disaster survivor, the minority spokesperson, the victim. The socially powerful tend to be familiar to us as individuals, the powerless or the voices of opposition are familiar mainly as social roles, which are filled by a variety of forgettable individuals. The elite, who appear repeatedly, bear the accumulated meanings of their past appearances. Because these are embodied in an individual they carry greater semiotic weight in our individualistic society than do the accumulated meanings of "roles," such as union organizer, victim, and so on. The social power of elite persons is underscored by the narrative power that familiarity confers.

News occurs in the public sphere (which is where elite people circulate) rather than the domestic. The domestic appears only when it is the site of extreme or violent crime, and can thus be constructed as a matter of public law and order. The public sphere is one that our society deems to be masculine and is thus peopled largely by men. News is largely about "the masculine" and aimed at a male audience, so it is hardly surprising that news stories are structured to provide a point of narrative closure that approximates that of masculine fictional narrative. News stories have to impose a closure upon the openness of ongoing events: recency must be tempered by completion.

News is negative. What is new is what disrupts the normal. What is absent from the text of the news, but present as a powerful force in its reading, are the unspoken assumptions that life is ordinarily smooth-running, rule- and law-abiding, and harmonious. These norms are of course prescriptive rather than descriptive, that is, they embody the sense of what our social life ought to be rather than what it is, and in doing this they embody the ideology of the dominant classes. This singular category of "the abnormal" means, for example, that murder and an industrial dispute can be seen as similarly disruptive, and the conceptual strategies that enable the news and its readers to construct similar ways of understanding such apparently disparate events are an important part of its ideological practice.

The unstated, ideological norms which make this conceptual strategy possible are those of *our* society. Negative events in another part of the world do not bear the same relationship to these norms and are therefore read differently. Third World countries are, for example, conventionally represented in western news as places of famines and natural disaster, of social revolution, and of political corruption. These events are not seen as disrupting *their* social norms, but as confirming ours, confirming our dominant sense that western democracies provide the basics of life for everyone, are stable, and fairly and honestly governed. When deviations from these norms occur in our own countries they are represented as precisely that, deviations from the norm: in Third World countries, however, such occurrences are represented as *their* norms which differ markedly from ours. For the western news media, the Third World is a place of natural and political disasters and not much else.

The common complaint that our news is always "bad" ignores the fact that "the bad" is treated and read as a deviation from the norm, which is therefore constructed as "good," and that this normative assumption is all the more powerful for being unspoken. It would be interesting to know how TV news is read by its viewers in the Soviet Union, for it is a convention of Soviet news to lead with positive stories such as factories meeting their quotas or agricultural successes. It is possible that a sector of Soviet viewers read such stories cynically, that is, as deviations from the norm of industrial inefficiency. Such oppositional readings would occur when the conventions of news fail to match the conventions by which people "read" their social experience. The relationship between these two sets of conventions is interactive: the conventions by which news stories are selected and told, and thus the sense that they propose, cannot impose themselves upon an unwilling or oppositional audience.

Reading the news cynically or angrily can deconstruct its conventions and demystify their attempted ideological practice. Trade unionists who are angered by the news convention that their actions are always represented as "demands" whereas employers are said to "offer" read this convention as further evidence of the power of the dominant classes to naturalize their social interests into "ordinary" common sense. It is, of course, only convention and its relationship to social power that prevents the news reporting that the unions "offered" to work for a 5 per cent wage increase but the employers "demanded" that they accept 2½ per cent. The word "offer" suggests that its agents, those who offer, are generous, take the interests of the other party into account, and are comfortably in control, whereas "demand" suggests that its agents are greedy, selfish, and having to struggle to gain control of the situation. Demand is a disruptive word which places the "demanders" within the negative forces that make news. Conventions such as these are an important part of news's struggle to contain and defuse the disruptive forces at work in society while fulfilling its obligation to represent them.

There is, of course, a connection between elitism and negativity: the positive or "normal" actions of elite people will often be reported whereas those without social power are considered newsworthy only when their actions are disruptive or deviant. In representing the dominant as performing positive actions and the subordinate as performing deviant or negative ones the news is engaging in the same ideological practices as fictional television. We saw in chapters 1 and 8 how heroes embodied socially central values, whereas villains and victims embodied deviant and disruptive ones. Violence, which is the dominant mode of representing the relationship between heroes and villains, is thus a concrete metaphor of social or class conflict.

Conflict is as important in making a good news story as it is in making a good fiction, and its relationship to the social system is similar. News values and fictional values stem from the same society, they both bear the same need to be popular, and it is not surprising that they are fundamentally similar. We will explore more of these similarities in this chapter (see "News narrative," p. 293).

It is perhaps paradoxical that a convention of news should be its "surprisingness." But the tension between the predictability of the conventions and the assumed unpredictability of "the real" demands some recognition. The whole operation of news gathering and reporting resists this unpredictability, for news stories are essentially prewritten; all that the reporter does is fill in local details. This conventionalization of the real must never be acknowledged, however, for to do so would expose the transparency fallacy. Surprisingness is therefore valued as a sign that the unpredictability of the real triumphs over the conventionality of news, that it is, finally, reality that determines the news. Surprisingness is a necessary bedfellow to the belief in the objectivity of the news.

☐ Subcategories

The primary classification, whose criteria have been outlined above, is that of news or not-news. Once an event or person has been selected as newsworthy, a further categorization takes place (the sequence of the levels of categorization is analytical, not chronological). Hartley (1982: 38–9) suggests that news is subdivided into the following categories: politics, the economy, foreign affairs, domestic news, occasional stories, and sport. We may wish to modify these categories, for instance, by adding the category of entertainment, or by dividing "domestic news" (as Hartley does) into the "hard" – stories of conflict and crime in the public sphere – and the "soft" – warm-hearted or human-interest stories. Similarly, we may wish to make a sub-category of "industrial" news within "the economy." The actual categories themselves are not hard and fast, but are indicative: it is the process of categorization as a major sense-making act that is the point at issue. Categorization constructs a conceptual grid within which "raw" events can be instantly located and thus inserted into a familiar set of conceptual relationships. Categories are normalizing agents. They also serve as simple but effective structuring principles for the building of news programs. "Industrial affairs" or "foreign affairs" categories are used to group stories and to place them in the conventional sequence of the news flow. These groupings are part of the strategy by which news masks its social process of representation and presents itself as objective, as driven by events in "the real." Thus "industry" and "foreign affairs" appear to be empirical categories based in nature, yet their operation is highly ideological. A story of an industrial dispute appears to be naturally, rather than ideologically, linked with one on employment or falling exports. Similarly stories on a famine in northern Africa, political corruption in Nicaragua, riots in Bengal, and guerrilla activity in Indonesia all appear to be naturally linked as part of "foreign affairs." Putting them in one category invites the reader to understand them in terms of their similarities rather than their differences, and the similarities, in both the industrial and foreign examples, make a sense that serves the interests of the western bourgeoisie.

But categories do not only link stories, they also separate them. Linking a story of an industrial dispute with one on unemployment is no more significant than separating it from stories of politics, of inner-city crime, or even of illiteracy rates. Categories fragment as well as cohere, and news follows the practice of the public sphere in compartmentalizing social life in order to make it both practically and semiotically more controllable. The semiotic and political practice of categorizing social life into neat compartments – the economy, education, crime, industry, etc. – is an essentially reactionary one, because it implies that a "problem" can be understood and solved within its own category: localizing the definition of problems encourages local "solutions" and discourages any critical interrogation of the larger social structure. Tracing links between categories, therefore, sees any one problem as symptomatic of the social structure and thus promotes a more radical, or socially literate, understanding.

The categorization of news and its consequent fragmentation is a strategy that attempts to control and limit the meanings of social life, and to construct the interests of the western bourgeoisie into "natural" common sense. Compartmentalization is central to news's strategy of containment.

287

□ Objectivity

Objectivity is an empiricist concept that has been under attack for most of the twentieth century, especially from structuralism, post-Einsteinian physics, and psychoanalysis, to name only some of its major theoretical challenges. Yet news professionals still cling to it as both an achievable goal and a central justification of their role in western democracies. It thus plays an important role in the ideology of news and the reading relations that news attempts to set up with its audiences. The impossibility of objectivity and the consequent irrelevance of notions of bias (based as they are upon an assumption that non-bias is possible) should be clear to readers of this book, but should not blind us to the ideological role that the concept of "objectivity" plays.

There are modal differences between the news and fiction, despite their similar conventions of representation. The news does appear to bear a closer relationship to "raw reality" than does fiction and consequently there are ifferences in the way that viewers read it. Children, for example, find death in the news far more disturbing than death in fiction television. News's high modality, its closer relationship to the indicative mood by which we normally represent the real, is central to a number of institutional values and practices.

It underlies, for instance, what Fiske and Hartley (1978) have termed "clawback." This is a structure of reporting that works to claw back potentially deviant or disruptive events into the dominant value system. Thus television news typically works with three stages of clawback that correspond with spaces that are both material and symbolic. The central space is that of the studio news reader, who does not appear to be author of his/her own discourse, but who speaks the objective discourse of "the truth." Paradoxically, the news reader's personal traits, such as reliability or credibility, are often used to underwrite the objectivity of the discourse. Locating this discourse in the institutional studio signifies its ideological conformity: no radical, disruptive voices speak in these accents or from this space.

Spatially positioned further away and discursively subordinated is the reporter, who signs off as both an individual and an institutional voice. Her/his function is to mediate between "raw reality" and the final truth spoken by the news reader. Different reporters can make different contributions to the same "truth"; they need individual signatures so that their "truths" appear subjective, "nominated" (Barthes 1973, see p. 290) and therefore lower in the discursive hierarchy than the "truth" of the news reader. Furthest from the studio, both geographically and discursively, is the eyewitness, the involved spokesperson, the actuality film, the voices that appear to speak the real, and that therefore need to be brought under discursive control. There is a vital contradiction here. The "truth" exists only in the studio, yet that "truth" depends for its authenticity upon the eyewitness and the actuality film, those pieces of "raw reality" whose meanings are actually made by the discourse of the studio, but whose authenticating function allows that discourse to disguise its productive role and thus to situate the meanings in the events themselves. This "actuality" film, of course, is frequently not of the events described in the script, but may be file tape from the library, or footage shot some time after the events occurred. Thus a story of political kidnappings in Lebanon was, on the ABC news of January 23, 1987, "authenticated" by film of an ordinary, peaceful Beirut street: what mattered was not the content of the film, but its authenticating function. Repressing the content of the film, which contradicted the meanings given to "the Middle East" by the story, is another typical example of news's strategies of containment at work.

Clawback then is the process by which potentially disruptive events are mediated into the dominant value system without losing their authenticity. This authenticity guarantees the "truth" of the interpretation that this mediating involves and thus allows, paradoxically, that which has been interpreted to present itself as objective. Objectivity is the "unauthored" voice of the bourgeoisie. (See "Exnomination" in chapter 3, and p. 290.)

Hand in glove with objectivity go authenticity and immediacy. Both these link news values in particular with qualities of television in general. For authenticity links with realisticness, and immediacy with "nowness" or "liveness," both of which are central to the experience of television. In news, both work to promote the transparency fallacy and to mask the extent of the construction or interpretation that news involves.

Immediacy is used not only to mask the production of news but also to promote television over the press and to divert attention from its means of gathering and distribution. New distribution technologies, particularly those of the satellite, have enabled the instantaneous distribution of news over the whole world. The instantaneity implies that there has been no time for editorializing or reworking, that television brings us events-as-they-happen. So television channels often promote their news programs in terms of their immediacy.

This emphasis on speed has another ideological effect. This is to divert attention away from the fact that satellites are very expensive means of distribution and that only large multinational news corporations can afford to have regular access to them. News is processed into tight satellite packages to be sold in every corner of the world. The stress on speed and immediacy diverts attention from the commodification of news whose criteria of production and selection are determined by the multinational corporations such as News Limited. News gathering is as expensive as news distribution, so poorer Third World countries often find themselves driven by economic factors to buy "white" news of themselves or of their neighbors.

□ **Exnomination and inoculation**

There are a number of textual devices of news that can be thought of as the tactics through which the strategies of containment are applied. The "impersonal" authority of the words of the studio news reader constructs a framework of objectivity within which the words and images which constitute other levels of reporting are situated.

The impersonal objectivity of this discourse "guarantees" its truth: it is an example of the ideological practice that Barthes (1973) calls "exnomination" (see chapter 3). Exnomination is the evacuation of a concept from the linguistic system with its structure of difference and alternatives. That which is exnominated appears to have no alternative and is thus granted the status of the natural, the universal, or that-which-cannot-be-challenged. Thus, in the news story analyzed below, the union view of the dispute is *nominated*; but that of the management is *exnominated*.

The differences between the two are quite clear in both vision and sound. Visually, the union spokespersons are shown as individuals, their names and union positions are given in subtitles, and a shot of their union badge on their office door merely underlines the process. The management point of view, however, is exnominated. There is no spokesperson, instead it is the "objective" voice of the news reader which speaks the management sense. On the sound track, or in the news script, the difference is more subtle, but equally, if not more, significant. The difference between the two social voices is embodied in the difference between the grammatical voices of active and passive. The active voice has a nominated subject and is thus appropriately used for union actions. For example, "The union executive was mapping out strategy" or "Assistant secretary Jack Marks told the men the issue struck at the core of unionism." On the other hand, management never appears as an agent in the conflict, its actions are described in the passive voice or impersonal mode: "Mr Duke could be reinstated immediately" or "Geoff Duke, whose dismissal at Port Hedland, for alleged misconduct, triggered the strike." The nomination of the union voice admits that alternative viewpoints are possible and thus discredits its status: the exnominated management voice, however, is given the status of truth. The process of nomination is a tactic of MacCabe's hierarchy of discourses (see chapter 3). Nominating discourses places them low in the hierarchy and thus licenses them to speak oppositionally or radically. The exnominated metadiscourse, however, speaks the final "truth," against which the partiality of the subordinated discourses can be assessed. Nominating disruptive discourses and exnominating that of social control is a common tactic of semiotic and ideological containment.

Equally common is the tactic of "inoculation" (Barthes 1973; see chapter 3). In this metaphor Barthes likens the social body to the physical body.

Literally, inoculation is the process in which the physical body takes into itself a controlled dose of a disease that threatens it in order to strengthen its defenses against that disease. Figuratively, the metaphor refers to news's convention of allowing radical voices a controlled moment of speech that is nominated and inserted into the narrative in such a way as to ensure that the social body is strengthened and not threatened by the contrast between it and the radical. The transcript of a TV news story given on pp. 296–301 contains examples of both exnomination and inoculation.

☐ Metaphor

News, as a form of realism, is generally considered to work through metonymy (Fiske 1982), that is, by a careful selection of people and incidents that stand for a more complex and fuller version of reality. But paradoxically (and the news is full of paradoxes) the objectivity of news is frequently conveyed in language that is metaphorical rather than literal. Unlike literature, news stories use metaphors that are so conventional that they have become clichés and their metaphorical nature is consequently unrecognized. A cliché is a piece of discourse that is frequently repeated because it bears a particularly close relationship with the dominant ideology. A cliché is a convention *in extremis* and it is this excessive conventionality that is the key to defusing the paradox. "Literal" language is no better than metaphorical language at conveying reality, for "reality" (or what passes for it in any given society) is a product of the dominant discourse. It is this view that enables Foucault to argue that the distinction between literal and figurative discourse is unproductive: all language is figurative and no language can bear the objective relation to an empirical reality that the description "literal" implies.

Metaphors, then, are not literary decoration or stimulants to the individual imagination, but are widespread and basic sense-making mechanisms. A metaphor explains the unfamiliar in terms of the familiar and is thus a conventionalizing agent. Following Lakoff and Johnson (1980), Mumby and Spitzack (1985) made a study of the language of television news in six political stories on three US networks and found a grand total of 165 metaphors.

Table 15.1 shows that war was the commonest metaphor for describing politics, followed by sport and drama. Making sense of politics by metaphors of war or sport constructs politics as a conflict between parties and not as a public sphere serving the good of the nation. Using the metaphor of drama makes sense of it as a "stage" upon which talented individuals "perform" as stars.

Table 15.1 *Occurrence of the principal metaphors in six news stories*

	Politics is war	Politics is a game	Politics is a drama	Total
AWACS Senate vote	35	30	9	74
OPEC negotiations	4	3	1	8
King Hussein	21	5	6	32
White House policy	19	5	0	24
Reagan budget policy	8	4	2	14
Administration feud	9	1	3	13
Total	96	48	21	165

The origins of these cliché metaphors lie in the institutional discourse shared between the news, the viewers, and, of course, the politicians. We should not question the accuracy of such metaphors in terms of assessing how appropriately they describe the way that politicians actually behave, for such questions presume that politicians' behavior precedes, and is independent of, the discourse by which they are represented. It is more productive to grant discourse a more formative role: the discourse is common to news producers and consumers, which of necessity includes politicians, and so the discourse forms the way politicians see themselves and their actions and thus plays an active role in shaping those actions.

Conventionalized metaphors make common sense. Lakoff and Johnson (1980) have shown, for example, how widespread is the metaphor that "time is money." The ordinariness of phrases such as "saving" or "wasting time," of "spending" time is evidence of how well the metaphor serves the ideology of the Protestant work ethic within capitalism.

The Australian news story analyzed on pp. 296–301 shows a typical use of metaphor in news. Here it is not politics but an industrial dispute which is represented by the metaphor of war. The effect of this is to construct the management as "us," and the unions as "them," the hostile invaders, and to deny any sense that society is composed of a series of legitimate and necessary conflicts of interest that cannot be properly understood from one point of view only. These conflicts occur *within* society, and not between us and an alien. The metaphor of war defines unionism as non-Australian and delegitimates the challenge it poses to the bourgeoisie: its clichéd invisibility gives to this construction the status of objective reality. The metaphor is "exnominated." It is not, like a literary one, foregrounded and ascribed to a named author, but is part of a conventional discourse whose conventions originate from a social location, not from an individual imagination.

This sort of metaphor has none of the self-awareness or excess of the bees-honey-flowers metaphor in the *Hart to Hart* segment discussed in chapter 6. The clichéd metaphors of the news do not draw attention to themselves as sense-making devices: they work to close meanings down rather than open them up and thus work quite differently from metaphors in poetry or the self-parodic excessive metaphor in *Hart to Hart*.

☐ News narrative

The categorizations and textual devices that control the sense of news are all embedded in a narrative form. In chapter 8 we outlined Todorov's account of the basic narrative structure in which a state of equilibrium is disrupted, the forces of disruption are worked through until a resolution is reached, and another state of equilibrium is achieved which may differ from or be identical to the first. This constitutes the basic structure of a television news story, just as it does of a sitcom or a cop show. In all three genres the final state of equilibrium is identical to, or at least closely approximates, that of the first and to this extent the form is reactionary or conservative.

The main narrative energy in news, as in other stories, lies in the central section in which the forces of disruption are explored and their conflict with the social order is enacted: the ideological energy, however, is expended in the resolution of this conflict and its relationship to the status quo embodied in the opening and closing states of equilibrium. In news stories the opening state of equilibrium performs its ideological work through its absence: it is the unspoken norm whose status as the taken-for-granted common sense obviates any need to articulate it. For Hall (1984) the ideological work performed by the form of news stories is more important than any notion of content:

> Those stories, or rather those ways of telling the stories, write the journalists. The stories are already largely written for them before the journalists take fingers to typewriters or pen to paper. . . .
> Let me make the point that if you tell a story in a particular way you often activate meanings which seem almost to belong to the stock of stories themselves. I mean you could tell the most dramatic story, the most graphic and terrible account of an event; but if you construct it as a children's story you have to fight very hard not to wind up with a good ending. In that sense those meanings are already concealed or held within the forms of the stories themselves. Form is much more important than the old distinction between form and content. We used to think form was like an empty box, and it's really what you put into it that matters. But we are aware now that the form is actually part of the content of what it is that you are saying. (p. 7)

The content of news stories will necessarily vary from day to day, but their constant form is one of their crucial strategies of containment and is common to both fiction and news. Hall (1984) believes that

> we make an absolutely too simple and false distinction between narratives about the real and the narratives of fiction. And you can find that in the news: the news is full of little stories which are very similar to war romances. And so there isn't, I think, any way of simplifying that relationship between reality and fiction. (p. 6)

The TV networks often exploit this increasingly uncertain relationship. Feuer (1986) gives two examples of the news and fiction being explicitly interwoven. In one, a news item about college students ritualistically watching *Dynasty* was broadcast as a promo during *Dynasty* and as an item in the news that followed.

> Similarly, following a "trauma drama" on teen suicide, the eleven o'clock news announced and subsequently presented "expert" psychological advice on how to recognise suicidal tendencies in "your" children. (p. 105)

It is in the interests of the TV networks to make the drama appear more real, for "realisticness" is central to the ideology of capitalist societies and thus so important in the reading practices in them. But they are only able to exploit the similarity because "news" is a discourse, as is fiction, and news works through stories that make sense of reality in just the same way as do fictional stories.

This blurring of the distinction between fiction and reality is also seen in the news's treatment of character. Clearly the news is peopled by real individuals, but in representing events through people the news is following the conventions of classic realism, for it assumes that the way to construct an understandable and authentic version of the real is through the actions, words, and reactions of the individuals involved. Social and political issues are only reported if they can be embodied in an individual, and thus social conflict of interest is personalized into conflict between individuals. The effect of this is that the social origins of events are lost, and individual motivation is assumed to be the origin of all action. The story of a strike and the story of *Hart to Hart* are identical in this respect.

As in classic realism, the individuals who people the news are first carefully selected and then carefully controlled by the way they are inserted into the narrative structure. A limited range of people is given access to the news, very few social positions are allowed to "speak." The British government, for instance, uses the concept of "the national interest" to "persuade" the BBC that Northern Irish "terrorists" (*sic*) should not be allowed to put their side of a story in their own words. The "accessed voices" (Hartley 1982) speak from a limited range of social positions, usually those contained within the safe limits of parliamentary democracy. Voices that appear too radical are not allowed to speak directly, but are reported, that is, mediated, if their point of view is represented at all.

These selectively accessed voices are controlled even more by the way they are written into the news narrative. Hartley (1982) makes the productive analogy between the accessed voices of news and dialogue in a novel:

> Even though the dialogue "belongs" to the characters who speak it, it is *produced* by the author. In television news the same principle holds. Whatever an individual character may say, its meaning will be determined not by his or her intentions or situation, but by the placing of the interview in the overall context of the story. (pp. 109–10)

Thus, in the story analyzed below, the trade unionist is only allowed to speak after the narrative has constructed him as the enemy/villain.

News controls the multivocality of the real by narrative structure and a careful selection of which voices are accessed. These voices are always located within familiar social roles – the political leader, the unionist, the trauma victim, and so on. These social roles are then organized into narrative functions. Bell (1983), in his detailed study of drug stories in print and television news, gives a good example of this process at work. First individuals were inserted into four main social roles: police and law enforcement officers, social and welfare workers, drug runners and dealers, and drug users. Then these social roles were constructed into the narrative functions of heroes, helpers, villains, and victims. Bell concludes that the media

> posit heroes and helpers acting on behalf of the administrative arm of society in just the right proportion to allay any excessive threat that the villainy of racketeers and the weakness of victims might arouse. (p. 118)

Bell found that these narrative and social roles were typically filled by the social types that embody the same ideological values as they do in fiction. Thus the villains (or drug runners/dealers) were typically not Anglo-Saxon or, if they were, they had their Asian or Latin connections stressed. Social or racial deviance is the sign and embodiment of evil in news as in fiction. The victims came from groups of minimal social power – the young, women, lower classes, the unemployed, the low achievers. The threat that their weakness posed was defused by being located in a position in the social structure designed to accommodate it. The heroes were active in the fight against evil and tended to be of socially central types, whereas the helpers were less active and more nurturing, and might be represented by social types who mediated between the heroes and the victims, and had characteristics of both.

As Hall (1984) points out, these formal characteristics are not just a familiar mold into which the bearer of meanings, the content, is poured: form and content make meaning together and to separate them out is finally an unproductive exercise. These stories are prewritten, they "write" the journalists, and their meanings are already in circulation. In using their forms, the news is inserting apparently new or surprising events into the familiar: their familiarity is central to news's strategies of containment.

☐ News analysis

To trace these strategies of containment at work, let us look at a typical news story in some detail. Shown on Channel Nine News, it concerns an industrial dispute in the State Energy Commission (the SEC), the provider of electricity and gas in Perth, Western Australia. It was the evening's lead story, and was followed by another "industrial" one, this time about rising unemployment figures.

☐ CHANNEL NINE NEWS

NEWS READER, RUSSEL GOODRICK:
The FBI investigating a bomb explosion on board a jumbo jet in flight between Japan and Hawaii.

The familiar news reader: his individuality hooks the viewer through identification and familiarity, but does not affect the impersonality (objectivity) of his words.

Good evening. A satellite report from Honolulu shortly. But tonight's lead report is the end of the power strike. Also in the bulletin, Australia's worst unemployment figures on record. And in sport, Wally.

satellite: connotation of immediacy, authenticity, speed

strike: the choice of the word implies union agency. Striking is what unions do and management suffers.

Grouping of dispute and unemployment stories can easily suggest a cause and effect relationship that imputes blame to the unions.

SPORTSCASTER, WALLY FORMAN:

Thanks Russ. Well, Val Cominah will attempt to win her fifth state golf title at the Royal Fremantle tomorrow and we go hobie catting on Sydney harbour. Barry has the weather.

The "headlines" foreground the segmented nature of the news and the struggle required to contain its potential unruliness.

WEATHERMAN, BARRY BARKLA:

Well, there'll still be a fair bit of cloud around, maybe one or two drops, but I wouldn't even worry about taking the umbrella. Russ.

The news "team" is an attempt to unify the fragmented news items. Hard news is disruptions to the norm – a bomb, a strike, and unemployment are equally disruptive. Soft news and sport reaffirm the norm.

NEWS READER, RUSSEL GOODRICK:

The crippling statewide power strike will end at midnight and the threat of further blackouts tonight is receding as generating stations begin winding up to full capacity. The dispute, which cost millions of dollars in lost production, plunged one-third of the city into darkness and contributed to the death

crippling: the consumer constructed as victim

blackouts: war metaphor

Concentration on effects, not causes, of the strike, constructs the reader as consumer-victim, a hostile viewpoint from which to "understand" union activity (conventional news practice).

297

of a pedestrian in a blacked-out street, has been settled through a compromise.

Conflict (unions) v. *compromise* (social norm)

REPORTER, JOHN COLLIS (VOICE-OVER):
As State Energy Commission staff battled to keep the power generators turning, hundreds of grim-faced strikers were forced to take the stairs to this morning's second floor meeting at the Labour Centre.

battled: ongoing war metaphor: SEC staff as heroes, unions as villains
grim-faced: potential contradictions with visuals; fictional convention for representing villains
take the stairs ... second floor meetings: "objective" facts, not of interest in themselves, guarantee the "truth" of the constructed story; moral judgment in the irony.

"nomination" – visual and verbal

In a nearby office the union executive was mapping out strategy for the meeting with its shop stewards. Among them 24-year-old Geoff Duke, whose dismissal at Port Hedland, for alleged misconduct, triggered the strike.

mapping out strategy: ongoing war metaphor, which implies links with the bomb-on-aircraft story: strikes are in the same conceptual category as terrorism. The sole mention of the cause of dispute – very nonspecific compared to its effects: cause is individualized, management "exnominated": *dismissal* is Duke's, not an act of management.

The "disruptive event" (Todorov) is the alleged misconduct of a worker (cf. "union duty" below).
Alleged by whom? By exnominated management.

REPORTER, JOHN COLLIS (LIVE SOUND):
How does it feel to have blacked out the city last night?

Individualization of reaction and responsibility depoliticizes the motive.
Duke "nominated" by visuals

JACK MARKS (UNION ASSISTANT SECRETARY):
Just leave him be, will you. We don't want any inflammatory discussions at this stage. We're trying to resolve this problem. If any one wants to throw a bucket of kerosene on the fire, well they can do it. But that's not our position. We've got idiots ringing and threatening to shoot the lot of us at the present time.

Problem of containment: is this inoculation or disruption? The structure of the story so far leads us to read this as "that's what the enemy would say, we have to know their point of view in order to discount it" – a clear example of inoculation. But its effectivity is doubtful (see pp. 301–8).

Marks "nominated" by visuals

REPORTER, JOHN COLLIS (VOICE-OVER):
Amid cheers of approval, Assistant Secretary Jack Marks told the men the issue

Unionists constructed as emotional, dangerous ideologues; the live film/sound shows no cheers.

struck at the core of unionism, the right of a shop steward to do his union duty.

Potential contradiction with the visuals which show the unionists as ordinary people-like-us. The structure of the story so far has worked to delegitimize this *right*. What the union calls "his union duty" the "objective" news reader, through "claw-back," has called "alleged misconduct."

But he saved his trump card until later. A compromise deal had already been hammered out with Premier Ray O'Connor. Mr Duke could be reinstated immediately in a review of the sacking. The vote to go back to work was unanimous. But if a compromise had been so easy, was yesterday's chaos so necessary?

trump card: game metaphor

been hammered out: passive mode denies the unions the power to act positively.

could be reinstated: passive mode ex-nominates management, which is never mentioned and grammatically constructed as passive; the union appears the agent of disruption. The restorative event is the act of a government agency.

Conflict of interest is implied to be a union invention: the power of the bourgeoisie is said to work through compromise/consensus.

JACK MARKS (LIVE):
The city was plunged into darkness last night because of managerial

Are the strategies of inoculation and ex-nomination enough to

decisions by the SEC, not by us.

REPORTER, JOHN COLLIS (VOICE-OVER):
The men will begin returning to work after midnight, and although power restrictions are still in force, everything should be back to normal by morning.

John Collis, Channel Nine News.

NEWS READER, RUSSEL GOODRICK:
In fact, the State Energy Commission says it now expects to be able to lift the power restrictions by about seven o'clock this evening but consumers have been asked to wait for the official all-clear and continue to conserve power.

contain this disruption? Marks is shot in extreme close-up – the code of the villain (see p. 7).

resolution: return to the same state of equilibrium as at the start of the story

SEC as heroes improving on an already acceptable resolution. SEC and consumers (i.e. the people) constructed as having identical interests in "defeating" the unions. *But* the unions are also consumers/people.

The management point of view has, through exnomination, become the objective point that reveals the "truth": the management *is* the SEC: the unions, paradoxically, are not.

Source: Bond Media, Perth, Western Australia.

☐ The forces of disruption

The strategies of containment are many, subtle, and tried and tested by time. They are essentially formal characteristics and thus bear the brunt of the ideological work. But the intense need that the news has for such strategies should not be seen merely as evidence of the desire of the dominant ideology to impose and naturalize itself, but also as evidence of the strength of the forces of disruption. By the forces of disruption I mean those aspects of the text, of the real, and of the audience, which threaten the sense that is used to contain oppositional, alternative, or unruly elements.

The social experience that news brings to us is itself *unruly*: its events do not easily fit the conventional shapes and sequences that news imposes. The "bits" left out in the news's metonymic selection do not necessarily stay silent and invisible, but may erupt and disrupt the smooth surface of the narrative. Hartley (1984a) demonstrates how a BBC news story on a shooting in Northern Ireland tried to set the incident within a domestic framework. The story constructed the victim as husband/father, his age, marital status, number and names of children were given, his ordinary house and neighbors were filmed. But during the filming of the house and interviews with neighbors, a military helicopter was hovering overhead, its engine clearly audible on the sound track. The political-military "sense" of the incident disrupted the domestic "sense" that the story was proposing. The "real" is too multifaceted, too contradictory, to submit easily to the control of the news conventions. There is simply "too much reality" for it to be contained. The unruliness of the real and the semiotic excess of television work together to ensure that multiple and contradictory meanings can never be finally ruled out. Their disruptive forces are always there, however marginalized and silenced, fighting against the strategies of containment and available for the appropriate reader.

We have seen how highly news values the "vox pop" for its authenticity and immediacy, but these values are inherently risky, their continuity with "the real" works not only to naturalize and guarantee the process of objectification (see above) but also, conversely, to disrupt it. Jack Marks's comment in the story above that "the city was plunged into darkness last night because of managerial decisions" cannot have *all* its oppositionality evacuated from it by inoculation and narrative placement. Indeed, its very authenticity paradoxically works to enhance its impact and thus to work against those strategies. The authenticity and immediacy of the vox pop necessarily makes it potentially unruly and disruptive, and thus available for oppositional readings by readers whose social position is closer to Jack Marks's than to the exnominated managerial voice of the studio news reader.

Lewis (1985) has shown how surprisingly ineffective the narrative strategies of news stories are in imposing their structure and its associated meanings upon the viewers. The content of a live "vox pop" segment made a greater impression on many of his subjects than did the studio-based introduction and narrative structure within which it was inserted. Lewis's study of

the news audiences shows us how limited is the power of the news conventions to impose their preferred meanings and ideologies upon the diverse
audiences that news reaches. In this bulletin there are clear contradictions
between Jack Marks's statement and the main narrative strategies of the rest
of the story, and Lewis's work shows us that even though all the firepower
appears to be held by the news conventions, there is no guarantee that they
will always win in the struggle for meaning between them and the vox pop
insert. The immediacy and authenticity of Jack Marks "live" will, for some
readers, have more power than the narrative attempts to contain and control
his voice.

Lewis's work follows Morley's (1980a), but unlike Morley, Lewis locates
the variety of the readings not in the social diversity of the audience but in the
ineffectiveness of the news conventions. He suggests that television news has
inherited from print news the (for it) inappropriate convention of starting
each story with the most important point and giving the other details in
descending order of importance. Clearly a newspaper and a television news
bulletin require different modes of reading: the reader of the newspaper can
select which story to read, and, more significantly for this argument, can
select how much of that story to read. The conventional structure of a news
story is, then, appropriate for print journalism. But television news selects
both the order of stories and their length and so has no need to use the
structure of print stories. The segmentation of the news, with its abrupt
changes from story to story, means, according to Lewis's findings, that the
opening moments of a new story are spent by the audience in adjusting to the
new topic. The details of the opening sentence are likely to be submerged in
this adjustment, so the print-derived structure of the television news story
quite often resulted in the loss of the information that the news had decided
was the key importance.

This inappropriate structure worked in another way to minimize, or even
counteract, the effectivity of the news narrative. By concentrating on solutions and conclusions, it denied what Barthes (1975a) calls "the hermeneutic
code" of narrative. This is the code that provides most of the motor power of
the plot, it is the code that poses enigmas and controls the way they are
resolved. According to Lewis, this code is the one that engages the audience
most closely with the narrative, it is the one that makes the audience care
about the outcome. Its comparative absence in television news weakens the
hold of the program upon its audience and thus opens up a space in which
"misreading" or "mismemory" can occur.

Thus, the opening statements in the SEC news may not position the reader
as the consumer-victim of the striking unionists as effectively as our earlier
analysis of the text would lead us to believe. If the audiences of this bulletin
behaved in the same way as Lewis's there would be a significant number who

would have no recall of this opening, framing statement, but who would remember clearly Jack Marks's comment that it was the management who put out the lights. Of course, they need not actually remember these framing statements in order to have been positioned by them: the statements' function in setting up the point of view from which to make sense of the rest of the story does not depend solely upon a conscious recall of their content. But many of Lewis's subjects remembered and *interpreted* the live insert (the equivalent of Jack Marks's comment) apparently free from any positioning effect of the (forgotten) introductory remarks.

Dahlgren (1985) lays more stress on the differences between viewers to explain the differences in news readings. His research team used themselves as subjects and tried to read the news "naively," that is, in their everyday social roles. They compared these "readings" with the ones they made later, in their roles as researchers when they analyzed a recording, and found, not surprisingly, large differences between the two sets of readings. Firstly they found that their memories were even more inefficient than they had expected: they instantly forgot enormous amounts of information, and came up with very different readings. More surprisingly, perhaps, their academic readings varied as much:

> Moreover we found that the interpretation, the "sense" of any given story, could vary considerably between us, even after repeated study. This had to do not only with the frames of reference we applied, our different stocks of knowledge, dispositions, chains of association, and so on, but also the "mind sets" with which we approached the stories. For example, if one of us happened to be on the alert for the message dimensions while the other was more orientated towards experiencing the visuals, our respective "readings" could be quite different. (p. 237)

The news is a montage of voices, many of them contradictory, and its narrative structure is not powerful enough to dictate always which voice we should pay most attention to, or which voice should be used as a framework by which to understand the rest.

News is not unique in this. Barthes (1975a) suggests that all narratives are an interweaving of different voices carried by the five codes, and that there can be no final hierarchical order amongst them. At any one reading, any one voice may speak more loudly than the rest. The codes that bear these voices are the means by which the text is invaded by other texts, by social experience of "life as culture" (p. 21). Jack Marks's statements working in Barthes's referential code (see chapter 8) may be invaded by our textual experience of other unionists on the media, of other media stories of industrial disputes. For students of the media, they may be invaded by the analytical and critical voices of secondary texts such as those of Glasgow Media Group. For others with direct experience of industrial disputes, either managerial or union experience, their "life as culture" will invade the text: their conversations and gossip, as tertiary texts, will be read back into the news itself. Codes, for Barthes, are bridges by which a diversity of textual/social experience gains access to the primary text and makes it meaningful at the moment of reading. This de-originates the text in two senses: it shows that the text-as-meaning is produced at the moment of reading, not at the moment of writing, and it takes away from that text the status of being the originator of that meaning. The meanings preexist the text in culture, and the text is a montage of quotations from what has already been said/thought/represented. If this is an appropriate description of a novel apparently originating in the imagination of a named author, it is even more obviously an explanation of the apparently unauthored or multi-authored news, which lays no claim to the unifying action of a single imagination, but instead flaunts the diversity of the world that it covers and creates while hiding the authorial process of narrativizing it.

Barthes does not theorize the role of the social location of the reader in opening up the polysemy of the text, but he does demonstrate in detail the extent of the work the reader has to perform to make the text make sense. And the reader's experience of the conventions of news is only a comparatively small part of the cultural "training" that underlies this process.

The strongly marked segmentation of the news also fights against the structure given by its narrative and works to open up its meanings. The collisions, the lack of the laws of cause and effect, and the surprising contradictions remain the manifest character of the news despite any latent ideological coherence. Grouping of stories into "political," "industrial," "foreign," and so on is an attempt to minimize these collisions but is of limited strategic effect. Segmentation is not only a structuring principle of the bulletin itself, but it works also on a micro level *within* stories, as well as between them. Thus the SEC dispute story is composed of a number of segments – the studio comments, the preparation for the meeting, the meeting itself, Marks's address to camera, and so on. The narrative may have attempted to put these in a chronological and semiotic order, but it could never finally disguise the montage that is a contradictory, and more open, structuring principle.

It is difficult to extrapolate precisely from a piece of ethnographic research to another situation, but the work of Lewis and Dahlgren does provide evidence in support of Barthes's theorizing of the text as a construct of the reader. But neither of these authors goes on to see the news text as the site of a struggle for meaning, and we must beware of allowing the ethnographic perspective on a single empirical moment to evacuate this moment from the larger perspective of the experience of, and possible resistance to, social power of which it is necessarily a part. Thus the different readings and remeberings of which Dahlgren and his colleagues were conscious were situated in a framework of unconscious meanings which were more ideological and thus oppositional to the apparent "freedom" of the reader. When commenting on the inadequacy of their memories during their naive readings, Dahlgren (1985) writes:

> Yet, at the same time, during these initial viewings we seldom *felt* very left out. Our failure in formal information absorption was apparently disguised by a strong experience of recognition of something familiar. Indeed, our spontaneous impressions were often a bit self-assured, and it was not until after repeated viewings of the videotapes and studies of the transcripts that we realised just how much we had missed. (pp. 236–7)

The "experience of recognition of something familiar" was due to the way that the dominant ideology was structured, by the news conventions, into the form of the text. It is this that is constant from day to day and that provides the ground rules by which we are led to interpret the daily differences, and it may be argued that this constancy makes the form of the news ideologically more powerful than the individual differences of reading which occur largely at the level of content and which are weakened by the inefficiency of memory. Another uncertainty is the origin of Dahlgren's "self-assurance." It may derive ideologically from the power of these ground rules to provide an adequate way of making sense that is common to the (comparatively minor) individual differences of senses that are actually made, or it may derive from the adequacy of each sense that is made to the subcultural requirements of its reader/maker. Probably different readers experience differently derived senses of "self-assurance." The uncertainty cannot be resolved empirically, but at least the contradictions between the inadequacy of memory and the sense of self-assurance, between the new information and the sense of familiarity, must lead us to realize that reading the news is as complex a cultural practice as reading any other text.

This similarity between reading the news and reading fiction is evidenced further by comparing some of Dahlgren's findings with those of Katz and Liebes (1985). Both turned to Jakobson's (1960) distinction between the referential and poetic functions of communication to explain a difference of reading practices that they found. The referential function is that served by a text's reference out to a sense of an extra-textual reality (contra Barthes's referential code): the poetic function is the text's reference to its own textuality, its structure and conventions. Dahlgren comments that for some viewers of the news,

> the reference to outer reality may appear weak, and meaning may be embodied more in the message's self-reference, fostering aesthetic involvement of some form. In Roman Jakobson's terms, the "referential function" may at times be subordinate to the "poetic function." (p. 238)

Katz and Liebes (1985) found that some non-American ethnic groups read *Dallas* referentially, that is, as representation of the American way of life, whereas others read it more poetically, as a structure of narrative conventions, characterization, and dramatic conflict. American ethnic groups, on the other hand, were more flexible and showed signs of reading it both referentially and poetically. Referential readings foreground the representational qualities of the text and poetic readings its discursivity.

The difference between the two reading strategies parallels the opposition between the conventions of news and the "reality" they construct/control. Sometimes these conventions are applied with such a sense of strain that one hardly needs empirical evidence to cast doubt on their effectiveness. The convention that every story must reach a point of closure is a case in point. In this story, the dispute was settled, the lights came back on, and life, apparently, returned to normal. But the story, in the way it was told, was not about this dispute in particular, but rather concerned a "war" between the unions and the rest of society. This "war" was structured by deep binary oppositions such as:

allies : enemies
Australian : non-Australian
victims : villains
management : unions
US : THEM

and there was no attempt to suggest that this deep conflict had been resolved by the (superficial) narrative closure of this individual story. On the contrary, as with most news stories the point of closure was formal and temporary: the conventionalization of the conflict that underlay it means that the conflict is always left unresolved and ready to disrupt the fragile equilibrium once again. In this way, the news is similar to the series drama or sitcom, for in all three genres the basic situation is never finally resolved. Ellis (1982) makes the point that the television series "implies the form of the dilemma rather than that of resolution and closure," and, like news, is "based on the repetition of a problematic" (p. 154).

This problematic is finally one of exerting discursive and social control over the unruliness and diversity of social life. Arguments that news should be more accurate or objective are actually arguments in favor of news's authority, and are ones that seek to increase its control under the disguise of improving its quality. News, of course, can never give a full, accurate, objective picture of reality nor should it attempt to, for such an enterprise can only serve to increase its authority and decrease people's opportunity to "argue" with it, to negotiate with it. In a progressive democracy, news should stress its discursive constructedness, should nominate *all* its

307

voices (not just the subordinated, disruptive ones) and should open its text to invite more producerly reading relations. Because news deals, in a high modality, with the very stuff of social conflict and social differences, it is politically healthy for news to encourage its readers to negotiate (often stubbornly) with it, to use its discursive resources to provoke and stimulate viewers to make *their* sense of, and validate *their* point of view on, the social experiences it describes.

The differences between news and fiction are only ones of modality. Both are discursive means of making meanings of social relations and it is important that readers treat news texts with the same freedom and irreverence that they do fictional ones.

A wider and more self-confident recognition of this essential fictionality of news might lead its masculine viewers to treat its texts with the same socially motivated creativity as do the feminine viewers of soap operas. Such a producerly reading strategy is harder to adopt for news, because the genre's forces of closure are strongly supported by its authoritative status in our society, and because masculine viewers in a patriarchy are less likely to have developed these sorts of cultural competencies than are feminine ones. It becomes an important task for the critic, then, to demystify news's discursive strategies and to discredit its ideology of objectivity and the truth.

For all its attempts to impose a masculine closure and sense of achievement, the news shares many characteristics with such drama as soap opera – lack of final closure, multiplicity of plots and characters, repetition and familiarity. The apparent formlessness of soap opera approximates to the multifacetedness of the real, so the struggle within the news to control the disruptive forces of reality is reflected in its formal dimension by the struggle of a masculine narrative form to impose its shape upon the feminine. The masculine principle invokes control and rules, the feminine disruption or at least evasion. The masculine attempts to control meanings and center the reader, the feminine to open them up and decenter him or her. The masculine bears the dominant ideology, the feminine enacts the strategies of resistance. It is this interplay of similarity and difference with a fictional form that underwrites our distrust of dividing television generically into fact and fiction, and justifies thinking of the news as masculine soap opera.

Chapter 16

Conclusion: the popular

economy

☐ The problem of the popular

Popularity is seductively easy to understand if we persist in the fallacious belief that we live in a homogeneous society and that people are fundamentally all the same. But it becomes a much more complex issue when we take into account that late capitalist societies are composed of a huge variety of social groups and subcultures, all held together in a network of social relations in which the most significant factor is the differential distribution of power.

In this book I have argued against the common belief that the capitalist cultural industries produce only an apparent variety of products whose variety is finally illusory for they all promote the same capitalist ideology. Their skill in sugar-coating the pill is so great that the people are not aware of the ideological practice in which they are engaging as they consume and enjoy the cultural commodity. I do not believe that "the people" are "cultural dopes"; they are not a passive, helpless mass incapable of discrimination and thus at the economic, cultural, and political mercy of the barons of the industry. Equally I reject the assumption that all that different people and different social groups have in common is baseness, so that art that appeals to many can only do so by appealing to what humans call "the animal instincts." "The lowest common denominator" may be a useful concept in arithmetic, but in the study of popularity its only possible value is to expose the prejudices of those who use it.

More recent Marxist thinking rejects the notion of a singular or monovocal capitalist ideology in favor of a multiplicity of ideologies that speak capitalism in a variety of ways for a variety of capitalist subjects. Their unity in speaking capitalism is fragmented by the plurality of accents in which they speak it. Such a view posits a multiplicity of points of resistance or accommodations whose only unity lies in the *fact* of their resistance or accommodation, but not in the *form* it may take.

This is a model that has far greater explanatory power in late capitalism and is one that grants some power to "the people." Despite the homogenizing force of the dominant ideology, the subordinate groups in capitalism have retained a remarkable diversity of social identities, and this has required capitalism to produce an equivalent variety of voices. The diversity of capitalist voices is evidence of the comparative intransigence of the subordinate.

Any discussion of popularity must account for opposing forces within it. The definition that serves the interests of the producers and distributors of the cultural commodity is one of head counting, often with some demographic sophistication so that heads of a particular socioeconomic class, age group, gender, or other classification can be collected, counted, and then "sold" to an advertiser. The greater the head count, the greater the popularity. Opposed to this is the notion that popular means "of the people" and that popularity springs from, and serves the interests of, the people amongst whom it is popular. Popularity is here a measure of a cultural form's ability to serve the desires of its customers. In so far as the people occupy different social situations from the producers, their interests must necessarily differ from, and often conflict with, the interests of the producers.

The term "the people" has romantic connotations which must not be allowed to lead us into a idealized notion of the people as an oppositional force whose culture and social experience are in some way authentic. We need to think rather of the people as a multiple and constantly changing concept, a huge variety of social groups accommodating themselves with, or opposing themselves to, the dominant value system in a variety of ways. In so far as "the people" is a concept with any validity at all, it should be seen as an alliance of formations which are constantly shifting and relatively transient. It is neither a unified nor a stable concept, but one whose terms are constantly under reformulation in a dialectic relationship with the dominant classes. In the cultural domain, then, popular art is an ephemeral, multifarious concept based upon multiple and developing relationships with the practices of the dominant ideology.

The term "people," then, refers to social groups that are relatively powerless and are typically interpellated as consumers, though they may not respond in this manner. They have cultural forms and interests of their own that differ from, and often conflict with, those of the producers of cultural commodities. The autonomy of these groups from the dominant is only relative, and never total, but it derives from their marginalized and repressed histories that have intransigently resisted incorporation, and have retained material, as well as ideological, differences usually through devalued cultural forms, many of which are oral and unrecorded. For some groups these differences may be small and the conflicts muted, but for others the gap is enormous. For a cultural commodity to be popular, then, it must be able to meet the various interests of the people amongst whom it is popular as well as the interests of its producers.

□ The two economies

The multiplicity and contradictory value of these interests does not mean that they cannot be met in the one commodity: they can, though only because the cultural commodity circulates in different though simultaneous economies, which we may call the financial and the cultural.

The workings of the financial economy cannot account adequately for all cultural factors, but it still needs to be taken into account in any investigation of popular art in a consumers' society. It *is* useful, if only up to a point, to be able to describe texts as cultural commodities, but we must always recognize crucial differences between them and other goods in the marketplace.

For instance, cultural goods do not have a clearly defined use-value, despite Marx's assertion that the production of aesthetic pleasure is a use-value, but this seems to be a metaphorical use of the term – the use-value of a work of art is different from that, say, of a machine gun or a can of beans, if only that it is very much more difficult to predict or specify. Cultural commodities do, however, have a more clearly identifiable exchange-value which the technology of reproduction has put under severe pressure. Photocopiers, audio and video recorders are agents of popular power, and thus the producers and distributors have had to argue for elaborations and extensions of copyright laws to maintain some control over exchange-value and its base in scarcity. Such legislation has largely failed: the copying of television programs and of records is not only widespread, but also socially acceptable.

The cultural commodity differs from other commodities in having comparatively high initial production costs and very low reproduction costs, so distribution offers a safer return on investment than production. Technical development and venture capital have, therefore, been concentrated on satellites, on cable and microwave distribution systems, or in the hardware of televisions, sound systems, and home entertainment centers.

But the cultural commodity cannot be adequately described in financial terms only: the circulation that is crucial to its popularity occurs in the parallel economy – the cultural. What is exchanged and circulated here is not wealth but meanings, pleasures, and social identities. Of course commodities primarily based in the financial economy work in the cultural economy too, consumer choice between similar commodities is often not between competing use-values, despite the efforts of consumer advice groups, but between cultural values: and the selection of one particular commodity over others becomes the selection of meanings, pleasures, and social identity for the consumer. With the shift of capitalist economies from production to marketing, the cultural value of material commodities has enormously increased in proportionate importance – one has only to look at the fashion industry, or the motor car industry, to find examples. None the less, such commodities still circulate within a primarily financial economy that retains their bases in use-value.

We need to look in a little more detail at the interaction between these separate, though related, economies, the financial and the cultural. The financial economy offers two modes of circulation for cultural commodities: in the first, the producers of a program sell it to distributors: the program is a straightforward material commodity. In the next, the program-as-commodity changes role and it becomes a producer. And the new commodity that it produces is an audience which, in its turn, is sold to advertisers or sponsors.

A classic example of the interdependence of these two financial "sub-economies" and the possibility of controlling them is provided by *Hill Street Blues*. MTM produces the series and sells it for distribution to NBC. NBC sells its audience (a higher socioeconomic group of both genders than most TV audiences) to Mercedes Benz who sponsor the series. The show rates respectably, but not spectacularly. MTM could, if they wished, modify the format and content of the series to increase the size of the audience. But such an increase would be in a lower socioeconomic group, and this is not a commodity that Mercedes Benz wish to buy. So the show stays as it is, one of the few on American television that has a strong class basis, though noticeably little class conflict. Furillo and Davenport, those embodiments of middle-class angst, care and suffer for their team of working-class cops. The program is built around the yuppie view of class, social conscience, and moral responsibility, which form the basis of the meanings and pleasures that it offers in the cultural economy.

The move to the cultural economy involves yet another role-shift from commodity to producer. As the earlier role-shift changed the role of the program from commodity to producer, so the move to the cultural economy involves the audience in a role-shift which changes it also from a commodity to a producer: in this case a producer of meanings and pleasures. The gap between the cultural and the financial economies is wide enough to grant the cultural economy considerable autonomy, but not too wide to be bridgeable. The producers and distributors of a program can exert some, if limited, influence over who watches and some, though limited, influence over the meanings and pleasures that the audiences (and we must shift to the plural in the cultural economy) may produce from it. The upscale target audience of *Hill Street Blues* is far from its only audience and the variety of audiences will presumably produce a variety of pleasures and meanings. *Dallas* not only tops the ratings in the USA and thus must gain a wide diversity of American audiences, it is also widely exported and arguably has the largest range of audiences of any fictional TV program. As we saw in chapter 6, Ien Ang (1985) found a Dutch Marxist and a feminist who were able to find pleasure in the program by discovering in its excess of sexism and capitalism a critique of those systems that it was apparently celebrating. Similarly, Katz and Liebes (1984, 1985) found that members of a Jewish kibbutz were clear that the money of the Ewings did not bring them happiness, whereas members of a rural North African cooperative were equally clear that their wealth gave them an easy life. Katz and Leibes's fifty different ethnic lower-middle-class groups produced a huge variety of meanings and found an equal variety of pleasures from the same show.

This book has argued that the power of audiences-as-producers in the cultural economy is considerable. This is partly due to the absence of any direct sign of their (subordinate) role in the financial economy which liberates them from its constraints – there is no exchange of money at the point of sale/consumption, and no direct relationship between the price paid and the amount consumed, people can consume as much as they wish and what they wish, without the restriction of what they are able to afford. But more importantly, this power derives from the fact that meanings do not circulate in the cultural economy in the same way that wealth does in the financial. They are harder to possess (and thus to exclude others from possessing), they are harder to control because the production of meaning and pleasure is not the same as the production of the cultural commodity, or of other goods, for in the cultural economy the role of consumer does not exist as the end point of a linear economic transaction. Meanings and pleasures circulate within it without any real distinction between producers and consumers.

In the financial economy consumption is clearly separate from production and the economic relations that bind them are comparatively clear and available for analysis. But the cultural economy does not work in the same way. Its commodities, which we call "texts," are not containers or conveyors of meaning and pleasure, but rather *provokers* of meaning and pleasure. The production of meaning/pleasure is finally the responsibility of the consumer and is undertaken only in his/her interests: this is not to say that the material producers/distributors do not attempt to make and sell meanings and pleasures – they do, but their failure rate is enormous. Twelve out of thirteen records fail to make a profit, TV series are axed by the dozen, expensive films sink rapidly into red figures *(Raise the Titanic* is an ironic example – it nearly sank the Lew Grade empire).

This is one reason why the cultural industries produce what Garnham (1987) calls "repertoires" of products; they cannot predict which of their commodities will be chosen by which sectors of the market to be the provoker of meanings/pleasures that serve *their* interests as well as those of the producers. Because the production of meaning/pleasure occurs in the consumption as well as the production of the cultural commodity the notion of production takes on a new dimension that delegates it away from the owners of capital.

□ Popular cultural capital

Cultural capital, despite Bourdieu's (1980) productive metaphor, does not circulate in the same way as economic capital. Hobson's (1982) viewers of *Crossroads,* for example, were vehement that the program was theirs, it was their cultural capital. And they made it theirs by the pleasures and meanings they produced from it, that articulated their concerns and identities. There is a popular cultural capital in a way that there is no popular economic capital, and thus Bourdieu's institutionally validated cultural capital of the bourgeoisie is constantly being opposed, interrogated, marginalized, scandalized, and evaded, in a way that economic capital never is.

This popular cultural capital consists of the meanings and pleasures available to the subordinate to express and promote their interests. It is not a singular concept, but is open to a variety of articulations, but it always exists in a stance of resistance to the forces of domination. Like any form of capital, either economic capital or the cultural capital of the bourgeoisie, it works through ideology, for, as Hall (1986) points out, we must not limit our understanding of ideology to an analysis of how it works in the service of the dominant. We need to recognize that there are resistive, alternative ideologies that both derive from and maintain those social groups who are not accommodated comfortably into the existing power relations: "an ideology empowers people, enabling them to begin to make some sense or intelligibility of their historical situation." (p. 16).

These ideologies that empower the subordinate enable them to produce resistive meanings and pleasures that are, in their own right, a form of social power. Power is not, according to Foucault, a one-way force, from the top down. When he talks of power coming from below, he alerts us to the fact that power is necessarily a two-way force: it can only work, in either direction, in opposition. This is just as true for "top down" power as it is for "bottom up" power.

If power is a two-way force, so, too, is the pleasure so closely associated with it.

> The pleasure that comes of exercising a power that questions, monitors, watches, spies, searches out, palpates, brings to light: and, on the other hand, the pleasure that kindles at having to evade this power, flee from it, fool it or travesty it. The power that lets itself be invaded by the pleasure it is pursuing: and opposite it, power asserting itself in the pleasure of showing off, scandalizing, resisting.
>
> (Foucault 1978: 45)

Television participates in both these modes of power-pleasure. It exerts the power of surveillance, revealing the world, spying out people's secrets, monitoring human activity, but an integral part of this power is the resistance, or rather resistances, to it. The two-way nature of power means that its resistances are themselves multiple points of power. Power, paradoxically, can thus liberate people from its own force to subject and discipline them.

Play, besides being a source of pleasure, is also a source of power. Children's "play" with television is a form of power over it. In incorporating its characters and scenarios into their own fantasy games they create their own oral and active culture out of the resources it provides. Sydney children in 1982 and 1983 were singing their own version of a beer commercial:

How do you feel
when you're having a fuck
under a truck
and the truck rolls off

I feel like a Tooheys', I feel like a Tooheys'
I feel like a Tooheys or two.

(Children's Folklore Archives, Australian Studies Centre, Western Australian Institute of Technology)

The production of a scatological playground rhyme out of a television commercial is a typical, and complex, cultural activity. At the most obvious level it is an empowering, creative response to television and an oppositional one. It is a clear example of "excorporation," that process by which the powerless steal elements of the dominant culture and use them in their own, often oppositional or subversive, interests. This is the verbal equivalent of Madonna's use of religious inconography to convey her independent sexuality and the opposite of the fashion industry's incorporation of elements of punk or of working-class dress into its own haute couture. It is also an example of Foucault's resistive power, the power to "travesty" the original power, the pleasure of "showing off, scandalizing, resisting."

This children's rhyme involves a powerful, playful, pleasurable misuse of television, in that the signifiers are changed as well as the signifieds. In chapter 5 we noted a similar "misuse" of *Dallas* (Katz and Liebes 1985), in which the narrative was distorted to meet the cultural needs of a particular audience. The Arab group who "rewrote" the program so that Sue Ellen returned with her baby to her father's home instead of her former lover's were "rewriting" or travestying television in a fundamentally similar way to that of the Sydney school children, and for much the same purposes. *Prisoner*, too, is easily rewritten in a way that allows school students to travesty its meanings and to make it a representation not of prison but of school (Hodge and Tripp 1986). Their ideology, deriving from, and making sense of, their social experience of subordination in both the school and the family, enabled them to partake in an active ideological practice: they were not cultural dopes at the mercy of the text or its producers, but were in control of their own reading relations. They were active producers of their own meanings and pleasures from the text.

Of course, the semiotic excess and the producerly reading relations it requires are not unique to television: any art form that is popular amongst widely differing audiences must allow for this overspill. Thus Michaels (1986) shows that Aboriginal viewers of *Rambo* found neither pleasure nor sense in his nationalistic, patriotic motivation. Instead, they "wrote" him into an elaborate kinship network with those he was rescuing, thus making "tribal" meanings that were culturally pertinent to themselves. The fact that the film was popular with both them and Ronald Reagan must not lead us to assume any similarity between the two, nor that the meanings and pleasures they produced from it were similar.

☐ Resistance and semiotic power

Resistance is a concept that has been woven throughout the argument of this book, for it is central to an understanding of popularity in a society where power is unequally distributed. As social power can take many forms, so too can the resistances to it. There is no singular blanket resistance, but a huge multiplicity of points and forms of resistance, a huge variety of resistances. These resistances are not just oppositions to power, but are sources of power in their own right: they are the social points at which the powers of the subordinate are most clearly expressed.

It may be helpful to categorize these resistances into two main types, corresponding to two main forms of social power – the power to construct meanings, pleasures, and social identities, and the power to construct a socioeconomic system. The first is semiotic power, the second is social power, and the two are closely related, although relatively autonomous.

The power domain within which popular culture works is largely, but not exclusively, that of semiotic power. One major articulation of this power is the struggle between homogenization and difference, or between consensus and conflict. The "top down" force of this power attempts to produce a coherent set of meanings and social identities around an unarticulated consensus whose forms serve the status quo. It attempts to deny any conflict of interest and to mobilize social differences in a structure of complementarity. It is a homogenizing, centralizing, integrating force that attempts to maintain semiotic and social power at the centre.

Volosinov argues that the multiaccentuality of the sign is crucial, for it is this that enables it to play an active role in the class struggle: its polysemic potential is always mobilized in and against a structure of domination, and the strategy of the dominant is to control polysemy, to reduce the multiaccentual to the uniaccentual.

316

The ruling class strives to impart a superclass, external character to the ideological sign, to extinguish or drive inward the struggle between social value judgements which occurs in it, to make the sign uniaccentual.

(Volosinov 1973: 23)

Resisting this is the diversity of social groups with their diversity of social interests. Their power is expressed in the resistances to homogenization, it works as a centrifugal rather than a centripetal force, it recognizes conflict of interest, it proposes multiplicity over singularity and it may be summed up as the exercise of the power to be different.

This power to construct meanings, pleasures, and social identities that *differ* from those proposed by the structures of domination is crucial, and the area within which it is exercised is that of representation. Popular culture is often denigrated by its critics for appearing to offer not representations of the world, but avenues of escape from it: "mere escapism" is an easy way of dismissing popular culture from the critical and social agenda. Underlying this is the notion that *representation* has a social dimension, whereas *escapism* is a merely personal flight into fantasy. Such an easy dismissal ignores the fact that escapism or fantasy necessarily involves both an escape from or evasion of something and an escape to a preferred alternative: dismissing escapism as "mere fantasy" avoids the vital questions of *what* is escaped from, *why* escape is necessary, and *what* is escaped to.

Asking these questions gives escapism or fantasy as strong a sociopolitical dimension as representation, and begins to erode the difference between the two. But the differences are still commonly believed to exist, and I wish to challenge them because maintaining them serves the interests of the dominant by devaluing many of the pleasures of the subordinate. As with many of the experiences of the subordinate, fantasy or escapism is often "feminized," that is, it is seen as a sign of feminine weakness resulting from women's inability to come to terms with (masculine) reality. It is a sort of daydreaming that allows women or children to achieve their desires in a way that they are never capable of in the "real" world, a compensatory domain which results from and disguises their "real" lack of power. Representation, however, is seen as a means of exercising power: not a means of escaping from the world but of acting upon it. Representation is the means of making that sense of the world which serves one's own interests: it is "the process of putting into concrete forms (that is, different signifiers) an abstract ideological concept" (O'Sullivan *et al.* 1983: 199). Its process of making ideology material, and therefore natural, is a highly political one that involves the power to make meanings both of the world and of one's place within it: it is therefore "appropriately" thought of as dominant or masculine: it is seen as a site of struggle for power, in a way that fantasy is not. Such a simplistic distinction that is so much a part of the structures of domination needs challenging.

317

McRobbie (1984) articulates this challenge when she argues convincingly that fantasy is a private, intimate experience which can be interpreted as

> part of a strategy of resistance or opposition: that is, as marking out one of those areas that cannot be totally colonised. (p. 184)

She makes the point that the apparently obvious distinction between fantasy and reality is open to question:

> [fantasy is] as much an *experience*, a piece of reality, as is babysitting or staying in to do the washing. (p. 184)

Fantasy is a means of representation whose privacy and intimacy do not prevent its acting just as powerfully upon the meanings of social experience as do the more public representations of language and the media. Its interiority does not disqualify it from political effectivity: the interior is, to coin a phrase, the political.

The argument that this is a pseudo-power that dissipates the drive to seize "real" political or economic power underestimates the extent to which the construction of subjectivity is political. Part of the argument asserts that resistive fantasies that occur only in the interior experience of the subject are not finally resistive at all, for resistance can only occur at the level of the social or the collective. This argument is based upon the belief that the material social experience of the subordinate can, of itself, be the origin of resistance. Against this I would argue that the origins of resistance lie not just in the social experience of subordination, but in the sense people make of it. There are meanings of subordination that serve the interests of the dominant, and there are ones that serve those of the subordinated. But the crucial point is that the separation of material social experience from the meanings given to it is an analytical and theoretical strategy only. In everyday life, there is no such neat distinction: our experience *is* what we make of it. Similarly, distinctions between the social and the interior are finally unproductive particularly when they value one over the other: social or collective resistance cannot exist independently of "interior" resistance, even if that is given the devalued name of "fantasy." The connections between the interior and the social cannot be modeled along the simple cause and effect lines that underlie the devaluation of interior resistance because it may not have the direct effect of producing resistance at the social level. The relationship between the interior and the social can only be explained by a model of a much more dispersed and deferred effectivity.

Popular culture that works in the interests of the subordinate is often a provoker of fantasy. These fantasies may take many forms, but they typically embody the power of the subordinate to exert some control over representation. Such a fantasy is no escape from social reality, rather it is a direct response to the dominant ideology and its embodiment in social relations. The challenge it offers lies both in *what* meanings are made and in *who* has the power and the ability to make them. Fantasy, at the very least, maintains a sense of subcultural difference, it is part of the exercise of semiotic power.

□ Diversity and difference

The "power to be different" is the power that maintains social differences, social diversity. The relationship between social diversity and a diversity of voices on television is one that needs to be carefully thought through. There is a familiar rhetoric that proposes that diversity of programs on television is a good thing, and few would take issue with that as a general principle. Conversely, homogeneity of programming is seen to be undesirable. The problem lies in deciding what constitutes homogeneity and what diversity and, equally problematically, what constitutes "a good thing." In one sense, the new technologies of distribution, satellites, cables, and optical fibers, can be viewed as potential agents of diversity, in that their economics demand that *more* be transmitted. But, as Bakke (1986) argues, in the European context, at least, new technologies such as satellites also permit a larger audience to be reached which produces a demand for noncontroversial content, a bland homogeneity that will offend no one and appeal in some, relatively superficial, way to everyone. Paradoxically, then, the increase in the means of distribution may actually decrease the variety of cultural commodities that are distributed.

But diversity is not simply to be measured in terms of the variety of programs transmitted: diversity of readings is equally, if not more, important. Paradoxically, diversity of readings may best be stimulated by a greater homogeneity of programming. A widely distributed single program, such as *Dallas*, whose openness makes it a producerly text, may not be such an agent of homogenization as it appears, for to reach its multitude of diverse audiences it must allow for a great deal of cultural diversity in its readings, and must thus provide considerable semiotic excess for the receiving subcultures to negotiate with in order to produce *their* meanings, rather than the ones preferred by the broadcasters. *Dallas* may be a singular, and highly profitable, commodity in the financial economy, but in the cultural it is a full *repertoire* of commodities: as Altman (1986) says, *Dallas* provides a "menu" from which the viewers choose.

A diversity of programs is a diversity that is deliberately constructed by television producers and schedulers in an attempt to segment the audience into the markets required by the advertisers, which may or may not coincide with the subcultural formations constructed by the people. A greater variety of closed, readerly texts that impose their meanings more imperialistically and that deliver market segments to advertisers may not be as socially desirable as a narrower range of more open texts, where the diversity is a function of the people rather than of the producers.

Wilson and Gutierrez (1985) argue that the new technologies, particularly cable, allow the media to exploit subcultural diversity, and to commodify ethnic and minority audiences in order to sell them to advertisers. *Dallas,* for all its apparent homogeneity, may well be a more diversified program than the variety of offerings of such multiple special-interest channels, and in so far as its diversification is audience-produced rather than centrally produced, it is, I argue, more likely to maintain cultural differences and to produce subculturally specific meanings and pleasures.

The same dilemma confronts us in the attempt to understand television's role and effects in the international arena. Hollywood, and, to a lesser extent, Europe, may dominate the international flow of both news and entertainment programming, yet there is little evidence of a global surge of popularity for the western nations and their values. The domination in the economic domain may not necessarily produce the equivalent domination in the cultural. Katz and Liebes (1987) have shown that Russian Jews, newly arrived in Israel, read *Dallas* as capitalism's self-criticism: "consuming" the program did not necessarily involve consuming the ideology.

A national culture, and the sense of national identity which many believe it can produce, which is constructed by the cultural industries or by politicians or cultural lobbyists, may not coincide with the social alliances that are felt to be most productive by subordinate groups within the nation. Thus Aboriginal cultural identity within contemporary Australia may serve itself best by articulating itself not with an Australian nation, but with blacks in other white-dominated, ex-colonial countries. And Michaels (1986) has indicated that the recent popularity of reggae amongst Aboriginal peoples is explained by some Aboriginals as the perception of a common social alliance amongst black subjected cultures. Black music, produced within and against colonialism, has a cultural and political effectivity that traverses national boundaries. Hodge and Tripp's (1986) Aboriginal children who constructed a single cultural category that included themselves, American Indians, and American black children were similarly forging their own cultural alliances in a way that can be neither controlled nor predicted by the cultural industries. Such a cultural consciousness is a prerequisite for political action, though it will not, of itself, produce it. But without it, any political movement to improve the Aboriginal situation will be insecurely based. MacCabe (1986) makes the point well:

> The crucial necessity for political action is a felt collectivity. It may be that cultural forms indicate to us that politically enabling collectivities are to be located across subcultures, be they national or international.   (pp. 9–10)

Conclusion: the popular economy

Hebdige (1979, 1982, 1987) has shown how American popular culture in the 1950s and 1960s was eagerly taken up by British working-class youth who found in its flashy streamlining a way to articulate their new class confidence and consciousness. Such symbolizations of their identity were simply not available in "British" culture which appeared to offer two equally unacceptable sets of alternatives – the one a romanticized cloth-cap image of an "authentic" traditional working-class culture, the other a restrained, tasteful, BBC-produced inflection of popular culture. The commodities produced by the American cultural industries were mobilized to express an intransigent, young, urban, working-class identity that scandalized both the traditional British working class and the dominant middle classes. The cultural alliance between this fraction of the British working class and their sense of American popular culture was one that served their cultural/ideological needs at that historical moment. Similarly, one might speculate about the cultural meanings of Madonna in Moscow (at the time of writing it is reported that her albums are changing hands for \$75 on the black market).

In a similar vein, Worpole (1983) has shown how the style of pre-Second World War American fiction, particularly that of Hemingway, Hammett, and Chandler, articulated a vernacular, masculine, critical stance towards urban capitalism that the British working class found pertinent to their social position. British popular literature, typified by the bourgeois rural milieu of Agatha Christie or the aristocratic, imperialist heroism of Bulldog Drummond, promoted a nostalgic class-specific Britishness that was more alien and hostile to the British working class than novels produced in America. Similarly Cohen and Robbins (1979) have shown how Kung Fu movies play a positive role as articulations of the subcultural norms of working-class London boys. The economic origin of the cultural commodity cannot account for the cultural use-value it may offer in its moment and place of reception and can neither control not predict the variety of meanings and pleasures it may provoke. The dominant ideological interests of the society that produces and determines the industry may well be imbricated in the conventions and discourses of the text, but they cannot comprise all of the textual fabric. In order for the text to be popular amongst audiences whose social position produces a sense of difference from that ideology, it must contain contradictions, gaps, and traces of counter-ideologies. Its narrative structure and hierarchization of discourses may attempt to produce a resolution in favor of the dominant, but various moments of reading can reveal this resolution to be much more fragile than traditional textual analysis would suppose it to be. Indeed, texts that are popular amongst a wide variety of audiences must hold this balance between the dominant ideology and its multiple oppositions on a point of extreme precariousness: it is no willful misreading to find in *Dallas* a critique of patriarchal capitalism, nor in *Prisoner* an exposure of the insensitivities of institutional power.

The unpredictability of the market for cultural commodities has forced the cultural industries into certain economic strategies, particularly the production of a repertoire of products (Garnham 1987), to ensure their profitability, and while these strategies have proved successful in maintaining the industries' domination in the financial economy, they necessarily weaken their ideological power in the cultural.

Those of us on the left may deplore the fact that, with some exceptions, it is the commercially produced commodities that most easily cross the boundaries of class, race, gender, or nation and that thus appear to be most readily accessible and pleasurable to a variety of subordinated groups. But alternative strategies are not easy to find, though the success of the BBC with working-class realist serials like *EastEnders* or the comedy series *Only Fools and Horses* does offer some hope. Otherwise, attempts to produce television by and for the working classes or other subordinate or minority groups, have only partially succeeded, if at all. Ang's (1986) account of the problems faced by a proletarian progressive television channel in Holland is exemplary here, and Blanchard and Morley (1984) have given an equally thoughtful account of the difficulties faced by Britain's Channel 4. It may well be that the subordinate maintain their subcultural identity by means other than television (schoolyard culture for children, gossip for women, etc.), and that television is popular to the extent that it intersects with these other cultural forces.

Cohen and Robbins (1979) try to account for the popularity of Kung Fu movies with British urban working-class males via the coming together of two forms of "collective representations," one of which is the oral tradition and interpersonal style of working-class culture, and the other is the industrially produced conventions of the genre. Morley (1981) summarizes the argument neatly:

> The oral traditions constitute forms of cultural competence available to these kids which make it possible for them to appropriate these movies – without forms of competence, the popularity of these movies would be inexplicable. (p. 11)

These points of intersection between mass and local or oral culture can only be activated by the viewers and cannot be deliberately or accurately produced by the cultural industries themselves, though they can, of course, be aimed at.

The industrial mode of production of television will necessarily separate its producers from its audiences culturally, socially, and ideologically: in the financial economy this gap clearly works to the advantage of the industry

322

which obviously would not like to see a series of popular, low-cost community stations develop, and thus it works to maximize the difference by developing more fully its high-cost production values. But in the cultural economy, the gap works to the industry's disadvantage and it seeks to close it, to stress its cultural closeness to its audiences. But in this it is rather like the lovesick suitor who can only hope to be chosen and who will never know if he will be nor the reasons why he was or was not.

The attempt to produce a culture for others, whether that otherness be defined in terms of class, gender, race, nation, or whatever, can never be finally successful, for culture can only be produced from within, not from outside. In a mass society the materials and meaning systems out of which cultures are made will almost inevitably be produced by the cultural industries: but the making of these materials into culture, that is, into the meanings of self and of social relations, and the exchange of these materials for pleasure is a process that can only be performed by their consumer-users, not by their producers. Thus, in the sphere of a "national" culture, it may be that *Miami Vice* is more "Australian" than a mini-series that sets out to document and celebrate a specific movement in Australian history. *Miami Vice* is a cultural form of a late capitalist, consumerist, pleasure-centered society, where drugs, sex, sun, sensuality, leisure, music, and, above all, style are the order of the day; its depicted society is a racial cocktail where the white Anglo-Saxon hero only just maintains his position of narrative dominance; this world of *Miami Vice* may offer most contemporary Australians a more pertinent set of meanings and pleasures than any of the mini-series, so beloved of the Australian television industries, in which white, male, British immigrants open up the bush and in so doing build their own and their nation's character.

The reception of Hollywood cultural commodities into the cultures of Third World and developing nations may be a very different matter indeed, though the work of Katz and Liebes and of Michaels has hinted at similar active and discriminating viewing practices. A lot more work needs to be done on the international reception of both news and entertainment programs and ways that the developed nations can help the less developed to produce their own cultural commodities that can genuinely challenge Hollywood's in the arena of popular taste rather than of political or economic policy.

For this can be achieved. While it is clear that the most popular cultural commodities tend to be produced in and exported by Hollywood and other western cultural industries, this tendency is far from total. The top twenty television programs (and records) in the USA, the UK and Australia may well exhibit striking similarities but they also contain very significant differences. There are locally popular cultural commodities as well as internationally popular ones.

323

We must also bear in mind that attempts to produce or defend a national culture, whether by a national broadcasting system or other means, have historically been dominated by middle-class tastes and definitions of both nation and culture, and have shown remarkably little understanding of popular pleasures or popular tastes. Thus is it almost without exception that in countries that have both a national public broadcasting system and a commercial one, that the commercial one will be more popular with the subordinated groups and classes, and the public one with the more educated middle classes. It is also generally true that the public channels will show more nationally produced programs, and the commercial channels more internationally produced, usually American, ones. The interesting exception to this is the public channel in the United States which tends to show more British programs, because in the United States "British" culture is strongly associated with higher-class, educated tastes.

If those with a public or social motivation wish to intervene effectively in the cultural economy, they need to devote more attention to understanding popular tastes and pleasures than they have in the past. It is all too easy to arrive at a set of values that are deemed to be in the public interest, but submitting those values to the test of popular pleasure and subcultural pertinence is a much less comfortable enterprise. The reconciliation of a sense of the public good with the diverse demands of popular pleasure may not be easy, but those who wish to attempt it have much to learn from Hollywood and its ilk, for these industries are sometimes adept at achieving an equally difficult reconciliation – that between an industrially centralized, economically efficient mode of production and a multiplicity of dispersed, subculturally determined, as opposed to industrially determined, moments of reception.

There will always, in industrialized cultures, be a conflict of interest between producers/distributors on the one hand and the various formations of the people on the other. The two economies, the financial and the cultural, are the opposing sides of this struggle. The financial economy attempts to use television as an agent of homogenization: for *it* television is centered, singular in its functionality, and is located in its centers of production and distribution. In the cultural economy, however, television is entirely different. It is decentered, diverse, located in the multiplicity of its modes and moments of reception. Television is the plurality of its reading practices, the democracy of its pleasures, and it can only be understood in its fragments. It promotes and provokes a network of resistances to its own power whose attempt to homogenize and hegemonize breaks down on the instability and multiplicity of its meanings and pleasures.

Despite a generation of television, that most centrally produced and widely distributed popular art form, western societies have resisted total homogenization. Feminists have shown that we do not all of us have to be patriarchs; other class, ethnic, age, and regional differences are also alive and well. Wilson and Gutierrez (1985) whose book is appropriately subtitled *Diversity and the End of Mass Communication* show how ethnic minorities in the USA have maintained and even strengthened their separate identities, despite the homogenizing thrust of the mass media. Labov has shown, too, that the difference between black English and white English has widened over the past ten years, despite the white dominance of the media and educational systems.

Carey (1985) argues that any theory of the popular media must be able to account for the diversity of social experiences within a contemporary society, and therefore the diversity of pleasures that the media offer:

> To strip away this diversity, even it if is described as relatively autonomous diversity, in order to reveal a deep and univocal structure of ideology and politics, is to steamroller subjective consciousness just as effectively as the behaviorists and functionalists did. One does not, on this reading, wish to trade the well-known evils of the Skinner box for the less well-known, but just as real, evils of the Althusserian box. Any movement, therefore, toward encompassing elements of social structure – class, power, authority – which explain away the diversity of consciousness is to head one down a road just as self-enclosing as the behaviorist terrain phenomenologists have been trying to evacuate for most of this century.   (pp. 35–6)

Mercer (1986a) also argues that the shift of critical attention from ideology to pleasure is one that rejects the supposed homogenizing power of the dominant ideology:

> The concern with pleasure then is a corresponding interrogation of the "fact" of ideology. It suggests a rejection of the ascribed unity and omniscience, of its depth and homogeneity, of its stasis within a given cultural form.   (p. 54)

Any theory of the popular must be able to account for this elaborated diversity of social formations.

The sort of diversity of programming that is often called for on television is one that diversifies the social positions of those who are granted access to it. This is unlikely to occur within a commercial broadcasting system, though cable networks in the USA and Channel 4 in the UK are making some moves in this direction. But, however valuable these moves are, they still remain minority voices speaking to minority audiences. The political battle of popularity is fought in the arena of commercial broadcast television, and it is on this struggle that I have concentrated in this book.

In this arena, the inevitable (because profitable) homogenization of programming, which means that one financial commodity is sold to as many different audiences as possible, may not be such an agent of cultural domination as many fear. Indeed, I would argue the opposite. Diversity of readings is not the same as diversity of programs, and a diversity of readings and the consequent diversity of subcultural identities is crucial if the popular is to be seen as a set of forces for social change.

This brings us to the relationship between entertainment and politics. These are two separate cultural domains which, in Althusserian terms, are relatively autonomous though overdetermined. The resistive readings and pleasures of television do not translate directly into oppositional politics or social action. Relatively autonomous cultural domains do not relate to each other in simple cause and effect terms. But the absence of a direct political effect does not preclude a more general political effectivity (see chapter 1). Resistive reading practices that assert the power of the subordinate in the process of representation and its subsequent pleasure pose a direct challenge to the power of capitalism to produce its subjects-in-ideology. The way that people understand themselves and their social relations is part of the social system itself. Any set of social relations requires a set of meanings to hold it in place (Hall 1984), and any set of social meanings has to be produced by, and in the interests of, a group or a formation of groups situated within a social system of power relations. The classes who dominate social relations also attempt to dominate the production of meanings that underpin them: social power and semiotic power are two sides of the same coin. Challenging meanings and the social group with the right to make them is a crucial part of asserting subcultural identities and the social differences that they maintain. The domain of entertainment is one of pleasures, meanings, and social identity: if this domain cannot maintain and promote the power of the subordinate to be different, there will be severely reduced motivation for change in the political domain. Maintaining subcultural diversity may not, in itself, produce any direct political effect, but at the more general level of effectivity its power is crucial.

And television is not neutral in this. Its success in the financial economy depends upon its ability to serve and promote the diverse and often oppositional interests of its audiences. In this sense it is the meanings and pleasures of the cultural economy that determine the extent of the economic return on that capital: the cultural economy drives the financial in a dialectic force that counters the power of capital. Television, as a mass-mediated popular art, must contain within it the opposing but linked forces of capital and the people if it is to circulate effectively in both financial and cultural economies. Far from being the agent of the dominant classes, it is the prime site where the dominant have to recognize the insecurity of their power, and where they have to encourage cultural difference with all the threat to their own position that this implies.

References

Allen, R. (1983) "On Reading Soaps: A Semiotic Primer" in E.A. Kaplan (ed.) (1983b) *Regarding Television*, Los Angeles: American Film Institute/University Publications of America, 97–108.

Allen, R. (1985) *Speaking of Soap Operas*, Chapel Hill: University of North Carolina Press.

Allen, R. (ed.) (1987) *Channels of Discourse: Television and Contemporary Criticism*, Chapel Hill: University of North Carolina Press.

Althusser, L. (1971) "Ideology and Ideological State Apparatuses" in *Lenin and Philosophy and Other Essays*, New York and London: Monthly Review Press, 127–86.

Althusser, L. (1979) *For Marx*, London: Verso.

Altman, R. (1986) "Television/Sound" in T. Modleski (ed.) (1986) *Studies in Entertainment: Critical Approaches to Mass Culture*, Bloomington and Indianapolis: Indiana University Press, 39–54.

Ang, I. (1985) *Watching Dallas*, London: Methuen.

Ang, I. (1986) "The Vicissitudes of 'Progressive Television'," paper presented at the International Television Studies Conference, London, July 1986.

Bakhtin, M. (1968) *Rabelais and his World*, Cambridge, Mass.: Massachusetts Institute of Technology Press.

Bakhtin, M. (1981) *The Dialogic Imagination*, Austin: University of Texas Press.

Bakke, M. (1986) "Culture at Stake" in D. McQuail and K. Siune (eds) (1986) *New Media Politics: Comparative Perspectives in Western Europe*, London: Sage, 130–51.

Barthes, R. (1968) *Elements of Semiology*, London: Cape.

Barthes, R. (1973) *Mythologies*, London: Paladin.

Barthes, R. (1975a) *S/Z*, London: Cape.

Barthes, R. (1975b) *The Pleasure of the Text*, New York: Hill & Wang.

Barthes, R. (1977a) *Image-Music-Text*, ed. and trans. S. Heath, London: Fontana.

Barthes, R. (1977b) "An Introduction to the Structural Analysis of Narratives" in R. Barthes (1977a) *Image-Music-Text*, ed. and trans. S. Heath, London: Fontana, 79–124 and S. Sontag (ed.) (1983) *Barthes: Selected Writings*, London: Fontana/Collins, 251–95.

Barthes, R. (1977c) "From Work to Text" in R. Barthes, *Image-Music-Text*, London: Fontana, 155–64.

Bell, P. (1983) "Drugs as News: Defining the Social," *Australian Journal of Cultural Studies* 1: 2, 101–19, also in M. Gurevitch and M. Levy (eds) (1985) *Mass Communication Review Yearbook Volume 5*, Beverly Hills: Sage, 303–20.

Belsey, C. (1980) *Critical Practice*, London: Methuen.

Bennett, T. (1982) "Text and Social Process: The Case of James Bond," *Screen Education* 41: 3–15.

Bennett, T. (1983a) "A Thousand and One Pleasures: Blackpool Pleasure Beach" in Formations (ed.) (1983) *Formations of Pleasure*, London: Routledge & Kegan Paul, 138–55.

Bennett, T. (1983b) "The Bond Phenomenon: Theorizing a Popular Hero," *Southern Review* 16: 2, 195–225.

Bennett, T. (1986) "Hegemony, Ideology, Pleasure: Blackpool" in T. Bennett, C. Mercer, and J. Woollacott (eds) (1986) *Popular Culture and Social Relations*, Milton Keynes and Philadelphia: Open University Press, 135–54.

Bennett, T., Boyd-Bowman, S., Mercer, C., and Woollacott, J. (eds) (1981) *Popular Television and Film*, London: British Film Institute/Open University.

Bennett, T., Mercer, C., and Woollacott, J. (eds) (1986) *Popular Culture and Social Relations*, Milton Keynes and Philadelphia: Open University Press.

Bennett, T. and Woollacott, J. (1987) *Bond and Beyond: Fiction, Ideology and Social Process*, London: Macmillan.

Berger, J. (1972) *Ways of Seeing*, Harmondsworth: Penguin.

Berne, E. (1964) *Games People Play: the Psychology of Human Relationships*, Harmondsworth: Penguin.

Blanchard, S. and Morley, D. (1984) *What's This Channel Fo(u)r?*, London: Comedia.

Blum, A. (1964) "Lower-class Negro television spectators: The concept of pseudo-jovial scepticism," in A. Shostak and W. Gomberg (eds) *Blue-Collar World*, Englewood Cliffs, NJ: Prentice-Hall.

Bordwell, D. (1985) *Narrative in the Fiction Film*, Madison: University of Wisconsin Press.

Bordwell, D. and Thompson, K. (1986) *Film Art: an Introduction* (2nd edn), New York: Knopf.

Bourdieu, P. (1968) "Outline of a Sociological Theory of Art Perception," *International Social Sciences Journal* 2: 225–54.

Bourdieu, P. (1980) "The Aristocracy of Culture," *Media, Culture and Society* 2: 225–54.

Bourget, J.-L. (1977/8) "Sirk and the Critics," *Bright Lights* 2, 6–11.

Bradley, A. C. (1904) *Shakespearean Tragedy*, London: Macmillan.

Brown, M. E. (1987a) "The Politics of Soaps: Pleasure and Feminine Empowerment," *Australian Journal of Cultural Studies* 4: 2, 1–25.

Brown, M. E. (1987b) "The Dialectic of the Feminine: Melodrama and Commodity in the Ferraro Pepsi Commercial," *Communication* 9: 3/4, 335–54.

Brown, M. E. and Barwick, L. (1986) "Fables and Endless Genealogies: Soap Opera and Women's Culture," paper delivered at the Australian Screen Studies Association Conference, Sydney, December 1986.

Brunsdon, C. (1981) *"Crossroads:* Notes on Soap Opera," *Screen* 22: 4, 32–7.

Brunsdon, C. (1984) "Writing about Soap Opera" in L. Masterman (ed.) (1984) *Television Mythologies: Stars, Shows, and Signs*, London: Comedia/MK Media Press, 82–7.

Brunsdon, C. and Morley, D. (1978) *Everyday Television: Nationwide*, London: British Film Institute.

Budd, M., Craig, S., and Steinman, C. (1985) "Fantasy Island: Marketplace of Desire" in M. Gurevitch and M. Levy (eds) *Mass Communication Review Yearbook, Volume 5*, Beverly Hills: Sage, 291–301.

Carey, J. (1985) "Overcoming Resistance to Cultural Studies" in M. Gurevitch and M. Levy (eds) (1985) *Mass Communications Review Yearbook, Volume 5*, Beverly Hills: Sage, 27–40.

Caughie, J. (1981) "Progressive Television and Documentary Drama" in T. Bennett, S. Boyd-Bowman, C. Mercer, and J. Woollacott (eds) (1981) *Popular Television and Film*, London: British Film Institute/Open University, 327–52.

Caughie, J. (1984) "Television Criticism: a Discourse in Search of an Object," *Screen* 25: 4/5, 109–20.

Cawelti, J. (1970) *The Six Gun Mystique*, Bowling Green: Bowling Green University Press.

Chambers, I. (1986) *Popular Culture: the Metropolitan Experience*, London: Methuen.

Chatman, S. (1978) *Story and Discourse: Narrative Structure in Fiction and Film*, Ithaca and London: Cornell University Press.

Chodorow, N. (1974) "Family Structure and Feminine Personality" in M. Rosaldo and L. Lamphere (eds) (1974) *Women, Culture and Society*, Stanford: Stanford University Press, 43–66.

Chodorow, N. (1978) *The Reproduction of Mothering*, Berkeley: University of California Press.

Cohen, P. and Robbins, D. (1979) *Knuckle Sandwich*, Harmondsworth: Penguin.

Cohen, S. and Young, J. (1973) *The Manufacture of News*, London: Constable.

Cook, P. (ed.) (1985) *The Cinema Book*, London: British Film Institute.

Coward, R. and Ellis, J. (1977) *Language and Materialism: Developments in Semiology and the Theory of the Subject*, London: Routledge & Kegan Paul.

Cunneen, C. (1985) "Working-Class Boys and Crime: Theorizing the Class/ Gender Mix" in P. Patton and R. Poole (eds) (1985) *War/Masculinity*, Sydney: Intervention Publications, 80–6.

Curran, J., Gurevitch, M., and Woollacott, J. (eds) (1977) *Mass Communication and Society*, London: Arnold.

Dahlgren, P. (1985) "The Modes of Reception: For a Hermeneutics of TV News" in P. Drummond and R. Paterson (eds) (1985) *Television in Transition*, London: British Film Institute, 235–49.

Davies, G. (1978/9) "Teaching about Narrative," *Screen Education* 29: 56–76.

Davies, J. (1983) "Sale of the Century – Sign of the Decade," *Australian Journal of Screen Theory* 13/14, 21–42.

Davies, J. (1984a) "Soap and Other Operas," *Metro* 65, 31–3.

Davies, J. (1984b) "The Television Audience Revisited," paper presented at the Australian Screen Studies Association conference, Brisbane, December, 1984

Davis, H. and Walton, P. (eds) (1983a) *Language, Image, Media*, London: Blackwell.

Davis, H. and Walton, P. (1983b) "Death of a Premier: Consensus and Closure in International News" in H. Davis and P. Walton (eds) (1983) *Language, Image, Media*, London: Blackwell, 8–49.

Dorfman, A. and Mattelart, A. (1975) *How to Read Donald Duck*, New York: International General.

Drummond, P. and Paterson, R. (eds) (1985) *Television in Transition*, London: British Film Institute.

Dunning, E. (ed.) (1971) *The Sociology of Sport: a Selection of Readings*, London: Cass.

Dyer, R. (1979) *Stars*, London: British Film Institute.

Dyer, R. (1981) "Stars as Signs" in T. Bennett, S. Boyd-Bowman, C. Mercer, and J. Woollacott (eds) (1981) *Popular Television and Film*, London: British Film Institute/Open University Press, 236–69 (an edited version of Dyer 1979).

Dyer, R. (1985) "Male Sexuality in the Media" in A. Metcalf and M. Humphries (eds) *The Sexuality of Men*, London: Pluto, 28–43.

Dyer, R. (1986) *Heavenly Bodies: Film Stars and Society*, New York: St Martin's Press.

Dyer, R., Geraghty, C., Jordan, M., Lovell, T., Paterson, R., and Stewart, J. (1981) *Coronation Street*, London: British Film Institute.

Easlea, M. (1983) *Fathering the Unthinkable: Masculinity, Scientists and the Nuclear Arms Race*, London: Pluto.

Eaton, M. (1981) "Television Situation Comedy" in T. Bennett, S. Boyd-Bowman, C. Mercer, and J. Woollacott (eds) (1981) *Popular Television and Film*, London: British Film Institute/Open University, 26–52.

Eco, U. (1972) "Towards a Semiotic Inquiry into the TV Message," *WPCS* no. 3, 103–26, in J. Corner and J. Hawthorn (eds) (1980) *Communication Studies: An Introductory Reader*, London: Arnold.

Eco, U. (1979) *The Role of the Reader; Explorations in the Semiotics of Texts*, Bloomington and London: Indiana University Press.

Ellis, J. (1982) *Visible Fictions*, London: Routledge & Kegan Paul.

Elsaesser, T. (1973) "Tales of Sound and Fury: Observations on the Family Melodrama" *Monogram* 4.

Feuer, J. (1983) "The Concept of Live Television: Ontology vs Ideology" in E. A. Kaplan (ed.) (1983b) *Regarding Television*, Los Angeles: American Film Institute/University Publications of America, 12–22.

Feuer, J. (1984) "Melodrama, Serial Form and Television Today," *Screen* 25: 1, 4–16.

Feuer, J. (1986) "Narrative Form in American Network Television" in C. MacCabe (ed.) (1986) *High Theory/Low Culture*, Manchester: Manchester University Press, 101–14.

Feuer, J. (1987) "Genre Study and Television" in R. Allen (ed.) (1987) *Channels of Discourse: Television and Contemporary Criticism*, Chapel Hill: University of North Carolina Press, 113–33.

Fiske, J. (1982) *Introduction to Communication Studies*, London: Methuen.

Fiske, J. (1983) "The Discourses of TV Quiz Shows or School + Luck = Success + Sex," *Central States Speech Journal* 34, 139–50.

Fiske, J. (1984) "Popularity and Ideology: A Structuralist Reading of Dr Who" in W. Rowland and B. Watkins (eds) (1984) *Interpreting Television: Current Research Perspectives*, Beverly Hills: Sage, 165–98.

Fiske, J. (1985a) "Television: A Multilevel Classroom Resource," *Australian Journal of Screen Theory* 17/18, 106–25.

Fiske, J. (1985b) "The Problem of the Popular," A. C. Baird Lecture, University of Iowa.

Fiske, J. (1986a) "Television and Popular Culture: Reflections on British and Australian Critical Practice," *Critical Studies in Mass Communication* 3: 2, 200–16.

Fiske, J. (1986b) "Television: Polysemy and Popularity," *Critical Studies in Mass Communication* 3:4, 391–408.

Fiske, J. (1986c) "MTV: Post Structural Post Modern," *Journal of Communication Inquiry* 10: 1, 74–9.

Fiske, J. (1987a) "British Cultural Studies" in R. Allen (ed.) (1987)

Channels of Discourse: Television and Contemporary Criticism, Chapel Hill: University of North Carolina Press, 254–89.

Fiske, J. (1987b) "Cagney and Lacey, Reading Character Structurally and Politically," *Communication* 9: 3/4, 399–426.

Fiske, J. and Hartley, J. (1978) *Reading Television*, London: Methuen.

Fiske, J., Hodge, R., and Turner, G. (1987) *Myths of Oz: Readings in Australian Popular Culture*, Sydney: Allen & Unwin.

Flitterman, S. (1983) "The *Real* Soap Operas: TV Commercials" in E. A. Kaplan (ed.) (1983b) *Regarding Television*, Los Angeles: American Film Institute/University Publications of America, 84–96.

Flitterman, S. (1985) "Thighs and Whiskers, the Fascination of *Magnum P.I.*," *Screen* 26: 2, 42–58.

Formations (ed.) (1983) *Formations of Pleasure*, London: Routledge & Kegan Paul.

Foucault, M. (1978) *The History of Sexuality*, Harmondsworth: Penguin.

Frow, J. (1986) "Spectacle, Binding: on Character," *Poetics Today* 7:2, 227–50.

Galtung, J. and Ruge, M. (1973) "Structuring and Selecting News" in S. Cohen and J. Young (eds) (1973) *The Manufacture of News*, London: Constable.

Garnham, N. (1987) "Concepts of Culture: Public Policy and the Cultural Industries," *Cultural Studies* 1: 1, 23–37.

Geraghty, C. (1981) "The Continuous Serial – a Definition" in R. Dyer, C. Geraghty, M. Jordan, T. Lovell, R. Paterson, and J. Stewart (1981) *Coronation Street*, London: British Film Institute, 9–26.

Gerbner, G. (1970) "Cultural Indicators: the Case of Violence in Television Drama," *Annals of the American Association of Political and Social Science* 338, 69–81.

Gilligan, C. (1982) *In a Different Voice: Psychological Theory and Women's Development*, Cambridge, Mass. : Harvard University Press.

Gitlin, T. (1982) "Prime Time Ideology: the Hegemonic Process in Television Entertainment" in H. Newcomb (ed.) (1982) *Television: the Critical View*, New York: Oxford University Press, 426–54.

Gitlin, T. (1983) *Inside Prime Time*, New York: Pantheon.

Glasgow Media Group (1976) *Bad News*, London: Routledge & Kegan Paul.

Glasgow Media Group (1980) *More Bad News*, London: Routledge & Kegan Paul.

Glasgow Media Group (1982) *Really Bad News*, London: Writers & Readers Publishing Co-operative Society.

Goffman, E. (1979) *Gender Advertisements*, London: Macmillan.

Greenfield, P. (1984) *Mind and Media*, London: Fontana.

Grossberg, L. (1984) "Another Boring Day in Paradise: Rock and Roll and the Empowerment of Everyday Life," *Popular Music* 4, 225–57.

Grossberg, L. (forthcoming) "The In-difference of Television, or Mapping TV's Popular (Affective) Economy," *Screen*.

Gurevitch, M., Bennett, T., Curran, J., and Woollacott, J. (eds) (1982) *Culture, Society and Media*, London: Methuen.

Gurevitch, M. and Levy, M. (1985) *Mass Communication Review Yearbook, Volume 5*, Beverly Hills: Sage.

Hall, S. (1973) "The Determination of News Photographs" in S. Cohen and J. Young (eds) (1973) *The Manufacture of News*, London: Constable, 176–90.

Hall, S. (1977) "Culture, the Media and the Ideological Effect" in J. Curran, M. Gurevitch, and J. Woollacott (eds) (1977) *Mass Communication and Society*, London: Arnold, 128–38.

Hall, S. (1980a) "Encoding/Decoding" in S. Hall, D. Hobson, A. Lowe, and P. Willis (eds) (1980) *Culture, Media, Language*, London: Hutchinson, 128–39.

Hall, S. (1980b) "The Message from the Box," *English Magazine*, 4–8.

Hall, S. (1981) "Notes on Deconstructing 'The Popular'," in R. Samuel (ed.) (1981) *People's History and Socialist Theory*, London: Routledge & Kegan Paul, 227–40.

Hall, S. (1982) "The Rediscovery of Ideology: the Return of the Repressed in Media Studies" in M. Gurevitch, T. Bennett, J. Curran, and J. Woollacott (eds) (1982) *Culture, Society and Media*, London: Methuen, 56–90.

Hall, S. (1983) "Ideology, or the Media Effect on the Working Class," address to La Trobe University, Melbourne, November 1983.

Hall, S. (1984) "The Narrative Construction of Reality," *Southern Review* 17: 1, 3–17.

Hall, S. (1986) "On Postmodernism and Articulation: An Interview with Stuart Hall" (edited by L. Grossberg), *Journal of Communication Inquiry* 10: 2, 45–60.

Hall, S., Connell, I., and Curti, L. (1976) "The Unity of Current Affairs Television," *Working Papers in Cultural Studies* no. 9, 51–94, also in T. Bennett, S. Boyd-Bowman, C. Mercer, and J. Woollacott (eds) (1981) *Popular Television and Film*, London: British Film Institute/Open University, 88–117.

Hall, S., Critcher, C., Jefferson, T., Clarke, J., and Roberts, B. (1978) *Policing the Crisis: Mugging, the State, and Law and Order*, London: Macmillan.

Hall, S., Hobson, D., Lowe, A., and Willis, P. (eds) (1980) *Culture, Media, Language*, London: Hutchinson.

Hamon, P. (1977) "Pour un status sémiologique du personnage," in R.Barthes, W.Kayser, W. Booth (eds) *Ph. Hamon, Poétique du récit*, Paris, Seuil, 115–80.

Hartley, J. (1982) *Understanding News*, London: Methuen.

Hartley, J. (1983) "Television and the Power of Dirt," *Australian Journal of Cultural Studies* 1: 2, 62–82.

Hartley, J. (1984a) "Encouraging Signs: TV and the Power of Dirt, Speech, and Scandalous Categories," in W. Rowland and B. Watkins (eds) (1984) *Interpreting Television: Current Research Perspectives*, Beverly Hills: Sage, 119–41.

Hartley, J. (1984b) "Regimes of Pleasure," *Eye* 2.

Hartley, J. (1985) "Invisible Fictions, Television Audiences and Regimes of Pleasure," unpublished paper, Murdoch University, Perth, WA.

Hartley, J. and O'Regan, T. (1987) "Quoting not Science but Sideboards, Television in a New Way of Life" in M. Gurevitch and M. Levy (eds) (1987) *Mass Communication Review Yearbook, Volume 7*, Beverly Hills: Sage.

Heath, S. and Skirrow, G. (1977) "Television: A World in Action," *Screen* 18: 2, 7–59.

Hebdige, D. (1979) *Subculture: the Meaning of Style*, London: Methuen.

Hebdige, D. (1982) "Towards a Cartography of Taste 1935–1962" in B. Waites, T. Bennett, and G. Martin (eds) (1982) *Popular Culture: Past and Present*, London: Croom Helm/Open University Press, 194–218.

Hebdige, D. (1987) *Hiding in the Light*, London: Comedia.

Henderson, J. (1986) unpublished research paper, Western Australian Institute of Technology.

Hewitt, M. (1986) "Advertising: Fashion, Food and the Feminine," unpublished paper, Curtin University, Perth.

Hite, S. (1981) *The Hite Report on Male Sexuality*, London: Macdonald.

Hobson, D. (1980) "Housewives and the Mass Media" in S. Hall, D. Hobson, A. Lowe, and P. Willis (eds) (1980) *Culture, Media, Language*, London: Hutchinson, 105–14.

Hobson, D. (1982) *Crossroads: the Drama of a Soap Opera*, London: Methuen.

Hodge, R. and Tripp, D. (1986) *Children and Television*, Cambridge: Polity Press.

Hogben, A. (1982) "Journalists as Bad Apples," *Quadrant*, January/February, 38–43.

Huizinga, J. (1949) *Humo Ludens*, London: Routledge & Kegan Paul.

Hunter, I. (1983) "Reading Character," *Southern Review* 16: 2, 226–43.

Jakobson, R. (1960) "Closing Statement: Linguistics and Poetics" in T.

Sebeok (ed.) (1960) *Style and Language*, Cambridge, Mass.: Massachusetts Institute of Technology Press.

Jenkins, H. (1986) *"Star Trek:* Rerun, Reread, Rewritten," unpublished paper, University of Wisconsin-Madison.

Johnston, C. (1973) *Notes on Women's Cinema*, London: Society for Education in Film and Television.

Johnston, C. (1985) "Film Narrative and the Structuralist Controversy" in P. Cook (ed.) (1985) *The Cinema Book*, London: British Film Institute, 222–50.

Jordan, M. (1981) "Realism and Convention" in R. Dyer, C. Geraghty, M. Jordan, T. Lovell, R. Paterson, and J. Stewart(1981) *Coronation Street*, London: British Film Institute, 27–39.

Kaplan, E. A. (1983a) *Women and Film: Both Sides of the Camera*, New York: Methuen.

Kaplan, E. A. (ed.) (1983b) *Regarding Television*, Los Angeles: American Film Institute/University Publications of America.

Katz, E. and Liebes, T. (1984) "Once upon a Time in Dallas," *Intermedia* 12: 3, 28–32.

Katz, E. and Liebes, T. (1985) "Mutual Aid in the Decoding of *Dallas:* Preliminary Notes from a Cross-Cultural Study" in P. Drummond and R. Paterson (eds) (1985) *Television in Transition*, London: British Film Institute, 187–98.

Katz, E. and Liebes, T. (1987) "On the Critical Ability of Television Viewers," paper presented at the seminar *Rethinking the Audience*, University of Tubingen, February 1987.

Kellner, D. (1982) "TV, Ideology and Emancipatory Popular Culture" in H. Newcomb (ed.) (1982) *Television: the Critical View*, New York: Oxford University Press, 386–421.

Kerr, P. (1981) *"Gangsters:* Conventions and Contraventions" in T. Bennett, S. Boyd-Bowman, C. Mercer, and J. Woollacott (eds) (1981) *Popular Television and Film*, London: British Film Institute/Open University, 73–8.

Kleinhans, C. (1978) "Notes on Melodrama and the Family under Capitalism," *Film Reader* 3, 40–8.

Kuhn, A. (1982) *Women's Pictures: Feminism and Cinema*, London: Routledge & Kegan Paul.

Kuhn, A. (1984) "Women's Genres," *Screen* 25: 1, 18–28.

Kuhn, A. (1985) "History of Narrative Codes" in P. Cook (ed.) (1985) *The Cinema Book*, London: British Film Institute, 208–20.

Lakoff, G. and Johnson, M. (1980) *Metaphors We Live By*, Chicago: University of Chicago Press.

Langer, J. (1981) "Television's Personality System," *Media, Culture and Society*, vol. 4, 351–65.

Lewis, J. (1985) "Decoding Television News" in P. Drummond and R. Paterson (eds) (1985) *Television in Transition*, London: British Film Institute, 205–34.

Lewis, L. (1985) "Consumer Girl Culture: How Music Video Appeals to Women," paper presented at the Society for Cinema Studies Conference, New Orleans, April 1985.

Lewis, L. (1987) "Form and Female Authorship in Music Video," *Communication* 3/4, 355–78.

Lopate, C. (1977) "Daytime Television: You'll Never Want to Leave Home," *Radical America* 2, 33–51.

Lovell, T. (1980) *Pictures of Reality: Aesthetics, Politics, Pleasure*, London: British Film Institute.

Lovell, T. (1981) "Ideology and *Coronation Street*" in R. Dyer, C. Geraghty, M. Jordan, T. Lovell, R. Paterson, and J. Stewart (1981) *Coronation Street*, London: British Film Institute, 40–52.

Lovell, T. (1983) "Writing like a Woman: a Question of Politics" in F. Barker (ed.) (1983) *The Politics of Theory 8*, Colchester: University of Essex.

McArthur, C. (1981) "*Days of Hope*" in T. Bennett, S. Boyd-Bowman, C. Mercer, and J. Woollacott (eds) (1981) *Popular Television and Film*, London: British Film Institute/Open University, 305–9.

MacCabe, C. (1976) "Theory and Film: Principles of Realism and Pleasure," *Screen* 17, 7–27.

MacCabe, C. (1981a) "Realism and Cinema: Notes on Brechtian Theses" in T. Bennett, S. Boyd-Bowman, C. Mercer, and J. Woollacott (eds) (1981) *Popular Television and Film*, London: British Film Institute/Open University, 216–35.

MacCabe, C. (1981b) "*Days of Hope*, a Response to Colin McArthur" in T. Bennett, S. Boyd-Bowman, C. Mercer, and J. Woollacott (eds) (1981) *Popular Television and Film*, London: British Film Institute/Open University, 310–13.

MacCabe, C. (1981c) "Memory, Fantasy, Identity: Days of Hope and the Politics of the Past" in T. Bennett, S. Boyd-Bowman, C. Mercer, and J. Woollacott (eds) (1981) *Popular Television and Film*, London, British Film Institute/Open University, 314–18.

MacCabe, C. (1986) "Defining Popular Culture" in C. MacCabe (ed.) (1986) *High Theory/Low Culture*, Manchester: Manchester University Press, 1–10.

McQuail, D. (ed.) (1972) *The Sociology of Mass Communications*, Harmondsworth: Penguin.

McQuail, D., Blumler, J., and Brown, J. (1972) "The Television Audience:

a Revised Perspective" in D. McQuail (ed.) (1972) *The Sociology of Mass Communications*, Harmondsworth: Penguin, 135–65.

McQuail, D. and Siune, K. (eds) (1986) *New Media Politics: Comparative Perspectives in Western Europe*, London: Sage.

McRobbie, A. (1984) "Dance and Social Fantasy" in A. McRobbie and M. Nava (eds) (1984) *Gender and Generation*, London: Macmillan, 130–61.

McRobbie, A. and Nava, M. (eds) (1984) *Gender and Generation*, London: Macmillan.

Marc, D. (1984) *Demographic Vistas: Television in American Culture*, Philadelphia: University of Pennsylvania Press.

Masterman, L. (ed.) (1984) *Television Mythologies: Stars, Shows and Signs*, London: Comedia/MK Media Press.

Mattelart, A. (1980) *Mass Media, Ideologies and the Revolutionary Movement*, Sussex: Harvester.

Mattelart, A. and Siegelaub, S. (eds) (1979) *Communication and Class Struggle* Vol. 1, New York: International General.

Mellencamp, P. (1977) "Spectacle and Spectator," *Cine-tracts* 1: 2, 28–35.

Mellencamp, P. (1985) "Situation and Simulation: an Introduction to 'I Love Lucy'," *Screen* 26: 2, 30–40.

Mercer, C. (1986a) "Complicit Pleasures" in T. Bennett, C. Mercer, and J. Woollacott (eds) (1986) *Popular Culture and Social Relations*, Milton Keynes and Philadelphia: Open University Press, 50–68.

Mercer, C. (1986b) "That's Entertainment: the Resilience of Popular Forms" in T. Bennett, C. Mercer, and J. Woollacott (eds) (1986) *Popular Culture and Social Relations*, Milton Keynes and Philadelphia: Open University Press, 177–95.

Metcalf, A. and Humphries, M. (eds) (1985) *The Sexuality of Men*, London: Pluto.

Michaels, E. (1986) "Aboriginal Content," paper presented at the Australian Screen Studies Association Conference, Sydney, December 1986.

Mills, A. and Rice, P. (1982) "Quizzing the Popular," *Screen Education* 41 Winter/Spring, 15–25.

Modleski, T. (1982) *Loving with a Vengeance: Mass Produced Fantasies for Women*, London: Methuen.

Modleski, T. (1983) "The Rhythms of Reception: Daytime Television and Women's Work" in E. A. Kaplan (ed.) (1985b) *Regarding Television*, Los Angeles: American Film Institute/University Publications of America, 67–75.

Modleski, T. (ed.) (1986) *Studies in Entertainment: Critical Approaches to Mass Culture*, Bloomington and Indianapolis: Indiana University Press.

Monaco, J. (1977) *How to Read a Film*, Oxford: Oxford University Press.

Morley, D. (1980a) *The Nationwide Audience: Structure and Decoding*, London: British Film Institute.

Morley, D. (1980b) "Texts, Readers, Subjects" in S. Hall, D. Hobson, A. Lowe, and P. Willis (eds) (1980) *Culture, Media, Language*, London: Hutchinson, 163–73.

Morley, D. (1981) "The *Nationwide* Audience – a Critical Postscript," *Screen Education* 39, 3–14.

Morley, D. (1983) "Cultural Transformations: the Politics of Resistance" in H. Davis and P. Walton (eds) (1983) *Language, Image, Media*, London: Blackwell, 104–19.

Morley, D. (1986) *Family Television*, London: Comedia.

Morse, M. (1983) "Sport on Television: Replay and Display" in E. A. Kaplan (ed.) (1983b) *Regarding Television*, Los Angeles: American Film Institute/University Publications of America, 44–66.

Morse, M. (1986) "Post Synchronizing Rock Music and Television", *Journal of Communication Inquiry* 10: 1, 15–28.

Moye, A. (1985) "Pornography" in A. Metcalf and M. Humphries (eds) (1985) *The Sexuality of Men*, London: Pluto, 44–69.

Mulvey, L. (1975) "Visual Pleasure and Narrative Cinema," *Screen* 16:3, 6–18, also in T. Bennett, S. Boyd-Bowman, C. Mercer, and J. Woollacott (eds) (1981) *Popular Television and Film*, London: British Film Institute/Open University, 206–15.

Mulvey, L. (1977–8) "Douglas Sirk and Melodrama," *Movie* 25, 53.

Mulvey, L. and Halliday, J. (eds) (1972) *Douglas Sirk*, Edinburgh: Edinburgh Film Festival.

Mumby, D. and Spitzack, C. (1985) "Ideology and Television News: A Metaphoric Analysis of Political Stories," *Central States Speech Journal* 34:3, 162–71.

Neale, S. (1977) "Propaganda," *Screen* 18: 3, 9–40.

Neale, S. (1981) "Genre and Cinema" in T. Bennett, S. Boyd-Bowman, C. Mercer, and J. Woollacott (eds) (1981) *Popular Television and Film*, London: British Film Institute/Open University, 6–25.

Neale, S. (1983) "Masculinity as Spectacle," *Screen*, 24: 6, 2–17.

Nelson, C. (1985) "Envoys of Otherness: Difference and Continuity in Feminist Criticism" in P. Treichler, C. Kramarae, and B. Stafford (eds) (1985) *For Alma Mater: Theory and Practice in Feminist Scholarship*, Urbana: University of Illinois Press.

Newcomb, H. (ed.) (1982) *Television: the Critical View*, New York: Oxford University Press.

Newcomb, H. (1984) "On the Dialogic Aspects of Mass Communication," *Critical Studies in Mass Communication* 1: 1, 34–50.

Newcomb, H. and Alley, R. (1983) *The Producer's Medium: Conversations with America's Leading Television Producers*, New York: Oxford University Press.

Newcomb, H. and Hirsch, P. (1984) "Television as a Cultural Forum: Implications for Research" in W. Rowland and B. Watkins (eds) (1984) *Interpreting Television: Current Research Perspectives*, Beverly Hills: Sage, 58–73.

Nowell-Smith, G. (1977) "Minelli and Melodrama," *Screen* 18: 2, 113–18.

Ong, W. (1982) *Orality and Literacy: the Technologizing of the Word*, London: Methuen.

Osborn, A. (1984) "Kids TV Sounding the Terrain," unpublished paper, Western Australian Institute of Technology.

O'Sullivan, T., Hartley, J., Saunders, D., and Fiske, J. (1983) *Key Concepts in Communication*, London: Methuen.

Palmer, P. (1986) *The Lively Audience: a Study of Children around the TV Set*, Sydney: Allen & Unwin.

Parkin, F. (1972) *Class Inequality and Political Order*, London: Paladin.

Patton, P. and Poole, R. (eds) (1985) *War/Masculinity*, Sydney: Intervention Publications.

Porter, D. (1977) "Soap Time: Thoughts on a Commodity Art Form," *College English* 38, 783.

Propp, V. (1968) *The Morphology of the Folktale*, Austin: University of Texas Press.

Radway, J. (1984) *Reading the Romance: Feminism and the Representation of Women in Popular Culture*, Chapel Hill: University of North Carolina Press.

Rogge, J. U. (1987) "The Media in Everyday Family Life – Some Biographical and Typological Aspects," paper presented to the seminar on *Rethinking the Audience*, University of Tubingen, February 1987.

Root, J. (1984) *Pictures of Women: Sexuality*, London: Pandora/Channel 4.

Rosaldo, M. and Lamphere, L. (eds) (1974) *Women, Culture and Society*, Stanford: Stanford University Press.

Ross, A. (1986) "Masculinity and *Miami Vice*: Selling In," *Oxford Literary Review* 8: 1 & 2, 143–54.

Ross, A. (1987) "*Miami Vice*: Selling In," *Communication* 9: 3/4, 305–34.

Rowland, W. and Watkins, B. (eds) (1984) *Interpreting Television: Current Research Perspectives*, Beverly Hills: Sage.

Said, E. (1984) *The World, the Text and the Critic*, Cambridge, Mass.: Harvard University Press.

Samuel, R. (ed.) (1981) *People's History and Socialist Theory*, London: Routledge & Kegan Paul.

Schiff, S. (1985) "What *Dynasty* Says about America," *Vanity Fair* 47: 12, 64–7.

Schlesinger, P., Murdock, G., and Elliott, P. (1983) *Televising Terrorism*, London: Comedia.

Schwichtenberg, C. (1987) "Sensual Surfaces and Stylistic Excess: the Pleasure and Politics of *Miami Vice*," *Journal of Communication Inquiry* 10: 3, 45–65.

Seal, G. (1986) "Play", paper delivered to the Gender and Television Group, Perth, Western Australia, February 1986.

Seiter, E., Kreutzner, G., Warth, E. M., and Borchers, H. (1987) "'Don't Treat Us Like We're So Stupid and Naive': Towards an Ethnography of Soap Opera Viewers," paper presented at the seminar on *Rethinking the Audience*, University of Tubingen, February 1987.

Showalter, E. (1985a) *The New Feminist Criticism: Essays on Women, Literature and Theory*, New York: Pantheon.

Showalter, E. (1985b) "Feminist Criticism in the Wilderness" in E. Showalter (ed.) (1985a) *The New Feminist Criticism: Essays on Women, Literature and Theory*, New York: Pantheon, 243–70.

Silverman, K. (1983) *The Subject of Semiotics*, Oxford: Oxford University Press.

Silverstone, R. (1981) *The Message of Television: Myth and Narrative in Contemporary Culture*, London: Heinemann.

Singer, J. L. and Singer, D. G. (1980) "Imaginative Play in Preschoolers. Some Research and Theoretical Implications," paper presented in symposium on *The Role of Pretend in Cognitive-Emotional Development*, American Psychological Association Annual Convention, Montreal, September 1980.

Sontag, S. (ed.) (1983) *Barthes: Selected Writings*, London: Fontana/ Collins.

Stephenson, W. (1967) *Play Theory of Mass Communication*, Chicago: University of Chicago Press.

Stone, G. (1971) "American Sports: Play and Display" in E. Dunning (ed.) (1971) *The Sociology of Sport: a Selection of Readings*, London: Cass, 47–59.

Tetzlaff, D. (1986) "MTV and the Politics of Postmodern Pop," *Journal of Communication Inquiry* 10: 1, 80–91.

Thorburn, D. (1982) "Television Melodrama" in H. Newcomb (ed.) (1982) *Television: the Critical View*, New York: Oxford University Press, 529–46.

Todorov, T. (1977) *The Poetics of Prose*, Oxford: Blackwell.

Tolson, A. (1977) *The Limits of Masculinity: Male Identity and Women's Liberation*, New York: Harper & Row.

Tolson, A. (1984) "Anecdotal Television," paper presented at the Australian Screen Studies Association Conference, Brisbane, 1984.

Treichler, P., Kramerae, C., and Stafford, P. (eds) (1985) *For Alma Mater:*

Theory and Practice in Feminist Scholarship, Urbana: University of Illinois Press.

Tribe, K. (1981) "History and the Production of Memories," in T. Bennett, S. Boyd-Bowman, C. Mercer, and J. Woollacott (eds) (1981) *Popular Television and Film*, London: British Film Institute/Open University, 319–26.

Tulloch, J. and Alvarado, M. (1983) *Dr Who, the Unfolding Text*, London: Macmillan.

Tulloch, J. and Moran, A. (1984) *"A Country Practice*: Approaching the Audience," paper delivered at the Australian Communication Association Conference, Perth, 1984.

Tulloch, J. and Moran, A. (1986) *A Country Practice: "Quality Soap,"* Sydney: Currency Press.

Turnbull, S. (1984) *"Prisoner*: Patterns of Opposition and Identification," unpublished paper, La Trobe University, November 1984.

Turner, G. (1985) "Nostalgia for the Primitive: Wildlife Documentaries on TV," *Australian Journal of Cultural Studies* 3: 1, 62–71.

Volosinov, V. (1973) *Marxism and the Philosophy of Language*, New York: Seminar Press.

Waites, B., Bennett, T., and Martin, G. (eds) (1982) *Popular Culture: Past and Present*, London: Croom Helm/Open University Press.

Watt, I. (1957) *The Rise of the Novel*, Harmondsworth: Penguin.

Wiebel, K. (1977) *Mirror Mirror: Images of Women Reflected in Popular Culture*, New York: Anchor.

Willeman, P. (1978) "Notes on Subjectivity: On Reading Edward Branigan's Subjectivity under Siege," *Screen* 19, 41–69.

Williams, R. (1974) *Television: Technology and Cultural Form*, London: Fontana.

Williams, R. (1977) "A Lecture on Realism," *Screen* 18: 1, 61–74.

Williamson, J. (1978) *Decoding Advertisements*, London: Marion Boyars.

Williamson, J. (1986) "The Making of a Material Girl," *New Socialist*, October, 46–7.

Wilson, C. and Gutierrez, F. (1985) *Minorities and Media: Diversity and the End of Mass Communication*, Beverly Hills: Sage.

Wollen, P. (1969) *Signs and Meaning in the Cinema*, London: Secker & Warburg.

Wollen, P. (1982) *Readings and Writings: Semiotic Counter Strategies*, London: Verso.

Wollen, P. (1986) "Ways of Thinking about Music Video (and Post-modernism)," *Critical Quarterly* 28: 1 & 2, 167–70.

Woollacott, J. (1977) "Messages and Meanings," *Open University Unit DE 353–6*, Milton Keynes: Open University.

Woollacott, J. (1982) "Messages and Meanings" in M. Gurevitch, T. Bennett, J. Curran, and J. Woollacott (eds) (1982) *Culture, Society and Media*, London: Methuen.

Worpole, K. (1983) *Dockers and Detectives*, London: Verso.

Name index

Subject index